T4-BBV-487

Register of

St. Philip's Parish

1754–1810

REGISTER

OF

ST. PHILIP'S PARISH,

CHARLES TOWN, or CHARLESTON, S. C.,

1754-1810.

EDITED BY

D. E. HUGER SMITH
and
A. S. SALLEY, JR.

University of South Carolina Press
Columbia, South Carolina

First Edition published by the South Carolina Society,
Colonial Dames of America, Charleston, S. C., 1927

This edition published in Columbia, S. C., by the
University of South Carolina Press, 1971

International Standard Book Number: 0-87249-217-6
Library of Congress Catalog Card Number: 77-153483

Library of Congress classification of 1927 edition
furnished by
McKissick Memorial Library of the University of South Carolina:

F
279
.C4
C4682

Manufactured in the United States of America by
Benson Printing Company

FOREWORD

The user of this volume should know that the index found in the front of the manuscript volume was not printed by D. E. Huger Smith and A. S. Salley, Jr. The editors did indicate the pagination of the manuscript volume, but the printed index refers to the pagination of the printed volume.

The manuscript volume has recently been laminated and rebound as two volumes: "Births and Baptisms, 1753–1810" and "Marriages and Burials, 1753–1810."

"Births and Baptisms, 1753–1810" contains the record of births from September 20, 1754, to March 8, 1774, and of baptisms from December 19, 1756, to August 10, 1810. The baptisms appear in the following order both in the manuscript and in the printed volumes: May 6, 1796, to December 28, 1802; March 16, 1796, to August 10, 1810; December 19, 1756, to November 17, 1782; and then, after a gap of over four years, from January 1, 1787, to October 10, 1801. The haphazard arrangment is due to the fact that later baptisms were recorded in the portion of the volume reserved for the entry of births after it was apparent that the record of births would occupy comparatively few pages.

"Marriages and Burials, 1753–1810" contains the records of marriages from June 28, 1755, to November 1, 1774; July 1, 1781, to August 18, 1782; November 14, 1774, to February 22, 1780; and then, after a blank of almost seven years, from January 14, 1787, to October 8, 1801; and April 27, 1796, to December 29, 1802. The records of burials cover the periods from November 19, 1753, to August 7, 1770; October 29, 1779, to November 12, 1782; and, after a blank of almost fourteen years, from August 24, 1796, to May 22, 1803.

The date 1810 is somewhat misleading as attached to the title of this volume. There are two other bound volumes in the church office with burial records prior to 1810. "Burials and Baptisms, 1796–1809" contains records of burials from May 26, 1803, to October 25, 1809, which were not transferred to the large volume for the years 1753–1810. "Burials, 1805–1853" has records of burials from 1805 to 1853 and, therefore, many entries prior to 1810. The editors may have omitted these not only because they had not been transferred to the larger volume, but also because they have more than a simple notation of burial. In "Burials and Baptisms, 1796–1809" the notation contains the following information: "Name, Age, Place of Nativity, Disease, Member or Stranger, Minister, Service." In "Burials, 1805–1853": "Date, Name, Age, Occupation or Profession, Place of Nativity, Disease or Casualty, Time of Residence, Member." Such entries are a storehouse of valuable information. The entry for the burial of Christopher Gadsden reads: "1805, Aug. 29, Christopher Gadsden, 81 yr. 6 mo., General, Charleston, Parlictic Stroke, 71 ys., Member." The user is, therefore, warned that though the final date is 1810 in the title some of the parish records for burials before 1810 still exist in manuscript form in the church office.

To rearrange all of the records in simple chronological order would have been to undertake an entirely new project. The decision has been made merely to reprint this volume in the exact form in which it first appeared. In that way those sponsoring the reprinting have been faithful to the original manuscripts. The index will help the searchers to bypass this problem of organization without any trouble.

George C. Rogers, Jr.
June 1971

Register of

St. Philip's Parish

1754–1810

PREFACE.

In 1904 Mr. Salley published the first volume of the register of St. Philip's Parish, which covered the period from 1720 to 1758, a part of the records of the first manuscript volume overlapping the first four years of the second manuscript volume.

The copy from which this volume has been printed was not made by Mr. Salley, as was the case with the first volume, but was made by an experienced typist for the South Carolina Society, Colonial Dames of America, about 1900. Mr. Salley has never compared the copy with the original to note differences, but Miss Marie H. Heyward, with the assistance of Mr. Smith, has and they have harmonized the differences. The copyist did not observe superior letters in copying, which accounts for the lack of characteristic superiors in abbreviations.

On October 1, 1764, the following notice appeared in the supplement to *The South-Carolina Gazette*:

THE REGISTER of *St. Philip's* parish *Charles-Town*, Berkley County humbly entreats all persons concerned, to send in an account of whatever births may happen in their respective families, with the Christian and Sir-name of each, and date of the month and year, within two months after such births, agreeable to an Act of the General Assembly of this province, in that case made and provided: And, as there have been no births registered for almost five years, (*the ill consequences of which neglect may in some cases prove prejudicial*); 'tis therefore hoped all such births, with those in future, will be given in which shall be duly and regularly registered, by

ELISHA POINSETT, *Register*.

Births.

Alex. Petrie	On the 20th. September 1754 Alexander Son of Alexander & Elizabeth Petrie was born
George Petrie	On the 16th. September 1756. George son of Alexander & Elizabeth Petrie was born
John Grindlay	On the 9th. day of December 1756 John son of James & Christian Grindlay was born
James Obrien Parsons.	On the first Day of November 1755 James Obrien son of James Parsons & Susanna his wife was born
William John Hale	On the 9th. day of August 1756. William John, son of Capt John Hale Esqr. Commander of His Majesty's Ship Winchelsea, & Gertrude his Wife was Born
Ann Roupell	On the 12th. Day of August 1756 Ann Daughter of George & Elizabeth Roupell was Born
Eliza. Grimke	On the 16th. Day of November 1757 Elizabeth Daughter of John Paul and Mary Grimke was Born
Benja. Smith	On the 10th. Day of January 1757 Benjamin Son of Thomas and Sarah Smith Junr. was Born
Jane Frier	On the 23 Day of November 1757 Jane Daughter of John & Susannah Frier was Born
Eliza. Garden	On the 28th. Day of December 1756 Elizabeth Daughter of Alexander and Elizabeth Garden was Born
Alexr. Garden	On the 4th. December 1757 Alexander Son of Alexander & Elizabeth Garden was Born
Harriott Oliphant	On the 23d Day of July 1757 Harriott Daughter of David & Hannah Oliphant was Born

Thomas Gadsden	On the 13th. Day of August 1757 Thomas Son of Christopher and Mary Gadsden was Born[1]
Richard Brooke Roberts	On the 15th. December 1757 Richard Brooke Son of Owen and Ann Roberts was Born[2]
Mickie Ann —	On the 14th. Day of September 1768, Ann Michie Daughter of Alexander and Heneritta Michie. was Born ....

Births 2.

Mary Linthwaite	On the 9th. Day of January 1757 Mary Daughter of Thomas and Ann Linthwaite was born ....
Mary Hindes	On the 2nd. Day of May 1757 Mary the Daughter of Patrick and Sarah Hindes was born ....
Sarah Poinsett	On the 7th. Day of October 1757 Sarah the daughter of John & Sarah Poinsett was born ....
Mary James	On the 6th. Day of October 1757 Mary the Daughter of John and Elizabeth James was born ....

---

[1]He was a captain in the 1st Regiment, South Carolina Line, Continental Establishment, and was taken prisoner at the fall of Charles Town, May 12, 1780. He married, October, 1778, Martha Fenwicke, daughter of Hon. Edward Fenwicke. He was lieutenant governor for a term between 1782 and 1790, and during the absence of the governor on one occasion acted as governor.

[2]He was a captain in the 4th (Artillery) Regiment, South Carolina Line, Continental Establishment, and was taken prisoner at the fall of Charles Town, May 12, 1780. He married, January, 1785, Everarda Catharina Sophia Houckgeest van Braam. He died at Burlington, N. J., in January, 1797.

Charles Pinckney	On the 26th. Day of October 1757 Charles Son of Charles Pinckney and Frances his Wife was born.[1] ....
Isabella Liston	On the 19th. Day of September 1757 Isabella the Daughter of Robert and Mary Liston was born. ....
John Cannon	On the 2nd. Day of April 1758 John Son of Daniel Cannon and Mary his Wife was born. ....
John Wilson	On the 28th. Day of May 1758 John Son of John & Mary Willson was born. ....
Gabriel Manigault	On the 17th. Day of March 1758 Gabriel Manigault Son of Peter Manigault and Elizabeth his wife was born.[2] ....

[1]His father, known later as Colonel Charles Pinckney, was a son of William Pinckney and Ruth Brewton, his wife, and a nephew of Charles Pinckney, sometime chief-justice of the province. His mother was Frances Brewton, daughter of Col. Robert Brewton, and her husband's first cousin. He was elected to the House of Representatives in 1779, when but a little over twenty-one. He was at that time a captain in the Charles Town Regiment of militia and participated in the siege of Savannah, October 9, 1779. He was several times a delegate to the Continental Congress and was one of South Carolina's delegates to the convention which framed the Constitution of the United States in 1787, and submitted thereto a plan which was largely used by the committee that prepared the Constitution. He was a delegate to the South Carolina convention which ratified the Constitution in 1788. In 1789, he was elected governor and was reëlected in January, 1791, for the short term ending in December, 1792, in accordance with the change made by the state constitution of 1790. He was president of the convention of 1790 which adopted a new constitution for the state. He was again elected governor in December, 1796, and in December, 1798, was elected United States Senator to succeed John Hunter, resigned, and also for the full term beginning March 4, 1799. In 1801, he was appointed by President Jefferson Minister to Spain; retired in 1805 and was returned to the state House of Representatives to fill a vacancy for Christ Church Parish, October 22, 1805; was elected governor for the fourth time, in December, 1806; was returned to the state House of Representatives in 1810 and 1812, and was sent to Congress in 1818, retiring March 4, 1821. He died October 24, 1824. (See *The South Carolina Historical and Genealogical Magazine*, Vol. II, pages 128-148.)

[2]For an account of the Manigault family see *Transactions* of the Huguenot Society of South Carolina, No. 4, page 64.

William Neufville	On the 13th. Day of December 1757 William Neufville Son of John and Elizabeth Neufville was born. ....
William Boone	On the 17th. Day of September 1758 William Son of William and Martha Boone was born ....
Samuel Roupell	On the 20th. Day of October 1758 Samuel Son of George and Elizabeth Roupell was born. ....
John Berisford	On the 27th. Day of May 1758 John Son of Richard and Sarah Berisford was Born. ....
Stobo	On the 21st. Day of December 1758........... Daughter of Richard Park Stobo and Mary his wife was born ....
Sophia Fesch	On the 26th. Day of December 1758 Sophia Chrischona Daughter of Andrew Fesch & Sophia his Wife was born ....
Martha Logan	On the 28th. Day of October 1758 Martha Daughter of William Logan and Margaret his Wife was born ....
Edie Taylor	On the 16th. Day of September 1758 Edie Daughter of David & Edie Taylor was born ....
Joshua Lockwood	On the 12th. Day of December 1758 Joshua Son of Joshua and Mary Lockwood was born ....

Births 3.

Ebenezer Simmons	On the 17th. Day March 1759 Ebenezer Son of Ebenezer Simmons Junr. and Jane his wife was born ....
John Ward Linthwaite	On the 24th. Day of February 1759 John Ward Son of Thomas and Ann Linthwaite was born ....

Margaret Philp	On the 8th. Day of January 1759 Margaret Daughter of Robert and Mary Philp was born[1] ....
Thos. Pinckney	On the 2nd Day of May 1760. Thomas the Son of Charles Pinckney & Frances his Wife was born. ....
Eliz. Chalmers	On the 7th. Day of September 1741 Elizabeth daughter of Lionel & Martha Chalmers was born ....
Martha Chalmers	On the 12th. day of May 1755 Martha daughter of Lionel .... & Martha Chalmers was born ....
Sarah Chalmers	On the 1st. day of June 1756 Sarah daughter of Lionel & Martha Chalmers was born ....
Ann Bensley Chalmers	On the 4th. day of September 1760 Ann Bensley daughter of Lionel & Martha Chalmers was born ....
Isaac Chalmers	On the 2nd. day of February 1762 Isaac Son of Lionel and .... Martha Chalmers was born ....
George Chalmers	On the 19th. day of February 1763 George Son of Lionel & Martha Chalmers was born ....
John Howell	On the 15th. day of September 1763 John, Son of John & Martha Howell was born....
Elizabeth Huger	On the 20th. day of October 1763 Elizabeth Daughter of Isaac & Elizabeth Huger was born ....

[1]She was married in December, 1780, to Lieutenant Archibald ("Mad Archie") Campbell, of the 71st (British) Regiment. He was killed at the battle of Videau's Bridge, in St. Thomas and St. Denis's Parish, and his wife died a few days after, leaving an infant, who was brought up by her great-grandmother, Mrs. Robert Williams. This infant, Margaret Philp Campbell, married in 1799, Robert Deas. The marriage of "Mad Archie" and Margaret Philp was an elopement and not an abduction, as stated by an account given in Johnson's *Traditions of the Revolution* and in *Katherine Walton,* by W. Gilmore Simms. The story has been variously distorted by the many writers who have made use of it. (See page 153 for marriage of her parents.)

Elizabeth Wood	On the 20th. day of November 1764 Elizabeth Daughter of George & Ann Wood was born ....
Thomas Bee	On the 20th. day of October 1764 Thomas son of Thomas & Susanna Bee was born ....
Elizabeth Hall	On the 5th. day of March 1765 Elizabeth Daughter of George Abbot & Lois Hall was born. ....
Joseph Smith	On the 14th. day of October 1764. Joseph, Son of Stephen & Ann Smith was born ....

Birth 4.

Anne Simmons	On the 19th. November 1755. Anne Simmons daughter of Ebenezer & Anne Simmons was born ....
Ebenezer Simmons	On the 17th. of March 1759 Ebenezer Son of Ebenezer & Anne Simmons was born....[1]
Mary Simmons	On the 13th. of February 1764. Mary daughter of Ebenezer & Anne Simmons was born ....
Thomas Simmons	On the 18th. of August 1765. Thomas Son of Ebenezer & Anne Simmons was born. ....
Thos. Simmons of Maurice	On the 11th. June 1765 Thomas of Maurice & Mary Simmons was born ....
Eleanor Gillmore	On the 2nd. May 1765 Eleanor of Anthony & Mary Gillmore was born ....
Webb Benjamin	On the 5th. of August 1766, Benjamin of Benjamin & Rebecca Webb was born in St. Philips Parish ....
Pinckney Mary	On 14th. June 1761 .... Mary of Charles & Frances Pinckney was born ....
Pinckney Wm. Robert	On the 1st. of Octor. 1765 William Robert of Charles & Frances Pinckney was born ....

---

[1]On page 8 there appears an entry of the same name as of the same date of birth, but of different parents. (?)

Mitchell Sarah	On the 9th. August 1761 Sarah of Moses & Sarah Mitchell was born ....
Mitchell Moses	On the 12th. Octor. 1763 Moses of Moses & Sarah Mitchell was born ....
Mitchell William	On the 28th March 1766 William of Moses & Sarah Mitchell was born ....
Chalmers Margaret	On the 2nd. July .... 1767. Margaret of Lionel & Elizabeth Chalmers was born
Pinckney Thomas[1]	On the 2nd. day of May 1760 Thomas Son of Charles & Frances Pinckney was born
Pinckney Miles Brewton	On the 18th. Day of December 1768 Miles Brewton Pinckney Son of Charles & Frances Pinckney was Born.

Birth 5

Doyley Margaret	On the 6th. Day of January 1757 Margaret Doyley, of Daniel & Anne Doyley was born .... in Charlestown
Doyley Ann	On the 19th. day of August 1759, Ann Doyley of Daniel & Ann Doyley was born, in Charlestown ....
Doyley Rebecca	On the 10th. day of August 1761 Rebecca Doyley of Daniel & Ann Doyley was born, in Charlestown
Doyley Daniel	On the 19th. day of March 1763. Daniel Doyley of Daniel & Ann Doyley was Born On Wexford farm, on Charles town Neck.
Huger Mary	On the 1st. day of Decmr. 1764 Mary Huger of Isaac & Elizabeth Huger was born ....
Huger Martha	On the 16th. Decmr. 1765 Martha Huger of Isaac & Elizabeth Huger was born ....
Huger Daniel	On the 17th. of May 1768 Daniel Huger of Isaac & Elizabeth Huger was born ....
Huger Isaac	On the 1st. day of March 1767 Isaac Huger Son of Isaac & Eliz. Huger was born ....

[1]Twice entered. See page 3.

Huger Francis	On the 26th. Day of July 1769 Francis Huger son of Isaac & Eliz. Huger was born ....
Stoll, Ann Baker	On the 5th. day of January 1766, Ann Baker Stoll, daughter of Justinus & Phoebe Stoll was born.
Skottowe Thos. Brittiffe	Dec. 22nd .... 1767, Thomas Brittiffe, of Thos. & Mary Lucia Skottowe was born[1]
Skottowe Nicholas Brittiffe	Sept. 24th. .... 1769, Nicholas Brittiffe, of Thos. & Mary Lucia Skottowe was born ....
Skottowe C. Brittiffe	Sept. 26th. .... 1770, Coulsin Brittiffe, of Thos. & Mary Lucia Skottowe was born ....
Telfair Mary Lucia	Oct. 24th. .... 1770, Mary Lucia, of William & Elizabeth Telfair, was born ....
Telfair Thomas	Apr. 30th. .... 1772, Thomas, of William & Elizabeth Telfair, was born ....
Skottowe, J. Bellinger	July 16th. .... 1772 John Bellinger, of Thos. & Mary Lucia Skottowe Was Born
Skottowe E. M. Bellinger	Mar. 8th. .... 1774, Edmund Massinberd Bellinger, of Thos. & Mary L. Skottowe, was born ....

Baptisms 36

McGregor	May 6 1796 James Smith,	Sons of Daniel and
Do.	Jacob, and	
Do.	Isaac	Magdalen McGregor.
Hook	" 15 " John Snyder son of Conrad and Susannah Hook.	
Byrd	" 20 " Elizabeth daughter of Samuel and Sarah Byrd.	
Dewees	June 8 " John son of William and Jane Dewees.	

[1] This and the subsequent entries on page 5 were evidently belated entries. Pages 6-35 are blank.

Mayers	" 12 " Ann Charlotte daughter of John G. and Charlotte Mayers.
Phipps	" 16 " William son of John and Jane Phipps.
Johnson	" 28 " James son of William and Sarah Johnson.
Gaillard	" " " Alfred Samuel son of Theodore and Elizabeth Gaillard.
Izard	July 16 " Henry son of Henry and Emma Philadelphia Izard.
Wilson	August 2 " Lionel Joseph son of John and Wilson.
Bockenaw	" 21 " Ann Felicity daughter of Charles and Sarah Bockenaw.
Doughty	" 27 " John son of William and Mary Doughty.
Dalton	Sept. 10 " Mary Ann daughter of Peter and LeGrace Dalton.
Harleston	" 15 " Elizabeth Pinckney daughter of William and Sarah Harleston.
Harvey	" 30 " Samuel William son of Samuel and Ann Harvey.
Smith	Oct. 23 " Thomas Moore (2 years old,) and Mary Barnwell, son and daughter of James and Mary Smith.
Johnson	" 23 " William Henry son of William and Sarah Johnson.
Coon	Nov. 24 " Mary daughter of Richard and Catharine Coon.
Stoll	Dec. 7 " Martha daughter of Jacob and Catharine Stoll.
Brock	Oct. 18. 1789 John son of Anthony Puntly and Mary Brock.
Wyatt	Dec. 26 " Eliza daughter of Peter and Mary Ann Wyatt.
Ravenel	Dec. 29 " Daniel son of Daniel and Catharine Ravenel.
Magwood	Jany. 15 1797 James Holmes son of Simon and Mary Elizabeth Magwood.

Dupre	" " Elizabeth Garnair daughter of Benjamin and Elizabeth Dupre.
Jones	" " Thomas son of Joseph and Frances Jones.
Do.	" 27 " Alexander son of Alexander and Frances Jones.
Crafts	Feby 26 " Henry and Margaret, son and daughter of William and Margaret Crafts.
Lehre	" 28 " Ann Judith daughter of William and Ann Lehre.
Derby	March 8 " Anna Elizabeth daughter of John and Arabella Derby.

Baptisms.

Baptisms 37

Frink	March 9. 1797. Thomas Blodget son of Rebecca Elizabeth and Thomas Frink.
Kirkland	" 12 " William Lenox son of John and Mary Ann Kirkland.
Hazard	" 21 " Daniel Browne son of William and Margaret Hazard.
Detmore	" 25 " Martha daughter of Henry and Abigail Detmore.
Harleston	April 2 " John son of Edward and Annabella Harleston.
Smith	" " " Roger son of Roger Moore and Ann Smith.
Dwight	" " Samuel Broughton son of Samuel and Esther Eliza Dwight.
Bell	" " John son of David and Sarah Bell.
Newton	" 16 " William son of William and Mary Newton.
Dowell	May 25 " John Caldwell born January 27. 1792, son of Stephen and Jane Dowell.
Fitsimons	June 2 " Christopher son of Christopher and Fitzsimons.

Pilor	" 7 " Caroline Matilda daughter of and Esther Pilor.
Bryant	Aug. 10 " Charles Henry son of John and Susanna Bryant.
Wood	Septr. 17 " Anne Elizabeth daughter of William and Margaret Wood.
Pinckney	" 23 " Richard Shubrick son of Roger and Susanna Pinckney.
Haskell	Oct. 15 " Harriott Julia daughter of Elnathan and Charlotte Haskell.
Middleton	Nov. 5 " Henry son of Henry and Emma Philadelphia Middleton.
Johnson	" 6 " Sarah daughter of Mary and Thomas Johnson.
Stioins	" " Maria Somersall daughter of Cotton Mather and Elizabeth Stioins.[1]
Smith	" 20 " Jane Maria daughter of John and Ann Smith.
Do	Dec. 10 " Quinton Hamilton son of William and Catharine Smith.
Lockey	" 17 " William son of George and Mary Lockey.
Mazyck	" " Isaac son of William and Elizabeth Mazyck.
Gaillard	" 24 " Ellinor St. Cecilia daughter of Theodore and Elizabeth Gaillard.
Brailsford	" 25 " Hannah Amelia daughter of William and Amelia Brailsford.
Snyder	" 30 " John Jacob son of John Paul and Elizabeth Snyder.
Joye	" " Mary Elizabeth daughter of Abraham and Elizabeth Joye.
Fowler	Jany 5 1798 Anna Elizabeth daughter of John and Mary Fowler.

---

[1]Stevens. See book P4, page 338, office of Register of Mesne Conveyances, Charleston County.

Do	” ” ” Elizabeth Ann daughter of John and Mary Fowler.
Middleton	” 27 ” Mary Elizabeth daughter of Solomon and Mary Middleton.
Coleman	” 31 ” Lack Henry son of George and Margaret Coleman.

Baptisms

Baptisms 38

Whealer	Jany 31 1798 William son of William and Elizabeth Whealer.
Edmonds	Feby 4 ” Elizabeth Mary daughter of James and Sarah Edmonds.
Vinri	” 7 ” John Warran son of Narbott and Sarah Vinri.
Prioleau	” 18 ” Elizabeth Clara daughter of John and Mary Ann Prioleau.
West	March 11 ” Edward Forrest son of William and Martha West.
Prince Do	” 18 ” Ann Elizabeth and William Morgan, son and daughter of Clement and Mary Prince.
Browne	” 19 ” William George son of William and Magdaline Browne.
McCrady	” 20 ” Eliza daughter of John and Jane McCrady.
Gaillard	” 27 ” Samuel son of John and Harriott Gaillard.
Page	April 1 ” Samuel son of Luke and Jane Page.
Loyd	” 4 ” Robert son of Robert and Mary Loyd.
Green	” 15 ” James Farquharson son of James Carey and Mary Manson Green.
Smith	” ” George Wilson son of Henry and Mary Smith.
Ditmore	” 22 ” Henry son of Henry and Abigail Ditmore.

Thackum	" 29 " Eloisa daughter of Thomas and Judith Thackum.
Jones	" 30 " Edward son of Edward and Ann Jones.
Frazer	" " " John Jacob son of John M. and Rebecca Frazer.
Ellis	May 5 " John son of Samuel and Ann Ellis.
McGregor	" " Susannah McGregor daughter of Daniel and Magdalen McGregor.
Marshall Do	" " Sarah Ann and Thomas Chandler, daughter and son of Thomas and Mary Susannah Marshall.
Mowbray	" 11 " Frances Donne daughter of William and Martha Mowbray. aged 5 years.
Frost	" " " Eleanor daughter of Thomas and Elizabeth Frost. aged 11 months.
Bailey	" 19 " William Edward and Louisa Caroline, son and daughter of Polly and Henry Bailey.
Bedont	" 22 " Margaret Ford daughter of Charles and Judith Bedont.
Gibbes	July 1 " Benjamin son of William and Mary Gibbes, of St. James Island.

Baptisms

Bessellieu	July 4. 1798. Benjamine Lewis son of Lewis and Elizabeth Bessellieu.
Hogarth	" 12 " William son of William and Mary Hogarth.
Gibbes	15 " Frances Margaret daughter of Benjamin and Elizabeth Gibbes.
Oswald	" 26 " Thomas son of David and Margaret Oswald.
Flagg	Sept. 7 " Thomas McCleish son of Samuel Howk and Elizabeth Flagg.
Ladson	" " " Sophia Josepha daughter of James and Judith Ladson.

Ball	" 23 " Elizabeth Ann daughter of John and Elizabeth Ball.
Guy	" 25 " William and Elizabeth, son and Daughter of James and Sarah Guy.
Elfe	" 27 " Benjamin son of Benjamin and Elizabeth Elfe.
Dewees	" " " Joseph son of Joseph and Elizabeth Dewees.
Perry	Oct. 7 " Edward Drayton son of Edward and Mary Perry.
Calwell	" 8 " Sarah daughter of Henry and Sarah Calwell.
Rivers	" " Mary daughter of Margaret Rivers.
Elfe Do.	" 24 " George and James sons of Thomas and Mary Elfe.
Doughty	" " Emma Julia daughter of William and Susanna Doughty.
Marshall	Nov. 28 " Elizabeth Mary daughter of William and Louisa Marshall.
Heyward	" " " Ann Miles daughter of William and Charlotte Heyward.
Smith	Dec. 13 " Richard son of Roger Moore and Anna Smith.
Pinckney	" " Elizabeth Pinckney daughter of Roger and Susannah Pinckney.
Hugfins (Four children)	" 20 " Charles, Charlotte Caroline, Nathan, and Mary Kazea, sons and daughters of Mary and Nathan Hugfins, at Santee.
Hazard	" 25 " Elsey daughter of Carder and Elsey Hazard, South Kingston, Rhode Island.
Do	" " " William son of William and Margaret Hazard.
Pritchard (2 sons)	" 26 " William and George sons of William and Mary Pritchard.

Baptisms.

Grainger	Decr. 30. 1798. Henry son of James and Ann Grainger.
Graiser	" " " Louisa Clarke daughter of Jacob and Ann Maria Graiser.
Bass	Jany. 1 1799. Frances Eliza daughter of Thomas and Dorothy Bass.
King	" 9 " Elizabeth Pinana daughter of Benjamin and Penina King.
Toomer	Feby. 11 " Sarah daughter of Thomas and Sarah Toomer.
Shanly	" 19 " Anna daughter of Ann and Patrick Shanly.
Flint	" 20 " Thomas Thompson son of Thomas and Sarah Flint.
Smith	" 25 " Elizabeth daughter of John and Elizabeth Smith.
Haskell	March 3 " Eugilia Dorothy, daughter of Elnathan and Charlotte Haskell.
Griffith	" 7 " Ralph son of Thomas Jones and Elizabeth Boswell Griffith.
Shmidt	" 17 " John Frederick son of John Frederick and Elizabeth Shmidt.
Dupre	" 18 " Mary Louisa daughter of Mary and Benjamin Dupré.
Hussey	" 20 " Edward son of Bryant and Susanna Hussey.
Fields	" " " Ann daughter of Agnes and William B. Fields.
Mitchell	" 24 " Margaret daughter of James and Ann Mitchell.
Burrows	April 3 " Elizabeth daughter of Mary and Frederic Burrows.
Elden	" 4 " Elizabeth Elden daughter of Benjamin and Elizabeth Elden.
Headright	" 7 " James son of James and Elizabeth Headright.

Edmonds	" " James son of James and Sarah Edmonds.
Smith	" " Elizabeth Catharine daughter of John and Ann Smith.
Moultrie Do Do	" 14 " Alexander, Eleanor Bellamy, and John, sons and daughter of James and Catharine Moultrie.
Miller	" 21 " Louisa Bennet daughter of John and Margaret Miller.

Baptisms.

Baptisms 41

Kelley	May 1. 1799. Elizabeth daughter of James and Sophia Kelley
Doane	" 5 " Maria Tunno daughter of Joseph and Mary Doane.
Gourdine	" 7 " Samuel son of Samuel and Mary Gourdine.
Pepoon	" 26 " Isabella Nott, and Carolina Deas, daughters of Benjamin and Lucy Pepoon.
Wish	June 9 " Anna Thetis daughter of William and Martha Wish.
Rutledge	" 12 " Francis Huger son of Hugh and Mary Golightly Rutledge.[1]
Newman	July 4 " Henry son of Morris and Catherine Newman.
Gaillard	" 7 " Augustus Theodore son of Theodore and Martha Gaillard.
Brailsford	" 14 " Anna Elizabeth daughter of John and Amelia Brailsford.
Mazyck	Sept. 8 " Edward son of William and Elizabeth Mazyck.

---

[1]He was rector of Christ Church Parish, 1825-1826; rector of Trinity Church, St. Augustine, Fla., 1839-1845; consecrated Bishop of Florida, October 15, 1851; died in Tallahassee, November 6, 1851.

Berkley	" 9 " John son of George and Ellenora Berkley.
Merlin	" 11 " Mary Stevens daughter of William and Elizabeth Merlin.
Dalton	" 22 " Louisa daughter of Peter and Grace Dalton.
Baxter	" " " Samuel Gaillard son of Joseph Sanford and Henrietta Catharine Baxter.[1]
Coburn	Oct. 6 " Eliza and John Robert, daughter and son of Eliza and James Coburn.[2]
Middleton	" 11 " Arthur, Henry, and Oliver Herring, sons of Henry and Mary Helen Middleton.
Prioleau	" 20 " John Cordes son of John Cordes and Mary Ann Prioleau.
Heyward	Nov. 2 " Henrietta daughter of Nathaniel and Henrietta Heyward.
Harleston	" 3 " Hannah Constantia daughter of William and Sarah Harleston.
Hickborne	" " " Barre Flagg son of Isaac Barre and Catherine Hickborne.
Jones	" " of Joseph and Frances Jones.
Dixon	" 16 " Williamson of Robert and Matilda Dixon.
Jones	" 24 " Edward son of Edward and Ann Jones.
Middleton	Dec. 1 " Eloise daughter of Solomon and Mary Middleton.
Smith	" 7 " William Skirving son of Thomas Rhett and Ann Rebecca Smith.

Baptisms

---

[1]A clerical error for Barker.

[2]The index of the original gives Colburn, but Coburn is correct.

Ball	Jany 1 1800, Mary Golf[1] Stevens daughter of John and Elizabeth Ball.
Phipps	" 6 " Sarah Elizabeth daughter of Jane and John Phipps
Prichard	" 8 " Aphra Ann daughter of William and Mary Prichard
Green	" " William Heyward, son of James Cary and Mary Manson Green.
Jones	" " Joseph son of Alexander and Mary Jones.
Huggins	" 28 " John Hartman son of Luke and Maria Huggins.
Cleapor	Feby 9 " William Henry son of Charles and Mary Cleapor
McCready	" 23 " Sarah daughter of John and Jane McCready.
Askew	" " " Harriett daughter of James and Mary Askew.
Doughty	" " " Georgiana Washington daughter of William and Susanna Doughty
Pinckney	" 28 " Jane Mary daughter of Susanna Bullin and Roger Pinckney.
Sterns	March 3 " Alice daughter of Caleb and Alice Sterns
Weyman	" " " Mary Rebecca daughter of Edward and Catharine Weyman.
Grimke	" 5 " Eliza Carolina daughter of J. F. and Mary Grimke.
Stoll	" 6 " of Jacob and Catharine Stoll
Elliott	" " " Barnard son of Barnard and Juliet Elliott.

[1]Gough.

Nirott	" 9 " Amelia daughter of Louis and Lucy Nirott
Harvey	" 16 " Mary Gracia Kiely and St. Sebastian Kiely daughter and son of Benjamin and Harvey
Marshall	" 22 " Louisa Frederica daughter of William and Louisa Frederica Marshall.
Smith	April 9 " Jane daughter of John Rutledge and Susannah Smith.
Galloway	" 23 " Sarah Elizabeth daughter of Alfred and Elizabeth Galloway.
Bocket	May 6 " Sarah Elizabeth daughter of John and Sarah Bocket

Baptisms.

McGregor	May 6 1800 Sarah Priscilla daughter of Magdalena and Daniel McGregor.
Smith	" 11 " Louisa daughter of Henry and Mary Smith.
Harvey	" 16 " William Pritchard son of Samuel and Ann Harvey.
Clarke	" 21 " Jane daughter of Zechariah and Susannah Clarke
Bonneau	" " " William Hoyland son of Francis and Eleanor Bonneau
Hext	" " Thomas James Hor son of John Briton and Mary Hext.
Mitchell	June 5 " Judith daughter of James and Ann Mitchell.
Handy	" 6 " Benjamin son of Thomas and Dorothy Handy.
Holland	" 16 " Martha daughter of John and Mary Holland.

Froit	" 19 " John le Jaw son of Thomas and Elizabeth Froit.[1]
Hogarth	" 26 " Ann daughter of William Hogarth Jr. and Mary Hogarth.
Manigault	July 25 " Emma and Maria daughters of Margaret Izard and Gabriel Manigault.
Graeser	August 2 " Eleanor daughter of Conrad Jacob and Anna Maria Graeser.
Holloway	" 27 " Jane daughter of Hervey and Eleanor Holloway.
Johnson	" 31 " Anna Huget daughter of William and Sarah Johnson.
Smith	Sept. 6 " Jacob son of John Frederic and Elizabeth Smith.
Minor	" " " Henry Peregrine son of Mathew and Elizabeth Minor.
Smith	Oct 19 " Eliza Sarah daughter of John and Elizabeth Smith.
Dranne	" 20 " William Henry son of Joseph and Mary Dranne.
Smith	" 22 " Mary Rutledge daughter of Thomas Rhett and Anna Rebecca Smith.
Duprie	" 23 " Benjamin David son of Benjamin and Mary Duprie.
Barker	Nov 21 " Eleanor daughter of Joseph Sanford and Catharine Henrietta Barker.
Ball	" 25 " Ann Scott daughter of Archibald and Mary Golf Ball

Baptisms.

Baptisms 44

Skirving	Nov 21 1800 Anne Holland daughter of William and Bethia Skirving
Nell	" " Stephen Browne son of Jesse and Ursula Nell.

[1]Frost is correct. LeJau was the middle name of the child.

Jones	" " Louisa daughter of Joseph and Frances Jones.
Rogers	" " Ann Missroon Rogers daughter of Christopher and Ann Rogers.
Prioleau	Jany 4 1801 Catharine Emily daughter of John Cordes and Mary Ann Prioleau.
Chandle	" 5 " Arthur Holmes son of Patrick and Ann Chandle.
Mayberry	" 8 " Thomas Read, Caroline Ballard, Maria Thompson, Ann Simons, children of Thomas and Mary Mayberry.
Aldergoe	" " " James Thompson son of Elizabeth Aldergoe, (an orphan)
Gaillard	" 13 " William Theodore son of Rebecca and Bartholomew Gaillard.
Gibbes	" 25 " Mary Anna daughter of Benjamin and Elizabeth Gibbes.
Vesey	" " " William Smith son of Charles and Mary Vesey.
Cherchsenbourne	" " " Thomas son of Jacob and Anna Cherchsenbourne
Ladson	Febry 3 " Josepha Adelaide daughter of James and Juda Ladson.[1]
Middleton	" 22 " Henry Augustus and Thomas sons of Thomas and Ann Middleton.
Heyward	" " " Ann daughter of Nathaniel and Henrietta Heyward.
Bonetheau	" " " Ann Elizabeth daughter of Gabriel Manigault and Anna Maria Bonetheau.
Browne	" " " James Cambridge son of Joshua and Harriott Browne
Heckborne	" 25 " James Crocker son of Isaac Barre and Catharine Heckborne.

---

[1]Probably Josephine Adela, daughter of James and Judith Ladson.

Gaillard	March 1 ” Mary Sarah daughter of Martha and Theodore Gaillard
Sharp	” 8 ” of John and Elizabeth Sharp.
Negrin	” ” 1801 Augusta Caroline daughter of John James and Elizabeth Negrin.

Heslop	March 12 1801 Joseph John son of Robert and Mary Heslop.
Browne	April 8 ” John son of John and Elizabeth Browne.
Miller	” 12 ” William Henry son of William and Magdalene Miller.
Lord	” 17 ” Maria daughter of Maria and Richard Lord.
Redman	” 18 ” Ann Martha daughter of James and Sarah Redman.
Pritchard	” ” Eliza Catharine daughter of Mary and William Pritchard
Manigault	” 22 ” Edward son of Gabriel and Margaret Manigault.
Chichester	” 24 ” Constantia daughter of John and Mary Chichester.
Middleton	” ” ” Solomon Washington son of Solomon and Mary Middleton
”	” ” Mary daughter of David and Mary Middleton.
Oliver	” 30 ” Stephen son of James and Alice Oliver.
Colliatt	May 2 ” Ary Ann Daughter of James and Eliza Colliatt.
Greene	” 7 ” Edward George Farquhar son of James Cary and Mary Manson Greene
Mazyck	” ” Alexander son of William and Elizabeth Mazyck.

Dolliver	July 14 " Mary Caroline daughter of Henry and Margaret Dolliver
Frost	" " " Edward son of Thomas and Elizabeth Frost.
Neufville	Aug. 1 " William son of Isaac and Mary Neufville.
Corker	" 16 " Eliza daughter of Thomas and Elizabeth Corker.
Williams	" " Louisa daughter of Ann and William Williams.
Marshall	" " Alexander Washington and Mary Caroline son and daughter of Thomas and Mary Marshall.
Mompoy	" 16 1801 Louisa daughter of Mary and Henry Mompoy.
Patch	" " Peter son of Robert and Susan Patch.
Thrackam	" " William and Nicholas sons of Thomas and Judith Thrackam.
Shivers	Sept 8 " Jane Holmes daughter of Richard and Ann Magdalen Shivers.

Baptism.

Baptisms 46

Cleapor	Sept 16 1801 Charles Thomas son of Charles and Mary Cleapor.
Watson	" 20 " James Alexander son of Alexander and Mary Watson.
Bessillieu	Oct. 12 " Mary Johanna daughter of Lewis and Elizabeth Bessillieu
Rutledge	" 21 " Ann Sarah daughter of Hugh and Mary Golightly Rutledge.
Browne	" " Magdalen Neuth daughter of William and Magdalen Browne.
Reed	" " Susanna daughter of William and Penina Reed.
Wilkinson	Nov. 4 " Martha Ruthy daughter of John and Mary Wilkinson.

Dart	" 5 " John Sanford son of Isaac Motte and Isabella Dart.
Griffith	" 10 " Thomas son of Thomas and Mary Breuer Griffith.
Corbett	" 11 " Richard son of Thomas and Elizabeth Corbett.
Jeannerett	" 22 " Maria Susanna daughter of Christopher and Elizabeth Jeannerett.
Dewees	" 23 " Jane daughter of William and Jane Dewees.
Elfe	" " Eleanora Sarah daughter of William and Elizabeth Elfe.
Heath	Dec 6 " Thomas Butler son of James and Ann Heath.
Deleisseline	" 11 " Thomas Verman, Ben Spurr, and Charlotte Ann, sons and daughter of John and Elizabeth Deleisseline.
Webb	" 16 " Martha Cecilia daughter of William and Mary Webb.
Williams	Jany 1 1802 John Coldham son of James and Jane Williams.
Boylston	" 24 " Nicholas Hallowell son of Nicholas and Mary Eliza Boylston.
Nell	" 30 " Ann Isabella daughter of Jesse and Rosella Nell.

Baptisms

Baptisms 47

Graddick	Jany. 31 1802 Angelina daughter of Pistin and Mary Graddick.
Kennedy	Febry. 3 " Edward son of James and Ann Kennedy.
Nowell	" " " Edward Saville, John Lascelles, Lionel Chalmers, Elizabeth Warden, children of Edward and Margaret Nowell.
Smith	" 4 " Mary daughter of Roger and Ann Smith.

Andrews	" 14 " Robert Lewis son of Rebecca and Robert Andrews.
Rutledge	" 24 " Elizabeth Pinckney daughter of Frederic and Harriott Rutledge.
Johnson	March 4 " John Williams son of David and Eleanor Johnson.
Harvey	" 12 " Grissel Jane daughter of and Capt. James Harvey.
Johnson	" 14 " Thomas Nightingale son of William and Sarah Johnson.
Hogarth	" 18 " Isaac Edwards son of William and Mary Magdalene Johnson.
Gregorie	" 21 " James Ladson son of James and Ann Gibbes Gregorie
McCredie	" 28 " Edward son of John and Jane McCredie.
Gray	April 13 " William Henry and Francis Children of Alexander and Frances Gray.
Phipps	" " " John and Mary, son and daughter of John and Sarah Phipps.
Woodrup	May 6 " of John and Ann Woodrup.
Farr	" 10 " William Robinson son of Joseph and Farr. Stono
Haskell	" 17 " Charles Thompson[1] son of Elnathan and Charlotte Haskell
FitzSimons	" " " Christopher son of Christopher and Catharine FitzSimons.
Pinckney	" 24 " Robert Quash son of Roger and Susanna Bullen Pinckney.

Baptisms.

Baptisms 48

Jones	June 2 " Caroline Flagg daughter of Ándrew and Mary Jones.

---

[1]Thomson. See *The South Carolina Historical and Genealogical Magazine*, Volume III, 107.

Wish	" " " William son of William and Martha Wish.
Hall	" 6 " Thomas son of William and Hall.
Carroll	" 18 " Mary Parsons daughter of James Parsons and Mary Carroll
Hume	" 22 " William son of John and Hume.
Greaser	" 27 " Caroline Clement daughter of Anna Maria and Jacob Greaser.
Rogers	July 11 " William son of Samuel and Elizabeth Rogers.
Galloway	" 18 " Amelia daughter of Alfred and Elizabeth Galloway.
Burrows	" " " Frederic son of Frederic and Mary Burrows.
Smith	" " " William Ladson son of J. R. and Susanna Smith.
Carroll	" 21 " Elizabeth Ann daughter of James Parsons and Mary Carroll.
Johnson	Aug. 4 " Esther Charlotte daughter of William and Anna Marie Johnson.
Chambers	" " " Ann daughter of William and Ann Chambers.
Bell	" 15 " David and Mary Prioleau, children of David and Sarah Bell.
Mitchell	" 20 " Ann Catherine daughter of James and Ann Mitchell.
Lord	" 23 " John Gascoinge son of Richard and Maria Lord.
Pritchard	" 28 " Sarah Charity daughter of William and Sarah Pritchard
Gaillard	" " " Charles Theodore son of Bartholomew and Rebecca Gaillard.
Schmidt	Oct 17 " William Branst son of John Frederic and Elizabeth Schmidt.
Browne	" " " William John son of Catharine and Browne

Darrell	" 24 " Henry James son of Nicholas and Mary Darrell
Corbett	Nov. 4 " Thomas Chapman son of Thomas and Ann Corbett.

Baptisms.

Oliver	Nov. 24 1802 Thomas Roberts son of James and Elizabeth Oliver.
Heyward	" 7 " Charles son of Nathaniel and Henrietta Heyward.
Fields	" " " Johanna daughter of William B. and Fields.
Drayton	" 14 " Harriott daughter of John and Esther Rose Drayton.
Butcher	" " " Sarah daughter of Abraham and Mary Butcher.
Church	" 21 " Elizabeth daughter of Slocum and Mary Church.
Rogers	" 26 " Harriet Eliza Stond daughter of Christopher and Ann Rogers.
Harleston	" " Sarah Hasell and Canstantia Hasell, daughters of Sarah and William Harleston.
Scott	Dec 6 " Sarah Margaret daughter of Harriot and William Scott.
Oliver	" 24 " Thomas Roberts son of James and Elizabeth Oliver.
Moncrief	" 8 " Andrew Schelpeler son of John and Sarah Clarke Moncrief.
Grimke "	" 14 " Charles Fauchereau, and Benjamin Smith, sons of John Fauchereau and Mary Grimke.
Martin	" 15 " Charles son of Lucy and Samuel Martin.
Browne	" 24 " James son of Jonathan and Mary Browne.
Ham	" 28 " Daniel son of Mary Haw and Samuel Ham.

Ball	" " " Elizabeth Jane Stiles daughter of Mary Gough and Archibald Ball.
Jones	" 26 " Edward son of Joseph and Frances Jones.
Just	July 23 " Thomas Just at 35.

Baptisms.

Baptisms. 50

Browne	March 16 1796 James son of Squire and Maria Browne.
Tate	" 23 " John son of Thomas and Jane Tate.
Granger	May 27 " Ann daughter of James and Ann Granger.
Smith	Decr. 25 " Sara Good daughter of John and Elizabeth Smith.
Good	" " " Elizabeth Good (an orphan.).
Norten	" " " Eliza daughter of John and Elizabeth Norton.
Armstrong	Jany. 1 1797 William George son of Fleetwood and Mary Armstrong.
Ellis	" " " Hester Ann daughter of Samuel and Ann Ellis.
Brown	" 22 " Elizabeth daughter of John and Elizabeth Brown.
Gabeau	Feby. 1 ." Susannah daughter of Anthony and Elizabeth Gabeau. (First child the Rev'd Mr. Mathews Baptised)
Moer	March 24 " Elizabeth daughter of William and Sara Moer.
Blake	May 12 " Elizabeth daughter of and Blake.
Halsell	July 13 " William Spinier son of William and Frances Halsall (Mr. Thompson)
Headright	" 30 " Eliza daughter of James and Elizabeth Headright.
McCall	Sept. 29 " Emma Washington daughter of James and Ann Amelia McCall. (Mr. Thompson

Tate	Decr. 13 " Sarah daughter of Thomas and Jane Tate.
Kelly	" 15 " Joseph son of William and Sophia Kelly.
Hursey	March 20 1799 Edward son of Bryan and Susanna Hursey.
Logan	" 24 " Francis son of George and Liddy Logan.
McIlhanney	" 27 " John Keeman son of James and Elizabeth McIlhanny.
Rutledge	" 29 " Edward Coatsworth son of Frederic and Harriott Pinckney Rutledge.[1]
Burrows	April 3 " Of Frederick and Mary Burrows.
Headright	" 7 " James son of James and Elizabeth Headright.
Browne Do	" 10 " Eleanor and Jane daughters of John and Elizabeth Brown.
Logan	August 2. " Mary Independentia daughter of William and Mary Doughty Logan.

Baptisms.

Baptisms. 51

Cheivers	Nov. 29. 1799 Ann Maria daughter of Richard and Ann Cheivers.
Lovely	Decr. 4 " Jeremiah John son of William and Margaret Lovely.[2]

[1]He was born October 16, 1798, and was an officer in the United States Navy, attaining the rank of captain; married Rebecca Motte Lowndes; died November 21, 1860. (See tombstone in Magnolia Cemetery.) He was the father of Mrs. Harriott Horry Ravenel, the author of *Charleston the Place and the People; Life of William Lowndes, Eliza Pinckney*, etc. This baptism was entered again on page 159.

[2]These were the the only entries on the original page 51. Page "51 Con" was an inserted page, and so was 52.

Cole	June 13 1800 John son of John and Grace Cole.
Calvert	" " " James Weathers son of William and Judith Calvert
Pogson "	Oct 24 1800 Francis Logan, " " " Mary Forghenson, } Rev. Mr. Pogson.
Gray	Nov 24 " Priscilla Ann daughter of William and Elizabeth Gray.
Ackes	June 27 1804 John Edward son of John Edward and Charlotte Ackes.
Winchester	July 12 " Edmund son of Jonathan and Mary Winchester.
Logan	" 22 " George William son of George and Margaret Logan.
Clarkson	Aug. 12 " Elizabeth Anderson daughter of William and Elizabeth Clarkson.
Johnson	Sept. 2 " David Clement son of David and Ellen Johnson.
Graeser	" 16 " Septima daughter of C. G. Graeser.
Annerly	" 27 " Maria daughter of George and Amelia Annerly.
Laval	" 29 " Richard son of Jacinth Laval.
Halloway	Oct. " " James son of Richard and Elizabeth Halloway.
Tucker	" " " Sarah daughter of Simon and Mary Tucker.
Hamett	" 7 " Rebecca Miller daughter of Thomas and Caroline Hamett
Drayton	" 14 " Sarah Butler daughter of John and Hester Rose Drayton
Lee	" " Stephen and Susan, son and daughter of Thomas and Keziah Lee.
Lee	" 23 " Catharine Lee (a free Mulatto)
Wigfall	" 28 " Harriett daughter of Thomas and Harriett Wigfall.

Baptisms 52

Monies	Nov. 2 1804 Isabella Monies (a free mulatto, an infant)
Smith	Febry. 22 1807 William Johnson Smith, born on the eighth day of November 1806, and baptised on the 22nd day of February 1807 by Dr Jenkins—Elizabeth and John Smith.
"	June 26 1803 Mary Smith, by the Rev. Mr. Frost, was born on the 11th day of June 1803, and baptised on the 26th of June 1803. daughter of John and Elizabeth Smith.
"	Caroline Smith was born on the 24th day of October 1804 and baptised on the 11th day of November by the Rev. Dr. Jenkins. daughter of John and Elizabeth Smith
Hicks	August 10 1810 Francis Hicks was baptised on the 10th day of August 1810, by the Rev. James D. Simons in St. Philips Church.

Christnings 82[1]

John Grindlay	On the 19th. December 1756 John the Son of James & Christian Grindlay was baptized by the Revd. Mr. John Baxter a Minister of of the Scotch Presbyterian Church.
Ann Roupell	On the Day of 1756 Ann Daughter of George & Elizabeth Roupell was baptized by the Revd. Mr. Andrews.
Eliza. Grimke	On the 4th. Day of November 1757 Elizabeth Daughter of John Paul and Mary Grimke was baptized by the Mr. Clarke Rector
Benja. Smith	On the Day of July 1757 Benjamin Son of Thomas & Sarah Smith was baptized by the Revd. Mr. Clarke

[1]Pages 53-81 are blank. Originally pages from 6-81 were evidently left blank and pages 6-52 subsequently used for making later records.

Eliza. Garden	On the 1st. Day of January 1757 Elizabeth Daughter of Alexander & Elizabeth Garden was baptized by the Revd. Mr. Clarke
Alexr. Garden	On the day of 175 Alexander son of Alexander & Elizabeth Garden was Baptized by Ditto.
Harriott Oliphant	On the Day of 175 Harriott daughter of David & Hannah Oliphant was baptized by the Revd. Mr. Martin of St. Andrews Parish
Thomas Gadsden	On the 20th. Day of August 1757 Thomas Son of Christopher & Mary Gadsden was baptized by the Revd. Mr. Clarke

Christnings 83

Richard Brooke Roberts	On the 1st. January 1758 Richard Brooke Son of Owen & Ann Roberts was Baptized by the Revd. Mr. Richard Clarke Rectoro

Christnings 84.

Mary Linthwaite	On the 10th. January 1758 Mary Daughter of Thomas & Ann Linthwaite was Privately Baptized by the Revd. Mr. Smith assistant to ye Rector
Mary Hindes	On the 2nd May 1757 Mary Daughter of Patrick & Sarah Hindes was Baptized by the Revd. Mr. Richard Clarke Rector ....
Sarah Poinsett	On 6th. March 1758 Sarah Daughter of John & Sarah Poinsett Was Baptized by the Revd. Mr. Robert Smith Assistant ....
Isabella Liston	On 6th. March 1758 Isabella Daughter of Robt. & Mary Liston was Baptized by the Revd. Mr. Robt. Smith..............................
Charles Pinckney	On the 15 May 1758 Charles Son of Charles & Frances Pinckney was Baptized by the Revd. Mr. Robt. Smith ....
Danl. Cannon	On the 19th. May 1758 Daniel Son of Daniel & Mary Cannon was Baptized by the Revd. Mr. Charles Martin ....

John Wilson	On the 12 July 1758 John Son of John & Mary Wilson was Baptized by the Revd. Mr. ....
Mary James	On the 18 July 1758 Mary Daughter of John & Elizabeth James was Baptized by the Revd. Mr. Richard Clarke Rector ....
Gabriel Manigault	On the 1758 Gabriel Son of Peter & Elizabeth Manigault was Baptized by the Revd. Mr. Robert Smith Assistant to the Rector ....
William Neufville	On the 20th. Day July 1758 William Son of John and Elizabeth Neufville was Baptized by the Revd. Mr. Robert Smith
William Boone	On the 25th Day September 1758 William Son of William and Martha Boone was Baptized by the Revd. Mr. Clarke
Saml. Roupell	On the Day of 1758 Samuel Son of George & Elizabeth Roupell was Baptized by the Revd. Mr. Martin of St. Andrews Parish
John Berisford	On the 29th. of December 1758 John Son of Richard & Sarah Berisford was Baptized by the Revd. Mr. Smith Assistant to the Rector
Sophia Chrischona Fesch	On the 10th. Day of January 1759 Sophia Chrischona Daughter of Andrew & Sophia Fesch was Baptized by the Revd. Mr. Smith.
Margaret Philp	On The 15 March 1759 Margaret Daughter of Robert & Mary Philp was Baptized by the Revd. Mr. Morrison of the Scotch meeting
Sarah Susannah Williams	On the 28th. January 1759 Sarah Susannah Daughter of John & Elizabeth Williams was Privately Baptized by the Reverend Mr. Robert Smith Rector ....
Marianne Blakeley	On the 31st January 1759 Marianne Daughter of Luke & Marianne Blakeley was privately Baptized by the Revd. Mr. Robt. Smith

John Peter Ward

On the 11 Day of February 1759, John Peter Son of John & Love Ward was privately Baptized by the Revd. Mr. Robt. Smith

On the 11th. Day of February 1759 Elizabeth Daughter of Samuel & Elizabeth Brailsford was publicly baptized by the Revd. Mr. Robt. Smith

Christnings 85.

Eliza. Maxey

On the 7th. Day of March 1759 Elizabeth Daughter of Joseph & Dor Maxey was privately baptized by the Reverend Mr. Robert Smith.

Sar. Bartley

On the 6th. Day of March 1759. Sarah, Daughter of John and Mara. Bartley was privately baptized by the Revd. Robert Smith.

Esther Perdriau

On the 11th. Day of March 1759 Esther Daughter of John & Esther Perdriau was privately baptized by the Reverend Mr. Robert Smith

Ann Butler or Legier

On the 22nd March 1759 Anne Daughter of John Butler & Margarett Legier was privately baptized by the Reverend Mr. Robert Smith

Hardy Crawford

On the 2nd Day of April 1759 Hardy Son of James & Kesiah Crawford was privately baptized by the Reverend Mr. Robert Smith.

Middleton

On the 21st. Day of May 1759 of Henry & Middleton was privately baptized by the Reverend Mr. Robert Smith

Eliz. Hutchins

On the 23rd. Day of May 1759 Elizabeth Daughter of John & Elizabeth Hutchins was privately baptized by the Reverend Mr. Robert Smith

Hazell Thomas

On the 24th. May 1759 Hazell Son of Samuel & Ann Thomas was privately baptized by the Reverend Mr. Robert Smith Rector.

James Macoon	On the 2nd Day of June 1759 James Son of James & Ann Macoon was privately baptized by the Reverend Mr. Robert Smith Rector.
Wm. Walker	On the 3rd. Day of June 1759 William Son of & Margaret Walker was privately baptized by the Reverend Mr. Robert Smith Rector
John Brailsford	On the 4th. June 1759 John Son of Morton & Ann Brailsford was privately baptized by the Reverend Mr. Robert Smith Rector.
Butler	On the 10th. Day of June 1759 of Peter and Butler privately baptized pr. the Revd. Mr. Robt. Smith Rector.
Wm. Austin	On the 17th. Day of June 1759 William Son of William & Barbary Austin was publicly baptized by the Reverend Mr. Robert Smith Rector.
Reb. Evance	On the 24th. June 1759 Rebeccah Daughter of Thomas & Evance was publicly baptized by the Reverend Mr. Robert Smith Rector
Wm. Martin	On the 1st. Day of July 1759 Wm. Son of John & Ann Martin was publicly baptized by the Reverend Mr. Robert Smith Rector
Mary Nicholson	On the 8th. Day of July 1759 Mary Daughter of Francis & Mary Nicholson was publickly Baptized by the Reverend Mr. Robt. Smith Rector.
Ann Mitchell	On the 23rd. Day of July 1759 Ann Daughter of John & Sarah Mitchell was publickly baptized by the Reverend Mr. Robert Smith Rector
Rosamond Thipping	On the 26th. Day of July 1759 Rosamond, Daughter of Joseph & Sar Thipping was privately baptized pr. the Reverend Robert Smith Rector

Mary Barber Row — On the 3rd. Day of August 1759 Mary Barber, Daughter of Morris & Mary Row was publickly baptized pr. the Reverend Mr. Robert Smith Rector.

Jane Remington — On the 13th. Day of August 1759 Jane, Daughter of John & Remington was privately baptized pr. the Reverend Mr. Robert Smith Rector ....

Christenings 86.

Mary Holzendorff — On the 24th. Day of August 1759 Mary Daughter of Frederic and Marianne Holzendorff was privately baptized pr. the Reverend Robt. Smith Rector

Robt. Lining — On the 25th. Day of August 1759 Robert Son of John and Linning was privately baptized pr. the Reverend Mr. Robert Smith Rector

John Logan — On the 26th. Day of August 1759 John Son of John & Logan was privately baptized pr. the Reverend Mr. Robert Smith Rector.

Frances Ewens — On the 27th. Day of August 1759 Frances Daughter of George & Priscilla Ewens was privately baptized pr. the Reverend Robert Smith Rector

Dan'el Tresvant — On the 6th. Day of September 1759 Daniel Son of Daniel & Elizabeth Tresvant was privately baptized pr. the Reverend Mr. Robert Smith Rector

Mar'a. Garrett — On the 10th. Day of September 1759 Martha Daughter of John & Garrett was privately baptized pr. the Reverend Mr. Robert Smith Rector.

Mary Gadsden — On the 17th. Day of September 1759 Mary Daughter of Christopher & Mary Gadsden was privately baptized pr. the Reverend Mr. Robert Smith Rector

Eliza. Russell — On the 18th. Day of September 1759 Elizabeth Daughter of & Mary Russell was privately baptized pr. the Reverend Mr. Robert Smith Rector

Chris'r Rogers	On the 28th. Day of September · 1759 Chris'r Son of & Elizabeth Rogers was privately baptized pr. the Reverend Mr. Robert Smith Rector
Fowler Axon	On the 28th. Day of September 1759 Fowler Son of Jacob & Eliza Axon was privately baptized pr. the Reverend Mr. Robert Smith Rector.
Dan'el Dwight or Maranneau	On the 10th. Day of October 1759 Daniel Son of Daniel Dwight and Mary Maranneau was publickly baptized pr. the Reverend Mr. Robert Smith Rector
Thos Pinckney	On the 27th. Day of February 1761 [or 2] Thomas Son of Charles Pinckney & Frances his wife was publickly baptized pr. the Revd. Mr. Robt. Smith Rector of St. Philips
John Snelling	On the 21st. Octr. 1759 John Son of John & Snelling was baptized .... by the Revd. Robt. Smith Rectr. ....
Abraham White	On the 27th. Octr. 1759 Abraham Son of Thomas & Frances White was baptized .... by the Revd. Robt. Smith Rectr. ....
Jacob Motte	On the 25th. of Octr. 1759 Jacob Son of Jacob & Rebecca Brewerton[1] was baptized .... by the Revd. Robt. Smith, Rectr. ....
Elizabeth Mayrant	On the 4th. Novr. 1759 Elizabeth, daughter of John & Elizabeth Mayrant was baptized .... by the Revd. Robt. Smith, Rectr. ....
William McKay	On the 9th. Novr. 1759 William Son of William & Elizabeth McKay was baptized .... by the Revd. Robt. Smith, Rectr. ....

[1]Jacob Motte, son of Jacob Motte and Rebecca (Brewton) Motte, his wife. (See *The South Carolina Historical and Genealogical Magazine*, II, 148.)

Jane Conway	On the 2d. Decbr. 1759 Jane, dautr. of John & Mary Conway was baptized .... by The Revd. Robt. Smith, Rectr. ....
Rebecca Wilkinson	On the 17th. Decbr. 1759 Rebecca daughter of Thomas & Martha Wilkinson was baptized .... by The Revd. Robt. Smith, Rectr. ....

Robt. Smith

Christenings 87

Mary Camel	On the 29th. Decbr. 1759 Mary, daughter of James & Ann Camel was baptized .... by the Revd. Robt Smith Rectr. ....
John Samway	On the 19th. Janry 1760 John, son of John & Mary Samway was baptized .... by The Revd. Robt Smith, Rectr. ....
Samuel Perkin	On the 22d. Janry 1760 Samuel, son of Samuel & Jane Perkin was baptized........ .... by The Revd. Robt Smith, Rectr.....
Francis Leigh	On the 24th. Janry 1760 Francis, son of Egerton & Martha Leigh, was baptized .... by The Revd. Robt Smith, Rectr. ....
Samuel Groves	On the 29th. Janry 1760 Samuel, son of Samuel & Groves was baptized .... by The Revd. Robt Smith, Rectr. ....
James Stephens	On the 30th. Janry 1760 James, son of David & Elizabeth Stephens was baptized .... by The Revd. Robt Smith, Rectr. ....
Martha Laurens	On the 9th. Febry 1760 Martha, daughter of Henry & Laurens was baptized .... by The Revd. Robt Smith, Rectr. ....
Jno. Melchior Armbristoe	On the 10th. Febry 1760 John Melchior, son of John & Elizabeth Armbristoe, was baptized .... by The Revd. Robt Smith, Rectr. ....

Hall — On the 10th. Febry 1760 of Hall, was baptized .... by The Revd. Robt Smith Rectr. ....

Thomas Linning — On the 12th. Febry 1760, Thomas, son of & Linning was baptized .... by the Revd. Robt Smith Rectr. ....

Violetta Lingard — On the 15th. Febry 1760 Violetta, daughter of Lingard, was baptized .... by The Revd. Robt Smith Rectr. ....

Jane Dewar — On the 15th. Febry 1760 Jane, daughter of Charles & Elizabeth Dewar was baptized .... by The Revd. Robt Smith Rectr. ....

Alexander Harvey — On the 17th. Febry 1760 Alexander of William & Harvey was baptized .... by The Revd. Robt Smith, Rectr. ....

Isabella Shaw — On the 24th. Febry 1760 Isabella, daughter of Lauchlan & Margaret Shaw was baptized .... by The Revd. Robt Smith, Rectr. ....

Margaret Remington — On the 25th. Febry 1760 Margaret, daughter of & Remington was baptized .... by The Revd. Robt Smith Rectr. ....

Lucretia Brailsford — On the 15th. Mar: 1760 Lucretia, daughter of Moreton & Brailsford was baptized .... By The Revd: Robt Smith Rectr. ....

James Obrien Parsons — On the 20th. Mar: 1760 James Obrien, of James & Susannah Parsons, was baptized .... by The Revd: Robt Smith Rectr. ....

Charles Gowdy — On the 20th. Mar: 1760 Charles, son of Charles & Lucina Gowdy, was baptized .... by The Revd: Robt Smith, Rectr.

Robt Smith

Doyley-Harrietta	On the 23rd. Mar: 1760 Harrietta of Daniel & Ann Doyley was baptized .... by The Revd: Robt Smith, Rectr. ....
Rutherforth-George	On the 22nd. Mar: 1760 George of Robert & Isabella Rutherforth was baptized .... by The Revd: Robt Smith, Rectr. ....
Timothy-Peter	On the 5th. April, Peter of Peter & Timothy was baptized .... by The Revd: Robt Smith, Rectr.
Beresford-William	On the 1st. April 1760 William of Richard & Beresford was baptized .... by The Revd: Robt Smith, Rectr. ....
Booden-Samuel	On the 5th. April 1760 Samuel of Thomas & Booden was baptized .... by The Revd: Robt Smith, Rectr. ....
Hutchins-Mary	On the 8th. April 1760 Mary, daughter of & Hutchins was baptized .... by The Revd: Robt Smith, Rectr. ....
McQueen-William	On the 11th. April 1760 William, son of John & McQueen was baptized .... by The Revd: Robt Smith, Rectr. ....
Sharp-Jane	On the 18th. April 1760: Jane, daughter of James & Elizabeth Sharp was baptized .... by The Revd: Robt Smith Rectr. ....
Johnson-Thomas	On the 21st. April 1760 Thomas, son of Joshua & Easter Johnson was baptized .... by The Revd: Robt Smith Rectr. ....
Brown-Ann	On the 3rd. May 1760, Ann, daughter of James & Ann Brown, was baptized .... by The Revd: Robt Smith, Rectr. ....
Roberson-Archibald	On the 11th. May 1760, Archibald, son of Archibald & Elizabeth Roberson was baptized .... by The Revd: Robt Smith, Rectr. ....

Massey-Mary	On the 18th. May 1760 Mary, daughter of John & Jane Massey was baptized .... by The Revd: Robt Smith, Rectr. ....
Prieleau-William Robert	On the 26th. May 1760, William Robert, son of Samuel & Provy Prieleau Was baptized .... by The Revd: Robt Smith, Rectr. ....
Wilson-Elizabeth Ann	On the 7th. June 1760, Elizabeth Ann, daughter of John & Mary Wilson was baptized .... by The Revd: Robt Smith, Rectr. ....
Pero-John	On the 7th. June 1760, John, son of Pedro & Pero, was baptized .... by The Revd: Robt Smith, Rectr. ....
McDonold-May	On the 13th. June 1760, May, daughter of Humphry & Isabella McDonold was baptized .... by The Revd: Robt Smith, Rectr. ....
Duckitt-Catharine Margaret	On the 29th. June 1760, Catharine Margaret, daughter of George & Ann Duckitt was baptized .... by The Revd: Robt Smith Rec: ....

Robt Smith

Christenings, 89

Adams-James	On the 4th. July 1760, Jane, daughter of Charles & Jane Adams was baptized .... by The Revd: Robt Smith, Rectr. ....
Bell-Robert	On the 12th. July 1760 Robert, son of Robert & Bell was baptized .... by The Revd: Robt Smith Rectr. ....
Yarnold-Benjamin	On the 29th. Septr: 1760 Benjamin, son of Benjamin & Yarnold was baptized .... by The Revd: Robt Smith, Rectr. ....

Warrant-Mary Anne	On the 13th. Octbr: 1760, Mary Anne, daughter of Joseph & Mary Warrant, was baptized .... by The Revd: Robt Smith Rectr. ....
Godin-Martha	On the 19th. Octbr: 1760 Martha, daughter of Isaac & Martha Godin was baptized .... by The Revd: Robt Smith Rectr. ....
Ferguson-Mary Booth	On the 25th. Octbr: 1760 Mary Booth, daughter of Thomas & Catharine Ferguson was baptized .... by The Revd: Robt Smith Rectr. ....
Rawlins-Jane	On the 10th. Octbr. 1760, Jane, daughter of Robert & Rawlins, was baptized .... by The Revd: Robt Smith Rectr. ....
Chalmers-Ann Bensley	On the 14th. Janry. 1761, Ann Bensley, daughter of Lionel & Martha Chalmers was baptized .... by The Revd: Robt Smith Rectr. ....
D'Frize-Christopher	On the 29th. Febry. 1761, Christopher, son of John & Elizabeth D'Frize was baptized ....by the Revd: Robt Smith Rectr. ....
McDonold-John	On the 18th. Mar: 1761, John, Son of Allen & Easter McDonold was baptized .... by The Revd: Robt Smith Rectr. ....
Logan-George Ogilvie	On the 25th. Mar: 1761 George Ogilvie, son of John & Logan, was baptized .... by The Revd: Robt Smith Rectr. ....
Tuckee-Elizabeth	On the 16th. April 1761, Elizabeth, daughter of James & Elizabeth Tuckee was baptized .... by The Revd: Robt Smith Rectr. ....

Rand-Ann	On the 22nd. April 1761 Ann, daughter of William & Ann Rand was baptized .... by The Revd: Robt Smith Rectr. ....
Browne-Mary	On the 26th. April 1761 Mary daughter of Thomas & Susannah Browne, was baptized .... by The Revd: Robt Smith Rectr. ....
Cony-Jane	On the 1st. May 1761 Jane, daughter of Philip & Biddy Cony was baptized .... by The Revd: Robt Smith Rectr. ....
Stobo-Ann	On the 17th. May 1761 Ann, daughter of Richard Park & Stobo was baptized .... by The Revd: Robt Smith Rectr. ....

....

Robt Smith

Christenings, 90

Cameron-Ann	On the 10th. June 1761 Ann, daughter of James & Ann Cameron was baptized .... by The Revd: Robt Smith Rectr. ....
Vain-Peter	On the 27th. June 1761 Peter, son of John & Ann Vain was baptized .... by The Revd: Robt Smith Rectr. ....
Donolsdon-James & Tiby	On the 27 June 1761, James & Tiby, son & daughter of James & Wall Donolsdon, was baptized .... by The Revd: Robt Smith Rectr. ....
Hyrn-Harriott	On the 1st. July 1761 Harriott, of Henry & Hyrn, was baptized .... by The Revd: Robt Smith Rectr. ....

Cromie-Alexander	On the 7th. Augst. 1761 Alexander, son of Alexander & Jane Cromie was baptized .... by The Revd: Robt Smith Rectr. ....
Gee-William	On the 17th. Augst. 1761, William, son of John & Ann Gee was baptized .... by The Revd: Robt Smith Rectr. ....
Brocknell-John	On the 6th. Septbr. 1761 John, son of John & Mary Brocknell, was baptized .... by The Revd: Robt Smith Rectr. ....
Courtonne-John Alexander	On the 25th. Sepbr. 1761 John Alexander, so of John & Courtonne was baptized .... by The Revd: Robt Smith Rectr. ....
Maxey-Thomas	On the 26th. Septbr. 1761 Thomas son of Joseph & Dorothy Maxey was baptized .... by The Revd: Robt Smith Rectr. ....
Gadsden-Philip	On the 11th. of Octbr. 1761 Philip, son of Christopher & Mary Gadsden was baptized[1] .... by The Revd: Robt Smith Rectr. ....
Cotter-Elizabeth	On the 13th. Octbr. 1761 Elizabeth, daughter of John & Elizabeth Cotter was baptized .... by The Revd: Robt Smith Rectr. ....
Redy-Philip	On the 11th. Novbr. 1761 Philip, son of Alexander & Catharine Redy, was baptized .... by The Revd: Robt Smith Rectr. ....

[1]He was the youngest son of Christopher and Mary (Hasell) Gadsden. He married, in November, 1783, Catherine Edwards. He was the father of Bishop Christopher Gadsden, of John Gadsden, U. S. District Attorney and James Gadsden, Minister to Mexico.

Smith-James — On the 11th. Novbr. 1761 James, son of Thomas & Smith was baptized .... by The Revd: Robt Smith Rectr. ....

Felder-Elizabeth — On the 12th. Novbr. 1761 Elizabeth, daughter of Henry & Elizabeth Felder was baptized .... by The Revd: Robt Smith Rectr. ....

McPherson-James — On the 13th. Novbr. 1761, James, son of James & Sarah McPherson, was baptized .... by The Revd: Robt Smith Rectr. ....

McKandlass-Ann — On the 15th. Novbr. 1761 Ann, daughter of John & Margaret McKandlass was baptized .... by The Revd: Robt Smith Rectr. ....

Robt Smith

Christenings, 91

Frazier-Simon — On the 23d. Novbr. 1761, Simon, son of Alexander & Margaret Frazier was baptized .... by The Revd: Robt Smith Rectr. ....

Berry-Elizabeth — On the 6th. Decbr. 1761 Elizabeth, daughter of Edward & Eleanor Berry, was baptized .... by The Revd: Robt Smith Rectr. ....

Mitchell- — On the 19th. Decbr: 1761 of Moses & Sarah Mitchell was baptized .... by The Revd: Robt Smith Rectr. ....

Shaw-William — On the 7th. Janry: 1762 William, son of William & Elizabeth Shaw was baptized .... by The Revd: Robt Smith Rectr. ....

Freer-Solomon	On The Febry 1762 Solomon, son of & Susannah Freer was baptized .... by The Revd: Robt Smith Rectr. ....
Johnston-Mary	On the 4th. Febry. 1762 Mary, daughter of Richard & Rebecca Johnston was baptized .... by The Revd: Robt Smith Rectr. ....
Hext-William Robt.	On the 10th. Febry 1762 William Robert, son of Alexander & Jane Hext, was baptized .... by The Revd: Robt Smith Rectr. ....
Bull-William Robt.	On the 10th. Febry: 1762 William Robert, son of William & Ann Bull, was baptized .... by The Revd: Robt Smith Rectr. ....
Stobo-Park	On the 26th. Febry. 1762 Park, son of Richard Park & Stobo, was baptized .... by The Revd: Robt Smith Rectr. ....
Chadwick Sarah	On the 1st. March 1762 Sarah, daughter of Thomas & Elizabeth Chadwick, was baptized .... by The Revd: Robt Smith Rectr. ....
Garret-Joseph	On the 11th. Mar: 1762 Joseph, son of John & Garret, was baptized .... by The Revd: Robt Smith Rectr. ....
Rawlins Eleanor	On June the 19th. 1762 Eleanor daughter of Robert & Rawlins was baptized....................by The Revd: Robt Smith Rectr. ....
Sarrazin	On the 6t. July 1762 of Jonathan & Sarazin was baptized............... by The Revd: Robt Smith Rectr. ....

E. Poinsett. (Registr.—

Curtis John	On The 13th. Septemr 1762 John, Son of Thos. & Frances Curtis was baptized .... by The Revd: Robt Smith Rectr. ....
Roupell Geo: Boone	On the 8d. Novemr. 1862. Geo. Boone son of Geo. & Eliz. Roupell was baptized .... by The Revd: Robt Smith Rectr. ....
Gardener John	On the 15th. decemr 1762, John, son of Simon & Barbara Gardener was baptized .... by The Revd: Robt Smith Rectr. ....

E Poinsett (Registr.)

Christenings 92

"Omitted from January the 4th. to November the 26th. 1762. Viz ...."

Lowndes-Mary	On the 9th. January 1762, Mary the daughter of Rawlins & Mary Lowndes was baptized .... by the Revd. Robt. Smith Rectr. ....
Burk-James	On the 12th. March 1762 James Son of John & Eliz: Burk was baptized .... by the Revd: Robt. Smith Rectr. ....
Nightingle John	On the 24th. March 1762, John Son of Thos. & Sarah Nightingle was baptized .... by the Revd. Robt. Smith Rectr. ....
Butler-Elizabeth	On the 24th. March 1762, Elizabeth, daughter of Peter & .... Butler Was baptized .... by the Revd. Robt. Smith. Rectr. ....
Stokes-Esther Eliz.	On the 25th. March 1762, Esther Eliz. Daughter of Joseph & Mary Stokes was baptized .... by the Revd. Robt. Smith Rectr. ....
Grey-Susanna	On April 7th. 1762. Susanna daughter of Henry & .... Grey was baptized .... by the Revd. Robt. Smith Rectr. ....

Harvey-Mary Cattell	On the 4th. June 1762, Mary Cattell daughter of Robt. & Eliz. Harvey was baptized .... by the Revd. Robt. Smith Rectr. ....
Sheener-Martha	On the 7th. June 1762, Martha, daughter of Charles & .... Sheener was baptized .... by the Revd. Robt. Smith Rectr. ....
Lybert-Isabella	On the 9th. June 1762 Isabella daughter of Henry & Mary Lybert was baptized .... by the Revd. Robt. Smith, Rectr. ....
Swallow-Margaret	On the 1st. August 1762, Margaret, daughter of Newman & Frances Swallow was baptized .... by the Revd. Robt. Smith Rectr. ....
Motte-Mary	On the 17th. August 1762, Mary daughter of Jacob & Rebecca Motte was baptized .... by the Revd. Robt. Smith Rectr. ....
Greene-Elizabeth	On the 22nd. Septemr. 1762, Elizabeth daughter of Nathan & Susanna Greene was baptized .... by the Revd. Robt. Smith Rectr. ....
Milligan-Wm. Johnson	On the 13th. October 1762 Willm. Johnson, son of George & Mary Milligan was Baptized .... by the Revd. Robt. Smith Rectr. ....

E. Poinsett (Registr.)

Christenings- 93

Fair--	On the 17th. November 1762 of Willm. & Catherine Fair was baptized .... by the Revd. Robt. Smith Rectr. ....
Shirer-Adam	On the 24th. November 1762, Adam, son of Michael & Barbary Shirer was baptized .... by the Revd. Robt. Smith Rectr. ....

Matty-Christiana	On the 26th. November 1762, Christiana daughter of Frederick & Margaret Matty was baptized .... by the Revd. Robt. Smith Rectr. ....
Backhouse-John	On the 18th. december 1762 John son of Benjamin & Catherine Backhouse was Baptized .... by the Revd. Robt. Smith Rectr. ....
West-William	On the 19th. december 1762, William, son of Edward & Elizabeth West was Baptized .... by the Revd. Robt. Smith Rectr. ....
Wood-david	On the 7th. January 1763, david Son of Joseph & Martha Wood was Baptized .... by the Revd. Robt. Smith Rectr. ....
Conner John	On the 14th. January 1763, John, son of John & Ann Conner was Baptized .... by the Revd. Robt. Smith Rectr. ....
Smith Samuel	On the 14th. January 1763, Samuel, son of Samuel & Mary Smith was Baptized .... by the Revd. Robt. Smith Rectr. ....
Williams John	On the 14th. January 1763, John, son of Jarvis & Edith Williams was Baptized .... by the Revd. Robt. Smith Rectr. ....
Redout, John	On the 17th. January 1763, John, son of Richard & Ann Redout was Baptized .... by the Revd. Robt. Smith Rectr. ....
Menzer Jno. Philip	On the 17th. January 1763, John Philip son of George & Barbara Menzer was Baptized .... by the Revd. Robt. Smith Rectr. ....
Hill- - -James Stevens	On the 17th. January 1763 James Stevens son of John & Susanna Hill was Baptized by the Revd. Robt. Smith Rectr. ....

David	On the 17th. January 1763 David son of Joseph & Martha was Baptized .... by the Revd. Robt. Smith Rectr.[1] ....
Gressun Sarah	On the 23d. February 1763 Sarah daughter of Charles & Lucia Gressun was Baptized .... by the Revd. Robt. Smith Rectr. ....

E. Poinsett (Regitr.)

Christenings 94

West- - - -William-	On the 23d. February 1763, William son of Edward & Elizabeth West- - - was Baptized .... by the Revd. Robt. Smith Rectr. ....
Anderson- -Ann	On the 23d. February 1763, Ann daughter of Lawrence & Elizabeth Anderson was Baptized .... by the Revd. Robt. Smith Rectr. ....
Rape- -Ruth	On the 23d. February 1763, Ruth daughter of Willm. & Elizabeth Rape was Baptized .... by the Revd. Robt. Smith Rectr. ....
Remeley- - -Elizabeth	On the 23d. February 1763 Elizabeth daughter of Martin & Ann Barbary Remeley was Baptized .... by the Revd. Robt. Smith Rectr. ....
Gressum- - William	On the 2d. March 1763, William, Son of Charles & Lucia Gressum was Baptized .... by the Revd. Robt. Smith Rectr. ....
Gressum- - Mary- -	On the 2d. March 1763, Mary daughter of Charles & Lucia Gressum was Baptized .... by the Revd. Robt. Smith Rectr. ....
Ellis- - James- -	On the 2d. March 1763 James, son of Abraham & Mary Ellis .... was Baptized .... by the Revd. Robt. Smith Rectr. ....

[1]Probably a garbled second entry of that above on the 7th.

Gressum- - Charles- -	On the 2d. March 1763 Charles, son of Charles & Lucia Gressum was Baptized .... by the Revd. Robt. Smith Rectr. ....
Keller- - Margaret	On the 10th. April 1763 Margaret daughter of Michael & Eliz. Keller was Baptized .... by the Revd. Robt. Smith Rectr. ....
Harvey- - - - Archibald	On the 13th. April 1763, Archibald son of Thomas & Eliz: Harvey ....was Baptized .... by the Revd. Robt. Smith Rectr. ....
Pickering- Francis	On the 28th. April 1763, Francis, son of Samuel & Mary Pickering was Baptized ....by the Revd. Robt. Smith Rectr. ....
Ainsetter- - - Christiana Juliana	On the 14th. May 1763, Christiana Juliana, daughter of Robt. & Barbara Ainsetter was Baptized .... by the Revd. Robt. Smith Rectr. ....
Coats- - - George	On the 15th. May 1763, George son of William & Mary Coats was Baptized .... by the Revd. Robt. Smith Rectr. ....
Tipping- - - - - Thomas	On the 18th. May 1763, Thomas, son of Joseph & Sarah Tipping was Baptized .... by the Revd. Robt. Smith Rectr. ....
Motte- - - - - Frances	On the 29th September 1763, Frances daughtr. of Jacob & Rebecca Motte was Baptized .... by the Revd. Robt. Smith Rectr. ....

E. Poinsett. (Registr.)

Christenings 95

[Copy mutilated in composing room.]	On the 1st. October 1763, Ann daughter of Christopher & Mary Gadsden was Baptized .... by the Revd. Robt. Smith Rectr. ....

	On the 23d. October 1763, Mary daughter of John & Mary Stevens was Baptized .... by the Revd. Robt. Smith Rectr. ....

Christenings Omitted to be Entered Viz.....

Deas John	On the 22d. April 1761 John—son of John & Eliz. Deas was Baptized .... by the Revd. Robt. Smith Rectr. ....
Jones Thomas	On the 26th. April 1761, Thomas of Thos & Christiana Jones was Baptized .... by the Revd. Robt. Smith Rectr. ....
Dawson Charles	On the 29th. April 1761 Charles of Charles & Martha Dawson was Baptized .... by the Revd. Robt. Smith Rectr. ....
Doiley Elizabeth	On the 11th. May 1761 Elizabeth, of Daniel & Ann Doily was Baptized .... by the Revd. Robt. Smith Rectr. ....
D'Harriette Ann	On the 11th. May 1761, Ann of John & Eleanor D'Harriette was Baptized .... by the Revd. Robt. Smith Rectr. ....
Dewar Ann	On the 20th. May 1761 Ann of Charles & Elizabeth Dewar was Baptized .... by the Revd. Robt. Smith Rectr. ....
Isaacs. Sarah	On the 20th. May 1761, Sarah of Saml. Caleb & Mary Isaacs. was Baptized............ by the Revd. Robt. Smith Rectr. ....
Watson William	On the 28th. May 1761, William of Archibold & Mary Watson was Baptized .... by the Revd. Robt. Smith Rectr. ....
Lance Mary	On the 28th. May 1761 Mary of Lambert & Lance was Baptized .... by the Revd. Robt. Smith Rectr. ....
Seward Thomas	On the 28th. May 1761, Thomas of Thomas & Mary Seward was Baptized .... by the Revd. Robt. Smith Rectr. ....
Yeates Mary	On the 7th June 1761 Mary of Joseph & Sarah Yeates was Baptized .... by the Revd. Robt. Smith Rectr. ....

Cateles Margaret	On the 17th. June 1761 Margaret of John & Eliz. Cateles was Baptized .... by the Revd. Robt. Smith Rectr. ....

E. Poinsett. (Registr.)

Two Soldier Boys	On the 7th. July 1761, Two Soldier Boys were Baptized by the Revd. Robt. Smith Rectr. ....
Cornish Christopher	On the 15th. July 1761 Christopher of Precilla Cornish was Baptized .... by the Revd. Robt. Smith Rectr. ....
Comberbeash Samuel	On the 15th. July 1761 Samuel of Saml. & Mary Comberbeash was Baptized by the Revd. Robt. Smith Rectr. ....
James Susanna	On the 17th. July 1761 Susanna, of John & Eliz. James was Baptized .... by the Revd. Robt. Smith Rectr. ....
Fley-Eliz. Catherine	On the 14th. August 1761 Eliz. Catherine of Saml. & Frances Fley was Baptized .... by the Revd. Robt. Smith Rectr. ....
Badger-Hannah Susanna	On the 14th. August 1761 Hannah Susanna of Ja^c^. & Mary Magdlin Badger was Baptized by the Revd. Robt. Smith Rectr. ....
Wood-John	On the 16th. October 1761 John of George & Ann Wood was Baptized .... by the Revd. Robt. Smith Rectr. ....
Whittle-Mary	On the 15th. November 1761 Mary of John & Margaret Whittle was Baptized .... by the Revd. Robt. Smith Rectr. ....
Britton Rosimond	On the 2d. decemr. 1761 Rosimond of Jno. & Allice Britton was Baptized .... by the Revd. Robt. Smith Rectr. ....
Elfe- - - - George	On the 2d. decemr. 1761 Geo. of Thos. & Elfe was Baptized .... by the Revd. Robt. Smith Rectr. ....
Kirk-Elizabeth	On the 2d. decemr. 1761 Eliz: of Thos. & Mary Kirk was Baptized .... by the Revd. Robt. Smith Rectr. ....

Keener-Precilla	On the 2d. decemr. 1761, Precilla of John & Mary Keener was Baptized .... by the Revd. Robt. Smith Rectr. ....
Smith-Bartley	On the 15th. January 1762 Bartley, of Robt. & Mary Smith was Baptized .... by the Revd. Robt. Smith Rectr. ....
Stevens-William	On the 5th. March 1762 William of John & Mary Stevens was Baptized .... by the Revd. Robt. Smith Rectr. ....

E. Poinsett (Registr.)

Smith Judith	On the 4th. June 1762 Judith of Benja. & Mary Smith Was Baptized .... by the Revd. Robt. Smith Rectr. ....
Lowndes-Mary	On the 9th. June 1762 Mary of Rawlins & Mary Lowndes was Baptized .... by the Revd. Robt. Smith Rectr. ....
Motte Elizabeth	On the 27th. August 1762 Elizabeth of Jacob & Rebecca Motte was Baptized .... by the Revd. Robt. Smith Rectr. ....
Harrison **Mary Eleonor**	On the 17th. February 1764 Mary Elionor of Saml. & Bathate Harrison was Baptized .... by the Revd. Robt. Smith Rectr. ....
Miles John	On the 4th. March 1764 John of Thos. & Elizabeth Miles was Baptized
Laurens-Henry	On the 18th. March 1764 Henry of Henry & Laurens was Baptized .... by
Snowden-Jno. Charles	On the 28th. March 1764 Jno. Charles of Joshua & Mary Snowden was Baptized .... by
Huger Elizabeth	On the 30th. March 1764 Elizabeth of Isaac & Elizabeth Huger was Baptized .... by
McClaring Margaret	On the 24th. April 1764, Margaret of David & Isabella McClaring was Baptized .... by

Stevens Ann	On the 9th. May 1764 Ann of Benj. & Elizabeth Stevens was Baptized .... by
Drayton Eliz. Hannah	On the 10th. June 1764 Eliz. Hannah of William & Mary Drayton was Baptized .... by
Swallow-Mary-Air	On the 3d. of August 1764 Mary-Air, of Newman & Frances Swallow was Baptized .... by
Drayton William	On the 8th. May 1764 William of William & Mary Drayton was Baptized .... by the Revd. Robt. Smith Rectr. ....
Motte Abraham	On the 16th. July 1764 Abraham of Jacob & Ann Motte was Baptized .... by the Revd. Robt. Smith Rectr. ....
Pickering Dorathy	On the 10th. August 1764 Dorathy of Samuel & Mary Pickering was Baptized .... by the Revd. Robt. Smith Rectr. ....
Forrister John	On the 11th. September 1764 John of John & Mary Forrister was Baptized .... by the Revd. Robt. Smith Rectr. ....

E. Poinsett. (Registr.)

Christenings 98

Shryock Mary	On the 5th. October 1764 Mary of Henry & Catherine Shryock was Baptized by the Revd. Robt. Smith Rectr. ....
Smith Joseph	On the 26th. October 1764 Joseph of Stephen & Ann Smith was Baptized .... by the Revd. Robt. Smith Rectr. ....
John	On the 15th. August 1764 John, a Negroe Belonging to Frances & Ann Kinlock was Baptized. Aged 70 Years ....
Roberson Joseph	On the 14th. december 1764 Joseph of William & Elizabeth Roberson was Baptized .... by the Revd. Robt. Smith Rectr. ....

Esmand Eliz. Isabel	On the 15th. decemr. Eliz. Isabel of George & Margaret Esmand was Baptized by the Revd. Robt. Smith Rectr.
Cochran Mary Eliz.	On the 19th. September 1764 Mary Elizabeth of Robert & Mary Cochran was Baptized
Fowler Richard	On the 19th. September 1764, Richard of Jonathan & Ann Fowler was Baptized
Perdu John	On the 23rd. September 1764 John of John & Christiana Perdu was Baptized
Dewar Sarah	On the 28th. September 1764 Sarah of Charles & Elizabeth Dewar was Baptized
Mitchell James	On the 10th. October 1764, James of John & Elizabeth Mitchell was Baptized
Hughes John	On the 17th. October 1764 John of John & Sarah Hughes was Baptized
Deas Wm. Allen	On the 19th. October 1764 William Allen of John & Elizabeth Deas was Baptized
Fearis Letitia	On the 16th. November 1764 Letitia of Denham & Mary Fearis was Baptized
Nowell John	On the 21st. November 1764 John of John & Elizabeth Nowel Was Baptized

E. Poinsett. (Registr.)

Christenings 99

Williams John	On the 30th. November 1764, John of Jarvis & Edith Williams was Baptized
Henderson John	On the 16th. January 1765—John of William & Margaret Henderson was Baptized

Hughes John	On the 16th. January 1765 John of John & Mary Julee Hughes .... was Baptized ....
Smith Joseph	On the 18th. January 1765, Joseph of Stephen & Ann Smith .... was Baptized ....
Blake Elizabeth	On the 27th. January 1765, Elizabeth of John & Elizabeth Blake .... was Baptized ....
Hicks Mary	On the 15th. February 1765, Mary of Thomas & Sarah Hicks .... was Baptized ....
Conner Wm. Robt.	On the 22d. February 1765, William Robt. of John & Ann Conner .... was Baptized ....
Nicholson, Cathrine Martha	On the 6th. March 1765, Cathrine Martha of Francis & Mary Nicholson .... was Baptized ....
Powell William	On the 6th. March 1765, William of Joseph & Ann Powell .... was Baptized ....
Moultrie John	On the 8th. March 1765, John of John & Eleanor Moultrie .... was Baptized ....
Moultrie Ann	On the 8th. March 1765, Ann of John & Eleanor Moultrie .... was Baptized ....
Mayrant Wm. Woodrop	On the 8th. March 1765, William Woodrop of John & Ann Mayrant .... was Baptized ....
Nicholson Francis	On the 8th. March 1765 Francis of Francis & Mary Nicholson .... was Baptized ....

E. Poinsett. (Registr.)

Christenings 100

Mayrant James	On the 8th. March 1765, James of John & Ann Mayrant .... was Baptized ....

Foster-Charlotte	On the 13th. March 1765 Charlotte of George & Isabella Foster .... was Baptized ....
Hall-Elizabeth	On the 9th. June 1765, Elizabeth of Geo. Abbot & Lois Hall .... was Baptized, at Johns Island by the Revd. Mr. Isaac Amory
Wood Elizabeth	On the 20th. November 1765, Elizabeth of George & Ann Wood was Baptized .... in St. Michaels Chh by the Revd. Mr. Hart, assistant
Strother Mary	On the 31st. January 1765, Mary of George & Mary Strother .... was Baptized ....
Walls Richard	On the 3d. February 1765, Richard of Benjamin & Ann Walls .... was Baptized ....
Manigault Judith	On the 7th. March 1765 Judith of Peter & Elizabeth Manigault .... was Baptized ....
Dickinson Joseph	On the 4th. July 1765, Joseph of David & Avis Dickinson .... Was Baptized ....
Burges Benjamin	On the 12th. July 1765, Benjamin of John & Rebecca Burges .... Was Baptized ....
Clark Louisa	On the 5th. August 1765 Louisa of Thomas & Ann Clark .... was Baptized ....
Clark Susanna	On the 5th. August 1765 Susanna of Thomas & Ann Clark .... was Baptized ....
Bacot Thos. Wright	On the 1st. August 1765 Thomas Wright of Peter & Eliz. Bacot .... was Baptized ....
Akin James	On the 27th. September 1765 James of James & Ann Akin .... was Baptized ....

E. Poinsett. (Registr.)

Bowen Daniel	On the 8th. October 1765, Daniel of John & Mary Bowen .... was Baptized ....
Boyd Elizabeth	On the 13th. October 1765 Elizabeth of Robert & Ann Boyd .... was Baptized ....
Moore Ann	On the 22d. Decemb 1765 Ann of John & Catherine Moore .... was Baptized ....
Roberson Joseph	On the' 10th. April 1765, Joseph of William & Elizabeth Roberson .... was Baptized ....
Lebby Aron	On the 24th. April 1765, Aron of Nathaniel & Elizabeth Lebby .... was Baptized ....
Russell George	On the 7th. June 1765 George of George & Mary Russell .... was Baptized ....
Harrison John	On the 19th. June 1765 John of John & Mary Harrison .... was Baptized ....
Rutledge Sarah	On the 23d of June 1765 Sarah of John & Elizabeth Rutledge .... was Baptized ....
Smith Ann	On the 28th. June 1765 Ann of Malcolm & Jane Smith .... was Baptized ....
Simmons Thomas	On the 10th. July 1765 Thomas of Maurice & Mary Simmons .... was Baptized ....
Hazlewood Elizabeth	On the 19th. July 1765, Elizabeth of William & Susanna Hazlewood .... was Baptized ....
Shoulds Christopher	On the 21st August 1765 Christopher of Daniel & Elizabeth Shoulds .... was Baptized ....
Bonetheau Ann	On the 7th Septemr. 1765 Ann of Peter & Ann Bonetheau .... was Baptized ....

E. Poinsett. (Registr.)

Ellis William	On the 16th. October 1765 William of William & Ellis Senr. was Baptized
Davies Mary Crosskeys	On the 13th. Septemr. 1765 Mary Crosskeys of Wm. & Mary Davies was Baptized
Shirer Mary	On the 1st. Novemr. 1761 Mary of Michael & Barbary Shirer was Baptized
Fair William	On the 11th. Decemr. 1765 William of William & Catherine Fair was Baptized
Lybert Isabella Wish	On the 29th. Decemr. 1765 Isabella Wish of Henry & Mary Lybert was Baptized
Harkenson Lidia	On the 7th. January 1766 Lidia of Joseph & Elizabeth Harkenson was Baptized
You Elizabeth	On the 15th. January 1766 Elizabeth of Thomas & Elizabeth You was Baptized
Gillmore Eleanor	On the 19th. January 1766 Eleanor of Anthony & Mary Gillmore was Baptized
Timothy Lewis	On the 21st. February 1766 Lewis of Peter & Ann Timothy was Baptized
Harleston Ann	On the 8th. March 1766 Ann of Nicholas & Ann Harleston was Baptized
Baldwin Sarah	On the 23d. March 1766 Sarah of Charles & Sarah Baldwin was Baptized
Trusler Edward	On the 11th. April 1764 Edward of William & Trusler was Baptized (private)
Brailsford Edward	On the 28th. March 1766 Edward of Samuel & Elizabeth Brailsford was Baptized

E. Poinsett (Registr.

Logan Geo Ogilvie	On the 24th. January 1761 Geo Ogilvie of John & Logan was Baptized
Logan Catherine	On the 20th. Septemr. 1762 Catherine of John & Logan was Baptized
Logan John	On the 14th. Septemr. 1764 John of John & Logan was Baptized
Huger Elizabeth	On the 20th. Octobr. 1763 Elizabeth of Isaac & Elizabeth Huger was Baptized
Huger Mary	On the 1st. Decemr. 1764 Mary of Isaac & Elizabeth Huger was Baptized
Huger Martha	On the 16th. Decemr. 1765 Martha of Isaac & Elizabeth Huger was Baptized
Huger Ann	On the Ann of Isaac & Elizabeth Huger was Baptized (private)
Tedder David	On the 17th. March 1765 David of Henry & Mary Eliz. Tedder of Orangeburgh was Baptized (do.)
Mims James	On the 28th. March 1765, James of James & Avis Mims, of Four holes was Baptized
Nickson William	On the 30th. March 1765—William of Thomas & Hannah Nickson was Baptized
Dewitt Ann	On the 6th. May 1765—Ann of William & Mary Dewitt was Baptized
Porcher Peter	On the 15th. May 1765—Peter of Joseph & Susanna Porcher was Baptized
Testard Robert	On the 15th. May 1765—Robert of Robert & Mary Testard was Baptized

E. Poinsett. (Registr.)

Risby Charles	On the 23d August 1765 Charles of Charles & Susanna Risby was Baptized
Cross Mathew Wm.	On the 28th. Septemr. 1765 Mathew William of William & Mary Cross was Baptized
Elliss William	On the 28th. Septemr. 1765, William of William Elliss (an Adult) was Baptized
Trusler William	On the 3d. October 1765 William of William & Trusler was Baptized
Dering Chalmondeley	On the 31st. Decemr. 1765 Chalmondeley of Chalmondely Dering & Duthy (Illigt.) was Baptized
Dewitt Rebecca	On the 19th. Novemr. 1765 Rebecca of Joseph & Jane Dewitt, of the Yewhaw's was Baptized
Wyly Mary	On the 25th. January 1766 Mary of Felix & Ann Wyly, of Christ Chh was Baptized
Herron Mary	On the 26th. January 1766 Mary of William & Eleanor Herron was Baptized
Dawson William	On the 26th. January 1766, William of Charles & Martha Dawson was Baptized
Tipping William	On the 16th. April 1766 William of Joseph & Sarah Tipping was Baptized
Minors Elizabeth	On the 20th. May 1766 Elizabeth of Charles & Sarah Minors was Baptized
McDonald Elizabeth	On the 26th. May 1766 Elizabeth of William & Margaret McDonald was Baptized
Pickering Samuel	On the 10th. July 1766 Samuel of Samuel & Mary Pickering was Baptized

E. Poinsett. (Registr.)

Smith Elizabeth	On the 10th. July 1766 Elizabeth of Walter & Catherine Smith was Baptized
Oliver Eleanor Catherine	On the 25th. July 1766 Eleanor Catherine of John & Jane Oliver was Baptized
Holloway Winefred	On the 4th. August 1766, Winefred of David & Mary Holloway Was Baptized
Wallis Samuel	On the 13th. October 1766 Samuel of Edward & Martha Wallis was Baptized
Mackensie Mary	On the 2d. Novemr. 1766 Mary of James & Jane Mackensie was Baptized
Gowdey William Charles	On the 10th. Septemr. 1764 William Charles of William & Mary Gowdey was Baptized
White John	On the 7th. March 1766 John of Sims & Mary White was Baptized
Testard Sarah	On the 27th. March 1766. Sarah of William & Sarah Testard was Baptized
Foster Mary	On the 29th. March 1766 Mary of Learon & Mary Foster was Baptized
Lowndes Harriot	On the 4th. April 1766 Harriot of Rawlins & Mary Lowndes was Baptized
Lowndes Thomas	On the 4th. April 1766, Thomas of Rawlins & Mary Lowndes was Baptized
Tebout Margaret	On the 9th. April 1766 Margaret of Tunis & Tebout was Baptized
Pinckney Mary	On the 30th. April 1766 Mary of Charles & Pinckney was Baptized

E. Poinsett. (Registr.)

Pinckney Wm. Robert	On the 30th. April 1766 William Robert of Charles & Pinckney was Baptized
Ball Agness	On the 27th. April 1766 Agness of Joseph & Ann Ball Junr. was Baptized
Pitt Elizabeth	On the 17th. May 1766 Elizabeth of James & Deborah Pitt was Baptized
Mitchell Sarah	On the 31st. April 1766 Sarah of Moses & Sarah Mitchell was Baptized
Mitchell Moses	On the 31st. April 1766 Moses of Moses & Sarah Mitchell was Baptized
Mitchell William	On the 31st. April 1766 William of Moses & Sarah Mitchell was Baptized
Dixon Margaret	On the 21st. May 1766 Margaret of Christopher & Susanna Dixon was Baptized
Lord Benjamin	On the 25th. May 1766, Benjamin of Benjamin & Ann Lord was Baptized
Deas David	On the 11th. July 1766 David of John & Elizabeth Deas was Baptized
Snowden William	On the 17th. August 1766. William of Joshua & Mary Snowden was Baptized
Devall Stephen	On the 17th. August 1766. Stephen of Stephen & Catherine Devall was Baptized
Beale	On the 10th. Septemr. 1766 of John & Beale was Baptized
Nevin Wm. Thomas	On the 17th. Septemr 1766 William Thomas of John & Isabella Nevin was Baptized

E. Poinsett. (Registr.)

Ham Thomas	On the 24th. Septemr. 1766 .... Thomas of Thomas & Sarah Ham was Baptized
You Harriott	On the 19th. July 1766 .... Harriott of Thomas & Elizabeth You .... was Baptized
Chalmers Margaret	On the 31st. July 1767 Margaret of Lionel & Elizabeth Chalmers .... was Baptized by the Revd. Mr. Jos. Darri Wilton
Gordon Cormos	On the 2d. August 1766 Cormos of James & Mary Magdelin Gordon was Baptized by the Revd Mr. Robert Smith Rectr. ....
Leigh Harriott Ann	On the 29th. August. 1766 Harriott Ann of Egerton & Martha Leigh .... was Baptized by the Revd. Mr. Robert Smith
Timothy Robert	On the 27th. Decemr. 1766, Robert of Peter & Timothy was Baptized by the Revd. Mr. Robt. Smith ....
Hatton Samuel	On the 13th. January 1767. Samuel of George & Elizabeth Hatton was Baptized by the Revd. Mr. Robt. Smith
Thomas Thos. Hazell	On the 19th. January 1767 Thomas Hazell of Samuel & Ann Thomas was Baptized by the Revd. Mr. Robt. Smith
Collins Sarah	On the 27th. January 1767, Sarah of Elizabeth Collins was Baptized by the Revd. Mr. Robt. Smith ....
Simons Maurice	On the 5th. August 1767. Maurice of Maurice & Mary Simons was Baptized by the Revd. Mr. Robt. Smith ....

Gadsden Jas. William — On the 22d September 1767 James William of Thomas & Mary Gadsden was Baptized by the Revd Mr. Robt. Smith ....

Wood Benjamin — On the 4th. October 1767.. Benjamin of John & Judith Wood .... was Baptized by the Revd. Mr. Robt. Smith ....

Akin Margaret — On the 30th. Septemr. 1767. Margaret of William & Ann Akin was Baptized by the Revd. Mr. Smith........

Sarah a free Wench — On the 2d. October 1767. Sarah (a free Negroe) formerly Belonging to Jno. Neufville, was Baptized. (Aged 64 Years)

E. Poinsett. (Registr.)

Christenings 108

Robertson Elizabeth — On the 6th. October 1767 Elizabeth of George & Margt. Robertson was Baptized by the Revd. Mr. Robt. Smith ....

Grey Benjamin — On the 6th. October 1767 Benjamin of Henry & Ann Grey was Baptized by the Revd. Mr. Robt. Smith ....

Simons Ann — On the 6th. October 1767. Ann of Benjamin & Ann Simons was Baptized by the Revd. Mr. Rt. Smith

Thompson William — On the 18th. Novemr 1767 William of John & Elizabeth Thompson was Baptized by the Revd. Mr. Robt. Smith ....

Howard Thomas — On the 3d. December 1767, Thomas of Robt. & Ann Howard was Baptized by the Revd. Robt. Smith....

Lebby Mary — On the 3d. Decemr. 1767, Mary of Nathaniel & Elizabeth Lebby was Baptized by the Revd. Mr. Robt. Smith

Lamer Thomas	On the 20th. January 1767 Thomas of Thomas & Catherine Lamer born Jan. 17— was Baptized by the Revd. Mr. J. D. Wilton.
Doughty Mary	On the 22d. January 1767. Mary of Thomas Doughty & Rebecca Gay was Baptized by the Revd. Mr. Wilton (a natural Child.)
Tyler William	On the 24th. January 1767 William of George & Elizabeth Tyler Was Baptd. by the Revd. Mr. Wilton (Born Decemr. 28th. 1766)
Backhouse Eleanor	On the 27th. January 1767.* Eleanor of Benjamin & Catherine Backhouse Was Baptd. by the Revd Mr. Wilton (born Decr. 11th. 1766—
Chambers Catherine	On the 27th. January 1767.. Catherine of William & Rose Chambers was Baptd. by the Revd. Mr. Wilton (born Decr. 14th. 1766—
Fickling Jane	On the 31st. January 1767, Jane of John & Mary Fickling Was Baptd. by the Revd. Mr. Wilton (born June 18th. 1766
Fickling Daniel	On the 13th. November 1766 Daniel of John & Mary Fickling was Baptd. by the Revd. Mr. Wilton ....

E. Poinsett Registr.

Christenings 109

Fenshaw Robert	On the 26th. April 1767 Robert of James & Hannah Fenshaw was Baptd. by the Revd. Mr. Wilton ....
McCallot John	On the 27th. April 1767 John of Archibald & Mary McCallot (of his Majesty's Ship Sardoine) was Baptd. by the Revd. Mr. Wilton ....
McMahone Ann	On the 6th. June 1767 .. Ann of Thomas & Catherine McMahone was Baptd. by the Revd. Mr. Wilton

Hogg Ann	On the 11th. June 1767 Ann of Richard & Elizabeth Hogg .... was Baptd. by the Revd. Mr. Wilton ....
Miller Elizabeth	On the 7th. July 1767.. Elizabeth of Jacob & Mary Miller was Baptd. by the Revd. Mr. Wilton
Robison James	On the 7th. July 1767. James of William & Elizabeth Robison was Baptd. by the Revd. Mr. Wilton
Worch John	On the 8th. July 1767 .... John of John & Eleanor Worch was Baptd.. by the Revd. Mr. Wilton
Bonetheau John	On the 9th. July 1767—John of Peter & Ann Bonetheau was Baptd. by the Revd. Mr. Wilton
Poaug Judith	On the 9th. July 1767—Judith of John Charlotte Poaug was Baptd. by the Revd. Mr. Wilton (June 18th. 1767)
Fickling George	On the 23rd. July 1767—George of George & Ann Fickling was Baptd. by the Revd. Mr. Wilton
Vane Ann	On the 25th. Augst. 1767. Ann of George & Ann Vane was Baptized by the Revd. Mr. Wilton
Dicks Alexr.	On the 7th. May 1767—Alexander Dicks was Baptzd. (Born 17th. Febry. 1767

E. Poinsett. (Registr............

Christenings 110.

Dawson Elizabeth	On the 24th. May 1767 Elizabeth of Charles & Martha Dawson was Baptd.
Young John	On the 13th. Decemr. 1767 John of David & Susanna Young was Baptized.
Gilling	On the 20th. Janry 1768 of & Gilling was Baptized

Hannah	On the 22d Janry. 1768 Hannah, negroe of Gabriel Manigault Esqr. was Baptized.
Cusek Sarah	On the 20th. Mar. 1788 Sarah of Adam & Frances Cusek was Baptized........... born Novr. 13th. 1766
Frasier Jas. Prioleau	On the 22d. Jany 1768 .... James Prioleau. of James & Margaret Frasier was Baptized.
Deas Seaman	On the 12th. Febry. 1768, Seaman of John & Elizabeth Deas was Baptized
Broadford Jane	On the 29th. Febry. 1768, Jane of Samuel & Jane Broadford Was Baptized
Izard Margaret	On the 21st Mar. 1768 Margaret of Ralph & Izard was Baptized ....
Clark Mary	On the 23d Mar. 1768, Mary of Richard & Catherine Clark was Baptized ....
Ruger Mary	On the 7th. April 1768—Mary of William & Christiana Ruger........ Was Baptized........
Montagu Eliz. Harriott	On the 18th. April 1768, Eliz. Harriott of Lord Charles Gaville[1] Montagu & Lady Elizer Harriott Montagu, was Baptized........
White Sarah	On the 18th. April 1768 Sarah of Sims & Mary White was Baptized........

....

E. Poinsett. Registr.

Christenings 111

Martin Mary	On the 18th. May 1768, Mary of James & Catherine Martin was Baptized........

[1]Greville.

Breuning Lewis	On the 4th. Mar. 1768 .... Lewis of Eugine & Mary Breuning........ was Baptized........
Smith Thomas	On the 18th. Mar. 1768 Thomas of Thomas & Ann Smith. was Baptized........
Cogdell Isaac	On the 21st. Mar. 1768 Isaac of John & Elizabeth Cogdell........ was Baptized........
Motte Francis	On the 31st. Mar. 1768 Francis of Jacob & Motte Was Baptized........
Leigh Charlotte Lucia	On the 16th. May 1768, Charlotte Lucia of Egerton & Martha Leigh, Was Baptized........
Michie Ann	On the 9th. October 1768 Ann of Alexander & Heneritta Michie was Baptized........
Bacot Eliz. Henrietta	On the 24th. August 1768 Elizabeth Henrietta of Peter & Elizabeth Bacot was Baptized........
Stephens Benjamin	On the 30th. August 1768 Benjamin of Benjamin & Elizabeth Stephens Was Baptized........
Gissinder John	On the 13th. September 1768 John of John & Lucretia Gissinder........ was Baptized........
Weyman Edward	On the 26th. October 1768, Edward of Edward & Rebecca Weyman was Baptized (born the 26th. September 1768)
Vaulton Harriett	On the 1st. Novembr. 1768 Harriett of Peter & Elizabeth Vaulton was Baptized ....
Burnham Thomas	On the 10th. November 1768 Thomas of Thomas & Mary Burnham........ was Baptized........
Cumings Hamilton	On the 20th. Novembr. 1768 Hambeton of James & Jane Cumings was Baptized........

Lennox John	On the 2d. of September 1768, John Lennox, son of Willm. & Judith Lennox was Born........ & Baptized the 7th. of Octor. 1768, by the Revd. Rt. Cooper.

E. Poinsett (Registr.)

Christenings 112

Cords Peter	On the 1st. of August 1766 Peter of Saml. & Elizabeth Cords Was Baptized........
Parks Ann	On the 1st. of August 1766 Ann of Thos & Ann Parks........ was Baptized........
Greeme, Ann	On the 8th. Septemr. 1766 Ann of & Greeme was Baptized........
McDonald John	On the 29th. October 1766 John of Donald McDonald was Baptized........
Gasser Jno. Abraham	On the 26th. November 1766 Jno. Abraham Gasser, & Hannah Mary, Was Baptized............[1]
Brennan Eugene	On the 4th. November 1766 Eugene of Eugene & Mary Brennan was Baptized .... born 26th. Octor. 1766
Gasser Jno. Eberhart	On the 26th. November 1766 Jno. Eberhart of John & Hannah Mary Gasser was Baptized............[1]
Hughes John Mathews	On the 14th. January 1767 John of John & Mary Hughes was Baptized........
Jones John	On the 1st. February 1767 John of William & Cliona Jones was Baptized........
Fowler John	On the 6th February 1767 John of Jonathan & Ann Fowler was Baptized........

[1]Two attempts at recording the same name.

Gowdey Elizabeth	On the 25th. February 1767 Elizabeth of William & Margaret Gowdey Was Baptized....
Bacot Peter	On the 29th. April 1767 Peter of Peter & Bacot was Baptized....
Trousiger Martha Eliz.	On the 29th. April 1767 Martha Eliz. of Peter & Elizabeth Trouseger was Baptized....
Prichard Ann	On the 15th. May 1767 Ann of Paul & Ann Prichard was Baptized....

E. Poinsett (Registr.........

Christenings. - - - 113

Holliss George	On the 7th. July 1767 George of John & Elizabeth Holliss Was Baptized
Lindzey Arabella	On the 12th. July 1767 Arabella of Thomas & Elizabeth Lindzey was Baptized....
Smith Margaret	On the 5th. August 1767 Margaret of Frederick & Mary Smith was Baptized....
Akins	On the 30th. Septemr. 1767 of William & Ann Akins was baptized....
Free Sarah	On the 2d. October 1767 Sarah a free Negroe .... was baptized....
Neufville	On the 2d. October 1767 of John & Neufville was baptized....
Young John	On the 13th. December 1767 John of David & Susanna Young was Baptized....
Gillon Mary	On the 20th. January 1768 Mary of Alexander & Mary Gillon was Baptized....

Manigault Hannah	On the 22d January 1768 Hannah a Free Negroe was Baptized .... Enterd. in 110........
Cuseck Sarah	On the 20th. March 1768 Sarah of Adam & Frances Cuseck was Baptized. Born the 13th. March 1766.
Bacot-Eliz. Henrietta	On the 24th. August 1768 Eliz. Henrietta of Peter & Elizabeth Bacot was Baptized .... Enterd. in 111....
Stevens Benjamin	On the 30th. August 1768 Benjamin of Benjamin & Elizabeth Stevens was Baptized .... Enterd in 111....
Gissindar John	On the 16th. Septemr. 1768 John of John & Lucretia Gissindar.... was Baptized .... Enterd. in 111....
Weyman Edward	On the 26th. October 1768 Edward of Edward & Rebecca Weyman was Baptized .... Enterd. in 111
Valton Harriett	On the 1st. November 1768 Harriett of Peter & Elizabeth Valton was Baptized .... Enterd. in 111

E. Poinsett. (Registr.

Christenings 114

Burnham Thomas	On the 10th. November 1768 Thomas of Thomas & Mary Burnham was Baptized .... Enterd. in 111
Cummings Hamilton	On the 20th. November 1768, Hamilton of James & Jane Cummings was Baptized .... Enterd. in 111....
Neufville Elizabeth	On the 14th. December 1768. Elizabeth of John & Neufville was Baptized....
Rush Elizabeth	On the 26th. December 1768 Elizabeth of Peter & Catherine Rush was Baptized....
Lebba Elizabeth	On the 30th. December 1768 Elizabeth of Nathaniel & Eliz. Lebba was Baptized....

Gravestork Ann	On the 13th. January 1769 Ann of William & Mary Gravestork was Baptized....
Hutton Jno. Morgot Hamilton	On the 13th. January 1769 Jno Morgot Hamilton of Geo. & Eliz Hutton was Baptized....
Wood Mary	On the 14th. January 1769 Mary of Jonathan & Jane Wood.... Was Baptized....
Walker James	On the 21st. January 1769, James of Joseph & Jane Walker was Baptized....
Wiley Alexander	On the 19th. February 1769 Alexander of Alexander & Ann Wiley Was Baptized
Clark Margaret	On the 26th. February 1769 Margaret of Richard & Hannah Clark was Baptized
Godin Eliz. Sarah	On the 1st. March 1769 Eliz. Sarah of Isaac & Godin was Baptized
Motte Jacob	On the 12th. May 1769 Jacob of Charles & Elizabeth Motte was Baptized
Hall Elizabeth	On the 9th. June 1765—Elizabeth of Geo. Abbot & Louisa Hall........ Was Baptized, by the Revd. Mr. Isaac Amory at St. Johns Colliton County.

E. Poinsett. (Registr.

Christenings 115

Poaug John	On the 23rd. July 1769 John of John & Charlotte Poaug was Baptized, & Born the 1st. Instant
Pinckney Thomas	On the 27th. day of February 1761 Thomas, son of Charles & Frances Pinckney, was Baptized by the Revd. Mr. Robt. Smith

Pinckney Miles Brewton	On the 25th day of October 1769, Miles Brewton Pinckney, Son of Charles & Frances Pinckney, was Baptized by the Revd. Mr. Purcell
Huger Isaac	On the 1st. March 1767 Isaac son of Isaac & Elizabeth Huger (Vide Births) Was Born
Knight Bulleine	On the 15th. Septemr 1769 Bulleine Son of Wm. & Elizabeth Knight was Baptized & Born 9th. Augst. 1768
Beale Othniel	On the 4th. October 1769 Othniel Son of John & Mary Beale was Baptized....
Holmes John	On the 11th. October 1769 John son of Paty & Jane Eliz. Holmes was Baptized....
Slade Ann Smiley	On the 13th. October 1769 Ann Smiley of Partianna Slade was Baptized....
Phillips Ann	On the 10th. Novemr. 1769 Ann of James & Phillips was Baptized....
Smith David	On the 24th. Novemr. 1769 David of David & Mary Smith was Baptized....
Harvey Elizabeth	On the 29th. Novemr 1769 Elizabeth of Thos. & Eliz. Harvey was Baptized....
Prichard William	On the 26th. Decemr. 1769 William of Paul & Ann Prichard was Baptized....
Tebout Elizabeth	On the 24th. January 1770 Elizabeth of Tunis & Deborah Tebout was Baptized....
Wish John	On the 26th. January 1770 John of Benja. & Thetus Wish Was Baptized....

E. Poinsett. (Registr.)

Harleston Sarah	On the 12th. of April 1770 Sarah of John & Elizabeth Harleston was Baptized....
Smith Mary	On the 27th. of April 1770 Mary of Thos. Laughton & Eliz. Smith was Baptized.....
Burges Elizabeth	On the 11th. May 1770, Elizabeth of John & Elizabeth Burges was Baptized....
Bacot Mary	On the 18th. May 1770 Mary of Peter & Eliza. Bacot was Baptized.
Doyley Margaret	On the 30th. Day of January 1757. Margaret of Daniel & Ann Doyley was Baptized by the Revd. Mr. Clark ....
Doyley Ann	On the 27th. day of September 1759 Ann of Daniel & Ann Doyley was Baptized by the Revd. Mr. Robt. Smith
Doyley Rebecca	On the 19th. day of May 1761, Rebecca of Daniel & Ann Doyley was Baptized by the Revd. Mr. Robt. Smith
Doyley Daniel	On the 3rd. Day of May 1763 Daniel of Daniel & Ann Doyley was Baptized by the Revd. Mr. Robt. Smith
Powell Ann	On the 13th. January 1770 Ann of Joseph & Ann Powell was Baptized....
Williams Peter	On the 13th. January 1770 Peter of Peter & Elizabeth Williams was Baptized....
Melyard Martha	On the 23rd. January 1770 Martha of William & Susanna Melyard was Baptized....
Spidell William	On the 4th. February 1770 William Hamon of Geo. & Mary Spidell was Baptized....

Nowell Charles	On the 17th. February 1770 Charles of John & Elizabeth Nowell was Baptized....
Granger James	On the 29th. April 1770 James of Henry & Eleanor Granger was Baptized....
Probey Barbary	On the 20th. May 1770 Barbary of Solomon & Barbary Proby was Baptized....
Mann Catherine	On the 10th. June 1770 Catherine of John & Christian Mann was Baptized....

E. Poinsett (Registr.........

Christenings 117

Mann Mary	On the 10th. June 1770 Mary of John & Christian Mann was Baptized....
Moore Catherine	On the 7th. July 1770 Catherine of William & Susanna Moore was Baptized....
Moore Jane	On the 7th. July 1770 Jane of William & Susanna Moore was Baptized....
Carter Celia	On the 8th. July 1770 Celia of James & Francis Carter was Baptized....
Woolford Mary	On the 10th. July 1770 Mary of Richard & Ann Woolford was Baptized....
Trusler William	On the 5th. Septemr. 1767—Mary of William & Sarah Trusler was Baptized....
Trusler Elizabeth	On the 10th. February 1770, Elizabeth of William & Sarah Trusler was Baptized....
Harleston Nicholas	On the 12th. August 1768, Nicholas of Nicholas & Ann Harleston was Baptized—pr Rev Mr. Hart

Reid Alexander	On the 27th. July 1770 Alexander, son of Alex. & Ried was Baptized....
Tyler Elizabeth	Sept. 18th. 1770 Elizabeth, of George & Elizabeth Tyler was Baptized....
Thomlinson James	Sept. 18th. 1770 James of James & Catherine Thomlinson Was Baptized....
Cunningham Andrew	Oct. 1st. 1770, Andrew of Andrew & Isabella Cunningham, was Baptized....
Gardner Anne	Oct. 5th. 1770, Anne, of Thomas & Mary Gardner, was Baptized....
Alexander Anne	Dec. 2nd. 1770, Anne of Alexander & Rachel Alexander, was Baptized
Sharp Barnett	Aug. 5th. 1770, Barnett, of .... & Anne Sharp, was Baptized—a natural child—
Reid Thomas	Sept. 17th. 1770, Thomas of .... & Rose Reid, Was Baptized....
Naylor Elizabeth Ann	Jan. 10th. 1771, Elizabeth Ann, of Rigby & .... Naylor, was Baptized....
Shrewsbury Mary Ann	Jan 11th. 1771, Mary Ann, of Stephen & Mary Ann Shrewsbury, was Baptized
McClich Mary	Feb. 6th. 1771, Mary of .... &............ McClich, was baptized....
Nowell - - - - -	Feb. .... 1771, ... of John & Elizabeth Nowell was Baptized

(Rodman Regst.)

Farquhar, Margaret,	Apr. 3rd. 1771, Margaret, of George & Elizabeth Farquhar, was baptized....
Sharp, Alexander,	Apr. 10th. 1771, Alexander, of Alexander & Ann Sharp was baptized....
Chalmers, Sarah,	May 4th. 1771, Sarah of Gilbert & Elizabeth Chalmers, was Baptized....
Wallace, Martha,	July 10th. 1771 Martha, of Edward & Martha Wallace, was baptized....
Wallace, Elizabeth,	July 10th. 1771, Elizabeth, of Edward & Martha Wallace, was baptized....
Whish, Benjamin,	July 20th. 1771, Benjamin, of Benjamin & Thetis Whish, was baptized....
Valton, Peter Smith,	Aug. 2nd. 1771, Peter Smith, of Peter & Elizabeth Valton, was baptized....
Murphy, William,	Aug. 6th. 1771, William, of William & Martha Murphy, was baptized....
Cole, John,	Sept. 17th. 1771 John, of Thomas & Ruth Cole, was baptized....
Wright J. Alexander	Sept. 18th. 1771, James Alexander, of Alexander & Elizabeth Wright, was baptized....
Gordon, J. Alexander,	Oct. 7th. 1771, John Alexander, of John & Elizabeth Gordon, was baptized....
Boen, Thomas,	Oct. 27th. 1771, Thomas, of John & Mary Boen, was baptized....
Blakie, Elizabeth,	Oct. 30th. 1771, Elizabeth, of John & Jennett Blakie, was baptized....

Atkerson, George	Oct. 1st. 1771, George, of William & Mary Atkerson, was baptized....
Taylor James,	Oct. 8th. 1771, James, of Christopher & Ann Taylor, was baptized....
Beale, Mary H.	Nov. 24th. 1771, Mary Hannah, of John & Mary Beale, was baptized....
Daniel, Mary.	Nov. 29th. 1771, Mary, of Robert & Elizabeth Daniel, was baptized....

[Bottom of page torn out.]

Christenings. 119

Rush, John,	Dec. 4th. 1771, John, of Peter & Catherine Rush, was baptized....
Dart, Isaac Motte,	Jan. 1st. 1772, Isaac Motte, of John & Martha Dart, was baptized....
Kennedy, Rachel,	Jan. 27th. 1772, Rachel, of Richard & Susannah Kennedy, was baptized....
Kennedy, John,	Jan. 27th. 1772, John, of Richard & Susannah Kennedy, was baptized....
Kennedy Sarah,	Jan 27th. 1772, Sarah, of Richard & Susannah Kennedy, was baptized....
Irons, John,	Feb. 20th. 1772, John, of Simon & Sarah Irons, was baptized....
Alexander, Elizabeth,	Mar. 16th. 1772, Elizabeth, of Alexander & Rachel Alexander, was baptized....
Harrison, Mary,	April 15th. 1772, Mary, of John & Sarah Harrison, was baptized....

Clark, Mary,	Apr. 18th. 1772, Mary, of John & Mary Clark, was baptized....
Neufville, Benjamin,	May 14th. 1772, Benjamin, of John &........ Neufville, was baptized....
Skottowe, Thos. Britiffe	July 1st, 1768, Thomas Britiffe, of Thos. & Mary Lucia Skottowe, was baptized....
Skottowe, Nicholas Brittiffe	June 9th. 1772, Nicholas Brittiffe, of Thos & Mary Lucia Skottowe, was baptized....
Skottowe, C. Brittiffe,	June 9th. 1772, Coulsin Brittiffe, of Thos & Mary Lucia Skottowe, was baptized....
Telfair, Mary Lucia,	June 9th. 1772, Mary Lucia, of William & Elizabeth Telfair, was baptized....
Telfair, Thomas,	June 9th. 1772, Thomas, of William & Elizabeth Telfair, was baptized....
Elsinor William,	June 14th. 1772, William, of Alexander & Elizabeth Elsinor, was baptized....

(Rodman Regst.)

Christenings. 120

Elsinor, Ann	June 14th. 1772, Ann, of Alexander & Elizabeth Elsinor, was baptized....
Kelly John,	June 20th. 1772, John, of John & Catherine Kelly, was baptized....
Cogdell, Richard,	July 19th. 1772, Richard, of John & Elizabeth Cogdell, was baptized....
Faesch, Harriott,	July 22nd. 1772, Harriott, of John & Sarah Faesch, was baptized....

Bull, William,	July 24th. 1772, William, of Thomas & Sarah Bull, was baptized....
Graham, Alexander,	July 24th. 1772, Alexander, of Faithful & Jane Graham, was baptized....
Guy, James,	Sept. 11th. 1772, James, of James & Sarah Guy, was baptized....
Marshall, Mary,	Nov. 7th. 1772, Mary, of Matthew & Mary Marshall, was baptized....
Smith, Mary,	Dec. 30th. 1772, Mary, of Roger & Mary Smith, was baptized....
Swallow, ...	Jan. 1st. 1773,...................., of Newman & Frances Swallow, was baptized....
Daniel, Mary,	Mar. 16th. 1773, Mary, of Thomas & Mary Daniel, was baptized....
Howard, Robert,	Mar. 17th. 1773, Robert, of Robert & Ann Howard, was baptized....
Goff, Mary Ann,	Mar. 17th. 1773, Mary Ann, of Richard & - - - - Goff, was baptized....
Quash, Sarah	Mar. 19th. 1773, Sarah, of Robert & Constantia Quash, was baptized....
Sanders, Mary,	Apr. 3rd. 1773, Mary, of John & Elizabeth Sanders, was baptized....

(C. Elmer Rodman Regst.)

Christenings. 121

Lord, Mary,	Apr. 4th. 1773, Mary, of John & Margaret Lord, was baptized....

You, Mary,	Apr. 5th. 1773, Mary, of Thomas & Elizabeth You, was baptized....
Shaw, Esther May,	Apr. 18th. 1773, Esther May, of Pott & Elizabeth Shaw, was baptized....
Wragg, Elizabeth,	Apr. 30th. 1773, Elizabeth, of William & Henrietta Wragg, was baptized....
Wright, John,	May 7th. 1773, John, Izard, of Alexander & Elizabeth Wright, was baptized....
Forinsby, Robert,	June 4th. 1773, Robert, of John & Ann Forinsby, was baptized....
Leigh, Sophia E.	June 4th. 1773, Sophia Egerton, of Egerton & Martha Leigh, was baptized....
Hatfield, Sarah,	June 20th. 1773, Sarah, of John & Sarah Hatfield, was baptized....
Pinckney, Rebecca,	July 11th. 1773, Rebecca, of Charles & Frances Pinckney, was baptized....
Clements, Anna Maria,	July 14th. 1773, Anna Maria, of John & Sarah Clements, was baptized....
Drayton, Sarah Motte,	Aug. 6th. 1773, Sarah Motte, of William & Mary Drayton, was baptized....
Pickerin, Samuel	Aug. 8th. 1773, Samuel, of Samuel & Mary Pickerin, was baptized....
Whaley, Joseph,	Aug. 9th. 1773, Joseph, of James & Sarah Whaley, was baptized....
Flagg, Sarah,	Sept. 7th. 1773, Sarah, of John & Mary Magdalen Flagg, was baptized....

Bonnetheau, Mary,	Sept. 12th. 1773, Mary, of Peter & Ann Bonnetheau, was baptized....
Cockran, ...	Nov. 14th. 1773, ... of Robert & .... Cockran, was baptized....
Mathews, James,	Dec. 8th. 1773, James, of John & .... Matthews, was baptized....
Crofts, Mary	Dec. 9th. 1773, Mary, of Robert & Judith Crofts, was Baptized....
Wakefield Mary,	Dec. 28th. 1773, Mary, of James & Sarah, Wakefield, was baptized....

(Charles E. Rodman Regst.)

Christenings 122

Smith Caroline,	Jan. 13th. 1774, Caroline, of Roger & Mary Smith, Was Baptized....
Bee, Sarah More,	Jan. 25th. 1774, Sarah More, of Thomas & Sarah Bee, was baptized....
Teulon, Peter	Mar. 3rd. 1774, Peter, of Charles & Comfort Teulon, was baptized....
Hort, Wm. H. Gibbes.	Apr. 18th. 1774, Wm. Haddrell Gibbes, of Wm. & Alice Hort, was baptized....
Parker P. Manigault,	May 22nd. 1774, Peter Manigault, of John & Mary Parker, was baptized....[1]
Dutton, William,	May 22nd. 1774, William, of Elizabeth Dutton, was baptized....

[1]He was born February 19, 1774. His mother's maiden name was Daniell. He was graduated at Yale, September 11, 1793; was rector of St. John's Parish, Berkeley, in 1796, and assistant rector of St. Philip's in 1802, dying in July of that year.

Shubrick, Sarah Motte,	July 9th. 1774, Sarah Motte, of Richard & Susannah Shubrick, was baptized....
Breedlove, Mary,	July 21st. 1774, Mary, of Nathaniel & Susannah Breedlove, was baptized....
Rutledge, Thomas,	July 22nd. 1774, Thomas, of John & Elizabeth Rutledge, was baptized....
Bland, Ann,	Aug. 8th. 1774, Ann, of George & Mary Bland, was baptized....
Cowan, John,	Aug. 14th. 1774, John, of George Kesson & Sarah Cowan, was baptized....
Doughty, Rachel,	Aug. 22nd. 1774, Rachel, of William & .... Doughty, was baptized....
Whitney, Lebbeus,	Sept. 19th. 1774 Lebbeus, of Lebbeus & Mary Ann Whitney, was baptized....
You, Mary,	Oct. 2nd. 1774, Mary, of Thomas & Elizabeth You, was baptized....
Shrewsbury, J. Dickerson,	Oct. 16th. 1774, John Dickerson, of Stephen & Mary Anne Shrewsbury, was Baptized....
Moon, Margaret	Oct. 23rd. 1774, Margaret of .... Moon, was baptized....
Garnier, Henry,	Oct. 23rd. 1774, Henry, of Melchior & .... Garnier, was baptized....
Parker, Wm. McKenzie,	Dec. 3rd. 1774, William McKenzie, of Jno. & Mary Parker, was baptized....
Follingsby, Mary,	Dec. 4th. 1774, Mary, of John & Elizabeth Follingsby, was baptized....

(C. E. Rodman)

Mills, Robert,	Dec. 5th. 1774, Robert, of Robert & Elizabeth Mills, was baptized....
Skottowe, J. Bellinger,	Dec. 16th. 1774, John Bellinger, of Thos. & Mary Lucia Skottowe, was baptized....
Skottowe E. M. Bellinger	Dec. 16th. 1774, Edmund Massinberd Bellinger, of Thos & Mary L. Skottowe, was baptized....
Reed Sarah,	Dec. 30th. 1774, Sarah, of Lavender & Susannah Reed, was baptized....
Shubrick Mary Elliot,	Jan. 15th. 1775, Mary Elliot, of Richard & Susannah Shubrick, was baptized....
Gibson, Charlotte,	Feb. 26th. 1775, Charlotte, of John & Martha Gibson, was baptized....
Rush, Samuel,	Mar. 20th. 1775, Samuel, of Peter & Catherine Rush, was baptized....
Wylley, Wm. Lettle,	Apr. 10th. 1775, William Lettle, of Alexander & Susannah Wylley, was baptized....
Weaver, Margaret,	Sept. 11th. 1775, Margaret, of William & Margaret Weaver, was baptized....
Clements, Sarah Clarke,	Nov. 17th. 1775, Sarah Clarke, of John & Sarah Clements, was baptized....
Smith, Sarah Motte,	Sept. 27th. 1775, Sarah Motte, of Rev. Robert & Sarah Smith, was baptized....
Huger, Daniel	Sept. 27th. 1775, Daniel, of John & Charlotte Huger, was baptized....
Brown, Samuel,	Dec. 8th. 1775, Samuel, of Samuel & Rachel Brown, was baptized....

Smith, J. Rutledge,	Jan. 6th. 1776, John Rutledge, of Roger & Mary Smith, was baptized....
Smyth, Ann Thomas	Feby. 16th 1776, Ann Thomas, of James & Ann Smyth, was baptized....
Bee Roger Smith	Feb. 18th. 1776, Roger Smith, of Thomas & Sarah Bee, was baptized....
Wish, Mary,	Mar. 20th. 1776, Mary, of Benjamin & Thetis Wish, was baptized....
Sansum, Mary Ann,	May 16th. 1776, Mary Ann, of John & Susannah Sansum, was baptized....

Christenings. 124

Sansum, Susannah,	May 16th. 1776, Susannah, of John & Susannah Sansum, was baptized....
Hogarth, William,	May 25th. 1776, William, of William & Ann Hogarth, was baptized....
James, John,	May 27th. 1776, John, of John & Elizabeth James, was baptized....
Elizabeth, James	May 27th. 1776, Elizabeth, of John & Elizabeth James, was baptized....
Huger Eliza,	July 12th. 1776, Eliza, of Benjamin & Mary Huger, was baptized....
Prioleau Phil. Gendrun	July 21st. 1776, Philip Gendrun, of Samuel & Catherine Prioleau, was baptized....
Simons, Benjamin,	Sept. 14th. 1776, Benjamin of Benjamin & Simons, was baptized....

Hainsdorff, Carolina,	Sept. 20th. 1776, Carolina, of Henry & Margaret Hainsdorff, was baptized....
Coram, John,	Nov. 22nd. 1776, John of John & .... Coram, was baptized....
Taylor, Paul,	Nov. 29th. 1776, Paul, of Barnard & Mary Taylor, was baptized....
Horry, Elizabeth B.	Dec. 3rd. 1776, Elizabeth Branford, of Thomas & Mary Horry, was baptized....
Callighan, John,	Dec. 26th. 1776, John, of John & Jane Callighan, was baptized....
Hall, Eliza Maria,	Apr. 19th. 1777, Eliza Maria, of Daniel & Susannah Hall, was baptized....
Hall Susannah M.	Apr. 19th. 1777, Susannah Matthews, of Daniel & Susannah Hall, was baptized....
Farr, Mary,	Apr. 19th. 1777, Mary, of Thomas & .... Farr, was baptized....
Baron, Alexander J.	July 20th. 1777, Alexander John, of Alexander & Sarah Baron, was baptized....
McGilvery, Mary,	July 20th. 1777, Mary, of William & Ann McGilvery, was baptized....

Christenings. 125

Shaddock, Abigail	July 20th. 1777, Abigail, Of Benjamin & Mary Shaddock, was baptized....
Hamett, Christopher	July 25th. 1777, Christopher, of Thomas & Charlotte Hamett, was baptized....

Dawson, William,	Aug. 1st. 1777, William, of John & .... Dawson, was Baptized....
Doile, Samuel,	Aug. 13th. 1777, Samuel, of Samuel & Mary Doile, was baptized....
.... Jane Blake,	Aug. 31st. 1777, Jane Blake, of .... & Rose .... was baptized....
Harper, William,	Sept. 6th. 1777, William, of Thomas & Elizabeth Harper, was baptized....
You, Sarah,	Sept. 6th. 1777, Sarah, of Thomas & Elizabeth You, was baptized....
Shrewsbury, Edward,	Sept. 24th. 1777, Edward, of Stephen & Mary Ann Shrewsbury, was baptized....
Smyth, Elizabeth,	Nov. 2nd. 1777, Elizabeth, of James & Anne Smyth, was baptized....
Smith, Press McP.	Nov. 11th. 1777, Press McPherson, son of Press & Elizabeth Smith, was baptized....
Simpson George,	Nov. 21st. 1777, George, of Archibald & Ann Simpson, was baptized....
Smith, Ben. Burgh,	Nov. 25th. 1777, Benjamin Burgh, of Roger & Mary Smith, was Baptized....
Bee, P. Smith,	Nov. 27th. 1777, Peter Smith, of Thomas & Sarah Bee, was baptized....
Reed, Margaret	Nov. 29th. 1777, Margaret, of John & Isabella Reed, was baptized....
Rind, Arabella A.	Dec. 14th. 1777, Arabella Ann, of David & .... Rind, was baptized....

Dorell, Nathaniel,	Dec. 17th. 1777, Nathaniel, Of .... & .... Dorell, was baptized....
Ward, Ann,	Jan. 1st. 1778, Ann, of Joshua & .... Ward, was baptized....
Alexander, William,	Jan. 4th. 1778, William, of Alexander & Rachel Alexander, was baptized....
Harleston, Elizabeth	Jan. 4th. 1778, Elizabeth, of John & .... Harleston, was baptized....
Motte, Rebeccah	Jan. 9th. 1778, Rebeccah Motte, of Jacob & Rebeccah Motte, was baptized....

Christenings. 126

Hoppen, Sarah	Jan. 10th. 1778, Sarah, of Thomas & Charlotte Hoppen, was baptized....
Wyatt, Mary L.	Feb. 14th. 1778, Mary Lingard, of John & Violetta Wyatt, was baptized....
Huger, Mary S.	Mar. 24th. 1778, Mary Shubrick, of John & Charlotte Huger, was baptized....
Heyward Thomas,	Mar. 25th. 1778, Thomas, of Thomas & Elizabeth Heyward, was baptized....
Frazier, Sabina	Apr. 23rd. 1778, Sabina, of Alexander & .... Frazier, was baptized....
Rooker, James R.	May 16th. 1778, James Lawrence, of William & Jane Rooker, was baptized....
Whitesides Thomas,	June 6th. 1778, Thomas, of Thomas & Jane Whitesides, was baptized....

Whitesides James,	June 6th. 1778, James, of Thomas & Jane Whitesides, was baptized....
Lowndes Sarah	Aug. 26th. 1778, Sarah, of Rawlins & Sarah Lowndes, was baptized....
Fish Arabella,	Sept. 6th. 1778, Arabella, of John & Sarah Fish was baptized....
Elliot, Barnard,	Oct. 6th. 1778, Barnard Elliot, ... was baptized....
Baker Richard B.	Oct. 6th. 1778, Richard Bohun Baker, ... was baptized....
Harvey, Thomas	Dec. 26th. 1778, Thomas, of Thomas & Elizabeth Harvey, was baptized....
*Tucker, Wm. Tucker,	Jan. 22nd. 1779 William Tucker, of Tucker & Christian Harris, was baptized....
M'Crady, Eliza	Feb. 3rd. 1779, Eliza, of Edward & Elizabeth M'Crady, was baptized....
Huger, Daniel,	Mar: 2nd. 1779, Daniel, of John & Charlotte Huger, was baptized....
Hort, Culcheth,	Mar. 2nd. 1779, Wm. Culcheth, of William & Alice Hort, was baptized....
Webber, John,	Mar. 3rd. 1779, John, of John & Ann Webber, Was baptized....
Darby, R. Andrew,	Feb. 3rd. 1779, Robert Andrew, of William & Joan Darby, was baptized....
Ross, John	Mar. 8th. 1779, John of John & Elizabeth Ross, was baptized....

*For *Tucker* read *Harris.*

Gervais, D. Sinclair,	Mar. 9th. 1779, David Sinclair, of John Lewis & Mary Gervais, was baptized....

Christenings. 127

Shaw, William A.	Mar. 10th. 1779, William Archibald, of Pott & Elizabeth Shaw, was baptized....
Hamilton, David A.	Mar. 10th. 1779, David Alexander, of David & Elizabeth Hamilton, was baptized....
McCan, Margaret	Mar. 17th. 1779, Margaret, of Patrick & Mary McCan, was baptized....
Smith, Henry M.	Apr. 7th. 1779, Henry Middleton, of Peter & Mary Smith, was baptized....
Smith Louisa C.	Apr. 7th. 1779, Louisa Columbia, of Thomas & Sarah Smith, was baptized....
Chalmers Harriot,	Apr. 9th. 1779, Harriott, of Gilbert & Sophia Chalmers, was baptized....
Lestarjette, Sophia E.	May 2nd. 1779, Sophia Elizabeth, of Lewis & Elizabeth Burnham Lestarjette, was baptized....
McFarlin, Andrew,	May 2nd. 1779, Andrew, of Mordecai & Mary McFarlin, was baptized....
Doughtty, Chiffele,	Aug. 20th. 1779, Chiffele, of William & Rachel Doughty, was baptized....
Graham, Abigail,	Aug. 22nd. 1779, Abigail, of William & ....Graham, was baptized....
Harris Thomas B.	Aug. 22nd. 1779, Thomas Boston, of Tucker & Christiana Harris, was baptized....

Bentham Sophia B.	Sept. 5th. 1779, Sophia Boswell, of James & .... Bentham, was baptized....
Ferguson, Thomas L.	Sept. 8th. 1779, Thomas Ladson, of Thomas & .... Ferguson, was baptized....
Dubois, ...	Sept. 8th. 1779, of & Dubois, was baptized....
Pinckney, Charles C.	Sept. 10th. 1779, Charles Cotesworth, of Charles Cotesworth & .... Pinckney, was baptized....[1]
Conyers, Susannah,	Sept. 14th. 1779, Susannah, of John & Susannah Conyers, was baptized....
Bolton, Elizabeth,	Sept. 23rd. 1779, Elizabeth, of Allen & Martha Bolton, was baptized....
Wyatt, James L.	Sept. 24th. 1779, James Lingard, of John & Violetta Wyatt, was baptized....
St. John, Mary G.	Sept. 25th. 1779, Mary Goff,[2] of James & Elizabeth St. John, was baptized....
Conyers, John,	Sept. 26th. 1779, John, of Daniel & Ann Conyers, was baptized....
Drayton, Caroline,	Sept. 29th. 1779, Caroline, of Charles & .... Drayton, Was baptized....

Christenings. 128

Davis, Mary,	Oct. 3rd. 1779, Mary of William & Elizabeth Davis, was baptized ....

[1]This was a son of Col. (subsequently Gen.) Charles Cotesworth Pinckney by his first wife, Sarah Middleton, to whom he had been married, September 28, 1773.

[2]Gough.

Miller, Cato Ash,	Oct. 16th. 1779, Cato Ash, of Solomon & Ann Miller, was baptized ....
Ward, Frances C.	Oct. 29th. 1779, Frances Carolina, of John & Love Ward, was baptized ....
Crofts Love L.	Oct. 29th. 1779, Love Legier, of George & Elizabeth Crofts, was baptized ....
Logan, Honoria M.	Nov. 10th. 1779, Honoria Muldrup, of George & .... Logan, was baptized ....
Radcliffe, Thomas	Dec. 8th. 1779, Thomas of Thomas & Lucretia Constant Radcliffe, was baptized ....
Alexander Rebekah & Ann	Dec. 16th. 1779, Rebekah and Ann, (twins) of Alexr. & Rachel Alexander, was baptized ....
Shubrick Sarah Alicia	Dec. 27th. 1779, Sarah Alicia, of Thomas & Mary Shubrick, were baptized ....
Pritchard, George W.	Dec. 28th. 1779, George Washington, of Paul & .... Pritchard, was baptized ....
You, John,	Feby. 6th. 1780, John, of Thomas & .... You, was baptized ....

Baptisms Continued 129

	N. B. The records of the Parish from 17 Nov. 1782 to 1787 have not been found up to this date Aug. 20. 1889. Reference will be made to them if they should be found.
Howard	Jan. 1787 1 Sarah Ann daughter of John & Elizabeth Howard.
Wells	" " Frances Singleton, daughter of Samuel & Suky Wells.

On the 20th. October 1779 James, (son of Anthony &) Gabeau Was Baptized

On the 29th. October 1779 Susannah Elizabeth, (daugr. of) Larry was Baptized

On the 3d. November 1779 Martha Mary, (daugr. of Thomas &) Holmes was Baptized

On the 12th. November 1779 Joseph, son of Joseph &) Atkinson was Baptized

On the 17th. November 1779 Ann Middleton (daughr of Alexr. &) Inglis was Baptized

On the 3d. December 1779 Mary (daughr. of) Gadsden was Baptized

On the 15th. December 1779 Robert, (son of Robert &) Weyman was Baptized

On the 22d December 1779 Robert, (son of Robert &) Howard was Baptized

On the 18th. January 1780 Grace, (a mulattoe servant to Mrs. Delahoy was Baptized

On the 28th. January 1780 Nancy, (daugr. of James &) Steadman was Baptized

On the 25th. August 1780, Stephen, (son of Peter &) Prow was Baptized

On the 11th. March 1781 Samuel, (son of & Phebe) Williams
Ditto George (son of Daniel & Smith
Ditto C. Timothy, (son of Cornelius &) Sullivant
Were Baptized

On the 13th. May 1781 Mary, (daugr. of John &) Todd was Baptized

On the 27th. May 1781 James, (son of William and) Ranken was Baptized

On the 27th. June 1781 David, (son of Jeremiah &) Clark was Baptized

On the 8th. July 1781 James (son of Alexander &) Smith was Baptized

Geo. Denholm C. S. & Regr.....

On the 3rd. August 1781 Elizabeth, (daugr. of Robert &) Nicholson Was Baptized

On the 17th. August 1781 Pearcy, (son of Charles &) Watson was Baptized

On the 24th. August 1781 Ann, (daugr. of a free Negroe Wench named Sucky Falconer was Baptized

On the 29th. August 1781 John, (son of John &) Sequin
Ditto Elizabeth, (daugr. of Daniel &) Martin
} were Baptized

On the 21st. September 1781 James, (son of James &) Wisdom was Baptized

On the 28th. September 1781 Delia, (a free negro-woman)
Ditto Joseph, (son of Joseph & Mary) Waring
} were Baptized

On the 30th. September 1781 Margaret, (daugr. of Nathaniel & Locke was Baptized

On the 12th. October Elsie, (daugr. of Charles &) Miller was Baptized

On the 21st. October 1781 Charlotte, (daugr. of Patrick &) Murphy
Ditto Elizabeth, (daugr. of Anthony &) Gabeau
were Baptized

On the 31st. October 1781 Henry, (son of Benjamin &) Wish was Baptized

On the 21st. November 1781 Rose, (a negroe-wench) was Baptized

On the 16th. December 1781 Ann, (daugr. of Christopher &) Brown was Baptized

On the 30th. December 1781 Alice, (daugr. of Thomas &) Chadwick was Baptized

On the 1st. January 1782 Sarah, (daugr. of Henry &) Newberry was Baptized

On the 13th. January 1782 Thomas, (son of Thomas &) Bouden was Baptized

On the 16th. January 1782 John Wary, (son of Major John &) Morrison Commissr. Genl. was Baptized

Geo. Denholm Regr.

On theh 3rd. February 1782 Peter, (son of Peter &) Geddis was Baptized

On the 17th. February 1782 Ann Mary, (daugr. William &) Easton was Baptized

On the 20th. February 1782 Sarah, (a mulattoe-Woman, N. B. Mr. Bentham, Mrs. Chalmers & Mrs. Stone were witnesses, was Baptized

On the 24th. February 1782 Elizabeth, (daugr. of Richard &) Bowling was Baptized

On the 25th. November 1781 John Joseph, (son of & Catherine) Lafar was Baptized

On the 11th. March 1782 Margaret Philip[1] orphan, daugr of Archd. & Margr. Campbell was Baptized privately

On the 13th. March 1782 James, (son of James &) Steadman was Baptized

On the 28th. March 1782 Sarah, (a negro-woman. N. B. Mr. Sheed, Mrs. Stone & Miss Mary Hall were witnesses, was Baptized

On the 10th. April 1782 Margaret, (daugr. of John & Margaret Coils was Baptized

On the 14th. April 1782 Nelly, (daugr. of Peter & Eleanor Friar (a young woman) was Baptized

On the 19th. April 1782 Ann, (daugr. of William & Ann Burt was Baptized

On the 24th. April 1782 John, (son of James & Sarah Gay
Ditto Sarah, (a negro-woman. N. B. Mr. Bacot, Mrs. Donaldson & Mrs. Perdrieau were witnesses.)
were Baptized

On the 28th. April 1782 Ann, daugr. of John & Rebecca Roiley was Baptized

On the 5th. May 1782 Elizabeth, (daugr. of Edward & Jane Sims was Baptized

On the 15th. May 1782 Thomas, (son of Richard & Sarah Wraingh was Baptized

Geo Denholm Regr.

---

[1]Philp. See page 9.

On the 5th. June 1782 Rose, (daugr. of John & Mary White was Baptized

On the 26th. June 1782 Robert, (son of Robert Patton & Mary a mulattoe woman was Baptized

On the 21st. July 1782 Charlotte, (daugr. of William & Mary Elson was Baptized

On the 11th. September 1782 Mary Isabella, (daugr. of Nicholas & Mary Abel Aleyne Smith was Baptized

On the 22nd Septemr. 1782 Daniel, (son of Joseph & Susannah Bell was Baptized

On the 25th. Septemr. 1782 Thomas, (son of Thos. & Elizabeth Harper was Baptized

On the 29th. May 1782 John Allison an adult was Baptized privately

On the 1st. August 1782 Isabella Ann, (daugr. of Robert and Sarah Barron was Baptized privately

On the 6th. August 1782 Daniel Cannon, (son of John and Mary Webb was Baptized privately

On the 20th. October 1782 William (son of David & Jean) Taylor was Baptized

On 6th. November 1782 Diana Lampton
Catherine Thorp
was Baptized } Yellow Girls { N. B. Mrs. Mary Chalmers was one of their Witnesses

On the 27th. October 1782 Elizabeth LeSerurier Mazyck was Baptized

On the 8th. November 1782 Rachael a yellow woman was Baptized { N. B. Mrs. John Webb & Mrs. Highland were Witnesses

On the 10th. November 1782 Margaret, (daugr. of) Nicholas & Martha) Gray was Baptized

On the 17th. November 1782 William (son of George & Hannah Forbes James (son of John & Ann) Siguina Ann } Mary } Mulattoe Girls Were Baptized	N. B. Mrs. Chalmers Mrs. Bonnetheau and Geo Denholm were Witnesses

.... Baptisms Continued 135

N. B. The records of the Parish from 17th Nov. 1782 to 1787, have not been found up to this date, August 20th. 1889., Reference will be made to them if they shall be found.

Howard	Jany 1787, Sarah Ann daughter of John and Elizabeth Howard
Wells	" 1 " Frances Singelton daughter of Samuel and Suky Wells.
Do.	" " " Thomas Bracey son of Samuel and Suky Wells.
Warham	" " " William Gibbes son of Charles and Mary Warham
Frogman	" 8 " James son of Richard and Jane Frogman. Bap.
Ferguson	" 12 " Samuel Wragg son of Thomas and Ann Ferguson. Bap.
Do.	" " " Richard Beresford son of Thomas and Ann Ferguson. Bap.
Clements	" 19 " Pinckney son of John and Sarah Clements
Sammers	" " " James son of John & Martha Sammers.
Taylor	" 31 " William Piercy son of Paul & Sarah Taylor.
Kennedy	Feby 7 " Lionel Henry son of James and Ann Bensley Kennedy.
Carnes	" 24 " Patrick son of Patrick and Susannah Carnes.
McKenzie	" 14 " Margaret Yetto daughter of John and Sarah McKenzie.

Holmes	" 18 " Stephen Richard son of Thomas and Sarah Holmes.
Manigault	" 8 " Elizabeth daughter of Gabriel and Margaret Manigault.
Izard	" " Caroline daughter of Ralph and Alice Izard.
Brown	" 14 " Anna Caroline daughter of Archibald and Mary Brown[1]
Bentham	" " Jane Boswell daughter of James and Mary Bentham.

Baptisms

.... Baptisms Continued 136

Hort	March 21 1787. Susannah Gibbes daughter of William and Alice Hort.
Grant	" 23 " John son of John and Mary Grant.
Elliot	" 25 " Benjamin son of Thomas Odingsill and Mary Elliot.
Peroneau	" 28 " Charles Honor son of John and Mary Peroneau.
Gadsden	" 31 " Emma daughter of Thomas and Martha Gadsden.
Garden	April 4 " Elizabeth daughter of Theodore and Elizabeth Gurdin.[2]
Bedam	" 5 " William son of William and Elizabeth Bedam.
Foster	" 6 " Thomas Edward son of Thomas and Mary Foster.
Shrowdy	" " Maria Tucker daughter of William and Eliz. Shrowdy.
Warley	" 8 " Felix Braneau son of Felix and Ann Warley.
Molton	" 9 " Mary Catherine daughter of William and Mary Molton.

[1]Broun is the correct name.
[2]Probably Gourdin.

Hogarth	" 10 " Sarah daughter of William and Ann Hogarth.
Hambleton	" 13 " Hannah Motte daughter of James & Elizabeth Hambleton.
McCall	" 15 " James son of John and Ann McCall.
Prioleau	" " Thomas Grimball son of Phillip and Alice Edith Prioleau.
Honywood	" " Richard son of Arthur and Elizabeth Honywood.
Poyas	" 18 " Louisa Dorothey daughter of John Lewis and Mary Madaline Poyas.
Crafts	" 20 " William son of Margaret and William Crafts.[1]
Tenant	May 1 " James son of John and Isabella Tenant.
Bullock	" 4 " Samuel son of Samuel and Rhoda Bullock.
Allen	" 4 " Richard Anderson son of Thomas and Martha Allen.
Blackallen	" 7 " Mary Ann daughter of Oliver and Martha Blackallen.

Baptisms

Lestargeth	May 25. 1787 Sophia Margaret daughter of Lewis and Elizabeth Burhham[2] Lettergeth.[3] Bap.
Robins	" " Mary daughter of Thomas and Mary Robins.
Gadsden	" 26. " Christopher Edwards son of Philip and Catherine Gadsden. — Elected Minister of the Church 1810.[4]

[1]Subsequently a noted lawyer, writer, editor and legislator, father of the legislation by which the State Lunatic Asylum was established. He died September 23, 1826.

[2]Burnham.

[3]Lestarjette.

[4]Subsequently (1840-1852) Bishop of South Carolina. He died June 24, 1852.

do.	" " John son of Philip and Catherine Gadsden.
McHugo	" 30 " Jane Teresa daughter of Anthony and Mary McHugo.
Fordham	July 10 " Richard son of Richard and Mary Fordham.
Hamilton	" 27 " Mary daughter of David and Elizabeth Hamilton.
Lining	Aug. 9 " Jane Savage daughter of Charles and Lining.
Crick	" 13 " Sarah daughter of Henry and Elizabeth Crick.
Stevenson	" 27 " Mary daughter of John and Mary Stevenson.
Simpson	" 24 " James son of James and Clementina Simpson.
Lyons	Oct. 10 " John son of Abraham and Ann Lyons.
Lance	" 10 " Sarah Louisa daughter of Sarah and Lambert Lance.
Russell	" 16 " Elizabeth Hartley daughter of Nathaniel and Sarah Russell.
Harris	" 21 " Sophia Harris daughter of Tucker and Christiana Harris.
Todd	Nov. 14. " Benjamin son of Todd.
Simple	" 21 " Catherine daughter of William and Sarah Simple. Bap.
Milligin	" 23 " Charlotte Maria daughter of James and Elizabeth Milligin. Bap.
Sheppard	Dec. 16. " Thomas son of Samuel and Jane Sheppard. Bap.
Do.	" " Samuel son of Samuel and Jane Sheppard. Bap.
Brock	" 24 " Anna Elizabeth daughter of Jacob and Mary Brock. Bap.

Wood — ” 25 ” Ann daughter of Margaret and William Wood.

Cready — Mary Elizabeth daughter of James Cready. Bap.

Baptisms.

.... Baptisms Continued 138

Jones. — Jan. 1st. 1788 Robert Williams son of Jesse and Margaret Jones.

Legare — 6 Sarah Ann daughter of Benjamin and Legare.

Hume — 11 Catherine daughter of John and Mary Hume.

Rout — 27 Robert William son of George and Ann Rout.

Cobye — Feb. 4 ” Sarah daughter of Michael and Susanna Cobye.

Miller — 17 Ann Judd daughter of John David and Ann Miller.

Sinkler — 23 William son of James and Sinkler. Bap.

Besileau — 28 Philip John son of Philip Anthony and Susanna Besileau. Bap.

Manigault — March 10 Peter son of Gabriel and Margaret Manigault

Brandford — 16 Barnaby son of Barnaby and Mary Magdaline Brandford.

Gibbes — 20 Eliza daughter of William Hasell and Eliza Gibbes.

Alger — 22 James son of James and Elizabeth Alger.

Bay — 28 Andrew son of Elihu Hall and Margaret Bay. Bap.

Bellinger — April 2 Claudia Margaret daughter of John and Rebecca Bellinger.

Sarah daughter of[1]

---

[1]Rest of the record not given.

Elsinore	9 William son of James and Elizabeth Elsinore Bap.
Foster	" Elizabeth Hall daughter of Thomas and Mary Foster. Bap.
Gadsden	10 Mary daughter of Thomas and Martha Gadsden. Bap.
Johnston	18 Peter son of William and Sarah Johnston. Bap.
Galloway	20 Catherine daughter of Robert & Elizabeth Galloway. Bap.
Campbell	23 Martin John son of McCartan & Sarah Campbell. Bap.
Gibson	25 Eliza daughter of Robert and Jane Gibson. Bap.
Williamson	William Franklin Jasper son of William & Elizabeth Ann Williamson. Bap.

Baptism

Sutton	May 4. 1788. Sarah daughter of John and Mary Sutton. Bap.
Miggins	7 John Todd son of Thomas Watt and Mary Miggins. Bap.
Crafts.	18 Caroline daughter of and William Crafts. Bap.
Meeks	June 7 Maria daughter of Joseph and Mary Meeks. Bap.
Bonnetheau	8 Robert son of Peter and Elizabeth Bonnetheau. Bap.
Williams	Francis son of Ann and Francis Williams. Bap.
Broughton	9 Mary daughter of Thomas and Mary Ann Broughton. Bap.
Lothrop	28 Martha Meed daughter of Seth and Sarah Lothrop. Bap.
McCall	Harriot daughter of John and Ann McCall. Bap.

Smith { 29 William Mason son of the Revd. Robert and Anna Smith.

Corbett { July 16 Elizabeth daughter of Thomas and Margaret Corbett. Bap.

Lining { Aug. 30 Charles Hill son of Charles and Polly Lining. Bap.

Wilson { Sep. 3 William Drayton son of Daniel and Mary Wilson. Bap.

Stewart { 10 Martha daughter of Robert and Martha Stewart. Bap.

Frost { 28 Mary Elizabeth Baughter daughter of Thomas and Elizabeth Frost.

Jones { " Mary Ann daughter of Joseph and Frances Jones. Bap

Miller { Oct. 2 James Trenholm son of James and Mary Miller.

Crocker { 10 Samuel Shaw son of John and Abigail Crocker. Bap.

Drayton { Mary Ann daughter of William and Hannah Drayton. Bap.

Simons { 22 Sedgewick Lewis son of Keating and Sarah Simons. Bap.

Sinkler { 30 Harriott Walker daughter of Peter and Mary Sinkler. Bap.

Baptisms

Harvey { Oct. 23. 1788 Benjamin son of Benjamin and Elizabeth Harvey. Bap.

Wearing { 31 Esther Marion daughter of Thomas and Elizabeth Wearing. Bap.

Simons { Mary Read daughter of Thomas and Elizabeth Simons. Bap.

Pinckney { Nov. 1. Rebecca Motte daughter of Thomas and Elizabeth Pinckney. Bap.

Roper { 2 Edward Steft son of William and Hannah Roper. Bap.

Jackson	27 Ann daughter of John and Ann Jackson. Bap.
Bacott	Dec. 17 Peter son of Thomas Wright and Jane Bacott. Bap.
Falker	25 Joseph son of John Casper and Rebecca Falker. Bap.
Do	Sarah daughter of John Casper and Rebecca Falker. Bap.
Morris	Christopher Gadsden son of Thomas and Mary Morris. Bap.

Shubrick	Jany 1. 1789 Richard son of Thomas and Mary Shubrick. Bap.
Do.	John Templer son of Thomas and Mary Shubrick. Bap.
Armstrong	12 George son of Alexander Fleetwood and Rebecca Armstrong. Bap.
White	Feb. 22 William son of Anthony Wharton and Sarah White. Bap.
Bentham	25 James son of James and Mary Bentham. Bap.
Ward	Susanna daughter of Thomas and Elizabeth Ward.
Guy	Jany 16 Joseph of James and Sarah Guy (Guy)
Dawes	Feb. 1. Hugh Peronneau son of Ralph and Margaret Dawes. Bap.
Roberson	4 Eliza Camell daughter of John and Mary Ann Roberson. Bap.
Legare	March 2. Sarah Hill daughter of Solomon and Mary Legare. Bap.
Hanahan	10 Sarah daughter of Edward and Sarah Hanahan. Bap.,

Baptisms

.... Baptisms Continued 141

Pinckney	March 14. 1789 Charles Cotesworth son of Thomas and Elizabeth Pinckney. Bap.

Grassel	16 Elizabeth Jane daughter of George and Sarah Grassel Bap.
Gaillard	18 Eleanor daughter of Theodore and Elizabeth Gaillard. Bap.
Peronneau	Elizabeth daughter of John and Mary Peronneau. Bap.
Huger	20 Alfred son of John and Ann Huger. Bap.[1]
Warley	22 William Kern son of Felix and Ann Warley. Bap.
Manigault	30 Gabriel Henry son of Gabriel and Margaret Manigault. Bap.
Calhoun	April 4 Mary daughter of John Ewing and Florida[2] Calhoun.[3] Bap.
Johnston	8 Isaac Emery son of William and Sarah Johnston. Bap.
Foster	12 Henry son of Thomas and Mary Foster. Bap.
Warham	14 Mary Mellen daughter of Charles and Mary Warham. Bap.
Gibbes	15 Harriott daughter of William Hasell and Eliza Gibbes. Bap.
Bee	" Mary daughter of Joseph and Susannah Bee. Bap.
Torrey	17 Elias son of Elias and Mary Torrey. Bap.
Thorn	" John Stock son of John Garding and Sarah Thorn.
Brailsford	May 3 Elizabeth daughter of William and Maria Brailsford. Bap.
Do	" Samuel son of William and Maria Brailsford. Bap.

---

[1]Subsequently a much revered citizen of Charleston. He was appointed postmaster of Charleston by President Jackson in 1832 and served continuously to the close of the Confederate War in 1865.

[2]Floride.

[3]Colhoun.

Harris	" Jane Campbell daughter of Tucker and Harris Bap.
Wyatt	6 Violetta daughter of John and Violetta Wyatt. Bap.
Robinson	9 Eliza Ann daughter of and Margaret P. Robinson. Bap.
Do	" Thomas Francis son of and Margaret P. Robinson. Bap.
Do.	" Robert Henry son of and Margaret P. Robinson. Bap.

Baptisms.

Farr	May 8. 1789 Susannah daughter of Joseph and Sarah Farr. Bap.
Boon	10 Susannah daughter of John and Boon. Bap.
Smith	June 2 Mary daughter of Peter and Elizabeth Smith. Bap.
Teasdale	3 Richard son of Mary and John Teasdale. Bap.
Drayton	" William Henry son of William and Hannah Drayton. Bap.
Parkinson	23 Sarah daughter of John and Catherine Parkinson. Bap.
Russell	26 Alicia Hopson daughter of Nathaniel and Sarah Russell Bap.
Cripps	28 Elizabeth, John, and William, daughter and sons of John and Elizabeth Cripps.
Heyward	" William son of Nathaniel and Henrietta Heyward. Bap.
Mayer	July 1 John George son of John George and Charlotte Mayer. Bap.
Ladson	20 Susannah daughter of Robert and Martha Ladson. Bap.
do.	" Robert son of Robert and Martha Ladson Bap.

Wallace	Aug. 12 Jane McNeal daughter of Edward and Elizabeth Wallace. Bap.
Doughty	16 Selina daughter of William and Susannah Doughty. Bap.
Prioleau	23 Elias son of Samuel and Catherine Prioleau. Bap.
Forest	George son of George and Catherine Forest. Bap.
Rice	Sept 13 William son of John and Mary Rice. Bap.
Izard	of of Ralph and Alice Izard. Bap.
Conner	Oct. 15. John son of Thomas and Letitia Conner. Bap.
Kennedy	19 William son of William and Kennedy. Bap.
Do.	Dec. 9 of James and Ann Bensley Kennedy. Bap.
Rogers	Rebecca daughter of Christopher and Mary Ann Rogers. Bap.

Temple	Jany 3. 1790 Ja[illegible]s Fair son of William and Sarah Temple. Bap.
Huger	6 Charlotte Motte daughter of John and Mary Huger. Bap.
Dupre	12 Amy Frances daughter of Benjamin and Mary Dupre. Bap.

Baptisms

Baptisms Continued 143

Barr	Feby 4 1790 John Thomas son of John and Frances Barr. Bap.
Peak	28 John son of John and Elizabeth Peak. Bap.
Frost	March 3 Richard Downes son of Thomas and Elizabeth Frost. Bap.

Hamilton	5	James son of James and Elizabeth Hamilton. Bap.[1]
Miller	14	Samuel Sterst Son of John David and Ann Miller. Bap.
Lenud	15	Eliza Love daughter of Henry and Lenud. Bap.
Cripps	19	Ann daughter of John Splatt and Elizabeth Cripps. Bap.
Lebby	21	William son of Nathaniel and Elizabeth Lebby. Bap.
Do.	21	Ann Hawkins daughter of Nathaniel and Elizabeth Lebby. Bap.
Wyatt		John Richardson son of Richard & Elizabeth Wyatt. Bap.
Dewees	April 2	William son of William and Jane Dewees. Bap.
Ash	"	Samuel son of Samuel and Hannah Ash. Bap.
Wingwood	11	Ann Elizabeth daughter of Samuel & Elizabeth Wingwood Bap.
Buckle		Ann Martha daughter of George and Elizabeth Buckle. Bap.
Brown	16	Mary daughter of Daniel and Margaret Brown. Bap.
Lining	18	Edward Blake Son of Charles and Polly Lining. Bap.
Wells	26	Elizabeth daughter of John and Elizabeth Wells. Bap.
Bay	May 5	William son of Elisha Hall[2] and Margaret Bay. Bap.
Simons	11	Thomas Grange son of Keating and Sarah Simons. Bap.

---

[1]Subsequently governor (1830-1832) of South Carolina. See *The South Carolina Historical and Genealogical Magazine*, Vol. III, 44-45, 172; XVIII, 189.

[2]Probably Elihu Hall Bay.

Mazyck	16	William son of William And Elizabeth Mazyck. Bap.
Guy		James son of William and Sarah Guy. Bap.
Porcher	July 8	Samuel son of Samuel and Harriott Porcher. Bap.
Foster	30	Edward Weyman son of Thomas And Mary Foster. Bap.
Doar	Sept. 10	Esther Susannah daughter of John and Esther Doar. Bap.
Gibbes	20	William son of William Hasell & Elizabeth Gibbes. Bap.
Ravenel	22	Henry son of Rene and Charlotte Ravenel. Bap.

Baptisms

.... Baptisms Continued 144

Mayer	Sept. 29 1790	Maria Juliana daughter of John George and Charlotte Mayer. Bap.
House		Caroline Stille daughter of Samuel and Sarah House. Bap.
Wyatt	Oct. 1	John son of John and Violetta Wyatt. Bap.
Fordham	4	Susanna daughter of Richard and Mary Fordham. Bap.
Hume	7	Robert son of John and Mary Hume. Bap.
Pinckney	27	Frances Henrietta daughter of Charles and Mary Eleanor Pinckney. Bap.
Kennon	28	Lavinia daughter of Henry and Elizabeth Sarah Kennon Bap.
Heyward	29	Nathaniel son of Nathaniel and Henrietta Heyward. Bap.
Ladson	Nov. 12	Sarah Reeve daughter of James and Judith Ladson. Bap.
Gourdin	20	Theodore Lewis son of Theodore and Elizabeth Gourdin. Bap.

Quash	26 Constantia daughter of Robert and Sarah Quash. Bap.
Penman	27 Jane Shaw daughter of Edward and Jane Penman. Bap.
Tart	28 Elizabeth daughter of Nathan and Elizabeth Tart. Bap.

Singleton	Jany 1. 1791. James Munroe son of Daniel and Mary Singleton. Bap.
Bacott	23 Jane Amelia DeSaussure daughter of Thomas Wright and Jane Bacott. Bap.
Legare	29 James Edward son of Benjamin and Alice Legare. Bap.
Doughty	Feb. 5 James son of William and Susannah Doughty. Bap.
	7 Legrand son of Robert and Magdalen Sutton. Bap.
Jones	13 Harriott Farquhar daughter of Alexander and Mary Jones. Bap.
Fitzsimons	March 6 Cashal son of Christopher and Catherine Fitzsimons. Bap.
Campbell	10 Harriott daughter of McCartan and Sarah Campbell. Bap.
Martin	April 5 Ann daughter of Samuel and Lucy Martin. Bap.
Hamilton	10 Christopher son of David and Elizabeth Hamilton. Bap.
Milligen	18 Susanna Melinda daughter of James and Elizabeth Milligen. Bap.
Harris	19 Catharine daughter of John H. and Mary Harris. Bap.
Monk	26 Mary Elizabeth daughter of James and Elizabeth Monk. Bap.
Frogatt	27 John Adding son of Adding and Ann Frogatt. Bap.

Baptisms

Jackson — May 16. 1791 John son of John and Ann Jackson. Bap.

Stoll — 20 William son of Jack and Catherine Stoll. Bap.

Morris — June 5 Thomas son of Thomas and Mary Morris. Bap.

Do — Samuel son of Thomas and Mary Morris. Bap.

Theus — 7 James Francis son of James and Theus. Bap.

Pagett — 8 Margaret daughter of and Margaret Pagett.

Manigault — 11 Ann daughter of Gabriel and Margaret Manigault. Bap.

Chambers — 12 Alexander son of Gilbert and Sophia Chambers.

Scott — July 3 Mary daughter of and Scott Bap.

Young — Lydia daughter of Gideon and Elizabeth Young. Bap.

Smith — 12 Ann Caroline daughter of William and Charlotte Smith. Bap.

Forrest — 27 Berkett son of George and Catherine Forrest. Bap.

Bryant — Aug. 18 James son of James and Hannah Bryant. Bap.

Lambert — " Mary Ann daughter of Elias and Mary Lambert. Bap.

Lothrop — 26 Sarah daughter of Seth and Sarah Lothrop. Bap.

Rout — 21 Elizabeth Rebecca daughter of George and Catharine Rout. Bap.

Porcher — 30 Samuel son of Samuel and Harriott Porcher. Bap.

Do.	Sept. 1	Philip son of Philip and Catharine Porcher. Bap.
Bryan	5	John son of John and Lidia Bryan. Bap.
Rambert	20	Elisha son of Matthew and Mary Rambert. Bap.
Morgan	Oct. 5	Alexander Russell son of Charles and Elizabeth Morgan. Bap.
Warley	9	Sarah Bond daughter fo Felix and Ann Warley. Bap.
Beneter	26	Justinus son of Justinus and Sarah Beneter. Bap.
Payne	27	Charles son of Jonas Parsley and Frances Rosalinda Payne. Bap.
Spindler	18	Ann daughter of Jacob and Mary Spindler. Bap.
Jones	23	William son of Joseph and Frances Jones. Bap.
Todd	Nov. 2	Richard Downing son of John and Elizabeth Todd. Bap.
Brally	12	Susannah Allison daughter of Thomas and Mary Brally. Bap.
Swain	15	Benjamin son of Luke and Rebecca Swain. Bap.
Beedon		Elizabeth daughter of William Ward and Elizabeth Beedon. Bap.
Moncrief	27	Caroline Young daughter of Richard and Elizabeth Moncrief. Bap.
Perry	29	Rebecca daughter of Joseph and Ann Perry. Bap.
Do.	"	John Rawlins son of Joseph and Ann Perry. Bap.

.... Baptisms Continued. 146

Cripps	Dec. 2. 1791	Caroline daughter of John Splatt and Elizabeth Cripps. Bap.

Caldwell { 9 Elizabeth daughter of Henry and Sarah Caldwell. Bap.

Stevens { 13 Mary Ann Jane daughter of Jervis Henry and Susannah Stevens. Bap.

Thorne { 25 Elizabeth daughter of John Gardner and Sarah Thorne Bap.

Mayers { 26 Elizabeth daughter of Thomas and Elizabeth Mayers. Bap.

Loyd { " Esther daughter of Joseph and Esther Loyd. Bap.

Morris { 30 Martha daughter of George and Martha Morris.

Grimke { Jany. 2. 1792. Polly daughter of John Faucheraud and Mary Grimke. Bap.

Do. { " Frederick son of John Faucheraud and Mary Grimke. Bap.

Armstrong { 4 Fleetwood son of Fleetwood and Rebecca Armstrong. Bap.

Gadsden { 29 Selina daughter of Thomas and Martha Gadsden. Bap.

Bay { " Margaret daughter of Elihu Hall and Margaret Bay. Bap.

Sheid { " Abraham Allen son of Christian Sheid. Bap.

Harleston { " Hannah Harleston daughter of Edward and Annabella Harleston. Bap.

Foster { Feby. 5. William Burrows son of Thomas and Mary Foster. Bap.

Bonnethea { " Elizabeth Bond daughter of Peter and Elizabeth Bonnetheau. Bap.

Eve { 19 Martha Henrietta daughter of Oswald and Ann Eve.

Gadsden { " Elizabeth daughter of Philip and Catharine Gadsden. Bap.

DeBow { " John son of John and Ann DeBow. Bap.

Sherrar	" William Belshazer son of William and Mary Sherrar. Bap.
Villepontoux	26 Frances Susannah daughter of Benjamin and Jane Villepontoux. Bap.
Ash	March 4 Thomas Jones son of Samuel and Hannah Ash. Bap.
Rowley	9 Susannah daughter of Thomas and Ann Rowley. Bap.
Wrainch	23 Louisa Margaret daughter of Richard and Sarah Wrainch. Bap.
Gibson	25 Robert son of Robert and Jane Gibson. Bap.
Bee	28 William son of Joseph and Susannah Bee. Bap.
Hort.	April 1. Benjamin Simons son of William and Catharine Hort. Bap.
Shubrick	3 Hannah Heyward daughter of Thomas and Mary Shubrick. Bap.

Baptisms.

Johnson	April 4. 1792. Mary Amory daughter of William and Sarah Johnson. Bap.
Oats	8 Ann daughter of Charles and Mary Oats. Bap.
Gabeau	" Benjamin son of Anthony and Elizabeth Gabeau. Bap.
Wyatt	10 Robert son of Richard and Elizabeth Wyatt. Bap.
Provieux	17 John Charles son of Adrian and Jane Knowles Provieux. Bap.
Leblong	May 2. Ann daughter of Henry and Rosanna Leblong. Bap.
Russel	Sarah daughter of Nathaniel and Sarah Russel. Bap.
Doughty	13 Ann daughter of William and Susannah Doughty. Bap.

Thomas	22 Hannah Harleston daughter of Edward and Elizabeth Thomas. Bap.
Parker	23 John son of John and Martha Parker. Bap.
Rodgers	Jane daughter of Lewis and Rodgers. Bap.
Darby	June 1. Elizabeth Mary daughter of William and Sarah Darby. Bap.
Course	10 Clement son of Isaac and Ann Course. Bap.
Gervais	15 Charles son of John Lewis and Mary Gervais. Bap.
Broun	July 12 Harriott daughter of Archibald and Mary Broun. Bap.
Blackaller	18 Louisa Ann daughter of Oliver and Martha Blackaller. Bap.
Crofts	21 Susannah daughter of Childermars and Ellen Crofts. Bap.
Mayer	Aug. 1. William Henry son of John George and Charlotte Dorothey Mayer. Bap.
Periman	7 Mary Catharine And Gracia Turnbull daughters of Edward and Jane Periman.
Lining	14 Mary Blake daughter of Charles and Polly Lining. Bap.
Smith	15 William son of Peter and Elizabeth Smith. Bap.
Buckle	29 Thomas Henry son of Thomas and Ann Buckle. Bap.
Trescot	31 George son of Edward and Catharine Trescot. Bap.
Bonnetheau	Sept. 4. Rebecca, Daniel and Thomas daughter and sons of Peter and Elizabeth Bonnetheau. Bap.
Milligen	9 Frances Jane daughter of James and Elizabeth Milligen. Bap.

Lestargeth	13 Lavinia daughter of Lewis and Elizabeth Lestargeth. Bap.
do	" Juliet Letitia daughter of Lewis and Elizabeth Lestargeth. Bap.
Bentham	18 Charlotte Bryn daughter of James and Mary Bentham. Bap.
Theus	19 Rosetta Charlotte daughter of James and Theus. Bap.
Porcher	22 Harriott daughter of Samuel and Henrietta Porcher. Bap.
Logan	26 Joseph son of Joseph and Ann Logan. Bap.

Baptisms.

.... Baptisms Continued 148

Allston	Sep. 29. 1792 Rebecca Brewton daughter of William and Mary Allston,. Bap.
Mazyck	30 William & Philip Porcher sons of William and Elizabeth Mazyck. Bap.
Morton	Oct. 7. William son of William and Mary Morton. Bap.
Hume	10 Charlotte daughter of John and Mary Hume. Bap.
Stoll	18 William Frederick son of Jacob and Catharine Stoll. Bap.
Rutledge	Nov. 6. John son of Sarah and John Rutledge Jun'r. Bap.
Pepoon	8 Maria daughter of Benjamin and Lucy Pepoon. Bap.
Quash	14 Andrew Hasell son of Robert and Sarah Quash. Bap.
Joel	18 Elizabeth Maria daughter of Thomas and Elizabeth Joel.
Pendarvis	" Kezia daughter of Josiah & Elizabeth Louisa Pendarvis.

Lee — 18 Harriott, Sarah-Dorothy, and Joseph Francis, daughters and son of William and Ann Lee. Bap.

Kennan — Dec. 4. Harriott Elizabeth daughter of Henry and Elizabeth Sarah Kennan. Bap.

Duvall — Jany 1. 1793 Mary Catharine daughter of John and Martha Duvall. Bap.

Foster — 13 Robert Smith son of Thomas and Mary Foster. Bap.

Andrews — 14 Moses son of Moses and Sarah Andrews. Bap.

McNeal — Archibald Agnaw son of Archibald and Elizabeth McNeal. Bap.

Rembert — 24 Martha Maria daughter of Isaac and Margaret Rembert. Bap.

Burnham — Feby 10. Mary Eugenia daughter of Charles and Harriott Rachel Cochran Burnham. Bap.

Patch — 16 Jacob Hendrickson son of Nathaniel & Frances Patch.

Dewees — 19 Ann Price daughter of William and Jane Dewees. Bap.

Bryan — 22 Martha Elizabeth daughter of Samuel and Susannah Bryan. Bap.

Besileau — 25 Susannah Elizabeth daughter of Philip and Susannah Besileau. Bap.

Kerr — March 3 Joseph son of John and Mary Kerr. Bap.

Townsend — 21 Benjamin son of Stephen and Sarah Townsend. Bap.

Gibbes — 24 Allston son of William Hasell and Eliza Gibbes. Bap.

Hort — April 2. Catharine Chicken daughter of William and Catharine Hort. Bap.

Sinkler	April 20. 1793 Margaret Ann daughter of James and Margaret Sinkler Bap.
Mitchell	May 4 Elizabeth daughter of John Hinckley and Ann Mitchell. Bap.
Miller	19 Mary Magdalen Grimball daughter of John David and Ann Miller. Bap.
Martin	31 John son of Samuel and Lucy Martin. Bap.
Hales	June 2 Alexander son of Daniel and Sarah Hales. Bap.
Paulton	3 Elizabeth Mary Righton daughter of Edward and Rachel Paulton. Bap.
Samford	5 Matthew son of John and Ann Samford. Bap.
Lance	7 Maurice Harvey son of Lambert and Sarah Lance. Bap.
Frost	.10 Anna Downes daughter of the Rev'd. Thomas and Elizabeth Frost. Bap.
Spindler	Thomas son of Jacob and Mary Spindler. Bap.
Crafts	16 Thomas son of William and Mary Crafts. Bap.
Do.	" Anna daughter of William and Mary Crafts. Bap.
Bouchenau	" William son of Charles and Sarah Bouchenau.[1] Bap.
Jones	Ann daughter of Joseph and Frances Jones Bap.
Teasdale	30 Caroline daughter of John and Mary Teasdale. Bap.
Do.	" Louisa daughter of John and Mary Teasdale. Bap.
Speissegger	July 7 Samuel Ladson son of John and Sarah Phoebe Speissegger. Bap.

[1]Bouchonneau.

Wyatt	12 Susannah Dunnovan daughter of Peter and Mary Wyatt. Bap.
Do	" Sarah Aklin daughter of Richard and Elizabeth Wyatt.
Buckle	18 Joel son of Joel and Elizabeth Buckle. Bap.
Elfe	26 Harriott Clarke daughter of Thomas and Mary Elfe. Bap.
Pinckney	Aug. 1. Roger son of Roger and Susannah Pinckney. Bap.
Todd	John Ball son of John and Elizabeth Todd. Bap.
Gabeau	of Anthony and Elizabeth Gabeau. Bap.
Ford	31 Elizabeth daughter of Isaac and Mary Ford. Bap.
Do	" Susannah daughter of Isaac and Mary Ford. Bap.
Pritchard	Sept. 10 Elizabeth Sarah daughter of William and Elizabeth Pritchard. Bap.
Baas	17 Eliza daughter of Thomas and Dorothy Baas. Bap.
Oats	21 Edward son of Edward and Catharine Oats. Bap.
Perry	27 James son of Edward and Mary Perry. Bap.
Doar	Aug. 1. Francis McCleiland son of John and Esther Doar. Bap.
Rutledge	Oct. 14. Robert Smith son of John and Sarah Motte Rutledge. Bap.

Baptisms.

.... Baptisms Continued. 150

Warley	Oct. 20. 1793 Jacob son of Felix and Ann Warley. Bap.

Porcher	Mary Elizabeth daughter of Thomas and Charlotte Porcher Bap.
Armstrong	27 Archibald son of Archibald and Mary Armstrong. Bap.
Ladson	Nov. 3 James son of James and Judith Ladson. Bap.
Heyward	" James Edward son of Nathaniel and Harriott Heyward. Bap.
Bee	8 James Templar son of Thomas and Susannah Bee. Bap.
Flagg	17 William Mason son of Samuel Hawk and Elizabeth Flagg. Bap.
Fordham	28 George John son of Richard and Mary Fordham. Bap.
Heriott	" Edward Thomas son of William and Mary Heriott. Bap.
Gibbes	29 Charlotte Withers daughter of Henry and Mary Gibbes. Bap.
Brown	Dec. 18 Thomas son of Squire and Maria Brown. Bap.
Alexander	22 Mary Bridgeman daughter of David and Mary Alexander. Bap.
Johnston	Nancy James, daughter of Thomas Nightingale and Nancy Johnston. Bap.
Graeser	26 Anna Maria daughter of Jacob Conrad and Anna Maria Greaser. Bap.
Jaudon	28 Elias son of James and Sarah Jaudon. Bap.
Michau	Charlotte daughter of Peter and Charlotte Michau. Bap.

Moore	Jany 15. 1794. Thomas son of William and Sarah Moore. Bap.
Pepoon	Benjamin son of Benjamin and Lucy Pepoon. Bap.

Pagett — 19 Eliza daughter of Thomas and Eliza Pagett. Bap.

Bay — " Grecia daughter of Elihu Hall and Margaret Bay. Bap.

Bacott — Henry William son of Thomas Wright and Jane Bacott. Bap.

Swain — 31 Margaret Eliza daughter of Luke and Elizabeth Swain. Bap.

Yates — Deborah Amelia daughter of Samuel and Deborah Yates. Bap.

Dupre — Feby. 2 Esther Mary daughter of Benjamin and Mary Dupre. Bap.

Hort — 16 Elias Ball son of William and Catharine Hort. Bap.

Baptisms

.... Baptisms Continued. 151

Farr — Feby. 17. 1794. John Freer Nathaniel son of Joseph and Sarah Farr. Bap.

Do. — " Mary Freer daughter of Joseph and Sarah Farr. Bap.

Do — " Jane Ladson Freer daughter of Joseph and Sarah Farr. Bap.

Moultrie — 23 James son of James and Catharine Moultrie.[1] Bap.

Rose — 19 James son of Hugh and Susannah Rose. Bap.

Haskell — 23 Charlotte daughter of Elnathan and Charlotte Haskell.

Cochran — Harriott Thompson daughter of Charles Burnham and Rachel Harriott Cochran. Bap.

Calhoun — March 6 Mary daughter of William and Lydia Calhoun. Bap.

---

[1]See *The South Carolina Historical and Genealogical Magazine*, V, 251.

Morgan	9	Elizabeth Jane daughter of Charles and Elizabeth Morgan. Bap.
Marshal	"	William Charles Garrison son of William and Louisa Marshal.
Ash	10	Andrew Deveaux son of Samuel and Hannah Ash. Bap.
Huger	12	Maria Huger daughter of Hugh and Mary Huger.[1] Bap.
Addison	16	Harriott daughter of James and Mary Ann Addison. Bap.
Gaillard	17	Martha Doughty daughter of Theodore and Martha Gaillard. Bap.
Elfe	20	Benjamin son of Thomas and Mary Elfe. Bap.
Smith		Elizabeth daughter of James and Mary Smith. Bap.
Prince	23	Clement Lempriere son of Clement and Mary Prince. Bap.
Caldwell	24	of Henry and Sarah Caldwell. Bap.
Frost	25	Thomas wnes son of the Rev'd Thomas and Mary Bap.
Chalmers	30	Alexander son of Gilbert and Sophia Chalmers. Bap.
Hogarth	April 7	Eleanor Yates daughter of William and Ann Hogarth. Bap.
Gourdine	8	Henrietta daughter of Theodore and Elizabeth Gourdine. Bap.
Doar		John son of John and Esther Doar. Bap.
Gaillard	13	John son of John and Harriott Gaillard. Bap.

[1]The entry is misleading. It was an attempt to record the baptism of Maria Huger, daughter of Hugh and Mary Golightly (Huger) Rutledge.

Nicholls	17	Mary Ann, Thomas, and Richard Moss, daughter and sons of Thomas and Sarah Nicholls. Bap.
Rogers	18	Charles son of Christopher and Mary Ann Rogers. Bap.
Moorhead	"	John Roberts son of John Alexander and Sarah Moorhead. Bap.

Baptisms.

.... Baptisms Continued 152

Bochet	April 30 1794.	Alexander Myott son of John Peter and Sarah Bochet. Bap.
Crofts	May 4.	Louisa daughter of Peter and Elizabeth Crofts. Bap.
Bee	7	Richard Moncrief son of Joseph and Susannah Bee. Bap.
Grimke	9	Ann Rutledge daughter of John Faucheraud and Mary Grimke. Bap.
Peak	14	William James son of Joseph and Elizabeth Peak. Bap.
McKoy	18	William West son of Abraham and Elizabeth McKoy Bap.
Guy	"	[illegible]h daughter of James and Sarah Guy. Bap.
Shepeler	21	John Clements son of John and Sarah Shepeler. Bap.
Theus	18	Mary Esther daughter of James and Theus. Bap.
Miller	24	Samuel Findlay son of Samuel and Ann Findlay Miller. Bap.
Granger	June 8.	Elizabeth Jane daughter of James and Anna Granger. Bap.
Gibbes	15	Anna Maria daughter of Benjamin and Elizabeth Gibbes. Bap.
Gibson	16	Thomas Callaghan son of Robert and Jane Gibson. Bap.

Mayer { 29 Joab Raymond son of John George and Charlotte Dorothea Mayer. Bap.

Simmons { July 18 Eliza Susannah daughter of Thomas and Elizabeth Simmons. Bap.

Weyman { 20 Edward son of Edward and Catherine Weyman. Bap.

Dorman { " Martha daughter of Robert and Martha Dorman. Bap.

Benney { Aug 11 Peter son of Peter and Benney. Bap.

Wyatt { 14 John son of John and Violetta Wyatt. Bap.

Strepper { 28 Nathaniel son of George and Rebecca Strepper. Bap.

Wyatt { 29 Elizabeth Mary daughter of Peter and Mary Wyatt. Bap.

Gray { Sept 1. Benjamin Francis son of Peter and Hannah Gray. Bap.

Hall { Robert Wilson son of William and Ann Hall. Bap.

Bignal { 3 Abiel George Story son of James and Hannah Bignal. Bap.

Collins { 10 Eliza daughter of Manasseth and Eliza Collins. Bap.

DeLesseline { 19 Lydia Elizabeth daughter of John and Elizabeth DeLesseline. Bap.

Baptisms

DeLesseline { Sept. 19. 1794 Isaac son of John and Elizabeth DeLesseline. Bap.

Boone { " Maria daughter of Boone. Bap.

Kenna { Oct. 2. Richard son of John and Martha Kenna. Bap.

Ball	4 Jane daughter of John and Ball. Bap.
Speed	5 Isabella daughter of William and Christiana Speed. Bap.
Gourdine	19 Mary daughter of and Mary Gourdine. Bap.
Penman	" Mary Edgar Cathrine daughter of James and Jane Penman. Bap.
Porcher	26 Charlotte daughter of Thomas and Charlotte Porcher. Bap.
Roberts	" John Samuel son of John and Hannah Roberts. Bap.
Smith	30 Sarah daughter of Peter and Elizabeth Smith. Bap.
Quash	Nov. 5 Francis Dallas son of Robert and Sarah Quash. Bap.
Beekman	9 Ann Lee daughter of Samuel and Ann Beekman. Bap.
Joel	" Thomas Lee son of Thomas and Elizabeth Joel. Bap.
Bonnetheau	16 James son of Peter and Elizabeth Bonnetheau. Bap.
Forster	Mary Elliott daughter of Thomas and Mary Forster. Bap.
Jones	Frances daughter of Joseph and Frances Jones. Bap.
Pendervais	Stobo son of Josiah and Elizabeth Louisa Pendervais. Bap.
Buckle	Dec. 3 Mary daughter of Thomas and Ann Buckle. Bap.
Manigault	12 Henrietta daughter of Gabriel and Margaret Manigault. Bap.
Heyward	" Joseph Manigault son of Nathaniel and Henrietta Heyward. Bap.

Stoll	Jany. 14. 1795. James Gregson son of Jacob and Catharine Stoll. Bap.

Morris	Feb. 9 James son of Thomas and Mary Morris. Bap.
Do.	" Mary Gadsden daughter of Thomas and Mary Morris. Bap.
Tarver	16 Maria Ann daughter of John and Maria Tarver. Bap.
Brooks	22 John son of John and Mary Brooks. Bap.
Dupre	Josiah James son of Benjamin and Mary Dupre. Bap.
Gibbes	Mar. 30 Washington son of William Hazell and Gibbes. Bap.
Bowers	April 15 Mary Martha daughter of Frederick and Mary Bowers. Bap.

Baptisms.

.... Baptisms Continued 154

Gadsden	April 19. 1795 Rebecca Harriott daughter of Philip and Catherine Gadsden. Bap.
Shubrick	28 Mary Rutledge daughter of Thomas and Mary Shubrick. Bap.
Do	" William Brandford son of Thomas and Mary Shubrick Bap.
Do.	" Edward Rutledge son of Thomas and Mary Shubrick. Bap.
Do.	" Eliza Susannah daughter of Thomas and Mary Shubrick. Bap.
Prestman	29 Stephen Wilkes son of William and Ann Ferguson Prestman. Bap.
Thomas	May 20 Ann Hasell daughter of Thomas Hasell and Ann Thomas. Bap.
Cordes	21 Margaret Catharine daughter of Thomas and Charlotte Cordes. Bap.
Lequeux	22 Harriott Walter daughter of Sims and Harriott Lequeux. Bap.
Gaillard	" Catharine daughter of Peter and Elizabeth Gaillard. Bap.

Roddom	23 Sarah Mary daughter of Joseph and Mary Roddom. Bap.
Moore	July 8 Ann daughter of William and Sarah Moore. Bap.
Ridgeway	Aug. 9. Joseph Meeks son of John and Rebecca Ridgeway. Bap.
Smith	Sept. 5 Mary daughter of Henry and Mary Smith. Bap.
Harth	Oct. 9 William son of Simon and Mary Harth. Bap.
Hunter	23 John Lingard son of Thomas and Mary Hunter. Bap.
Bruce	25 Alexander son of Alexander and Sarah Bruce. Bap.
Graeser	Nov. 11. Sarah daughter of Conrad Jacob and Ann Maria Graeser. Bap.
Trescott	18 Henry son of Edward and Catharine Trescott. Bap.
Pritchard	Dec. 9 Catherine daughter of William and Elizabeth Pritchard. Bap.
Baas	27 Francis Charles son of John and Frances Baas. Bap.

.... Baptisms. Continued 155

Corbett	Jan. 20. 1796 Martha daughter of Edward and Martha Corbett. Bap.
Tait	Feby. 12 Elizabeth Sarah daughter of Henry and Hannah Tait. Bap.
Frost	18 Henry Rutledge son of Thomas and Elizabeth Frost. Bap.
Grimke	16 Sarah Moore daughter of John Faucheraud and Mary Grimke. Bap.
Do.	26 Ann Rutledge daughter of John Faucheraud and Mary Grimke. Bap.
Gibbes	28 Elizabeth Fisher daughter of Benjamin and Elizabeth Gibbes. Bap.

Bentham	" Caroline Hardy daughter of James and Mary Bentham. Bap.
Do.	" Susannah Boswell daughter of James and Mary Bentham. Bap.
Boylston	" Henry son of Nicholas and Mary Boylston. Bap.
Simons	March 5 Thomas son of Thomas and Simons. Bap.
Porcher	12 Peter son of Samuel and Henrietta Porcher. Bap.
Browne	18 Oliver son of Squire and Mary Browne. Bap.
Speissegger	" Ann Heriott son of John and Sarah Speissegger. Bap.
Wigfall	19 of Thomas and Harriott Wigfall. Bap.
Gaillard	20 Edwin son of John and Mary Gaillard. Bap.
Neufville	" John son of Isaac and Ann Neufville Bap.
Rutledge	April 1 Elizabeth Rutledge daughter of John and Sarah Motte Rutledge. Bap.
Hort	10 John Ball son of William and Catharine Hort. Bap.
Clarkson	" Henrietta Christiana daughter of William and Elizabeth Anderson Clarkson. Bap.
Rutledge	" Jane Smith daughter of Edward and Jane Smith Rutledge. Bap.
Porcher	May 1. Thomas son of Thomas and Charlotte Porcher. Bap.
Pownal	5 Louisa Delia daughter of Hugh and Mary Ann Pownal. Bap.

Baptisms.

.... Baptisms Continued 156

Eve	May 29. 1796 Oswald son of Oswald and Ann Eve. Bap.

Kingdon	June 22 James son of Thomas and Sarah Kingdon. Bap.
Mayer	29 Mary Charlotte daughter of John George and Charlotte Dorothy Mayer. Bap.
Swain	Sept. 9 Mary daughter of Luke and Rebecca Swain. Bap.
Pendleton	Susannah Mary daughter of Oliver and Catharine Pendleton. Bap.
Morgan	Nov. 6 Henry son of Charles and Elizabeth Morgan. Bap.
Wyatt	27 Elizabeth daughter of Richard and Elizabeth Wyatt. Bap.
Nicholls	" George Parker son of Thomas and Sarah Nicholls.
Hume	Dec. 4 Charlotte daughter of John and Mary Hume. Bap.

Warley	Jany. 18. 1797 Charles son of Felix and Ann Warley. Bap.
Lining	29 Charles son of Charles and Sarah Lining. Bap.
Hill	Feb. 13 John son of Charles and Charlotte Hill. Bap.
Tarver	14 John son of John and Elizabeth Tarver. Bap.
Wilson	21 Elizabeth daughter of John and Mary Wilson. Bap.
Harvey	24 Robert James son of Robert and Mary Harvey. Bap.
Neufville	April 2. Carolina daughter of Isaac and Ann Neufville, Bap.
Gibbes	30 Henry son of William Hasell and Gibbes. Bap.
Baas	June 21 Thomas Emanuel son of Thomas and Dorothy Baas. Bap.
Fordham	22 Eliza daughter of Richard and Mary Fordham. Bap.

Cart	July 23 Martha daughter of John and Susannah Cart. Bap.
Teasdale	" Matilda daughter of Hichard and Mary Teasdale. Bap.
Hussey	30 Catharine Eliza daughter of Brian and Susannah Hussey. Bap.
Hunter	Oct. 11 James Wyatt son of Thomas and Mary Linguard Hunter. Bap.
Rutledge	25 Jane Harleston daughter of Edward and Jane Smith Rutledge.

Baptisms.

.... Baptisms Continued 157

Rutledge	Sept. 2. 1797 Sarah Rutledge daughter of John and Sarah Motte Rutledge. Bap.
Rout	5 William son of George and Catharine Rout. Bap.
Chichester	Nov. 12 Alicia Powell daughter of John and Mary Beatrix Chichester. Bap.
Corbett	13 Thomas son of Thomas and Elizabeth Corbett Jun'r. Bap.
Edwards	19 Daniel Cannon of Edward and Mary Edwards Edwards. Bap.
Drayton	Dec. 3. Esther Tidyman daughter of John and Esther Rose Drayton. Bap.
Simmons	7 Thomas Young son of Morris and Elizabeth Simmons. Bap.

Capers	Jany 29. 1798. Charles William son of William Henry and Abigail Capers. Bap.
Do	" Priscilla Ann daughter of William Henry and Abigail Capers. Bap.
Townshend	Feby 5 Sarah daughter of Stephen and Sarah Townshend. Bap.
Clarkson	27 Caroline Maria daughter of William and Elizabeth Clarkson. Bap.

Huger — March 10 Benjamin Huger son of Hugh and Mary Huger.[1] Bap.

Smith — 14 Francis Harth son of Peter and Elizabeth Smith. Bap.

Weyman — April 8. Joseph son of Edward and Catharine Weyman. Bap.

Roddom — 9 Frances Ann daughter of Joseph and Mary Roddom. Bap.

Bonnetheau — May 27 Henry Brentneil son of Peter and Elizabeth Bonnetheau. Bap.

Clarke — June 11 Zachariah Hasell son of Zachariah and Susanna Clarke. Bap.

Prestman — July 15 Maria daughter of William and Ann Ferguson Prestman. Bap.

Baptisms.

.... Baptisms Continued. 158

Rutledge — Aug. 3. 1798 Nancy Cosslet daughter of William and Ann Rutledge. Bap.

Gadsden — Sept. 14 Thomas son of Philip and Catharine Gadsden. Bap.

Do — " Philip son of Philip and Catharine Gadsden. Bap.

Hume — Oct. 15 John son of John and Mary Hume. Bap.

Johnstone — Nov. 25. Anna Maria daughter of William and Anna Maria Johnstone. Bap.

Allston — Dec. 4 Jacob Motte son of William and Mary Allston. Bap.

Magwood — 5 Eleanor Mary daughter of Simon and Mary Elizabeth Magwood. Bap.

McCall — Jany 20 1799 Maria Clementina daughter of James and Ann Amelia McCall Bap.

Hort — 24 Edward Simons Thomas son of William and Catharine Hort. Bap.

---

[1]Benjamin Huger, son of Hugh and Mary Golightly (Huger) Rutledge.

Roux — Feby 3 Albert Frederick son of Lewis and Ann Roux. Bap.

Gray — March 17 Elizabeth Sarah daughter of William and Elizabeth Gray Bap.

Corbett — 30 John Harleston son of Thomas and Eliza Corbett. Bap.

Lining — April 21. Thomas son of Charles and Sarah Lining. Bap.

Shubrick — June 11. Decima Cecilia daughter of Thomas and Mary Shubrick. Bap.

Do — " Irwin son of Thomas and Mary Shubrick. Bap.

Gibbes — July 15 Maria Ann Elizabeth daughter of William and Mary Gibbes. Bap.

Cripps — Oct. 8 Charlotte daughter of John Splatt and Elizabeth Cripps. Bap.

Do — " Octavius, Cecilia Septima, Clementia Elizabeth Farr, (3 children) son and daughters of John Splatt and Elizabeth Cripps.

Corbett — 11 John Harleston son of Thomas Corbett Jun'r and Elizabeth. Bap.

Lowndes — 17 Rawlins son of Thomas and Sarah Bond Lowndes. Bap.

Baptisms

Brown — Oct. 17 1799, Rawlins Lowndes son of Joseph and Harriott Brown. Bap.

Nowell — 20 Anna Maria daughter of John and Mary Nowell. Bap.

Warley — Nov. 1 Ann Eliza daughter of Felix and Ann Warley. Bap.

Purcell — 13 Edward Henry son of Henry and Sarah Purcell. Bap.

White — 15 John son of John and Jane Pogson White. Bap.

Lord	17 Richard son of Richard and Maria Lord. Bap.
Gibbes	21 Edwin son of William Hasell and Eliza Gibbes. Bap.
Allston	Dec. 1 Elizabeth Laura daughter of William and Mary Allston. Bap.

Gadsden	Feby 9 1800 Margaret daughter of Philip and Catharine Gadsden. Bap
Morris	23 Henry and Edward, two sons of Thomas and Mary Morris. Bap
Rutledge	March 27 Edward Cotesworth son of Frederick and Harriott Pinckney Rutledge.[1] Bap.
McCay	April 4 Frances Elizabeth Bacot daughter of Joseph R. and Frances McCay bap.
Bee	May 2 Sarah Love daughter of Peter Smith and Frances Caroline Bee Bap.
"	" " Emma Frances daughter of Peter Smith and Frances Caroline Bee. bap.
Bacot	July 22 Francis Augustus son of Thomas W. and Jane Bacot. Bap.
Johnson	Nov 6 Sarah Elizabeth daughter of William and Maria Johnson Bap
Jenkins	9 Ann Maria daughter of Elias and Elizabeth Jenkins. Bap
Pinckney	" Edward Rutledge son of Thomas and Frances Pinckney. Bap
Lowndes	30 Mary Ion daughter of Thomas and Sarah Bond Lowndes Bap
Ward	Dec 1 Sarah Hartley daughter of John and Mary Ward. Bap

Baptisms.

Baptisms 160

White	July 22 1801 Jane Purcell daughter of John and Jane Pogson.[2] Bap.

---

[1]This baptism had already been entered on page 50.
[2]John and Jane Pogson White, it should have been.

Hall	Feby 3 Anna Maria daughter of William and Hall. Bap.
Rolain	8 Robert son of Robert and Hannah Rolain. Bap.
Rutledge	27 Frederick son of Frederick and Harriott Pinckney Rutledge. Bap.
Deas	March 18 Elizabeth Allen daughter of William Allen and Ann Deas
Lining	23 Richard Hill son of Charles and Sarah Lining Bap
Miles	Polly Blake daughter of William and Mary Ann Blake Miles Bap.
Nowell	April 5 John Francis son of John and Mary Nowell. Bap.
Sutcliffe	" Louis Samuel Eli son of Eli and Anna Adelaid Sutcliffe Bap.
Hildreth	" Ann daughter of Benjamin and Mary Hildreth.
McKenzie	" Benjamin and Elizabeth, son and daughter of Canada and Ann McKenzie. Bap.
Gibbes	19 Benjamin the son of William Hasell and Eliza Gibbes Bap
Roux	23 Frances Lewis son of Lewis and Ann Roux. Bap.
Sinkler	May 3 James son of James and Margaret Sinkler Bap.
Heyward	24 William son of William and Charlotte Manley Heyward. Bap.
McCay	June 2 Jane Reid daughter of Joseph and Frances McCay. Bap.
Roper	July 25 Hazard son of William and Lydia Roper. Bap.
Shubrick	Sept 2 Elizabeth Susanna daughter of Thomas and Mary Shubrick Bap
Teasdale	6 Joseph son of John and Mary Teasdale. Bap.

Harleston	12 Harleston	Edward son of Edward and Jane Smith Bap.
Harris		Tucker Harris son of James and Sarah Tucker Harris. Bap
Gadsden	Oct 4 Gadsden.	Ann daughter of Philip and Catharine Bap.
Edwards	10 Edwards.	Edward Henry son of Edward and Mary Bap.
"	Martha Canon daughter of Edward and Mary Edwards. Bap.	

Marriages 163[1]

Buckles & Brown	On the 28th. June 1755 Thomas Buckles & Margaret Brown were married by Lic: by the Revd. Mr. Richd. Clarke Rector of St. Philips.
Roberts & Cattle	On the 2d. July 1755 Owen Roberts & Anne Cattle Widow were married pr. Lic. By Mr. Clarke.
Bayne & Heywood	On the 5th. July 1755 Daniel Bayne & Mary Heywood were married by Lic. by the Revd. Mr. Clarke
Coon & Manuel	On the 12th. July 1755 John Coon & Eleanor Manuel Spin. were married by Lic. by the Revd. Mr. Clarke.
Rivers & Gracia	On the 6th. September 1755 Isaac Rivers & Mary Gracia were married by Lic. by the Revd. Mr. Clarke.
Duval & Braithwaite	On the 27th. September 1755 Stephen Duval & Sarah Braithwaite were married by Lic. pr the Revd. Mr. Clarke.
Mayne & Michie	On the 2d. October 1755 Charles Mayne Mrchr. & Martha Michie Spinstr. were married pr Lic. by the Revd. Mr. Clarke.
Grindlay & Govan	On the 11th. October 1755 James Grindlay & Christian Govan were married pr. Lic. by the Revd. Mr. Clarke.

[1]Pages 161-162 are blank.

D'harriette & Fowler	On the 16th. October 1755 Benjamin D'harriette & Martha Fowler were married pr. Lic. by the Revd. Mr. Clarke........
Wilson & Lupton	On the 21 October 1755 John Wilson & Alice Lupton were married pr. Lic. by the Revd. Mr. Clarke ....
Cannon & Doughty	On the 30th. October 1755 Daniel Cannon & Mary Doughty were married pr Lic. by the Revd. Mr. John Andrews Assistant to the Rector ....
Bissett & Loyer	On the 30th. October 1755 William Bissett & Catherine Loyer were married pr Lic. by the Revd. Mr. Andrews ....
Calvert & Clarke	On the 13th. November 1755 John Calvert & Mary Clarke were married pr. Lic. by the Revd. Mr. Clarke ....
Urquehart & Young	On the 25th. November 1755 Alexander Urquehart & Martha Young were married pr. Lic. by the Revd. Mr. Clarke.
Hood & Bunker	On the 30th. November 1755 William Hood & Catherine Bunker were married pr Lic. by the Revd. Mr. Clarke. ....
Cain & Colcock	On the 3d December 1755 James Cain & Sarah Colcock were married pr Lic. by the Revd. Mr. Clarke ....
Bull & Woodward	On the 18th. December 1755 Stephen Bull & Elizabeth Woodward were married pr Lic. by the Revd. Mr. Clarke. ....
Garden & Peronneau	On the 25th. December 1755 Alexander Garden[1] & Elizabeth Peronneau were married pr Lic. ....
Clarke & Roberts	On the 26th. December 1755 The Revd. Mr. Richard Clarke[2] & Mary Roberts Spinster were married pr. Lic. by the Revd Mr. John Andrews. ....

[1]This was the distinguished physician and botanist after whom Linnæus named the gardenia. He died in London in 1791; his widow in Cheltenham, in March, 1805.

[2]For sketches of Mr. Clarke see Dalcho's *Protestant Episcopal Church in South Carolina* and Ramsay's *History of South Carolina*, Vol. II.

Gadsden & Hazell	On the 29th. December 1755 Christopher Gadsden & Mary Hazel Spinster were married pr Lic. by the Revd. Richd. Clarke ....
Elfe & Prideau	On the 29th. December 1755 Thomas Elfe & Rachel Prideau were married pr. Lic. by Mr. Clarke. ....
Garnes & Spencer	On the 11th. January 1756 William Garnes & Hannah Spencer Spin were married pr Lic. Mr. Clarke ....
Leigh & Bremar	On the 15th. January 1756 Egerton Leigh & Martha Bremar[1] Spinster were married pr Lic. by Mr. Clarke ....
Doyley & Pinckney	On the 18th. January 1756 Daniel Doyley[2] & Anna Pinckney Spinster Were married pr. Lic. by Mr. Clarke ....
Ward & Cavenah	On the 31st. January 1756 John Ward & Elizabeth Cavenah were married pr. Lic. by Do. ....
Pratt & Marsh	On the 5th. February 1756 James Pratt & Mary Marsh Widow were married pr. Lic. by Do. ....
McLaughlan & Kelly	On the 7th. February 1756 Hugh McLaughlan & Johanna Kelly were married pr. banns by Do. ....
Legare & Seabrook	On the 26 February 1756 Thomas Legare & Mary Seabrook Widow were married pr. Lic. by Do. ....
Massey & Holmes	On the 27th. February 1756 William Massey & Catherine Holmes Spins. were married pr. Lic. by Do. ....

[1]Egerton Leigh was a son of Chief Justice Peter Leigh. He was Attorney General, member of His Majesty's Council for South Carolina and Judge of the Admiralty in 1761. He was created a baronet in 1772.

[2]D'Oyley. He was one of the Assistant Judges, Rawlins Lowndes and Benjamin Smith being the other two, who opened court in 1766 after Chief-Justice Shinner had adjourned it because of the absence of stamped paper.

McGilveray & Chandler	On the 11th. March 1756 Alexander McGilveray & Elizabeth Chandler Spins. were married pr. Lic. by Do.
Bryan & Boddett	On the 30th. March 1756 John Bryan & Elizabeth Boddett Spinster were married pr. Lic. by Do.
Jones & Brandford	On the 6th. April 1756 John Jones & Ann Brandford were married pr. Lic. by Do.
Nelson & Easton	On the 7th. April 1756 James Nelson & Ann Easton Widow were married pr. Lic. by Do.
Simpson & Bull	On the 12th. April 1756 William Simpson & Elizabeth Bull Spinster were married pr. Lic. by Do.
Wood & Kempland	On the 18th. April 1756 Joseph Wood & Mary Kempland Spinster were married pr. Lic. pr. Do.
Ficklin & Coomer	On the 21st. April 1756 George Fickling & Mary Coomer were married pr. Lic. by Do.
Poinsett & Cattle	On the first May 1756 John Poinsett & Mary Cattle Widow were married pr. Lic. pr. Do.
Liston & Toomer	On the first May 1756 Robert Liston & Mary Toomer were married pr. Lic. by Do.
Baker & Elliott	On the 6th. May 1756 Richard Baker & Elizabeth Elliott Spinster were married pr. Lic. by Do.
Bee & Swan	On the 6th. May 1756 William Bee & Rachael Swan Widow were married. pr. Lic. by Do.

Marriages 165

Andrews & Rothmahler	On the 16th. May 1756 The Revd. John Andrews & Mary Rothmahler were married pr. Lic. by the Revd. Richard Clarke Rector.

Howarth & Croft	On the 27th. May 1756 Probert Howarth[1] & Ann Croft Spinster were married pr. Lic. by Do.
Samways & Holditch	On the 5th. June 1756 John Samways & Mary Holditch were married pr. Lic. by Ditto
Evans & Smith	On the 1st. July 1756 Thomas Evance & Margaret Smith Spinster were married pr. Lic. by Do.
Grimbal & Jenkins	On the 8th. July 1756 Paul Grimbal & Ann Jenkins Spinster were married pr Lic. by Do.
Dempsey & Gravell	On the 2d. August 1756 Edward Dempsey & Jane Graveell Widow were Married pr. Lic. by Do.
Talbert & Herberson	On the 28th. August 1756 James Talbert & Ann Herberson Spinster were married pr. Lic. by Do.
Prichard & Bulloch	On the 9th. September 1756 James Prichard & Eleanor Bulloch Spinster were married pr Lic. by Do.
Fitch & Rose	On the 16th. September 1756 James Fitch & Ann Rose Spinster were married pr. Lic. by Do.
Lochan & Poyas	On the 14th. October 1756 Veireus Lochon & Mary Poyas widow were married pr. Lic. by Do.
Edes & Goodwin	On the 23d October 1756 James Edes & Mary Goodwin Spinster were married pr. Lic. by Do.
Thompson & Hackness	On the 30th. October 1756 Archebald Thompson & Mary Hackness Spinster were married pr. Lic. by Do.
Powel & Smith	On the 31st. October 1756 George Powel & Ruth Smith widow were married pr Lic. by Do.

[1]Col. Probart Howarth was for some years prior to tne Revolution governor of Fort Johnson.

Ladson & Fenling	On the 18th. November 1756 Samuel Ladson & Sarah Fendling Spinster were married pr. Lic. by Do.
Porchee & Mazyck	On the 2nd. December 1756 Peter Philip Porchee & Mary Mazyck Spinster were married pr. Lic. By Do.
Stevens & Liverooke	On the 19th. December 1756 David Stevens & Elizabeth Liverooke Spinster were married pr. Lic. by Do.
Hern & Burn	On the 26th. December 1756 Hern & Margaret Burn Spinster were married pr. Lic. by Do.
Ward & Leger	On the 27th. December 1756 John Ward & Love Leger Spinster were married pr. Lic. by Do.
Legge & Smith	On the 6th. January 1757 Edward Legge & Elizabeth Smith Spinster were married pr. Lic. by Do.
Tuffs & Lloyd	On the 30th. January 1757 Simon Tuffs & Rebecca Lloyd Spinster were married pr. Lic. by Do.
Robertson & Baker	On the 24th. March 1757 William Robinson & Sarah Baker widow were married pr. Lic. by Do.

Marriages 166

Coats & Green	On the 17th. November 1757 William Coats and Mary Green Spinster were married pr. Lic. by the Revd. Mr. Richd. Clarke
Oliver & Trushee	On the 10th. April 1757 Peter Oliver & Martha Trushee Spinster were married pr. Lic. by Do.
Bruce & Fitchett	On the 10th. April 1757 Peter Henry Bruce & Elizabeth Fitchett widow were married pr. Lic. by Do.
Ash & Levingstone	On the 14th. April 1757 John Ash & Elizabeth Levingstone Spinster were married pr Lic. by Do.

Frier & Boone	On the 14th. April 1757 John Frier & Susanna Boone Spinster were married pr. Lic. by Do.
Bullard & Harris	On the 16th. April 1757 Edward Bullard & Sarah Harris widow were married pr. Lic. by Do.
Linn & Bower	On the 7th. May 1757 Thomas Linn and Agnes Bower Spinster were married pr. Lic. by Do.
June & Steele	On the 12 May 1757 Stephen June & Lydia Steele Widow were married pr. Lic. by Do.
Philips & Mathews	On the 12th. May 1757 Benjamin Philips & Sarah Mathews were married pr. Lic. by Do.
Burnet & Hamilton	On the 21st. May 1757 Henry Burnet & Mary Hamilton Widow were married pr. Lic. by Do.
Smith & Clarke	On the 24th. May 1757 Stephen Smith & Ann Clarke Spinster were married pr. Lic. by Do.
Lance & St. John	On the 2d June 1757 Lambert Lance & Mary St. John widow were married pr. Lic. by Do.
Logan & Crockatt	On the 21st June 1757 William Logan & Margaret Crockatt Spinster were married pr. Lic. by Do.
Lockwood & Lee	On the 23d June 1757 Joshua Lockwood & Mary Lee Spinster were married pr Lic. by Do.
Bowden & Powers	On the 22d July 1757 Thomas Bowden & Esther Powers widow were married pr. Lic. by Do.
Thomas & Hasell	On the 24th. July 1757 Samuel Thomas & Ann Hasell Spinster were married pr. Lic. by Do.
Mason & Jenkins	On the 25th. August 1757 William Mason (Schoolmaster) & Mary Jenkins widow were married pr. Lic. by Do.

Vinson & Vardill	On the 27th. August 1757 John Vinson & Mary Vardill Spinster were married pr. Lic. by Do.
Williams & Woodside	On the 17th. September 1757 Nicholas Williams & Sarah Woodside widow were married pr. Lic. by Do.
Lovell & Mackay	On the 22nd. September 1757 William Lovell & Elizabeth Mackay widow were married pr. Lic. by Do.

Marriages 167

Lander & Simpson	On the 16th. October 1757 Francis Lander & Elizabeth Simpson Spinster were married pr Lic. by the Revd. Mr. Richard Clarke
Dehay & Dringat	On the 30th. October 1757 John Andrews Dehay and Margaret Dringat Widow were married pr. Banns by Ditto
Tonge & Glazir	On the 3d Novr. 1757 James Tonge and Magdalen Glasie Spinster were married pr. Licence by Ditto.
Stobo & Harvey	On the 24th. November 1757 Richard Park Stobo and Mary Harvey Spinster were married pr. the Revd Mr. Charles Martin of St. Andrews Parish
Ash & Daniel	On the 12th. December 1757 Richard Cockran Ash and Ann Daniel Widow were married pr. Licence by Ditto.
Guerey & LeGrand	On the 15th. December 1757 Peter Guerey and Mary Ann LeGrand were married pr. Lic. by Ditto.
West & Dalton	On the 18th. December 1757 Samuel West and Mary Dalton Spinster were married pr. Lic. by Ditto.
Stone & Benoist	On the 20th. December 1757 John Stone and Margaret Benoist Spinster were married pr. Lic. by Ditto.
Nicholson & Willis	On the 25th. December 1757 Francis Nichelson and Mary Willis Spinster were married pr. Lic. by Ditto.

Lowcock & Irish	On the 27th. Jany 1758 Joseph Lowcock and Sarah Irish Widow were married pr. Lic. by Ditto.
Wallace & Vanderdussen	On the 26th. January 1758 Thomas Wallace and Elizabeth Vanderdussen Spins were married pr. Lic. by the Revd. Mr. Robert Smith Assistant to the Rector.
Colwell & Lewis	On the 9th. March 1758 John Colwell and Elizabeth Lewis Widow were married pr. the Revd. Mr. Clarke.
Caton & Vickery	On the 26th. March 1758 Benjamin Caton and Ann Vickery Spinster were married pr. Lic. pr. Ditto.
Remington & Willkins	On the 23d. March 1758 John Remington Jun'r & Jane Willkins were married pr. Lic. pr Ditto.
Pendergrass & More	On the 2d. June 1758 Darvey Pendergrass and Sarah More Widow were married pr. Lic. pr. Ditto.
Smith & Pagett	On the 9th. July 1758 The Revd. Robert Smith and Elizabeth Pagett Spinster were married pr. Licence pr. the Revd. Mr. Charles Martin Rector of St. Andrews Parish
Grove & Kean	On the 26th. August 1758 Samuel Grove and Jane Kean widow were married pr. Licence pr. the Revd. Mr. Clarke
Lehree & Brown	On the 14th. Sepr. 1758 John Lehre and Mary Brown widow were married pr. Licence pr. Ditto.
Gowdey & Barlow	On the 15th. October 1758 William Gowdey and Lucina Barlow Spinster were married pr. Lic. pr. Ditto
Mayrant & Woodroope	On the 25th. October 1758 John Mayrant and Ann Woodroope Spinster were married pr. Lic. pr. Ditto.
Young & Marsh	On the 11th. February 1758 Thomas Young and Margaret Marsh Widow were married pr. Lic. pr. Ditto.

McCarthy & Webb	On the 26th. January 1758 Thomas McCarthy and Mary Webb Widow was married pr. Licence pr. the Revd. Mr. Clarke Rector.
Bonar & Hanson	On the 25th. September 1758 William Bonar and Jane Hinson Spinster was married pr. Lic. pr. the Revd. Mr. Clarke Rector.
Mouncey & Boyland	On the 8th. August 1758 John Mouncey and Jane Boyland Widow was married pr. Lic pr. the Revd. Mr. Richard Clarke Rector.
Tamplet & Jeuning	On the 2d January 1758 John Tamplet & Sarah Jeuning Spinster was married pr. Licence pr. Ditto.
Powell & Young	On the 8th. January 1758 Joseph Powell & Ann Young Spinster was married pr. Lic. pr. Ditto.
Michew & Sutton	On the 26th. January 1758 Peter Michew and Constant Sutton Widow was married pr. Lic. pr. Ditto.
Skinner & Reid	On the 4th. February 1758 Samuel Skinner & Catherine Reid Widow was married pr. Banns pr Ditto.
Fray & Pyfrin	On the 9th. February 1758 George Fray and Christian Pyfrin Spinster was married pr. Lic pr Ditto.
Marshal & Graham	On the 16th. February 1758 James Marshal & Isabella Graham Widow was married pr. Lic. pr. Ditto.
Law & Jones	On the 16th. February 1758 Joseph Law and Mary Jones Spinster was married pr. Lic. pr. Ditto.
Aldridge & Hadding	On the 12th. March 1758 Robert Aldridge and Jane Hadding Spinster was married pr Lic. pr. Ditto.
Belton & Johnson	On the 18th. March 1758 James Belton and Agnes Johnson Spinster was married pr. Lic. pr. Ditto.

Cultender & Brit
On the 20th. March 1758 Abraham Cultender & Rebecca Brit Widow. was married pr. Lic. pr Ditto. ....

Carirne & Beckett
On the 22d March 1758 Samuel Carirne & Sarah Beckett Spinster was married pr. Banns pr. Ditto. ....

Shields & Moore
On the 1st. April 1758 Lambert Shields & Ann Moore Spinster was married pr. Ditto pr. Ditto. ....

Tipping & Rush
On the 1st. April 1758 Joseph Tipping & Sarah Rush Spinster was married pr. Lic pr. Ditto. ....

Edwards & Peronneau
On the 11th. April 1758 John Edwards & Margaret Peronneau Spinster was married pr. Lic. pr. Ditto. ....

Wagner & Boquette
On the 16th. April 1758 John Wagner and Ann Boquette Spinster was married pr. Lic. pr Ditto. ....

Easton & Lee
On the 19th. April 1758 Christopher Easton & Susannah Lee Spinster was married pr. Lic. pr Ditto. ....

Middleton & Mongin
On the 8 May 1758 Lewis Middleton & Priscilla Mary Mongin Spinster was married pr. Lic. pr. the Revd. Mr. Charles Martin of St. Andrews Parish

Motte & Brewton
On the 11th. June 1758 Jacob Motte Junr and Rebecca Brewton Spinster was Married pr. Lic. pr the Revd. Mr. Richd. Clarke Rector of St. Philips

(Chs. Town

Marriages 169

Douxsaint & Hendrick
On the 28th. June 1758 Paul Douxsaint and Mary Hendrick Spinster was married pr. Licence pr the Revd. Mr. Richd. Clarke. ....

Wilkinson & Spencer
On the 2d. July 1758 Thomas Wilkinson & Martha Spencer was married pr. Lic. pr. Ditto. ....

Fly & Guignard	On the 5th. July 1758 Samuel Fly and Frances Guignard Widow was married pr. Lic. pr. Ditto.
Mookinfost & Smith	On the 11th. July 1758 Joseph Mookinfost & Cathrine Smith Spinster was married pr. Lic pr. Ditto.
Lee & Bee	On the 20th. July 1758 Thomas Lee and Jane Bee widow was married pr. Lic. pr. Ditto.
Holzendorf & Miller	On the 26th. July 1758 Frederick Holzendorf & Mary Ann Miller Spinster was married pr. Lic. pr. Ditto.
Sullivan & Queen	On the 7th. August 1758 James Sullivan & Elianor Queen was married pr. Banns pr. Ditto.
Evans & Young	On the 9th. August 1758 John Evans & Hannah Christian Young Widow was married pr. Lic. pr. Ditto.
Lewis & Gannaway	On the 2d. September 1758 John Lewis & Mary Gannaway Widow was married pr. Lic. pr. Ditto.
Dill & Mason	On the 7th. September 1758 Joseph Dill & Susannah Mason Spinster was Married pr. Lic. pr. Do.
Stiles & Garden	On the 10th. September 1758 Copeland Stiles & Ann Garden Spinster was married pr. Lic. pr. Do.
Clarke & Hammond	On the 18th. September 1758 James Clarke & Rachel Hammond was married pr. Banns pr. Do.
Alliems & Smith	On the 7th. October 1758 Thomas Alliems & Hannah Smith Widow was married pr. Lic. pr. Do.
White & Leecraft	On the 15th. October 1758 Thomas White & Elizabeth Leecraft Widow was married pr. Lic. pr. Do.
Axson & Tookerman	On the 9th. November 1758 Jacob Axson & Elizabeth Tookerman Spinster was married pr. Lic. pr. Do.

Mitchell & Roper	On the 20th. December 1758 John Mitchell & Elizabeth Roper was married pr. Lic. pr. Do.
Guerin & McMurdy	On the 26th. December 1758 Andrew Guerin and Elizabeth McMurdy Widow was married pr. Lic. pr. Do.
Philp & Hartley	On the 10th. April 1758 Robert Philp & Mary Hartley Spinster was married pr. Lic. pr. the Revd. Mr. Alexr. Barron of St. Pauls Parish
Stone & Guerin	On the Thomas Stone Junior and Frances Guerin Spinster were married pr. Lic. pr. Revd. Mr. Robt. Smith, Rector of St. Philips Charles Town.

Marriages 170

Calwell & Norman	On the 11th. January 1759 John Calwell and Rebecca Norman were married pr. Lic. pr. the Revd. Mr. Richard Clarke Rector.
Græme & Mathews	On the 21st. January 1759 David Græme Esqr. and Ann Mathews[1] Spinster were married pr. Lic. pr. the Revd. Mr. Clarke Rector.
Cormack & Godwin	On the 13th. January 1759 Alexander Cormack and Mary Godwin Spinster were married pr. Lic. pr. the Revd. Mr. Clarke
Rutledge & Bennitt	On the 17th. January 1759 Andrew Rutledge & Rebecca Bennitt Widow were married pr. Lic. pr. Ditto.
Howell & Edwards	On the 17th. January 1759 John Howell & Martha Edwards Widow were married pr. Lic. pr. Ditto.
Ragg & Clarke	On the 27th. January 1759 John Ragg and Ann Clarke Widow were married pr. Lic. pr. Ditto.

[1]Mathewes. Græme attended the Middle Temple, London. He was subsequently a member of the Commons House of Assembly and Attorney General.

Dawes & Varnor	On the 13th. February 1759 James Dawes & Elizabeth Varnor Spinster were married pr. Licence pr. the Revd. Mr. Richard Clarke Rector.
Matthews & Ragnous	On the 24th. February 1759 John Matthews and Ann Ragnous Widow were married pr. Lic. pr. Ditto.
Davison & King	On the 15th. March 1759 John Davison and Susannah King Widow were married pr. Lic. pr. Revd. Mr. Sergant Rector of Christ Church Parish.
Cardozo & Allen	On the 3d. January 1759 Abraham Cardozo & Hannah Allen Widow was married pr. Lic. pr. the Revd. Mr. Clarke Rector.
Ran & Spencer	On the 23d. January 1759 William Ran & Ann Spencer Spinster was married pr. Lic. pr. Ditto.
Russ & Nichols	On the 28th. January 1759 Jacob Russ & Mary Ann Nichols Spinster was married pr. Lic. pr. Do.
Harvey & Drain	On the 8th. January 1759 George Harvey & Sarah Drain Widow was married pr. Lic. pr. Ditto.
Ravenell & Mazyck	On the 11th. February 1759 Daniel Ravenell & Charlotte Mazyck was married pr. Lic. pr. Do.
Thomson & Fisher	On the 27th. Feby. 1759 Michael Thomson & Ann Fisher Spinster was married pr. Lic. pr. the Revd. Mr. Clarke.
Wall & Shepard	On the 18th. March 1759 Robert Wall and Margaret Shepard Widow was married pr. Lic. pr. the Revd Mr. Robt. Smith
Wilson & Chisolme	On the April 1759 Wilson and Mary Chesholme Spinster was married pr. Lic. pr. Ditto.
Reid & Gray	On the 26th. February 1759 David Reid & Margaret Gray Spinster were married per Licence pr. the Reverend Mr. Robt. Smith Rector.

Mckay & Parsons — On the 11th. March 1759 William Mckay & Elizth. Parsons were married per By the Revd. Mr. Robert Smith Rector. ....

Marriages. 171

Wall & Sheppard — On the 18th. March 1759 Robert Wall & Margarett Sheppard Widow were married pr. License by the Revd. Mr. Robert Smith.

Watson & Dowdle — On the 21st. March 1759 Andrew Watson & Mary Dowdle were married pr. banns by the Reverend Mr. Robert Smith Rector. ....

Butter & Doujon & — On the 29th. March 1759 John Butter & Eleanor Doujon were married pr. Banns by the Reverend Mr. Robert Smith Rector. ....

Mckenny & Grant — On the 22nd. April 1759 Michael Mckenny & Margt. Grant were married pr. Banns by the Reverend Mr. Robert Smith Rector. ....

Simmons & Holmes — On the 22nd April 1759 James Simmons & Ann Holmes Spinster were married pr. License by the Revd. Mr. Robert Smith Rector. ....

Deas & Allen — On the 3d. May 1759 John Deas & Elizabeth Allen were married pr. License by the Reverend Mr. Robert Smith Rector ....

Stone & Guerin — On the 3d. May 1759 Thomas Stone and Frances Guerin were married pr. License by the Reverend Mr. Robert Smith Rector. ....

Holmes & Bee — On the 8th. May 1759 Isaac Holmes & Rebeccah Bee Spinster were married pr. License by the Reverend Mr. Robert Smith. ....

Fowzer & Lawry — On the 24th. May 1759 John George Fowzer & Sarah Lawry were married pr. Banns by the Reverend Mr. Robert Smith Rector. ....

Plunkett & Scully	On the 3d. June 1759 Thomas Plunkett & Elizabeth Scully Widow were married pr. License by the Reverend Mr. Robert Smith Rector.
Botton & Decker	On the 10th. June 1759 Peter Botton & Mary Decker were married pr. Banns by the Reverend Mr. Robt. Smith Rector.
Remington & Dalton	On the 10th. June 1759 John Remington Junior & Jane Dalton were married pr. License by the Reverend Mr. Robt. Smith Rector.
Speaks & Philips	On the 15th. June 1759 William Speaks and Sarah Philips were married pr. Banns by the Reverend Mr. Robert Smith Rector.
Day & Austin	On the 20th. June 1759 George Day and Sarah Austin were married pr License by Reverend Mr. Robt. Smith Rector.
Boomer & Phyfer	On the 21st. June 1759 John Boomer & Barbara Phyfer were married pr. License by the Reverend Mr. Robert Smith Rector.
Lord & Mace	On the 24th. June 1759 Benjamin Lord & Ann Mace were married pr. License by the Reverend Mr. Robert Smith Rector.
Amos & Dobson	On the 24th. June 1759 James Amos & Jane Dobson Widow were married pr. License by the Reverend Mr. Robert Smith Rector.
McClenachen & Beckworth	On the 1st. July 1759 James McClenachen & Eleanor Beckworth Widow, were married. pr. License by the Reverend Mr. Robert Smith
Nellum & Wm. son	On the 1st. July 1759 Wm. Nellum and Sarah Williamson were married pr Banns by the Reverend Mr. Robert Smith Rector.

Hones & Nunamaker	On the 14th. July 1759 Wm. Hones & Ann Nunamaker were married pr. Licence by the Reverend Mr. Robert Smith Rector.
Combe & Geautier	On the 19th. July 1759 Paul Combe & Charlotte Geautier were married pr. Licence by the Reverend Mr. Robert Smith Rector

Marriages 172

McCullough & Collier	On the 15th. August 1759 Andrew McCullough & Elizth. Collier were married per Licence by the Reverend Mr. Robert Smith Rector
Caismire & Lentry	On the 21st. August 1759 Claimance Caismire & Susannah Lentry were married per Banns by the Revd. Mr. Robert Smith Rector.
Mckenny & Blake	On the 1st. September 1759 William Mckenny & Agnes Blake were married pr. License by the Reverend Mr. Robert Smith Rector.
Stiles & Staples	On the 13th. September 1759 Benjamin Stiles & Sarah Staples were married pr License by the Revd. Mr. Robert Smith Rector.
Garden & Eliz. Har. Bremar	On the 16th. September 1759 Benjamin Garden & Eliza. Harry Bremar were married pr. Licence by the Revd. Mr. Robert Smith Rector.
Godin & Matthewes	On the 4th. October 1759 Isaac Godin & Mara. Matthewes were married pr. Licence by the Reverend Mr. Robert Smith Rector.
Benfield & Colcock	On the 7th. October 1759 John Benfield & Ann Colcock were married pr. Licence by the Reverend Mr. Robert Smith Rector.
Murphy & Martin	On the 3d. February 1760 Timothy Murphy & Jane Martin Widow were married pr. Banns by the Reverend Mr. Robert Smith Rector.

Robinson & Rybolt	On the 11th. Novbr. 1759 Thomas Robinson & Mary Rybolt, were married pr. Licence. .... by The Revd. Mr. Robert Smith—Rector. ....
Thornton & Rivers	On the 18th. Novbr. 1759 Samuel Thornton & Mary Rivers, wid. were married pr. Licence. ....by the Revd. Mr. Robt. Smith—Rector. ....
Benet & Benet.	On the 14th. Janry. 1760 William Benet & Mary Benet, Spin: were married pr Licence .... by the Revd. Mr. Robt. Smith.—Rectr. ....
Bocquet & Oliver	On the 23d. Feb: 1760 Peter Bocquet & Martha Oliver, Wid. were married pr Banns. .... by the Revd. Mr. Robt. Smith.—Rectr. ....
Connoway & Lee	On the 7th. April 1760 John Connoway & Mary Lee, were married pr Banns. .... by the Revd. Mr. Robt. Smith.—Rectr. ....
Atkin & McKenzy	On the 1st. May 1760. Edmund Atkin & Anne McKenzy, were married pr. Licence .... by the Revd. Mr. Robt. Smith.—Rectr. ....
Savage & Holmes	On the 1st. May 1760. William Savage & Martha Holmes, Spin: were married pr. Licence .... by the Revd. Mr. Robt. Smith.—Rectr. ....
Stone & Sayer	On the 20th. May 1760 William Stone & Mary Sayer, were married pr Licence .... by the Revd. Mr. Robt. Smith Rectr. ....
Cooper & Perenneau	On the 22d. May 1760 The Revd. Robert Cooper[1] & Ann Perenneau Spin. were married pr Licence .... by the Revd: Robt Smith Rectr. ....

[1]Said by Dalcho to have come to South Carolina in 1758 as rector of Prince William's Parish, and in 1759 became assistant rector of St. Philip's.

Frazier & Forbes	On the 25th. May 1760 Alexander Frazier & Margaret Forbes, were married pr. Banns. .... by the Revd: Robt. Smith Rectr. ....
Vensant & Smoke	On the 25th. May 1760. Garrard Vensant & Susannah Smoke, were married pr. Banns. .... by the Revd: Robt. Smith Rectr. ....

Robt. Smith.

Garns & D'Hay	On the 9th, June 1760 William Garns & Margaret D'Hay Wid. were married pr. Licence .... by the Revd: Robt. Smith Rectr. ....
Hagen & McCartney	On the 21st. June 1760 Dennis Hagen & Catharine McCartney, Wid. were married pr. Licence .... by the Revd: Robt. Smith Rectr. ....
White & Wilkins	On the 24th. June 1760. Sims White & Mary Wilkin were married pr. Licence .... by the Revd: Robt. Smith Rectr. ....
Proctor & Alexander	On the 28th. June 1760. William Proctor & Catharine Alexander, were married pr. Licence .... by the Revd: Robt. Smith Rectr. ....
Wood & Reid	On the 6th. July 1760 Adam Wood & Sarah Reid, Spin: were married pr Licence .... by the Revd: Robt. Smith Rectr. ....
Dawson & Goodbye	On the 17th. July 1760 Charles Dawson & Martha Goodbye, were married pr Licence. .... by the Revd: Robt. Smith Rectr. ....
Butler & Parrott	On the 9th. Aug. 1760 Samuel Butler & Catharine Parrott, Spin. were married pr. Licence. .. .. by the Revd: Robt. Smith Rectr. ....

Dulaney & Keighly	On the 13th. Sepbr. 1760 James Dulaney & Jane Keighly, Wid: were married pr. Licence. ....by the Revd: Robt. Smith Rectr. ....
Mathew & Coats	On the 27th. Sepbr. 1760 William Mathew & Catharine Coats, Spin: were married pr. Licence. .... by the Revd. Robt. Smith Rectr. ....
Smith & Wragg	On the 2d. Octbr 1760 Benjamin Smith & Mary Wragg, Spin: were married[1] pr. Licence. ....by the Revd: Robt. Smith Rectr. ....
Potter & Miller	On the 4th. Octbr. 1760 James Potter & Martha Miller, Wid. were married pr. Licence. .... by the Revd: Robt. Smith Rectr. ....
Ward & Hunley	On the 5th. Octbr. 1760 John Ward & Anne Hunley, Spin: were married pr. Licence. .... by the Revd: Robt. Smith Rectr. ....
Dixon & Black	On the 8th. Octbr. 1760 Christopher Dixon & Susannah Black, were married pr. Banns. .... by the Revd: Robt. Smith Rectr. ....
Wood & Smith	On the 11th. Octbr. 1760 George Wood & Anne Smith, Spin: were married pr. Licence. .... by the Revd: Robt. Smith Rectr. ....
Patureau & Grimbal	On the 23d. Octbr. 1760 William Patureau & Anne Grimbal, Wid: were married pr. Licence .... by the Revd: Robt. Smith Rectr. ....
Farr & Holmes	On the 23d Novbr. 1760 Thomas Farr & Elizabeth Holmes: Spin: were married pr. Licence .... by the Revd: Robt. Smith Rectr. ....
Smyth & Scott	On the Novbr. 1760 Robert Smyth & Mary Scott Spin: were married pr. Licence .... by the Revd: Robt: Cooper, Assistant ....

Robt. Smith.

[1]See *The South Carolina Historical and Genealogical Magazine,* IV, 244.

Mitchell & Hincley	On the Novbr. 1760. Moses Mitchell & Sarah Hincley were married pr. Licence .... by the Revd: Robt. Cooper. Assistant. ....
Vandalus & Wight	On the 10th. Decbr. 1760 John Vandalus & Martha Wight, Spin. were married pr. Licence .... by the Revd. Robt. Smith Rectr. ....
Fair & Devaux	On the 11th. October 1760 William Fair & Catharine Devaux, Spin: were married pr. Licence .... by the Revd: Robt. Smith, Rectr. ....
Hinds & Rivers	On the 1st. Janry. 1761 Patrick Hinds & Anne Rivers, Spin: were married pr. Licence .... by The Revd: Robt. Smith, Rectr. ....
Morris & Wainwright	On the 1st. Janry. 1761 Mark Morris & Wainwright, Wid. were married pr. Licence .... by The Revd: Robt: Cooper, Assistant. ....
Bates & Hall	On the 16th. Janry. 1761 John Bates & Mary Hall, Wid. were married pr. Banns .... by The Revd: Robt: Smith, Rectr. ....
Wallace & Bates	On the 28th. Janry. 1761 John Wallace & Ann Bates, Wid: were married pr. Licence .... by The Revd: Robt. Smith, Rectr. ....
Michael & Stronach	On the 3d. Febry. 1761 Lambert Michael & Priscilla Stronach, were married pr. Licence .... by The Revd: Robt: Smith, Rector. ....
Balentine & Hirst	On the 12th. Febry 1761 James Balentine & Sarah Hirst, were married pr. Banns .... by The Revd: Robt: Smith, Rectr. ....
Ellis & McKoy	On the 12th. March 1761 William Ellis & Lidia McKoy, were married pr Licence .... by The Revd: Robt: Smith, Rectr. ....

Connell & Rannels	On the 24th. March 1761 John Connell & Ann Rannels Wid: were married pr. Licence .... by The Revd: Robt: Smith, Rectr. ....
Monro & Neilson	On the 29th. March 1761 Daniel Monro & Sarah Neilson, Wid: were married pr. Licence .... by The Revd: Robt: Smith, Rectr. ....
Swallow & Blake	On the 31st. March 1761 Newman Swallow & Frances Blake, Spin. were married pr. Licence .... by The Revd: Robt: Smith, Rectr: ....
Howarth & Mayne	On the 6th. April 1761 Henry Howarth & Martha Mayne, Wid: were married pr. Licence .... by The Revd: Robt: Smith, Rectr: ....
Hill & Burrey	On the 8th. April 1761 John Hill & Susannah Burrey, Spin: Were married pr. Licence .... by The Revd: Robt: Smith, Rectr: ....
Elsinore & Worth	On the 7th. May 1761 James Elsinore & Margaret Worth, Spin: were mard: pr. Licence .... by The Revd: Robt: Smith, Rectr: ....
Hardy & Jenkins	On the 17th. May 1761 Robert Hardy & Hannah Jenkins, Spin: were married pr. Licence .... by The Revd: Robt: Smith, Rectr: ....

Robt. Smith

Marriages 175

Menott & Butler	On the 28th. May 1761 John Menott & Sarah Butler, Spin: were married pr. Licence .... by The Revd: Robt: Smith, Rectr: ....
Motte & Diall	On the 31st. May 1761 Charles Motte & Hannah Diall, Wid: were married pr. Licence .... by The Revd: Robt: Smith, Rectr: ....

Raven & Smith	On the 7th. June 1761 William Raven & Henrietta Smith, were married pr. Licence .... by The Revd: Robt: Smith, Rectr: ....
McKrott & Underwood	On the 7th. June 1761 John Lewis McKrott & Frances Underwood, Spin: were married pr. Licence .... by The Revd: Robt: Smith, Rectr: ....
Sams & Norton	On the 13th. June 1761 John Sams & Ann Norton, Spin: were married pr. Licence .... by The Revd: Robt: Smith, Rectr: ....
Fitts & Burns	On the 16th. June 1761 John Fitts & Elizabeth Burns, Spin: were married pr. Licence by The Revd: Robt: Smith, Rectr:
Edings & Codnor	On the 28th. June 1761 Joseph Edings & Provy Codnor, Spin: were married pr. Licence .... by The Revd: Robt: Smith, Rectr: ....
Bury & Richard	On the 9th. July 1761 John Bury & Margaret Richard, were married pr. Licence .... by The Revd: Robt: Smith, Rectr: ....
Sturgeon & Duncan	On the 20th. July 1761 John Sturgeon & Ann Duncan Wid: were married pr. Licence .... by The Revd: Robt. Smith, Rectr: ....
Rowl & Sprunton	On the 20th. July 1761 William Rowl & Ann Sprunton, were married pr. Licence .... by The Revd: Robt: Smith, Rectr: ....
Blazdell & Wemiss	On the 22d July 1761 Charles Blazdell & Susannah Wemyss, Wid were married pr. Licence .... by The Revd: Robt: Smith, Rectr: ....
Piggott & Clifford	On the 23d. July 1761 John Butler Piggott & Sarah Clifford, Spin: were married pr. Licence .... by The Revd: Robt: Smith, Rectr: ....

Barnes & Minott

On the 24th. July 1761 William Barnes & Ann Minott, Spin: were married pr. Licence .... by The Revd: Robt: Smith, Rectr: ....

Stroboll & Shram

On the 12th. Augst: 1761 John Stroboll & Mary Shram, Wid: were married pr. Licence .... by The Revd: Robt: Smith, Rectr: ....

Adair & Black

On the 22d. Augst. 1761 William Adair & Hannah Black, Wid: were married pr. Licence .... by The Revd: Robt: Smith, Rectr. ....

Johnston & Blanchard

On the 1st. Sepbr. 1761 Robert Johnston & Susannah Blanchard, Spin: were married pr. Lic. .... by The Revd: Robt: Smith, Rectr: ....

Robt Smith

Marriages, 176

Harris & Stillman

On the 2d. Sepbr. 1761 Samuel Harris & Mary Stillman, Spin: married pr. Licence .... by The Revd: Robt: Smith, Rectr: ....

Bampfield & Cook

On the 11th. Octbr. 1761 William Bampfield & Rebecca Cook, Spin: married pr. Licence .... by The Revd: Robt: Smith, Rectr: ....

Corbett & Harrison

On the 22d. Octbr. 1761 Joseph Corbett & Margaret Harrison, married pr. Banns .... by The Revd: Robt: Smith, Rectr: ....

Davis & Crim

On the 1st. Novbr. 1761 George Davis & Ann Crim, were married pr. Banns .... by The Revd: Robt: Smith, Rectr: ....

Trindle & Hill

On the 1st. Novbr. 1761 Edward Trindle & Elizabeth Hill, wid: were married pr. Banns .... by The Revd: Robt: Smith, Rectr: ....

Davis & Mann	On the 12th. Novbr. 1761 John Davis & Martha Mann, were married pr. Banns .... by The Revd: Robt: Smith, Rectr: ....
Larod & Warrant	On the 17th. Novbr. 1761 John Larod & Mary Warrant, were married pr. Banns .... by The Revd: Robt: Smith, Rector: ....
Fletcher & McIntoish	On the 22d. Novbr. 1761 William Fletcher & Elizabeth McIntoish were married pr. Banns .... by The Revd: Robt: Smith, Rectr: ....
Wood & Jones	On the 22d. Novbr. 1761 John Wood & Lucy Jones, were married pr. Banns .... by The Revd: Robt: Smith, Rectr: ....
Senior & Scriben	On the 23d. Novbr. 1761 Samuel Senior & Mary Scriben, were married pr. Banns .... by The Revd: Robt: Smith, Rectr: ....
Leonard & Benet	On the 30th. Novbr. 1761 George Leonard & Susannah Benet, were married pr. Banns .... by The Revd: Robt: Smith, Rectr: ....
Tong & Webb	On the 13th. Decbr. 1761 James Tong & Catharine Webb, were married pr. Banns .... by The Revd: Robt: Smith, Rectr: ....
Penkins & Weatherly	On the 16th. Decbr. 1761 Christopher Penkins & Mary Weatherly were married pr. Banns .... by The Revd: Robt: Smith, Rectr: ....
Gowdy & Beedle	On the 20th. Decbr. 1761 John Gowdy & Ann Beedle were married pr. Banns .... by The Revd: Robt: Smith, Rectr: ....
Hines & Farey	On the 20th. Decbr. 1761 William Hines & Ann Farey, were married pr. Banns .... by The Revd: Robt: Smith, Rectr: ....

Withers & Culloway	On the 1st. Janry. 1762 William Withers & Mary Culloway Wid. were married pr. Banns. .... by The Revd: Robt: Smith, Rectr: ....

Robt Smith

Marriages, 177

Smith & Finley	On the 2d. Janry 1762 Nicholas Smith & Margaret Finley, were married pr. Banns .... by The Revd: Robt: Smith, Rectr: ....
Larkin & Gray	On the 4th. Janry. 1762 Samuel Larkin & Sarah Gray, were married pr. Banns. .... by The Revd: Robt: Smith, Rectr: ....
Couliatt & Gunn	On the 7th. Janry. 1762 David Couliatt & Eleanor Gunn, Spin: were married pr. Licence .... by The Revd: Robt: Smith, Rectr: ....
Gibson & Burnett	On the 8th. Janry 1762 William Gibson & Mary Burnett, were married pr. Banns .... by The Revd: Robt: Smith Rectr: ....
Norton & Dixon	On the 26th. Janry. 1762 William Norton & Catharine Dixon, were married pr. Banns .... by The Revd: Robt: Smith, Rectr: ....
Davis & McGregar	On the 4th. Febry. 1762 Benjamin Davis & Mary Ann McGregar, were married pr. Banns .... by The Revd: Robt: Smith, Rectr: ....
Baker & Breed	On the 26th. Janry. 1762 John Baker & Eunis Mary Breed, Spin: were married pr. Licence .... by The Revd: Robt: Smith, Rectr: ....
Clayton & Roberson	On the 12th. Febry. 1762 David Clayton & Ann Roberson, were married pr. Banns .... by The Revd: Robt: Smith, Rectr: ....

Ehney & Hennegen	On the 5th. Mar: 1762 Unrick Ehney & Elizabeth Hennegen, Wid. were married pr. Licence .... by The Revd: Robt Smith, Rectr: ....
Boomer & Wagner	On the 6th. Mar: 1762 Jacob Boomer & Christiana Wagner, Spin: were married pr. Licence .... by The Revd: Robt: Smith, Rectr: ....
Reardon & McDugall	On the 8th. Mar: 1762 Timothy Reardon & Margaret McDugall, were married pr. Banns .... by The Revd: Robt Smith, Rectr: ....
Harcout & Boyer	On the 8th. Mar: 1762 John Harcout & Mary Boyer, Wid: were married pr. Banns. .... by The Revd: Robt Smith, Rectr: ....
Huger & Chalmers	On the 23d. Mar: 1762 Isaac Huger[1] & Elizabeth Chalmers, Spin: were married pr. Licence .... by The Revd: Robt Smith, Rectr: ....
Stobo & Chapman	On the 24th. Mar: 1762 Archibald Stobo, & Mary Chapman, Spin: were married pr. Licence .... by The Revd: Robt Smith, Rectr: ....
Barry & Barry	On the 25th. Mar: 1762 John Barry & Martha Barry, were married pr. Banns .... by The Revd: Robt: Smith, Rectr: ....
Cummins & Winton	On the 26th. Mar: 1762 Lawrence Cummins & Ann Winton, were married pr. Banns .... by The Revd: Robt Smith, Rectr: ....

Robt Smith

Marriages 178

Pond & Richardson	On the 26th. Mar: 1762 Richard Pond & Phoebe Richardson, Spin: were married pr. Lic: .... by The Revd: Robt Smith, Rectr: ....

[1]Born at Limerick plantation, March 19, 1742\|3; subsequently brigadier general, Continental Establishment; died October 7, 1797. (See *Transactions*, Huguenot Society of South Carolina, No. 4.)

Waters & Bary	On the 4th. April 1762 Philemon Waters & Mary Bary, were married pr. Banns .... by The Revd: Robt Smith Rectr: ....
Loyd & Boon	On the 22d. April 1762 Caleb Loyd & Esther Boon, Spin: were married pr. Licence .... by The Revd: Robt Smith, Rectr: ....
Cooper & Smith	On the 9th. May 1762 John Cooper & Sarah Smith, were married pr. Banns .... by The Revd: Robt Smith, Rectr: ....
Rideout & Thomson	On the 9th. May 1762 Richard Rideout & Ann Thomson were married pr Banns .... by The Revd: Robt Smith, Rectr: ....
Reily & Russel	On the 9th. May 1762 Charles Reily & Elizabeth Russel, Spin: were married pr. Lic: .... by The Revd: Jo: Wilton, Assistant ....
Burch & Fisher	On the 11th. May 1762 Joseph Burch & Mary Ann Fisher, were married pr. Licence .... by The Revd: Jo: Wilton, Assistant ....
Campbell & Lee	On the 17th. May 1762 John Campbell & Catharine Lee, Wid: were Married pr. Licence .... by The Revd: Robt Smith, Rectr: ....
Rossetter & Cotta	On the 24th. May 1762 Thomas Rosetter & Joanna Cotter, were married pr. Banns .... by The Revd: Robt Smith, Rectr: ....
Beekman & Courtonne	On the 26th. May 1762 Charles Beekman & Mary Courtonne, Spin: were married pr. Licence .... by The Revd: Robt Smith, Rectr: ....
Eden & Evans	On the 14th. Novbr. 1759 William Eden & Rachel Evans, were married pr. Banns .... by The Revd: Robt Smith, Rectr: ....

169

Kelly & Stoosin	On the 1st. June 1762 John Kelly & Regina Stoosin were married pr. Licence .... by The Revd: Robt Smith, Rectr: ....
Beaird & Schingler	On the 1st. June 1762 John Beaird & Catharina Schingler Wid: were married pr. Lic: .... by The Revd: Robt Smith, Rectr: ....
Harrison & Gorden	On the 9th. June 1762, Edward Harrison & Elander Gorden, were married pr Banns .... by The Revd: Robt Smith, Rectr: ....
George & Smidmore	On the 9th. June 1762, Edward George & Rebecca Smidmore, were married pr. Banns .... by The Revd: Robt Smith, Rectr: ....
Perenneau & Hudson[1]	On the 10th. June 1762, Arthur Perenneau & Mary Hudson, were married pr. Licence .... by The Revd: Robt Cooper, Rectr: St. Michls ....

Robt Smith

Marriages 179

Burton & Stewart	On the 11th. June 1762 Thomas Burton & Elizabeth Stewart Spin: were married pr. Licence .... by The Revd: Robt Smith, Rectr: ....
Weston & Hollybush	On the 18th. July 1762 Plowden Weston & Alice Hollybush, Spin: were married pr. Lic. by The Revd: Robt Smith, Rectr:....
Foskey & Underwood	On the 5th. Sepbr 1762 Bryan Foskey & Mary Underwood Widow, were married pr. Lic. .... by The Revd: Robt Smith, Rectr: ....
Bowman & Davies	On the 6th. Septem: 1762 John Bowman & Mary Davies Spin: were married pr. Lic .... by The Revd: Robt Smith, Rectr: ....

[1]Mary Hudson should read Mary Hutson. She was the daughter of the Rev. Wm. Hutson, of the "White" Meeting House, now the Circular Church.

Boyd & Walker	On the 19th. Septem 1762 Robert Boyd & Ann Walker Spin: were married pr. Licence .... by The Revd Robt Smith, Rectr: ....
Walker & Jones	On the 19th. Septem 1762, Robert Walker & Ann Jones, were married pr Banns .... by The Revd: Robt Smith, Rectr ....
Smith & Jones	On the 20th. Septem. 1762, George Smith & Elizabeth Jones were married pr. Banns .... by The Revd: Robt Smith, Rectr: ....
Holsen & Hamilton	On the 23d. Septemr. 1762, Christopher Holsen & Eliz. Hamilton Spin: was married pr. Licence .... by The Revd: Robt Smith, Rectr: ....
Godfrey & DelaChappelle	On the 25th. Septemr. 1762, John Godfrey & Patience DelaChappelle Wid. were married pr. Licence .... by The Revd: Robt Smith, Rectr: ....
Easton & Ratford	On the 14th. October 1762, Caleb Easton & Mary Ratford Spin: were marrd. pr. Licence .... by The Revd: Robt. Smith Rectr: ....
Ham & McConnell	On the 6th. Novemr. 1762 Thomas Ham & Sarah McConnell Spin were married pr. Licence .... by The Revd. Robt. Smith Rectr: ....
Snowden & Blain	On the 7th. Novemr. 1762 Joshua Snowden & Mary Blain Spin. were married pr. Licence .... by The Revd. Robt. Smith, Rectr. ....
Spidle & Copio	On the 7th. decemr. 1762, Adam Spidle & Rachell Copio widow, were married pr. Licence .... by The Revd: Robt. Smith Rectr ....
Poaug & Wragg	On the 1st. January 1763, John Poaug & Charlotte Wragg Spin. were married pr. Licence .... by the Revd. Robt. Smith Rectr. ....

E. Poinsett (Registr)

Schad & Aikler	On The 1st. January 1763 Abraham Schad & Mariam Aikler, were married pr. Licence .... by the Revd. Robert Smith Rectr. ....
Simpson & Eady	On the 3d. January 1763 James Gilchrist Simpson & Sarah Eady, Spin: were married pr. Licence by the Revd. Robert Smith Rectr. ....
Mackelish & Colfin	On the 27th. January 1763 Thomas Mackelish & Mary Colfin Spin, were married pr. Licence .... by the Revd. Robert Smith Rectr. ....
Cockran & Elliott	On the 3d. February 1763 Robert Cockran & Mary Elliott, Spin: were married pr. Licence .... by the Revd. Robert Smith Rectr. ....
Comefoord & Pendroos	On the 27th. February 1763, James Comefoord & Margaret Eliz. Pendroos were married pr. Banns .... by the Revd. Robert Smith Rectr. ....
Bayley & Cameron	On the 27th. March 1763, William Bayley & J'hatherine Cameron were marrd. pr. Banns. .... by the Revd. Robert Smith Rectr. ....
Stocker & Bedon	On the 16th. April 1763, Charles Stephen Stocker & Mary Bedon Spin: were marrd. pr Licence .... by the Revd. Robert Smith Rectr. ....
Campbell & Izard	On the 17th. April 1763 The Right Honble Lord Willm. Campbell & Sarah Izard, Spin. were married pr. Licence, by the Revd. Robt. Smith Rectr. ....[1]

[1]He was the fourth son of the Duke of Argyll and was a captain in the Royal Navy, Commanding H. M. S. *Nightingale;* was subsequently governor of Nova Scotia and on June 15, 1775, arrived in South Carolina as the Royal Governor. In consequence of the Revolutionary proceedings in South Carolina he retired from Charles Town to a British man-of-war in the harbour, September 15, 1775, and on June 28, 1776, he participated in the battle of Fort Moultrie as a volunteer on Sir Peter Parker's flag-ship and was wounded. (See *The South Carolina Historical and Genealogical Magazine*, II, 234-235.

Peak & Irvine	On the 9th. May 1763 Stephen Peak & Mary Ann Irvine Spin. were married pr. Licence .... by the Revd. Robt. Smith Rectr. ....
Nixon & Mondoza	On the 17th. May 1763, John Bently Nixon & Ann Mondoza Spin. were marrd pr. Licence .... by the Revd. Robt. Smith, Rectr. ....
Baker & Chambers	On the 14th. June 1763 John Barker & Isabella Chambers, were marrd pr. Banns. .... by the Revd Robt. Smith Rectr. ....
Haler & Coulin	On the 16th. June 1763, Siphorus Haler & Sarah Coulin, were married pr Banns .... by the Revd. Robt. Smith Rectr. ....
Scott & Wetherston	On the 16th. June 1763 Thomas Scott & Ann Wetherston, were married pr. Licence .... by the Revd. Robert Cooper ....
Pickering & Maxey	On the 20th. June 1763 Samuel Pickering & Mary Maxey were married pr. Licence .... by the Revd. Robt. Smith Rectr. ....

E. Poinsett (Regstr.)

Marriages — 181

White & Bowen	On the 18th. July 1763 Jacob White & Ephe Bowen Spin, were married pr. Licence .... by the Revd. Robt. Smith Rectr. ....
Orrett & Levrick	On the 30th. July 1763 Peter Orrett & Mary Levrick Spin. were married pr. Banns .... by the Revd. Robt. Smith Rectr. ....
Robison & Filput	On the 5th. August 1763 William Robison & Elizabeth Filput Wid. were marrd pr. Licence .... by the Revd. Robt. Smith Rectr. ....

Tray & Baldwin — On the 21st. August 1763, George Tray & Elizabeth Baldwin Spin. were marrd. pr. Licence .... by the Revd. Robt. Smith Rectr. ....

Reeves & Elliott — On the 8th. Septemr. 1763, Henry Reeves & Charlotte Elliott Spin. were marrd pr. Licence .... by the Revd. Robt. Smith Rectr. ....

Hays & Thompson — On the 25th. Septemr. 1763, Thomas Hays & Mary Thompson Widow, were marrd. pr. Banns. .... by the Revd. Robt. Smith Rectr. ....

Sarrazin & Lance — On the 29th. Septemr. 1763 Jonathan Sarrazin & Lucia Lance Spin. were mard. pr. Licence .... by the Revd. Robt. Smith Rectr. ....

Perry & Mouncey — On the 17th. Septemr. 1763, Francis Perry & Jane Mouncey Widow, were marrd. pr. Licence .... by the Revd. Robt. Smith Rectr. ....

McDonold & McNaught — On the 23d. October 1763, Alexander McDonold & Elizabeth McNaught were marrd. pr. Licence .... by the Revd. Robt. Smith Rectr. ....

Little & Gough — On the 29th. October 1763 James Little & Ann Gough Spin, were married pr. Licence .... by the Revd. Robt. Smith Rectr. ....

Frank & Lybfritz — On the 15th. Novemr. 1763 Simon Frank & Rebecca Lybfritz widow were married pr. Licence .... by the Revd. Robt. Smith Rectr. ....

Guerin & Elliott — On the 24th. Novemr 1763 William Guerin & Mary Elliott Spin were married pr. Licence .... by the Revd. Robt. Smith Rectr. ....

Glazier & Wildiers — On the 4th. decemr. 1763 Frederick Glazier & Mary Wildiers Spin. were marrd pr. Banns .... by the Revd. Robt. Smith Rectr. ....

Troise & Smith	On the 4th. decemr 1763 Christian Troise & Frances Smith Spin. were married pr. Banns .... by the Revd. Robt. Smith Rectr. ....

E. Poinsett 'Registr.)

Marriages 182

Motte & Smith	On the 15th. decemr. 1763, Isaac Motte & Ann Smith, Spin. were married pr. Licence .... by the Revd. Robt. Smith Rectr. ....
Farrow & Burnham	On the 22d. decemr. 1763 William Farrow & Elizabeth Burnham Spin. were marrd pr. Licence .... by the Revd. Robt. Smith Rectr. ....
Himeli & Russ	On the 8th. January 1764, Revd. Bartholomew Henry Himeli & Rachel Russ were married pr. Licence, by the Revd. Jos. Dacri Wilton Assistant St. Philips ....
Russel & Wigg	On the 13th. March 1764 George Russel & Mary Wigg were married pr. Licence, ... by the Revd. Jos. Dacri Wilton ....
Clinton & Burkmire	On the 25th. June 1764 John Clinton & Mary Burkmire were married pr. Licence .... by the Revd. Jos. Dacri Wilton ....
Shrewsbury & Talbot	On the 9th. August 1764 Stephen Shrewsbury & Mary Ann Talbot were married pr. Licence by the Revd. Jos. Dacri Wilton ....
Shulds & Sumner	On the 6th. February 1764 Daniel Shulds & Eliz. Sumner were married pr. Licence .... by the Revd. Robt. Smith Rectr. ....
Fearis & Hendley	On the 6th. February 1764 Denham Fearis & Mary Hendley were marrd. pr. Licence .... by the Revd. Robt. Smith Rectr. ....
Hazell & Brandford	On the 8th. February 1764 William Hazell & Susannah Brandford Spin. were mard. pr. Licence, by the Revd. Robt. Smith Rectr.

Lebby & Howard	On the 4th. March 1764 Nathaniel Lebby & Eliz. Howard were marrd. pr. Licence .... by the Revd. Robt. Smith Rectr. ....
McLaron & McNab	On the 17th. March 1764 Thomas McLaron & Agnes McNab were marrd. pr. Licence .... by the Revd. Robt. Smith Rectr. ....
Barlow & Ledbette	On the 29th. March 1764 Thomas Barlow & Catherine Ledbette were marrd. pr. Licence .... by the Revd. Robt. Smith Rectr. ....
Duval & Tousiger	On the 3d. April 1764 Stephen Duval & Catherine Tousiger were marrd. pr. Licence by the Revd. Robt. Smith Rectr. ....
Simmons & Frampton	On the 5th. April 1764 John Simmons & Theodora Frampton widow [?] were marrd. pr. Licence by the Revd. Robt. Smith Rectr. ....

E. Poinsett (Regist.)

Marriages —— 183

Dewis & Bell	On the 8th. April 1764 William Dewis & Mary Ann Bell were married pr. Licence .... by the Revd. Robt. Smith Rectr. ....
Howard & Norris	On the 13th. April 1764 Robert Howard & Mary Norris, Spin: were married pr. Licence .... by the Revd. Robt. Smith Rectr. ....
Holmes & Griffin	On the 16th. April 1764 James Holmes & Ann Griffin Spin: were married pr. Licence .... by the Revd. Robt. Smith Rectr. ....
Norris & Brown	On the 1st. May 1764 William Norris & Ruth Brown Widow were married pr. Licence .... by the Revd. Robt. Smith Rectr. ....
Loocock & Harramond	On the 3d. May 1764 William Loocock & Henriette Harramond Spin: were married pr. Licence by the Rev. Robt. Smith Rectr.

Emer & Marronete

On the 6th. May 1764 Abraham Emer & Ann Marronette Widow were married pr. Licence, by the Revd. Robt. Smith Rectr.....

Parker & Peronneau

On the 13th. May 1764 George Parker & Ann Peronneau Spin: were married pr. Licence .... by the Revd. Robt. Smith Rectr. ....

Morris & Allen

On the 16th. May 1764 Owen Morris & Mary Allen Spin: were married pr. Licence .... by the Revd. Robt. Smith Rectr. ....

Coulbourn & Dring

On the 19th. May 1764 Charles Coulbourn & Elizabeth Dring Spin: were married pr. Licence by the Revd. Robt. Smith Rectr.....

Fowler & Watkins

On the 20th. May 1764 Jonathan Fowler & Ann Watkins Widow were married pr. Licence by the Revd. Robt. Smith Rectr.....

Akins & Deveaux

On the 2d. June 1764 James Akins & Ann Deveaux Spin. were married pr. Licence .... by the Revd. Robt. Smith Rectr. ....

Fitch & Campbell

On the 28th. July 1764 James Fitch & Helena Campbell Spin. were married pr. Licence, by the Revd. Robt. Smith Rectr.

Threadcraft & Dewis

On the 30th. August 1764 Thomas Threadcraft & Sarah Dewis Spin: were married pr. Licence by the Revd. Robt. Smith Rectr. ....

Baxter & Bates

On the 6th. September 1764 Robert Baxter & Eliz. Richmd. Bates Spin: were married pr. Licence, by the Revd. Robt. Smith Rectr ....

E. Poinsett. (Regist.)

Marriages 184

Davis & Viart

On the 16th. September 1764, William Davis & Mary Viart Widow were married pr. Licence .... by the Revd. Robt. Smith Rectr. ....

McCullough & McKenzie	On the 18th. October 1764 John McCullough & Mary McKenzie Spin. were married pr. Licence by the Revd. Robt. Smith Rectr.
Bacot & Harramond	On the 11th. November 1764 Peter Bacot & Elizabeth Harramond Spin: were married pr. Licence by the Revd. Robt. Smith Rectr.
Bowen & Bargee	On the 28th. November 1764 John Bowen & Mary Bargee Spin were married pr. Licence by the Revd. Robt. Smith Rectr.
Ball & Scott	On the 20th. december 1764 Joseph Ball Junr. & Ann Scott Spin. were married pr. Licence by the Revd. Robt. Smith Rectr.
Postell & Douxsaint	On the 30th. december 1764 James Postell & Catherine Douxsaint, Spin. were married pr. Licence by the Revd. Robt. Smith Rectr.
Tebout & Darling	On the 1st. January 1765 Tunis Tebout & Sarah Darling Spin were married pr. Licence by Do.
Kelley & McCrott	On the 6th. January 1765 William Kelley & Frances McCrott widow were married pr. Licence pr Do.
Dart & Motte	On the 22d. January 1765 John Dart & Martha Motte Spinr. were married pr. Licence by Do.
Fendin & Norton	On the 26th. January 1765 Abraham Fendin & Mary Ann Norton Spinr. were married pr. Licence by Do.
Hackett & White	On the 14th. February 1765 Michael Hackett & Elizabeth White Widow were married pr. Licence by Do.
Pritchard & Conner	On the 17th. February 1765, Paul Pritchard & Ann Conner Widow were married pr. Licence by Do.

Greenwood & Wilson	On the 26th. February 1765, John Greenwood & Elizabeth Wilson Spinr. were married pr. Licence by Do.

E. Poinsett. (Registr.)

Marriages — 185

Hart & Williams	On the 7th. March 1765. Arthur Hart & Mary Williams Spinr. were married pr. Licence by Do.
Agelton & Parker	On the 3d. April 1765. John Agelton & Ann Parker Widow were married pr. Licence by Do.
Furgusson & Cordoza	On the 10th. April 1765 John Furgusson & Hannah Cordoza widow were married pr. Licence by Do.
Timrod & White	On the 13th. June 1765, Henry Timrod & Mary White Widow were married pr. Licence by Do.
Simmons & Stanyarne	On the 12th. December 1754 Ebenezer Simmons & Jane Stanyarne Spins. were married by Do.
Lance & Carne	On the 21st. February 1765 Lambert Lance & Ann Magdelene Carne Spinster were married per Lic. by Do.
Peet & Robinson	On the 4th. July 1765 James Peet & Debarah Robinson Spinsr. were married pr. Lic. by Do.
Horn & Pulla	On the 19th. August 1765 Peter Horn & Elizabeth Pulla Widow were married pr. Lic. by Do.
Taylor & Minors	On the 9th. August 1765 George Taylor & Elizabeth Minors Spinst. were married pr. Licence by Do.
Saltridge & Ellis	On the 14th. October 1766 William Saltridge & Lidia Ellis Widow were married pr. Lic. by Do.
Honour & Stock's	On the 14th. July 1762 Thomas Honour & Mary Stock's Widow were married pr. Lic. by the Revd. Mr. J. D. Wilton

Hattfield & Sheppard	On the 24th. Septemr 1763 John Hattfield & Mary Sheppard Spinstr. .... were married pr. Lic. by the Revd. Mr. J. D. Wilton ....
Jehne & Phillips	On the 24th. February 1763, August Jehné & Elizabeth Phillips Widow .... were married pr. Lic. by the Revd. Mr. J. D. Wilton ....

....

E. Poinsett. (Registr.)

Marriages — 186

Webb & Pinckney	On the 12th. May 1763 Benjamin Webb & Rebecca 'Pinckney Spinster .... were married pr. Lic. by the Revd. Mr. J. D. Wilton
Davis & Sarverance	On the 7th. April 1763 William Davis & Ann Sarverance, Widow .... were married pr. Lic. by the Revd. Mr. J. D. Wilton
Dorman & Barnes	On the 21st. Septemr. 1763 Michael Dorman & Margaret Barnes .... were married pr. Licence by the Revd. Mr. J. D. Wilton
Shrewsberry & Talbert	On the 9th. August 1764 Stephen Shrewsberry & Mary Ann Talbert Widow Entered in (182) .... were married pr. Lic. by the Revd. Mr. J. D. Wilton
Clinton & Birkmire	On the 25th. June 1764 John Clinton & Mary Birkmire Spinster ....Entered in (182) .... were married pr. Lic. by the Revd. Mr. J. D. Wilton
Russell & Wigg	On the 13th. March 1764 George Russell & Mary Wigg Widow .... Entered in (182) .... were married pr. Lic. by the Revd. Mr. J. D. Wilton

Himeli & Russ	On the 7th. January 1764 Bartholemew Henry Himeli[1] & Rachel Russ widow .... entered in (182) .... were married pr. Lic. by the Revd. Mr. J. D. Wilton
Gordon & Hawkes	On the 14th. January 1765 Thomas Gordon & Mary Hawkes Spinstr. .... were married pr. Lic. by the Revd. Mr. J. D. Wilton
Wells & Harriss	On the 21st. January 1765 Jeremiah Wells & Mary Harriss Widow .... were married pr. Lic. by the Revd. Mr. J. D. Wilton
Evans & Chapman	On the 15th. June 1765, Stephen Evans & Rebecca Chapman Spinstr. .... were married pr. Lic. by the Revd. Mr. J. D. Wilton
McNish & Black	On the 18th. May 1765 John McNish & Ann Black Spinstr. .... were married pr. Lic. by the Revd. Mr. J. D. Wilton
Donnam & Poo	On the 18th. May 1765 Ebenezer Donnom & Mary Poo. Spinstr. .... were married pr. Lic. by the Revd. Mr. J. D. Wilton
Clouney & Trezvant	On the 14th. February 1765 Joseph Clouney & Elizabeth Trezvant Spinstr. .... were married pr. Lic. by the Revd. Mr. J. D. Wilton
Hutchins & Watts.	On the 1st. March 1765 John Hutchins & Elizabeth Watts Spinstr. .... were married pr. Lic. by the Revd. Mr. J. D. Wilton —

Marriages ——— 187

Trezvant & Blackledge	On the 29th. June 1765 Daniel Trezvant & Mary Blackledge Spinstr. .... were married pr. Lic. by the Revd. Mr. J. D. Wilton

[1]He was pastor of the Huguenot Church in Charles Town, 1759-1772 After residing twelve years in Switzerland he returned to Charleston and was again pastor of that Church, 1785-1789. (See *Transactions*, Huguenot Society of South Carolina, No. 7, 60-61.

Barksdale & Patterson	On the 31st. October 1765 George Barksdale & Elizabeth Patterson Spinstr. .... were married pr. Lic. by the Revd. Mr. J. D. Wilton
McKintoch & Smith	On the 17th. October 1765 Lachlin McKintoch[1] & Elizabeth Smith Spinstr. .... were married pr. Lic. by the Revd. Mr. Robt. Smith Rectr
Scott & Brailsford	On the 17th. October 1765 William Scott & Sarah Brailsford Spinstr. .... were married pr. Lic. by the Revd. Mr. Rt. Smith (Rectr.)
Grimboll & Rippon	On the 29th. October 1765 Joshua Grimboll & Hannah Rippon Widow .... were married pr. Lic. by the Revd. Mr. J. D. Wilton
Feltham & Dike	On the 30th. October 1765 Joseph Feltham & Honra Dike Spinstr. .... were married pr. Lic. by the Revd. Mr. J. D. Wilton
Furman & Hartman	On the 10th. Novr. 1765 Josiah Furman & Sarah Hartman Spinstr. .... were married pr. Lic. by the Revd. Mr. Robt Smith (Rect)
Marden & Langley	On the 1st. Decemr. 1765 Thomas Marden & Jane Langley Spinstr. .... were married pr. Banns by the Revd. Mr. Rt. Smith (Rectr.)
Merritt & Bates	On the 1st. Decemr. 1765 John Merritt & Sarah Bates Widow .... were married pr. Banns by the Revd. Mr. Rt. Smith (Ret.)
Boquet & Smith	On the 3d January 1766 Peter Boquet & Martha Smith Spinstr. .... were married pr. Lic. by the Revd Mr. J. D. Wilton

[1]McIntosh. He had been "an officer in one of the independent companies that were disbanded upon the peace." She was a daughter of Francis Smith of Stono.

Law & Gill	On the 9th. January 1766 Richard Law & Mary Gill .... were married pr. Banns pr. the Revd. Mr. Rt. Smith rect
Hibben & Wingood	On the 13th. January 1766 Andrew Hibben & Elizabeth Wingood Widow .... were married pr. Lic. by the Revd. Mr. Rt. Smith Rectr.
Fowler & Jervis	On the 23d January 1766 Richard Fowler & Ann Jervis .... were married pr. Lic. by the Revd. Mr. J. D. Wilton

E. Poinsett (Registr.)

Marriages 188

Harleston & Fauchereaud	On the 17th. April 1766 John Harleston & Elizabeth Fauchereaud Spinstr. .... were married pr. Licence by the Revd. Mr. J. D. Wilton.
Barker & Maxwell	On the 28th. April 1766 Thomas Barker & Elizabeth Maxwell widow .... were married pr. Lic. by the Revd. Mr. J. D. Wilton
Robertson & Godfrey	On the 10th. May 1766 James Robertson & Mary Godfrey widow .... were married pr. Lic. by the Revd. Mr. J. D. Wilton
Jones & Jones	On the 14th. June 1766 William Jones & Mary Jones Widow .... were married pr. Lic. by the Revd. Mr. J. D. Wilton
Samways & Tinnable	On the 18th. June 1766 Samuel Samways & Ann Tinnable Spinstr. .... were married pr. Lic. by the Revd. Mr. J. D. Wilton.
Mason & Fairchild	On the 12th. July 1766 William Mason & Susanna Fairchild Spinstr. .... were married pr. Licence by the Revd. Mr. J. D. Wilton

Muncreff & Fley	On the 4th. Octor. 1766 John Muncreff & Mary Fley Spinstr. .... were married pr. Lic. by the Revd. Mr. J. D. Wilton
Chambers & Dane	On the 4th. Septemr. 1766 William Chambers (of the 31st. of Marines) & Rose Dane .... were married by the Revd. Mr. J. D. Wilton
Chalmers & Warden	On the 24th. August 1766, Lionel Chalmers & Elizabeth Warden Spinstr. were married pr. Licence by the Revd. Mr Robt. Smith Rect
Hume & Quash	On the 24th. April 1766 Robert Hume & Frances Susanna Quash Spinster were married pr. Lic. by the Revd. Mr. Robt. Smith
Hamilton & Macrea	On the 6th. May 1766 William Hamilton & Mary Macrea Widow were married pr Lic. by the Revd. Mr. Robt. Smith
Newman & Harrison	On the 3d. June 1766 William Newman & Elizabeth Harrison Widow were married pr. Banns by the Revd. Mr. Robt. Smith
Goulling & Lawson	On the 28th. July 1766 John Goulling & Ann Lawson were married by the Revd. Mr. Robt. Smith

E. Poinsett, (Registr.)

Chalmers & Warden	On the 24th. August. 1766 Lionel Chalmers & Elizabeth Warden Spinstr. .... were married pr. Lic. by the Revd. Mr. Robt Smith Entered before
Page & Eady	On the 7th. August 1766 George Page & Sarah Eady Widow .... were married pr. Lic. by the Revd. Mr. Robt. Smith
Butler & Freeman	On the 20th. Septemr. 1766 James Henry Butler & Sarah Freeman Spinster .... were married pr. Lic. by the Revd. Mr. Robt. Smith

Waud & Sullivan	On the 4th. Octr. 1766 Robert Waud & Ann Sullivan Widow .... Were married pr. Lic. by the Revd. Mr. Robt Smith
James & Dargan	On the 3d. Decemr. 1766 John James & Mary Dargan Spinster .... were married pr. Licence by the Revd. Mr. Robt. Smith
Hunt & Ball	On the 25th. Decr. 1766 John Hunt & Ann Ball Spinster .... were married pr. Lic. by the Revd. Mr. Robt. Smith
Smith & Oliver	On the 8th. Jany 1767 Thomas Smith & Margaret Oliver Spinster .... were married pr. Lic. by the Revd. Mr. Robt. Smith
Golsman & Bomgardner	On the 13th. Jany 1767 John Golsman & Margaret Bomgardner Widow .... were married pr. Lic. by the Revd. Mr. Robt. Smith
Johnston & Thompson	On the 13th. Jany 1767 Samuel Johnston & Mary Thompson Widow .... were married pr. Lic. by the Revd. Mr. Robt. Smith
Oates & Walker	On the 15th. Mar 1767 Edward Oates & Elizabeth Walker Spinster .... were married pr. Lic. by the Revd. Mr. Robert Smith
Page & Powers	On the 29th. Mar. 1767 John Page & Mary Powers Widow .... were married pr. Banns by the Revd. Mr. Robt. Smith
McCluer & Davies	On the 21st. April 1767 John McCluer & Mary Davies Spinster .... were married pr. Lic. by the Revd. Mr. Robt. Smith
Delahowe & Boyd	On the 23d. April 1767 John Delahowe & Ann Boyd Widow .... were married pr. Lic. by the Revd. Mr. Robt. Smith

E. Poinsett. (Registr.)

Johnston & Hunter	On the 22d. April 1767 John Johnston & Mary Hunter Widow were married pr. Lic. by the Revd. Mr. Robt. Smith
Varambaut & Latu	On the 27 July 1767 Francis Varambaut & Ann Latu Widow were married pr. Lic. by the Revd Mr. Robt. Smith
Disher & E'hney	On the 3d. Augst. 1767 Henry Disher & Catherine E'hney Widow were married pr. Lic. by the Revd. Mr. Robt. Smith
Capon & Lasberry	On the 17th. Augst. 1767 Luke Capon & Eleanor Lasberry were married pr. Banns by the Revd. Mr. Robt. Smith
James & Turnbull	On the 23d. Augst. 1767 John James & Elizabeth Turnbull Spinster were married pr. Lic. by the Revd. Mr. Robt. Smith
Meyers & Muckinfuss	On the 29th. Augst. 1767 Charles Meyers & Mary Ann Muckinfuss Spinstr were married pr. Lic. by the Revd. Mr. Robt. Smith
St. Leger & Dales	On the 5th. Septemr. 1767 John St. Leger & Justina Dales Spinster were married pr. Lic. by the Revd. Mr. Robt. Smith
Crosswell & Fenwick	On the 25th. Septemr. 1767 James Crosswell & Sarah Fenwick Spinster were married pr. Lic. by the Revd. Mr. Robt. Smith
Thompson & Gibbes	On the 27th. Septemr. 1767 Edward Thompson & Ann Gibbes Spinster were married pr. Lic. by the Revd. Mr. Robt. Smith.

Rutledge & Gadsden	On the 29th. Septemr. 1767 Andrew Rutledge[1] & Elizabeth Gadsden Spinster were married pr. Lic. by the Revd. Mr. Robt. Smith
McGill & Gambell	On the 2d. October 1767 Samuel McGill & Elizabeth Gambell Spinster were married pr. Lic. by the Revd. Mr. Robt. Smith

E. Poinsett. (Registr.)

Marriages 191

Alexander & Anderson	On the 22d. Octor. 1767 Alexander Alexander & Rachel Anderson Spinster were married pr. Lic. by the Revd. Mr. Robt. Smith
Valton & Timothy	On the 1st. November 1767 Peter Valton & Elizabeth Timothy Spinster were married pr. Lic. by the Revd. Mr. Robt. Smith
Creighton & Skette	On the 17th. Novr. 1767 William Creighton & Elizabeth Skette Widow were married pr. Lic. by the Revd. Mr. Robt. Smith
Capers & Spencer	On the 29th. Novr. 1767 Richard Capers & Rachel Spencer Spinster were married pr. Lic. by the Revd. Mr. Robt. Smith
Sands & Dewick	On the 29th. Novr. 1767 James Sands & Hannah Dewick Spinster were married pr. Lic. by the Revd. Mr. Robt. Smith
Milne & Brown	On the 6th. Decr. 1767 William Milne & Carolina Brown Widow were married pr. Lic. by the Revd. Mr. Robt. Smith

[1]A son of Dr. John and Sarah (Hext) Rutledge. He died in 1772 and she (who was a daughter of Christopher Gadsden) married, in August, 1774, Thomas Ferguson.

Capers & Guy	On the 8th. Decr. 1767 Thomas Capers & Elizabeth Guy Spinster were married pr. Lic. by the Revd. Mr. Robt. Smith
Seymour & Levimore	On the 21st. Jany 1768 Peter Seymour & Eleanor Levimore Spinster were married pr. Lic. by the Revd. Mr. Robt. Smith
Harley & Jackson	On the 9th. Jany 1768 Joseph Harley & Elizabeth Jackson Spinster were married pr. Licence by Do.
Milne & Vanderhorst	On the 16th. Jany. 1768 James Milne & Jane Vanderhorst, Widow were married pr. Lic. by Do.
Horry & Pinckney	On the. 15th. Feby 1768 Daniel Horry & Harriot Pinckney Spinster were married pr. Lic. by Do.

E. Poinsett. (Registr........

Marriages 192

Payne & Graves	On the 17th. Febry. 1768 James Payne & Eleanor Graves Widow were married pr. Lic. by the Revd. Mr. Robert Smith Rectr.
Balderkin & Clarivendike	On the 18th. Febry. 1768 George Balderkin & Hellina Clarivendike (Say Vandike were married pr. Banns by Do.
Akin & Christie	On the 18th. Febry. 1768 Thomas Akin & Ann Christie Spinster were married pr. Lic. by Do.
Shepperd & Radclitf	On the 18th. Febry. 1768 Charles Sheppard & Elizabeth Radclitf Spinster were married pr. Lic. by Do.
Benison & Walker	On the 12th. Mar. 1768 William Benison & Joanna Walker Spinster were married pr. Lic. by Do.
Egan & Miller	On the 29th. Mar. 1768 Dennis Egan & Eleanor Miller Widow were married pr. Lic. by Do.

Smith & Rutledge	On the 7th. April 1768 Roger Smith & Mary Rutledge[1] Spinster were married pr. Lic. by Do.
Nailor & Cardy	On the 3d. March 1768 William Rigby Nailor & Margaret Cardy Spinster were married pr. Lic. by Do.
Roundtree & Duthy	On the 12th. May 1768 Jethro Roundtree & Jane Duthey Widow were married pr. Lic.
Donavan & Ross	On the 23d. May 1768 Mathew Donavan & Mary Ross were married pr. Lic. by the Revd. Mr. Robt. Cooper
Long & Dart	On the 30th. June 1768 Samuel Long & Elizabeth Dart were married pr. Lic. by Do.
Colcock & Jones	On the 30th. October 1768 John Colcock & Millicent Jones, Spinster were married pr. Lic. by Do.
Rivers & Laws	On the 20th. November 1768 Nehemiah Rivers & Beaulah Laws were married pr. Lic. by Do.

E. Poinsett. (Regstr.)

Christie & Rose	On the 22d. November 1768 James Christie & Hephziba Rose Were married pr. Lic—by the Revd. Mr. Robt. Cooper
Webb & Doughty	On the 3d. January 1769 John Webb & Mary Doughty Spinster were married pr. Lic. by Do.

[1]She was a daughter of Dr. John and Sarah (Hext) Rutledge. Her portrait, with her infant son Edward, was painted by Romney, in London, in 1786. It was sold to Lord Masham about 1895 for £4000. (See *The South Carolina Historical and Genealogical Magazine*, IV, 46-47.)

Drayton & Waring	On the 24th. January 1769 Stephen Drayton Esqr. & Elizabeth Waring were married pr. Lic. by Do.[1]
Wragg & Wragg	On the 5th. February 1769 William Wragg Esqr. & Henrietta Wragg Spinster were married pr. Lic. by Do.
Lee & Theus	On the 26th. February 1769 William Lee & Ann Theus Spinster were married pr. Lic. by Do.
Raper & Marchand	On the 15th. February 1763 William Raper & Elizabeth Marchand as appears by an Affidavit as a voucher (Vide end of the Book) were married by the Revd. Mr. Jos. Dacre Wilton
Skirving & Mathews	On the 16th. March 1769 James Skirving & Charlotte Mathews Widow were married pr. Lic. by the Revd. Mr. Robt. Cooper
Mackinzie & Smith	On the 3d. April 1769 John Mackinzie & Sarah Smith Spinster were married pr. Lic. by the Revd. Mr. Robt. Cooper
Anslett & Banell	On the 8th. April 1769 John Anslett & Benedicta Banell were married pr. Lic. by the Revd. Mr. Robt. Cooper
Swanson & Smilie.	On the 31st. May 1768 David Swanson & Mary Smilie Spinster were married pr. Lic. by the Revd. Mr. Saml. Hart
Creighton & Robinson	On the 2d. June 1768 George Creighton & Clementine Robinson Spinster were married pr. Lic. by the Revd. Mr. Saml Hart
Whithill & Shaw	On the 9th. July 1768 John Whithill & Sarah Shaw were married pr. Lic. by the Revd. Mr. Saml Hart

[1]See "Draytons of South Carolina and of Philadelphia", Genealogical Society of Pennsylvania, March, 1921; *The South Carolina Historical and Genealogical Magazine*, XXIV, for Waring.

Skarp & Maxey	On the 23d. July 1768 Alexander Skarp & Ann Maxey were married pr. Lic. by the Revd. Mr Saml Hart
Maxcey & Ellisson	On the 30th. July 1768 Joseph Maxcey & Amelia Ellisson

E. Poinsett Registr.

Marriages — 194

Williams & Oram	On the 17th. Septemr. 1768 Jno. Mortimor Williams & Frances Oram, Widow were married pr. Lic. by the Revd. Mr. Saml. Hart
Breedlove & Lary	On the 17th. Septemr. 1768 Nathaniel Breedlove & Susanna Lary, Spinster, were married pr. Licence by the Revd. Mr. Hart
Richardson & Guinard	On the 13th. October 1768 William Richardson & Ann Guinard, Spinstr. were married pr. Lic. by the Revd. Mr. Hart
Knight & Grandon	On the 15th. October 1768 William Knight & Elizabeth Grandon Spinstr. were married pr. Lic. by the Revd. Mr. Hart
Thomas & Douxsaint	On the 30th. October 1768 Samuel Thomas & Jane Douxsaint, Spinstr. were married pr. Lic. by the Revd. Mr. Hart
Fesh & Varnon	On the 18th. Novemr. 1768 John Fesh & Sarah Varnon .... were married pr. Lic. by the Revd. Mr. Hart
Wish & Poe	On the 20th. Novemr. 1768 Benjamin Wish & Ann Thewtus Poe, Spinstr. were married pr. Lic. by the Revd. Mr. Hart
Williams & Cart	On the 27th. Novemr. 1768 Joseph Williams & Mary Cart, Spinstr. were married pr. Lic. by the Revd. Mr. Hart

White & Bessellew	On the 24th. Decemr. 1768 John White & Mary Bessellew, Spinster, were married pr. Lic. by the Revd. Mr. Hart
Chaplin & Westcoat	On the 19th. January 1769 William Chaplin & Ann Westcoat Widow were married pr. Lic. by the Revd. Mr. Hart
Burrows & Scott	On the 24th. Jany 1769 John Burrows & Eliz Scott Spinster were married pr. Lic. by the Revd. Mr. Hart
Schermerhorn & Mackey	On the 23d. February 1769 Arnott Schermerhorn & Mary Mackey, Spinstr. were married pr. Lic. by the Revd. Mr. Hart
Yorke & Prout	On the 17th. March 1769 Michael Yorke & Jane Prout Spinstr. were married pr. Lic. by the Revd. Mr. Hart
Williams & Addison	On the 23d. March 1769 David Williams & Leah Addison Spinstr. were married pr. Lic. by the Revd. Mr. Hart

E. Poinsett. (registr.

Walter & Lesesne	On the 26th. March 1769 Thomas Walter & Ann Lesesne Spinster Were married pr. Lic. by The Revd. Mr. Hart
Purcell & Meredith	On the 7th. June 1769 John Purcell & Margaret Meredith, Widow were married pr. Lic. by the Revd. Mr. Hart
Burt & Fallows	On the 20th. June 1769 Peter Burt & Mary Fallows Spinster were married pr. Lic. by the Revd. Mr. Hart

Gordon & Scott	On the 26th. June 1769 John Gordon & Elizabeth Scott Spinster were married pr. Lic. by the Revd. Mr. Hart
Roper & Burnham	On the 13th. July 1769 John Roper & Ann Burnham Spinst were married pr. Lic. by the Revd. Mr. Hart
Shannon & Simpson	On the 30th. July 1769 John Shannon & Elizabeth Simpson Spinster were married pr. Lic. by the Revd. Mr. Hart
Ancrum & Porcher	On the 26th. Novemr. 1769 George Ancrum & Cath Porcher Spinster were married pr. Lic. by the Revd. Mr Hart
Forst & Wiar	On the 23d. Decemr. 1769 Henry Forst & Elizabeth Wiar, Widow were married pr. Lic. by the Revd. Mr. Hart
Blott & Parks	On the 27th. January 1770, John Blott & Ann Parks, Widow were married pr. Lic. by the Revd. Mr. Hart
Clark & Long	On the 14th. January 1770 Robert Clark & Mary Long Spinster were married pr. Lic. by the Revd. Mr. Robt. Smith
McCants & Donnald	On the 18th. January 1770 James McCants & Agnes Donnald, Widow were married pr. Lic. by the Revd: Robt. Smith
Mann & Carpenter	On the 22d. January 1770 Henry Mann & Margaret Carpenter, Widow were married pr. Lic. by the Revd. Robt. Smith
Actkin & Wilson	On the 22d. January 1770 John Actkin & Elizabeth Wilson .... were married pr. Lic. by The Revd. Mr. Cooper

Farquhar & Sherwood	On the 5th. February 1770 George Farquhar & Eliz Sharwood Spinster were married pr. Lic. by the Revd. Robt. Smith

---

E. Poinsett, (Registr.

Doughty & Porcher	On the 22d. February 1770 William Doughty & Rachel Porcher Spinster were married pr. Lic.
Cole & Lloy'd	On the 25th. February 1770 Richard Cole & Ann Lloy'd Spinster were married pr. Lic.
Harper & Spencer	On the 3d. March 1770 Donald Harper & Mary Spencer Spinster were married pr. Lic.
Rivers & Spencer	On the 7th. March 1770 Thomas Rivers & Ann Spencer Spinster were married pr. Lic.
Gilchrist & Hanson	On the 27th. March 1770 Bryan Gilchrist & Eliz Hanson Spinster were married pr. Lic.
Lowry & Barr	On the 12th. April 1770 Robert Lowrey & Ann Barr Spinster were married pr. Lic.
St. John & Boomer	On the 12th. April 1770 James St. John & Eliz. Boomer Spinster were married pr. Lic.
Smith & Taylor	On the 18th. April 1770 Robert Smith & Isabell Taylor Spinster were married pr. Lic.
Grice & Burt	On the 24th. April 1770 James Grice & Mary Burt Widow were married pr. Lic.
Hayward & Sinclair	On the 26th. April 1770 Thomas Hayward & Ann Sinclair Spinster were married pr. Lic.
Howard & Cartman	On the 26th. April 1770 Robert Howard & Ann Cartman .... were married pr. Lic.

Charles & Hoof	On the 8th. May 1770 George Charles & Eliz Hoof Spinstr. were married pr. Lic.
Galaspie & Rogers	On the 12th. May 1770 David Galaspie & Mary Rogers, Widow were married pr. Lic.
Norcliff & Little	On the 27th. May 1770 William Norcliff & Ann Little, Widow were married pr. Lic.
Dewes & Minors	On the 29th. June 1770 Cornelius Dewes & Sarah Minors Widow were married pr. Lic.

Flagg & Anderson	On the 14th. July 1770 George Flagg & Mary Magdelene Anderson Spinster. were married pr. Lic.
Sarrasen & Prioleau	On the 22d. July 1770 Jonathan Sarrasen & Sarah Prioleau, Widow were married pr. Lic.
Greensword & Fellows	On the 9th. Novemr. 1769 Samuel Greensword & Ann Fellows were married pr. Lic.
Downing & Singleton	On the 5th. Decemr. 1769 Samuel Downing & Catherine Singleton were married pr. Lic.
Beekman & Scott	On the 14th. Decemr 1769 Barnard Beekman & Eliz. Scott Widow were married pr. Lic.[1]
Hawie & Lessesne	On the 14th. Decemr. 1769 Robert Hawie & Susanna Lessesne were married pr. Lic.
Worshing & Cobias	On the 30th. August 1769 George Worshing & Mary Cobias were married pr. Lic.

[1]He was colonel of the 4th Regiment (artillery), South Carolina Line, Continental Establishment from June 20, 1779, to the end of the Revolution. She was a daughter of James Lesesne, of Daniell's Island, and widow of Joseph Scott.

Simpson & Frederick	On the 7th. October 1769 James Simpson & Mary Frederick, Widow were married pr. Lic.
Kysell & Fulker	On the 24th. October 1769 Conrod Kysell & Hester Fulker, were married pr. Lic.
Montgomery & Commander	On the 20th. August 1770 John Montgomery & Mary Commander were married pr. Banns....
Bentham & Phillips	On the 4th. May 1772 James Bentham & Eleanor Phillips were married pr. Lic. pr. the Revd. Robert Cooper
Bentham & Hardy	On the 4th. June 1775 Jas. Bentham & Mary Hardy Spinster were married pr. Lic. pr. the Revd. Robert Smith ....

Marriages 198

Creighton & Piggot	Aug. 26th. 1770, William Creighton & Sarah Piggot, Widow were married, pr. License —
Hall, & Glare,	Sept. 6th. 1770, Thomas Hall & Susanna Glare, spinster were married, pr. License —
Lafield, & Garnes,	Sept. 17th. 1770, George Lafield & Hannah Garnes, Spinster. were married, per License —
Florentine, & Bishop,	Sept. 19th. 1770, Simeon Florentine & Ann Bishop, spinster, were married, per License —
DeLancey, & Berrisford,	Oct. 1st. 1770, Peter DeLancey & Elizabeth Berrisford[1], spinster, were married, pr. License —
Sayler, & Stoll,	Oct. 6th. 1770, John Sayler & Jacobina Catharine Stoll, widow were married, per license —

[1]Beresford. DeLancey was His Majesty's Deputy Postmaster General for the Southern District of North America. He was killed in a duel in August, 1771.

Wilkie, & Hext,	Oct. 27th. 1770, John Wilkie & Jane Hext, widow, were married, per license —
Carruthers, & Wertzer,	Nov. 14th. 1770, William Carruthers & Jean Wertzer, widow, were married, per license —
Morgan, & Thomas,	Nov. 16th. 1770, William Morgan & Sarah Thomas, widow, were married, per Justice's Warrant —
Kirk, & Bennet,	Nov. 19th. 1770, Edward Kirk & Charlotte Bennet, spinster, were married, per license, by Revd. Robt. Purcell --
Harris, & Wirth,	Dec. 4th. 1770, Thomas Harris & Susannah Wirth, widow were married, per license —
Taylor, & Newcombe,	Dec. 7th. 1770, Christopher Taylor & Ann Newcombe, spinster, were married, per license —
May, & Baynard,	Dec. 16th. 1770, John May, of St. Bartholemew's, & Elizabeth Baynard, widow, of Edisto Island, were married, per license —
Allen, & Cunningham,	Dec. 24th. 1770, John Allen & Mary Cunningham, were married, per license —
Graham, & Raven,	Jan. 1st. 1771, William Graham & Elizabeth Diana Raven, were married, per License —
Brewton, & Weyman,	Jan. 7th. 1771, John Brewton & Mary Weyman, spinster, were married, pere licence —
Clements, & Smith,	Jan. 22nd. 1771, John Clements & Sarah Smith, spinster, were married, per license —

Johnson, & Forester,	Jan. 24th. 1771, Richard Johnson & Catharine Forester, widow were married, per license —

Waring, & Ball,	Jan. 27th. 1771, Richard Waring & Ann Ball, spinster, were married, per license —
Mitchell, & Somervill,	Feb. 3rd. 1771, John Mitchell & Mary Somervill, were married, per license —
Mallery, & Russel,	Feb. 20th. 1771, Joseph Mallery & Mary Russel, were married, per license, by Revd. Robt. Purcell —
Webb, & Cane,	Feb. 25th. 1771, Matthew Webb, a free negro, & Susanna Cane, a free negress, were married, per license ....
Howard, & Harker,	Mar. 18th. 1771, James Howard & Jemima Harker, spinster, were married, per license —
Marshall, & Boomer,	Mar. 21st. 1771, John Marshall & Dorothy Boomer, were married, per license, by Rev. Robt. Purcell —
Lloyd, & Conolly,	Mar. 24th. 1771, Martin Lloyd & Elizabeth Conolly, were married, per license —
Elsinore, & Blake,	Mar. 31st. 1771, Alexander Elsinore & Elizabeth Blake, widow, were married, per license —
Spence, & Browne,	Apr. 7th. 1771, Peter Spence & Fanny Browne, spinster, were married, per license —
Gordon, & Hawthorn,	Apr. 4th. 1771, William Gordon & Margaret Hawthorn, spinster, were married, per license, by Rev. Robt. Purcell —
Besseleu, & Mason,	Apr. 10th. 1771, Philip Besseleu & Susanna Mason, spinster, were married, per license —
Tobias, & Neil,	Apr. 13th. 1771, Benjamin Tobias & Elizabeth Neil, spinster, were married, per license —

Roper, & Dart,
May 5th. 1771, William Roper & Hannah Dart, spinster,
were married, per license —

Bull, & Simpson
May 11th. 1771, Thomas Bull & Sarah Simpson, spinster,
were married, per license —

Buckingham, & Falker,
June 13th. 1771, Elias Buckingham, & Margaret Falker, spinster,
were married, per license, by Revd. John Ballman —

Marriages. 200

Jacobs, & Racus,
June 25th. 1771, Philip Jacobs & Amelia Racus, spinster,
were married, per license, by Revd. Robt. Purcell —

Legg, & Dewees,
June 29th. 1771, Samuel Legg & Mary Dewees, spinster,
were married, per license —

Willply, & McGaw,
June 30th. 1771, Benjamine Willply & Sarah McGaw, spinster,
were married, per license, by Revd. Robt. Purcell —

Harrison, & Evans,
Aug. 11th. 1771, John Harrison & Sarah Evans, spinster,
were married, per license —

Horn, & Conroy,
Aug. 26th. 1771, Donald Horn & Mary Conroy, widow,
were married, per license —

Carman, & Helligess,
Aug. 27th. 1771, Joseph Carman & Susannah Helligess, spinster,
were married, per license —

Yeadon, & Lining,
Sept. 5th. 1771, Richard Yeadon & Mary Lining, spinster,
were married, per license —

Heyward, & Simons,
Sept. 8th. 1771, Daniel Heyward & Elizabeth Simons, spinster,
were married, per license —

:. 9th. 1771, James Perdriau & Jane
wn, spinster,
e married, per license —

t. 9th. 1771, John Imrie & Elizabeth
ssell,
re married, per license —

pt. 14th. 1771, John Collings & Ann
ızick,
re married, per license —

pt. 15th. 1771, John Smith & Mary Hol-
idge, widow,
ere married, per license —

ept. 17th. 1771, Edward Simons & Lydia
all, spinster,
vere married, per license —

Horger, & Inabnit, — Oct. 17th. 1771, Jacob Horger & Margaret Inabnit, spinster, were married, per license .... by Rev. Henry Purcell —

Swallow, & Prince, — Oct. 26th. 1771, William Swallow & Sarah Prince, spinster, were married, per license ....

Knight, & Gascoign, — Oct. 31st, 1771, John Knight & Sarah Gascoign, spinster, were married, per license —

Bath, & Baker, — Nov. 2nd. 1771, William Bath & Elizabeth Baker, widow, were married, per license —

Myot, & Harden, — Nov. 17th. 1771, John Myot & Frances Harden, were married, per license —

Conaway, & Easton, — Nov. 26th. 1771, Robert Conaway & Juliana Easton, spinster, were married, per license —

Wakefield, & Cannon, — Nov. 26th. 1771, James Wakefield & Sarah Cannon, spinster, were married, per license —

Burn, & Ancrum,	Nov. 28th. 1771, Samuel Burn & Mary Ancrum, spinster, were married, per license —
Guy, & Hargrave,	Dec. 10th. 1771, James Guy & Sarah Hargrave, were married, per license —
Jeffrys, & Morrell,	Dec. 12th. 1771, James Jeffrys & Mary Morrell, spinster, were married, per license —
Hatten, & Richardson,	Dec. 15th. 1771, John Hatten & Elizabeth Richardson, widow, were married, per license —
Steadman, & Kelsey,	Dec. 18th. 1771, James Steadman & Elizabeth Kelsey, spinster, were married, per license—by Revd. Robt. Purcell.
Garner, & Murray,	Dec. 19th. 1771, William Garner & Sarah Murray, spinster, were married per lic. by Revd. Robt. Purcell ....
Blake, & Squeal,	Dec. 28th. 1771, John Blake & Frances Squeal, were married, per license —
Lyon, & Embleton,	Jan. 2nd. 1772, John Lyon & Elizabeth Embleton, spinster, were married, per license —
Ratcliffe, & Daniel,	Jan. 7th. 1772, James Ratcliffe & Prudence Daniel, widow were married, per license —
Hort, & Gibbes,	Jan. 7th. 1772, William Hort & Alice Gibbes, spinster, were married, per license —

Marriages. 202

Scott, & Wallace,	Jan. 14th. 1772, Robert Scott & Catharine Wallace, Spinster were married, per License —
Collins, & McWhennie,	Jan. 26th. 1772, John Collins & Mary McWhennie, spinster, were married, per License —

Follingsby, & Cadman,	Feb. 25th. 1772, John Follingsby & Ann Cadman, spinster, were married, per License —
Brewer, & Donolly,	Feb. 26th. 1772, Albert Brewer & Catharine Donolly, were married, per License —
Smyth & Richardson	Apr. 25th. 1772, John Smyth & Susannah Richardson, Spins. were married, per license —
Lynch Jr. & Shubrick,	May 14th. 1772, Thomas Lynch Junior[1] & Elizabeth Shubrick, spinster, were married, per license —
Gaultier, & Nichols,	May 7th. 1772, Joseph Gaultier & Mary Nichols, spinster, were married, per license by the Rev. Jno. Lewis.
Andrews, & Cellar,	May 8th. 1772, Samuel Andrews and Sarah Cellar, widow, were married, per Lic., by the Revd. Jno. Lewis —
Bagshaw, & Fardoe,	May 9th. 1772, Thomas Bagshaw & Bridget Fardoe, widow, were married, per lic., by the Rev. Jno. Lewis.
Segwalt, & Keller,	June 6th. 1772, Christian Segwalt & Mary Keller, widow, were married, per license —
Miller, Briegle,	June 6th. 1772, John Miller & Margaret Briegle, widow, were married, per license —

[1]He was one of the five delegates from South Carolina to the Continental Congress at the time of the adoption of the Declaration of Independence and was one of the four South Carolina delegates to sign that document. The fifth delegate was Thomas Lynch, father of this delegate. The elder Lynch was ill when the declaration was passed and was enable to sign it. He died at Annapolis, Md., the following December and was buried there. There is a vacant space on the Declaration for his signature. The younger man and his wife were lost at sea in 1779 leaving no issue.

Bryan, & Sanks,	June 11th. 1772, John Bryan & Mary Esther Sanks, widow, were married, per license —
Williman & Spidle,	June 27th. 1772, Jacob Williman & Mary Spidle, widow, were married, per license —
Wealth, & Heeness,	July 23rd. 1772, Adam Wealth & Anna Maria Heeness, widow, were married, per license —
Hanser, & Younker,	July 25th. 1772, Elias Hanser & Elizabeth Younker, spinster, were married, per license —

Chambers, & Hamilton,	July 30th. 1772, Joseph Chambers & Eleanor Hamilton, were married, per license —
Harttung, & Gotsman,	Aug. 13th. 1772, Philip Harttung & Mary Gotsman, widow, were married, pr. lic. by the Revd. Henry Purcell —
Hurst & Igen,	Aug. 19th. 1772, Robert Hurst & Jean Igen, spinster, were married, per lic. by the Rev. Robt. Purcell —
Strickland, Hennington,	Aug. 30th. 1772, James Strickland & Elizabeth Hennington, spinster, were married, per license —
Brown, & Hullman,	Feb. 19th. 1772 Casper Brown & Mary Hulman, widow, were married, per license —
Downes & Lindsay,	Sept. 1st. 1772, William Downes & Jane Lindsay, widow, were married, per license —
Turner, & Clark,	Sept. 16th. 1772, Thomas Turner & Ann Clark, widow, were married, per license —
Eden, & Newman,	Sept. 17th. 1772, James Gottier Eden & Mary Newman, spinster, were married, per license —

Marion, & Collis,	Sept. 22nd. 1772, Joseph Marion & Elizabeth Collis, spinster, were married, per license —
Brown, & Nipper,	Sept. 24th. 1772, Joseph Brown & Hannah Nipper, widow, were married, per license —
Mills, & Taylor,	Sept. 24th. 1772, William Mills & Ann Taylor, spinster, were married per. license—
Shubrick, & Bulline,	Oct. 1st. 1772, Richard Shubrick & Susannah Bulline, spinstr. were married, per license —
Brown & Easton,	Oct. 8th. 1772, Hugh Brown & Mary Easton, widow, were married, per license —
Fisher, & Minnick,	Oct. 8th. 1772, Ferdinand Fisher & Rosanna Minnick, widow were married, per License, —
Tidyman, & Rose,	Oct. 31st. 1772, Philip Tidyman & Hester Rose, spinster, were married, per license —

Brown & O'Hara,	Oct. 16th. 1772, Charles Brown & Mary O'Hara, widow, were married, per license —
Proctor, & Vinson	Oct. 18th. 1772, Richard Proctor & Mary Ann Vinson, spinster, were married, per license.
Morrell, & Feltham,	Oct. 17th. 1772, Francis Morrell & Honora Feltham widow, were married, per license, by the Rev. Henry Purcell —
Drummond, & Seller,	Oct. 19th. 1772, James Drummond & Mary Seller, spinster, were married, per license —
Mathews, & Royal,	Oct. 31st. 1772, James Mathews & Elizabeth Royal, spinster, were married, per license —

Nicoll, & Friets,	Oct. 31st. 1772 Stewart Nicoll & Elizabeth Friets, spinster, were married, per license —
Ellison, & Potts,	Nov. 6th. 1772, Robert Ellison & Elizabeth Potts, spinster, were married, per license, by the Rev. Henry Purcell,
Higgins, & Quash,	Nov. 8th. 1772, Thomas Higgins & Rachel Quash, spinster, were married, per license —
Byers, & Graham,	Nov. 21st. 1772, Robert Byers & Elizabeth Graham, widow, were married, per license —
Huger, & Kinloch,	Dec. 1st. 1772, Benjamin Huger[1] & Mary Kinloch, spinster, were married, per license —
Franks & Sabina,	Dec. 23rd. 1772, Ulrick Franks & Sophia Sabina, widow, were married, per license —
Simpson, & Barlow,	Dec. 13th. 1772, Andrew Simpson & Ann Barlow, spinster, were married, per lic. by the Rev. Robert Purcell —
Baron, & Cleiland,	Dec. 31st. 1772, Alexander Baron & Sarah Cleiland, spinster, were married, per license —
Harris & Christie,	Dec. 31st. 1772, Charles Harris & Elizabeth Christie, Spinster, were married, per license —
McCullough, & McKnight,	Jan 1st. 1773, Hugh McCullough & Jane McKnight, spinster, were married, per license —
Stevenson, & Snelling.	Jan. 7th. 1773, Peter Stevenson & Mary Jones Snelling, spinster, were married, per license —

[1]He was born at Limerick plantation, St. John's Parish, Berkeley County, December 30, 1746; was major of the 5th Regiment, South Carolina Line, Continental Establishment, when killed before Charles Town, May 11, 1779. (See *Transactions*, Huguenot Society of South Carolina, No. 4.)

Smith & Jenkins,	Feby. 13th. 1773, Christian Smith & Mary Jenkins, widow, were married, per license —
Henion, & Willis,	Feb. 13th. 1773, Peter Henion & Esther Willis, widow, were married, per license —
Davis & Curliss,	Feb. 18th. 1773, Charles Davis & Elizabeth Curliss, widow, were married, per license —
Godfrey, & Darling,	Feb. 3rd. 1773, Benjamin Godfrey & Abigail Darling, spinster, were married, per lic. by the Rev. Robt. Purcell. —
Deramus, & Cooney,	Feb. 7th. 1773, John Deramus & Margaret Cooney, spinster, were married, per lic. by the Rev. Robt. Purcell —
Bee & McKinsey,	Mar. 16th. 1773, Thomas Bee & Sarah McKinsey, widow, were married, per license. —
Smith & Thomas.	Mar. 18th. 1773, James Smith & Ann Thomas, spinster, were married, per lic. by the Rev. Robt. Purcell. —
Eveleigh, & Simmons	Mar. 23rd. 1773, Thomas Eveleigh, & Ann Simmons, spinster, were married, per lic., by the Rev. Robt. Purcell —
Shud & Elliott,	Mar. 29th. 1773, William Shud & Eleanor Elliott, spinster, were married, per lic., by the Rev. Robt. Purcell —
Davis, & McClaran,	Apr. 21st. 1773, Alexander Davis & Ann McClaran, spinster, were married, per license —
Fearow, & Ross	Apr. 22nd. 1773, John Fearow & Sarah Ross, spinster, were married, per license —

Smith & Tipper,	Apr. 28th. 1773, Thomas Smith & Susannah Tipper, Spinster, were married, per license —
Cusack & Brown,	Apr. 29th. 1773, James Cusack & Anna Brown, spinster, were married, per license —
Hogan & Wood,	May 3rd. 1773, Patrick Hogan & Sarah Wood, spinster, were married, per license —
Darby & Elliott,	May 4th. 1773, James Darby & Margaret Elliott, spinster, were married, per license —

Marriages. 206

Bentham & Phillips,	May 5th. 1773, James Bentham, & Eleanor Phillips, widow, were married, per license. —
Coachman & Johnston,	May 6th. 1773, James Coachman & Ann Johnston, widow, were married per license —
Meurset, & Haunbaum,	May 16th. 1773, Peter Meurset & Eberhardina Haunbaum, spins. were married, per license —
Ogilvie, & Simmons,	May 18th. 1773, Henry Ogilvie & Hannah Simmons, widow, were married, per license —
Jamison & Simons,	May 25th. 1773, James Jamison & Rebecca Simons, spinster, were married, per license —
Dunscom, & Hennien,	June 20th. 1773, Durham Dunscom & Esther Hennien, widow, were married, per license —
Reynerson & Caruthers,	July 15th. 1773, George Reynerson & Jane Caruthers, widow, were married, per license —
Bliston, & Vine,	July 8th. 1773, Charles Bliston & Elizabeth Vine, spinster, were married, per license by the Rev. Robt. Purcell.

Smith, & Luft,
July 27th. 1773, Melchior Smith & Margaret Luft, widow,
were married, per license —

Patrick, & Cobia,
Aug. 21st. 1773, Casimer Patrick & Ann Cobia, spinster,
were married, per license —

Carr, & Freglith,
Aug. 26th. 1773, John Carr & Mary Freglith, spinster,
were married, per license —

Lestarjette, & Elliott,
Sept. 9th. 1773, Lewis Lestarjette & Elizabeth Burnham Elliott,
spinster, were married, per license —

Davidson, & Rogers.
Sept. 25th. 1773, George Davidson & Elizabeth Rogers, spinster,
were married, per license —

Johnson, & Schacho.
Sept. 26th. 1773, Richard Johnson & Elizabeth Schacho, widow,
were married, per license —

Lindfors, & Martin,
Oct. 3rd. 1773, Charles Jacob Lindfors & Ann Martin, widow,
were married, per license —

Clarendon, & Meek,
Oct. 9th. 1773, Smith Clarendon & Margaret Meek, widow,
were married, per license —

Wilson & Bonneau.
Oct. 12th. 1773, John Wilson & Mary Bonneau, spinster,
were married, per license —

Whitney, & Ham.
Oct. 14th. 1773, Lebbeus Whitney & Mary Ann Ham, widow,
were married, per license —

Cobia & Spidell.
Oct. 23rd. 1773, Francis Cobia & Christiana Elizabeth Spidell, spinster,
were married, per license —

Smith, & Mensinger,
Nov. 1st. 1773, John Smith & Dorothea Mensinger, spinster,
were married, per license —

Farr, Jr. & Waring.	Nov. 18th. 1773, Thomas Farr, Jr. & Elizabeth Waring, were married, per license—by Rev. Robt. Purcell —
Schero, & Hawkins,	Jan. 8th. 1774, John Schero & Rosanna Hawkins, widow, were married, per license —
Moore, & Smilie.	Jan. 12th. 1774, Patrick Moore & Elizabeth Smilie, spinster, were married, per license —
Prioleau & Broadbelt.	Jan. 27th. 1774, John Prioleau & Jane Broadbelt, spinster, were married, per license —
Alexander, & Murray	Feb. 6th. 1774, Alexander Alexander & Elizabeth Murray, spinster, were married, per license —
Bruce, & Lockhart.	Feb. 14th. 1774, Donald Bruce & Margaret Lockhart, spinster, were married, per license —
Cross, & Nockliffe.	Mar. 19th. 1774, Paul Cross & Ann Nockcliffe, widow, were married, per license —
Smith, & Shubrick,	Feb. 17th. 1774, The Revd. Robert Smith[1] & Sarah Shubrick, spins. were married, per lic. by the Rev. Robt. Purcell —

Marriages. 208

Warnock, & Lochon	Mar. 24th. 1774, Samuel Warnock & Elizabeth Lochon Spins. were married per license by the Rev. Robt. Purcell.
McConnell, & Blakeley.	April 6th. 1774, Thomas McConnell & Mary Blakeley, were married, per license —

[1]He was born at Worsted, County of Norfolk, England, August 25, 1732; arrived in Charles Town, November 3, 1757; was the first Protestant Episcopal Bishop of South Carolina; died October 28, 1801. This was his second marriage. (See Dalcho's *Protestant Episcopal Church in South Carolina.*)

Remington, & Donovan.	Apr. 7th. 1774, John Remington & Sarah Donovan spinster, were married, per license —
Oliver & Snistrunck.	Apr. 10th. 1774, Thomas Oliver & Elizabeth Snistrunck, spins. were married, per license —
Eveleigh, & Shubrick.	May 5th. 1774, Nicholas Eveleigh & Mary Shubrick, spinster, were married, per license —
Pike, & Inman.	June 11th. 1774, Thomas Pike & Mary Inman, were married, per license —
Bothwell, & Hill.	June 12th. 1774, John Bothwell & Susannah Hill, widow, were married, per license —
Tucker, & Evans.	July 3rd. 1774, Thomas Tudor Tucker[1] & Esther Evans, spinster, were married, per license —
Henderson, & Sands.	May 10th. 1774, James Henderson & Hannah Sands, widow, were married per lic. by the Rev. Robt. Purcell
Pugh, & Johnston.	May 19th. 1774, Thomas Pugh & Deborah Johnston, spinster, were married, per lic. by the Rev. Robt Purcell —
Brenan, & Quire.	May 20th. 1774, Eugene Brenan & Mary Quire, spinster, were married, per lic. by the Rev. R. Purcell —
Chalmers, & Boddington.	June 23rd. 1774, Gilbert Chalmers & Sophia Boddington, were married, per lic. by the Rev. R. Purcell —
Ramaje & Swallow.	June 28th. 1774, Charles Ramaje & Frances Swallow, were Married, per lic. by the Rev. R. Purcell —

[1]A native of Bermuda; was sometime Treasurer of the United States; died in Washington, May 2, 1828.

Dollar, & Strobler.	July 19th. 1774, John Morgan Dollar & Elizabeth Strobler, spins. were married, per license —
Fickland & Elphinston,	July 21st. 1774, George Fickland & Elizabeth Elphinston, widow, were married, per license —
Door, & Little.	July 22nd. 1774, John Door & Mary Little, spinster, were married, per license —
Miller, & Stead.	June 18th. 1774, William Miller & Susannah Stead, spinster, were married, per license—by the Rev. Robt. Purcell —
Yarborough, & Miles.	Aug. 2nd. 1774, James Dandridge Yarborough & Ann Miles, widow, were married, per license —
Ferguson, & Rutledge.	Aug. 4th. 1774, Thomas Ferguson[1] & Elizabeth Rutledge, widow, were married per license —
Simpson, & Arnon.	Aug. 14th. 1774, Archibald Simpson & Ann Arnon, spinster, were married, per license —
Hickling, & Thorpe.	Aug. 20th. 1774, Ephraim Hickling & Hannah Thorpe spinster, were married, per lic. by the Rev. Henry Purcell —
Dutargue, & Gaillard.	Aug. 23rd. 1774, John Dutargue & Lydia Gaillard, spinster, were married, per license —
Singleton, & Strother.	Aug. 25th. 1774, Thomas Singleton & Mary Strother, widow, were married, per license —

[1]He was born in 1737, the son of James Ferguson and Mrs. Anne (Barker) Skipper, his wife; served in the Commons House of Assembly and the Provincial Congress, and was a member of the Council of Safety, 1775-1776. His mother was a half sister of John Parker, of Parker's Ferry. This was his third marriage. She was the widow of Andrew Rutledge and daughter of Christopher Gadsden. He survived her and married a fourth and a fifth time.

Swain, & Peaton. — Sept. 4th. 1774, Luke Swain & Rebecca Peaton, spinster, were married, per license —

Murray, & Oats. — Sept. 22nd. 1774, Patrick Murray & Margery Gorbett Oats, spins. were married, per license —

Imrie, & Esdmond. — Oct. 2nd. 1774, John Imrie & Margaret Esdmond, widow, were married, per license —

Broughton, & Lessene. — Nov. 1st. 1774, Thomas Broughton & Elizabeth Lessene, spin. were married, per license —

Cogdell, & Wilkie. — Nov. 1st. 1774, Charles Cogdell & Jane Wilkie, widow, were married, per license —

.... Marriages 210

Williams & Bury. — On the 1st. July 1781 John Williams & Charlotte Bury, were married pr. Licence by the Revd. Mr. Robert Cooper

Skrine & Dill — On the 3d. July 1781 William Skrine & Susannah Dill were married pr. Licence by The Revd. Mr. Robert Cooper

Duva & Rowser — On the 6th. July 1781 James Duva & Mary Rowser, were married pr. Licence by the Revd. Mr. Robert Cooper

Gready & Postell — On the 11th. July 1781 James Gready & Judith Postell were married pr. Licence by The Revd. Mr. Robert Cooper

Egan & Little — On the 18th. July 1781 John Egan & Catharine Little were married pr. Licence by The Revd. Mr. Robert Cooper

Keowin & Eshmore — On the 25th. July 1781 John Keowin & Sarah Eshmore, were married pr. Licence by The Revd. Mr. Robert Cooper

Champneys & Wilson	On the 15th. August 1781 John Champneys & Mary Wilson widdow, were marrd. pr. Lce. by The Revd. Mr. Robert Cooper
Smith & Brisbane	On the 18th. August 1781 John Smith & Margaret Brisbane, were marrd. pr. Lce. by The Revd. Mr. Robert Cooper
Waters & Rougemont	On the 19th. August 1781 Philip Waters & Ann Rougemont were married pr. Licence by The Revd. Mr. Cooper
Rattery & Bailey	On the 25th. August 1781 Alexander Rattery & Abigail Bailey, were married pr. Lce. by The Revd. Mr. Robert Cooper.
Carter & Wilson	On the 30th. August 1781 Stepney Carter & Mary Wilson, were married pr. Lce. by The Revd. Mr. Robert Cooper
Paterson & Jenkins	On the 13th. Septemr. 1781 John Paterson & Mary Jenkins, were marrd. pr. Lce by The Revd. Mr. Robert Cooper
Stoll & Henry	On the 16th. Septemr. 1781 Jacob Stoll & Elizabeth Henry, were married pr. Licence by The Revd. Mr. Robert Cooper
Brown & Tallman	On the 16th. Sepemr. 1781 Stephen Brown widdower & Elizabeth Tallman widdow, pr. Lce. by The Revd. Mr. Robert Cooper
Bay & Holmes	On the 19th. Septemr 1781 Elihu Hall Bay & Margaret Holmes, were marrd pr Lce. by the Revd. Mr. Robert Cooper
Duvall & Murray	On the 7th. Octobr. 1781 John Duvall & Rebecca Murray, were married pr. Lce. by The Revd. Mr. Robert Cooper

Geo. Denholm (Regr.

Johnston & Garner	On the 18th. October 1781 Samuel Johnston & Frances Garner, were married pr. Licence by The Revd. Mr. Robert Cooper
Tunno & Rose	On the 18th. October 1781 John Tunno & Margaret Rose, were married pr. Licence by The Revd. Mr. Robert Cooper
Dewees & Rogers	On the 25th. October 1781 William Dewees & Jane Rogers, were married pr. Licence by The Revd. Mr. Robert Cooper
Napier & Clark	On the 26th. October 1781, Robert Napier & Elizabeth Clark, were married pr. Licence by The Revd. Mr. Robert Cooper
Wernicke & Bishop	On the 29th. October 1781 Lewis Wernicke & Ann Bishop, were married pr. Licence by The Revd. Mr. Robert Cooper
Raper & Kane	On the 1st. November 1781 William Raper & Sarah Kane, were married pr. Licence
Denholm & Haines	On the 12th. November 1781 George Denholm & Alice Haines, were married pr. Licence
Wraingh & McKenzie	On the 13th. November 1781 Richard Wrainch & Sarah McKenzie, were married pr. Licence the preceding three marriages by The Revd. Mr. Robt. Cooper
Bowing & For	On the 18th. November 1781 George Bowing & Mary For, was married pr. Licence by The Revd. Mr. Robert Cooper
Follingsby & Johnson	On the 24th. November 1781 John Follingsby & Rhoda Johnson, were married pr. Licence by The Revd. Mr. Robert Cooper

Jones & Lampert	On the 29th. November 1781 William Cox Jones & Mary Lampert, were married pr. Licence by The Revd. Mr. Robert Cooper
Fickling & Bridgett	On the 30th. November 1781 Francis Fickling & Elizabeth Bridget, were married pr. Licence by The Revd. Mr. Robert Cooper
Oliphant & Ham	On the 7th. December 1781 Alexander Oliphant & Elizabeth Ham, were married pr. Licence by The Revd. Mr. Robert Cooper
Hearne & Rivers	On the 18th. December 1781 Peter Hearne & Elizabeth Rivers, were married pr. Licence by The Revd. Mr. Robert Cooper
Petrie & Campbell	On the 20th. December 1781 Ninian Petrie & Catharine Campbell, were married pr. Licence by The Revd. Mr. Robert Cooper
Jozie & Egan	On the 8th. January 1782 Patrick Jozie & Rebecca Egan, were married pr. Licence by The Revd. Mr. Robert Cooper

Geo. Denholm (Regr.

.... Marriages 212

Carnes & Wilkie	On the 15th. January 1782 Lawrence Carnes & Ann Wilkie, were married pr. Licence by The Revd Mr. Robert Cooper
Williams & Bullock	On the 2nd. February 1782 Mortimore Williams & Sarah Bullock, were married pr. Licence by The Revd. Mr. Robert Cooper
McKenzie & Mylley	On the 5th. February 1782 Kennedy McKenzie & Ann Mylley, were married pr, Licence by The Revd. Mr. Robert Cooper

Mellichamp & Styles	On the 7th. February 1782 Saintlo Mellichamp & Rebecca Styles, were married pr. Licence by The Revd. Mr. Robert Cooper
Gemmel & Simpson	On the 12th. February 1782 John Gemmel & Sarah Simpson, were married pr. Licence by The Revd. Mr. Robert Cooper
Crawford & Coates	On the 25th. February 1782 Peter Crawford & Elizabeth Coates, were married pr. Licence by The Revd. Mr. Robert Cooper.
Williams & Williams	On the 27th. February 1782 George Robert Williams & Catharine Williams were married pr. Licence by The Revd. Robert Cooper.
Coats & George	On the 7th. March 1782 Thomas Coats & Catharine George, were married pr. Licence by The Revd. Mr. Robert Cooper.
Calder & Whitfield	On the 9th. March 1782 James Calder & Margaret Whitfield, were married pr Lce. by The Revd. Mr. Robert Cooper
Peterson & Milton	On the 26th. March 1782 George Peterson & Sarah Milton, were married pr. Licence by The Revd. Mr. Robert Cooper.
VanAssendelft & Gruenswig	On the 31st. March 1782 William Van Assendelft & Mary-Ann Gruenswig, were married pr. Licence by The Revd. Mr. Robert Cooper.
Watson & White	On the 1st. April 1782 William Watson & Sarah White, were married pr. Licence by The Revd. Mr Robert Cooper.
Lloyd & Burt	On the 4th. April 1782 John Lloyd & Henny Burt, were married pr. Licence.

Green & Butler	On the 15th. April 1782 Henry Green & Elizabeth Butler, were married pr. Licence.
Fillery & Harriot	On the 15th. April 1782 Stephen Fillery & Elizabeth Harriot, were married pr. Licence. The preceding three marriages by The Revd. Robert Cooper.
Milligan & McMillan	On the 7th. May 1782 John Milligan & Sarah McMillan, were married pr. Licence by The Revd. Mr. Robert Cooper —

Geo. Denholm (Regr.

Honeywood & Howser	On the 7th. May 1782 Arthur Honeywood & Elizabeth Howser, were married pr. Licence by The Revd. Mr. Robert Cooper
McGaver & Smith	On the 9th. May 1782 Donald McGaver & D. Smith, were married pr. Licence by The Revd. Mr. Robert Cooper.
Brimingham & O'Neal	On the 14th. May 1782 Richard Brimingham & Ann O'Neal, were married pr. Licence by The Revd. Mr. Rober Cooper.
Thomson & Bine	On the 18th. May 1782 William Thompson & Mary Hester Bine, were married pr. Licence by The Revd. Mr. Robert Cooper.
Askew & Dunning	On the 19th. May 1782 Leonard Askew & Catharine Dunning, were married pr. Licence by The Revd. Mr. Robert Cooper.
Gosling & Roof	On the 24th. June 1782 William J. Gosling & Mary Ann Roof, were married pr. Licence by The Revd. Mr. Robert Cooper.

Sanders & Garrett	On the 27th. June 1782 Roger Sanders & Elizabeth Garrett, were married pr. Licence. by The Revd. Mr. Robert Cooper.
Wilkinson & Wanton	On the 7th. July 1782 Capt. John Wilkinson & Elizabeth Wanton, were married pr. Lce. by The Revd. Mr. Robert Cooper.
Turner & Badger	On the 8th. July 1782 Shadrach Turner & Susannah Badger, were married pr. Lce. by The Revd. Mr. Robert Cooper.
Keen & McKenzie	On the 21st. July 1782 Thomas Keen & Mary McKenzie by The Revd. Mr. Robert Cooper —
Duncan & Thomson	On the 21st. July 1782 Benjamin Duncan & Elizabeth Thomson were married pr Licence. by The Revd. Mr. Robert Cooper.
Gilmore & Ripley	On the 23rd. July 1782 John Gilmore & Mary Ripley were married pr. Licence by The Revd. Mr. Robert Cooper.
Boden & Mayfield	On the 31st. July 1782 Joseph Boden & Mary Mayfield, were married pr. Licence. By The Revd. Mr. Robert Cooper.
Miller & Bounetheau	On the 10th. August 1782 John David Miller & Ann Bounetheau, were married pr. Lce. by The Revd. Mr. Robert Cooper.
Gilbert & McIntosh	On the 18th. August 1782, Francis Gilbert & Sophia McIntosh, were married pr. Lce. by The Revd. Mr. Robert Cooper.

Geo. Denholm (Regr.

Marriages 214

Holman & Hoof,	Nov. 14th. 1774, Conrad Holman & Eve Mary Hoof, widow were married, per license —

Hamilton & Reynolds	Nov. 20th. 1774, David Hamilton & Elizabeth Reynolds, spins., were married, per license —
Ross & Kerr.	Dec. 3rd. 1774, James Ross & Elizabeth Kerr, spinster, were married, per license —
Rhind & Cleland	Dec. 22nd. 1774, David Rhind & Elizabeth Cleland, spinster, were married, per license. -
Burton & Remington.	Jan. 15th. 1775, Isaac Burton & Ann Remington, spinster, were married, per license —
Hall & Mathews	Feby. 23rd. 1775, Daniel Hall & Susanna Mathews, spinster., were married, per license
Grant & Filbing,	Feb. 26th. 1775, John Grant & Elizabeth Filbing, widow, were married, per license —
McMahan, & Grimes	Jan. 19th. 1775, Arthur McMahan & Eleanor Grimes, spin., were married, per license —by the Rev. Robt. Purcell
Purvis, & Richard.	Jan. 26th. 1775, John Purvis & Eliza Ann Richard, spin., were married, per lic., by the Rev. Robt. Purcell —
Walter Jr. & Stevens,	Mar. 14th. 1775, John Walter Jr. & Jannett Stevens, spinster, were married per License —
Bradwell & Loyd	Mar. 30th. 1775, John Bradwell & Elizabeth Loyd, spinster, were married, per license —
Hodgens, & Bent	Mar. 9th. 1775, William Hodgens & Ann Bent, widow, were married, per license — by the Rev. Robt. Purcell
Burt & Jones,	Apr. 20th. 1775, William Burt & Ann Jones, spinster, were married, per license—by the Rev. R. Purcell —

Genscel, & Jeyser,	Apr. 20th. 1775, John Genscel & Margaret Jeyser, spin., were married, per lic. by the Rev. R. Purcell —

Marriages — 215

Kneeshaw & Sutcliffe	On 18th. Febry. 1783 Jno. Kneeshaw & Elizth. Sutcliffe were Married pr. Lice. pr. the Revd. Mr. Purcell —
Clarkson, & Hutchinson,	May 4th. 1775, William Clarkson & Ann Hutchinson, spinster, were married, per lic., by the Rev. R. Purcell —
Taylor & Kelsey,	May 6th. 1775, David Taylor & Jane Kelsey, spinster, were married, per license —
Cordes & Banbury,	May 11th. 1775, John Cordes & Judith Banbury, spinster, were married, per lic., by the Rev. R. Purcell —
Wallace & Shannon,	May 21st. 1775, Edward Wallace & Elizabeth Shannon, widow, were married, per lic., by the Rev. R. Purcell —
Burger & Cleator,	June 4th. 1775, David Burger & Catharine Cleator, spin., were married, per license —
Mathews, & Holmes,	June 8th. 1775, John Mathews & Elizabeth Holmes, spin., were married, per license —
Fyfe, & Dott	July 2nd. 1775, John Fyfe & Sarah Dott, widow, were married, per license —
Moore, & Short,	July 21st. 1775, Charles Moore & Catharine Short, spin., were married, per license —
Cudworth Jr. & Sheppard,	Aug. 5th. 1775, Benjamin Cudworth Jr. & Catharine Sheppard, widow, were married, per license —

Ellis & Glaze,	Aug. 10th. 1775, Thomas Ellis & Ann Glaze, spinster, were married, per license —
Sheppard & Gibbes,	Aug. 27th. 1775, Charles Sheppard & Elizabeth Gibbes, spin., were married, per license —
Brickin & Henderson,	Sept. 2nd. 1775, James Brickin & Sarah Henderson, spinster, were married, per license —
Laffelle & Oats	Sept. 17th. 1775, Nicholas Laffelle & Mary Oats, spinster. were married, per license —
Wyatt & Lingard,	Oct. 21st. 1775, John Wyatt & Violetta Lingard, spinster, were married, per license —
Savage & Clifford,	Nov. 26th. 1775, Richard Savage & Mary Clifford, were married, per license —
Elliott, & Smith.	Jan. 1st. 1776, Barnard Elliott[1] & Susanna Smith, were married, per license. —
Bouston & Starling	Jan. 6th. 1776, Hugh Bouston & Ann Starling, widow, were married —
Middleton, & Ainslie,	Jan. 16th. 1776, Henry Middleton & Mary Ainslie, widow, were married —[2]
Gordon & Gordon,	Jan. 18th. 1776, John Gordon & Penelope Gordon, were married —

[1]See *The South Carolina Historical and Genealogical Magazine,* XV, 70-71.

[2]He was the owner of The Oaks plantation, St. James's Parish, Goose Creek, and the founder of Middleton Place, St. Andrew's Parish. This was his third marriage and her fourth. She was one of the daughters of George, fourth Earl of Cromartie. (See *The South Carolina Historical and Genealogical Magazine,* I, 239.)

Harper & Edwards, — Jan. 19th. 1776, Thomas Harper & Elizabeth Edwards, spin., were married —

Allston, & Browne. — Mar. 12th. 1775, Jonas Allston & Esther Browne, spinster, were married —

Bonsell, & St. Martin — Mar 14th. 1776, Samuel Bonsell & Elizabeth St. Martin, spinster, were married —

Simpson & Bregard, — Mar. 19th. 1776, Francis Simpson & Keziah Bregard, were married —

Sline, & Bregar — Mar. 19th. 1776, Bartholemew Sline & Hannah Bregar, spinster. were married —

Gadsden & Wragg, — April 14th. 1776, Christopher Gadsden & Ann Wragg, spinster, were married, per license —

Mathews & Saltus, — May 2nd. 1776, George Mathews & Mary Saltus, spinster, were married, per license —

Piercy & Elliott, — May 18th. 1776, William Piercy[1] & Catharine Elliott, spinster, were married, per license —

Legaré & Hoyland, — May 21st. 1776, Samuel Legaré & Eleanor Sarah Hoyland, spin., were married, per license —

Battoon, & Guy, — May 25th. 1776, John Battoon & Ann Guy, widow, were married, pr. License —

Austin & Frazer, — May 26th. 1776, Robert Austin & Catharine Frazer, spinster, were married, per license —

---

[1]See Dalcho's *History of the Protestant Episcopal Church in South Carolina*, 236-241.

Bellamy & Baker	Aug. 8th. 1776, William Bellamy & Esther Baker, widow, were married, per license —
Strickland, & Wallace.	Aug. 11th. 1776, James Strickland & Mary Wallace, were married, per license —
Yates & Lennox.	Sept. 12th. 1776, Seth Yates & Elizabeth Lennox, were married, per license —
Smith & Miles.	Sept. 19th. 1776, Press Smith & Elizabeth Miles, were married, per license —
Sanders, & Lowndes,	Sept. 23rd. 1776, Roger Parker Sanders & Amarinthia Lowndes, were married, per license —
Caskin & Weston,	Sept. 24th. 1776, John Caskin & Deborah Weston, were married, per license —
Fosky & Powell,	Oct. 13th. 1776, Brian Fosky & Ann Powell, widow, were married, per license —

Weir & Baird,	Oct. 14th. 1776, James Weir & Elizabeth Baird, widow, were married per license —
Gibbes, & Baddely,	Oct. 20th. 1776, John Walters Gibbes & Amarinthia Baddely, spinster, were married, per license —
Smith, & Middleton,	Nov. 19th. 1776, Peter Smith & Mary Middleton, spinster, were married, per license —
Bennis & Mace,	Nov. 23rd. 1776, William Bennis & Rebecca Mace, spin., were married, per license —
Rout & Nicholson,	Nov. 24th. 1776, George. Rout & Mary Nicholson, widow, were married, per license —

Poyas & Schwartskopff,	Nov. 24th. 1776, John Ernest Poyas & Magdalen Schwartskopff, wid. were married, per license —
Dunning & Scott,	Nov. 24th. 1776, James Dunning & Catharine Scott, widow, were married, per license —
Martin & Kaller,	Nov. 26th. 1776, Henry Martin & Eve Kaller, widow, were married, per license —
Jordan & Hier,	Nov. 27th. 1776, Christopher Jordan & Catharine Hier, widow, were married, per license —
Hamett & Kirk,	Dec. 1st. 1776, Thomas Hamett & Charlotte Kirk, widow, were married, per license —
Gough & Hext.	Dec. 2nd. 1776, John Gough & Rebecca Hext, spinster, were married, per license —
Hill & Green,	Dec. 5th. 1776, Thomas Hill & Susannah Green, widow, were married, per license —
Wainwright & Dewar	Dec. 10th. 1776, Richard Wainwright & Ann Dewar, spins. were married, per license —
Tallman & Snell	Dec. 15th. 1776, John Richard Tallman & Elizabeth Snell, wid., were married, per License —

Young, & Swince,	Dec. 22nd. 1776, Archibald Young & Mary Swince, widow, were married, per license —
Abercrombie & Mitchell,	Jan. 4th. 1777, John Abercrombie & Sarah Mitchell, widow, were married, per license —
Miller & Ash —	Jan. 9th. 1777, Solomon Miller & Ann Ash, spinster, were married, per license —

Bontiton, & Air.	Jan. 9th. 1777, Peter Bontiton & Mary Air, widow, were married, per license —
Eagan & Jeasop	Jan. 9th. 1777, Thomas Eagan & Ann Jeasop, were married, per license —
Bonetheau, & Weyman.	Jan. 14th. 1777, Peter Bonetheau & Elizabeth Weyman, Spin., were married, per license —
Davie & Williams.	Jan. 14th. 1777, William Davie & Mary Williams, widow, were married, per license —
Pinckney & Cannon,	Jan. 21st. 1777, Hopson Pinckney & Elizabeth Cannon, spin., were married, per license —
Pinder, & Lecraft.	Jan. 21st. 1777, William Pinder & Rebecca Lecraft, widow, were married, per license —
Freer & Mathews.	Feb. 2nd. 1777, Solomon Freer & Ann Mathews, widow, were married, per license —
Sawyer & Blake	Feb. 13th. 1777, Elisha Sawyer & Ann Blake, spinster, were married, pr. lic., by the Rev. Ch. Fred. Moreau —
Kaylor & Johnston.	Feb. 19th. 1777, Richard Kaylor & Mary Johnston, spinster, were married, per license —
Jervis & Ash.	Feb. 20th. 1777, John Jervis & Priscilla Ash, spinster, were married, per License —
Campbell & Fenwick —	Feb. 24th. 1777 Macartan Campbell & Sarah Fenwick, spinster, were married, per lic. by the Rev. John Lewis —
Dubose & Dutarque.	Feby. 27th. 1777, Isaac Dubose & Catharine Dutarque, spinster, were married, per lic. by the Rev. Henry Purcell

Fomea & Taylor.	Mar. 5th. 1777, Andrew Fomea & Elizabeth Taylor, widow, were married, per license —
Rudhall & Meyer	Mar. 25th. 1777, William Rudhall & Mary Miller Meyer, were married, per lic. by the Rev. Henry Purcell —
McCray & Fitig.	Mar. 27th. 1777, Alexander McCray & Susannah Fitig, were married, per lic. by the Rev. C. F. Moreau —
Dobbins & Brown.	Mar. 19th. 1777, Joseph Dobbins & Elizabeth Brown, were married, per license —
McCall Jr. & Lesesne.	Apr. 3rd. 1777, John McCall Jr. & Ann Lesesne, spinster, were married, per lic. by the Rev. C. F. Moreau —
Sansum & Stoll.	Apr. 6th. 1777, John Sansum & Mary Stoll, spinster, were married, per lic. by the Rev. C. F. Moreau —
Toussiger & Ball.	Apr. 10th. 1777, James Toussiger & Margaret Ball, were married, per lic. by the Rev. C. F. Moreau —
Air & Legaré.	Apr. 8th. 1777, James Air & Elizabeth Legaré, spinster, were married per lic. by the Rev. C. F. Moreau —
Stewart & Watt.	Apr. 16th. 1777, Thomas Stewart & Mary Watt, spinster, were married, per license —
Keckley & McKinfuss.	Apr. 21st. 1777, George Keckley & Margaret McKinfuss, were married, per lic. by the Rev. C. F. Moreau —

Bryan & Simons.	Apr. 24th. 1777, John Bryan & Rachel Simons, spinster, were married, per lic. by the Rev. C. F. Moreau —
Muckinfuss & Nuffer.	Apr. 27th. 1777, Michael Muckinfuss & Mary Nuffer, widow, were married, per license —
Trescott, & Boquet.	May 1st. 1777, Edward Trescott & Catharine Boquet, spinster, were married, per license —
Harleston & Lynch.	May 1st. 1777, John Harleston & Elizabeth Lynch, spinster, were married, per license —

McCall, & Dart.	May 5th. 1777, James McCall & Ann Amelia Dart, were married, per license —
Barnwell, & Hutsón.	May 8th. 1777, John Barnwell & Ann Hutson, spinster, were married, per lic. by the Rev. C. F. Moreau —[1]
Cogdell & Steevens.	May 11th. 1777, George Cogdell & Mary Ann Elizabeth Steevens, were married, per lic. by the Rev. C. F. Moreau —
Miller & Morgan.	May 14th. 1777, Samuel Miller & Hester Morgan, spinster, were married, per lic. by the Rev. C. F. Moreau —
Brown & Barklay.	May 18th. 1777, William Brown & Sarah Barklay, spinster, were married, per license —
Blackburn & Backstill.	May 23rd. 1777, James Blackburn & Elizabeth Backstill, widow, were married per license —

[1]See *The South Carolina Historical and Genealogical Magazine*, Vol. II, 46-88, for Barnwell; Vol. IX, 127-140, for Hutson.

Boyer & Delky.	May 27th. 1777, Henry Boyer & Katharine Delky, spinster, were married, per lic. by the Rev. C. F. Moreau —
Clancey & Caskie.	May 28th. 1777, William Clancey & Christian Caskie, spinster, were married, per lic. by the Rev. C. F. Moreau —
Cole & Boomer.	May 29th. 1777, Richard Cole & Ann Boomer, spinster, were married, per lic. by the Rev. C. F. Moreau —
Turner & Warner —	June 6th. 1777, John Turner & Elizabeth Warner, spinster, were married, per lic. by the Rev. C. F. Moreau—
Sucker & Gaspel.	June 5th. 1777, Richard Sucker & Charlotte Gaspel, spinster, were married, per lic. by the Rev. C. F. Moreau —
Pafford & Marshall.	June 5th. 1777, John Pafford & Hannah Marshall, spinster, were married, per. lic. by the Rev. John Lewis —
Long & Kirkwood.	June 22nd. 1777, William Long & Elizabeth Kirkwood, widow, were married, per license —
Glover & Young.	June 24th. 1777, William Glover & Margaret Young, spinster, were married, per lic. by the Rev. C. F. Moreau —

Marriages. 222

Hiltonbrand & Henrykinn.	June 30th. 1777, Adam Hiltonbrand & Margaretta Henrykinn were married per license —
Saunders & Hunt	July 9th. 1777, John Saunders & Martha Hunt, widow, were married, per lic. by the Rev. C. F. Moreau —

Dubois & Muncreef.	July 10th. 1777, David Dubois & Susannah Muncreef, spinster, were married, per. license —
Hendlen & Arnold,	July 13th. 1777, Thomas Hendlen & Amy Arnold, widow, were married, per license —
Cook & Wade	July 17th. 1777, George Cook & Eleanor Wade, widow, were married per license —
Cline & Shirer.	Aug. 3rd. 1777, George Cline & Ann Shirer, spinster, were married, per license —
Nicoll & Howser.	Aug. 3rd. 1777, William Nicoll & Dorothea Howser, spinster, were married, per license —
Hampton & King	Aug. 7th. 1777, John Hampton & Gracia King, spinster, were married, per license —
Burgess & Churchill	Aug. 28th. 1777, John Burgess & Mary Ann Churchill, were married —
McCrea, & Wells.	Sept. 3rd. 1777, Thomas McCrea & Mary Wells, widow, were married, per license —
Clifford, & Perry.	Sept. 11th. 1777, Charles Clifford & Elizabeth Perry, spinster, were married, per license —
Joyner & Russlett.	Sept. 25th. 1777, John Joyner & Benedicta Russlett, widow, were married, per license —
Walker & Philips.	Sept. 26th 1777, Gilbert Kennady Walker & Elizabeth Philips, widow, were married, per license —

Markley, & Gasser.	Oct. 5th. 1777, Abraham Markley & Mary Gasser, spinster, were married, per license —

Rudley, & Sheers.	Oct. 15th. 1777, Michael Rudley & Elizabeth Sheers, spinster, were married, per license —
Murray & Ruger.	Oct. 21st. 1777, Samuel Murray & Catharine Tora Ruger, spinster, were married, per license —
Smith & Young.	Nov. 4th. 1777, Thomas Smith & Jane Young, spinster, were married, per license —
Cheney & Wood.	Nov. 4th. 1777, Thomas Cheney & Elizabeth Wood, spinster, were married, per license —
Burger, & Elms.	Nov. 5th. 1777, David Burger & Mary Elms, spinster, were married, per license —
Wyatt & Fogartie.	Nov. 9th. 1777, William Wyatt & Rebecca Fogartie, spin., were married, per license —
Smith & Dry.	Nov. 18th. 1777, Benjamin Smith[1] & Sarah Dry, spinster, were married, per license —
Miller & Lord.	Nov. 25th. 1777, John Miller & Jane Lord, spinster, were married, per license —
Shaddock & Thompson.	Nov. 27th. 1777, John Shaddock & Ann Thompson, widow, were married, per license —
McKinzie, & Chapman.	Dec. 6th. 1777, Alexander McKinzie & Jean Chapman, spinster, were married, per license —
Cockran & Hewie.	Dec. 18th. 1777, Thomas Cockran & Susannah Hewie, widow, were married, per license —

[1]See *The South Carolina Historical and Genealogical Magazine*, IV, 41.

Perry & Hunt.	Dec. 18th. 1777, James Perry & Frances Hunt, spinster, were married, per lic. by the Rev. John Lewis —
Griffiths, & Walker.	Dec. 30th. 1777, Thomas Griffiths & Allen Walker, widow, were married, per license —
Delany, & Walker.	Dec. 30th. 1777, Marquis Delany & Allen Walker, spins., were married, per license —
Heyward & Shubrick.	Jan. 1st. 1778, William Heyward & Hannah Shubrick, spins. were married, per license —
Moore & Taylor.	Jan. 1st. 1778, Joseph Moore & Ann Taylor, widow, were married, per license —
Cambridge & Wood.	Jan 1st. 1778, Tobias Cambridge & Elizabeth Wood, spin., were married, per license —
Giles & Colleton.	Jan. 5th. 1778, Othniel Giles & Jane Colleton, widow, were married, per license —
Garvin & Day,	Jan. 11th. 1778, Ebenezer Garvin & Margaret Day, widow, were married, per license —
Gordon & Reed.	Jan. 14th. 1778, Peter Gordon & Sarah Reed, spinster, were married, per license —
Hendlin & Graey.	Jan 15th. 1778, Thomas Hendlin & Isabel Graey, spinster, were married, per license —
Mouatt & Ash	Jan. 20th. 1778, John Mouatt & Mary Ash, spinster, were married, per license —
Saltridge & Bull.	Jan 22nd. 1778, William Saltridge & Mary Bull, spin., were married, per license —

Taylor & Miller.	Jan. 25th. 1778, Paul Taylor & Martha Miller, spinster, were married, per license —
Wise & Beaty.	Jan. 29th. 1778, Samuel Wise & Ann Beaty, widow, were married, per lic. by the Rev. Henry Purcell —
Taggart & Haly.	Feb. 3rd. 1778, William Taggart & Mary Haly, widow, were married, per lic. by the Revd. Henry Purcell —
Knight & Ginnis.	Feb. 8th. 1778, Samuel Knight & Ann Ginnis, widow, were married, per license —
Cruger & Liston.	Feb. 12th. 1778, Frederick David Cruger & Isabella Liston, spin., were married, per license —
Vail & Sanders.	Feby. 24th. 1778, John Vail & Margaret Sanders, Spinster, were married, per license —
Conyers & Snell.	Mar. 8th. 1778, Clement Conyers & Frances Snell, spinster, were married, per license —
Clarke & Hall,	Mar. 18th. 1778, William Clarke & Lucretia Hall, widow, were married, per license —
Hewgill & Lindsay.	Mar. 23rd. 1778, John Hewgill & Eleanor Lindsay, spin., were married, per license —
Hanscombe & Gray.	Mar. 31st. 1778, William Hanscombe & Margaret Gray, widow, were married, per license —
Shubrick, Jr. & Branford.	Apr. 9th. 1778, Thomas Shubrick Jr. & Mary Branford, spin., were married, per license —
Peak & Harvey.	Apr. 19th. 1778, John Peak & Elizabeth Harvey, spinster, were married, per license —

Roach & Campbell.

Apr. 19th. 1778, William Roach & Mary Campbell, spinster, were married, per license —

Caylove, & Coffman.

Apr. 26th. 1778, Frederick Caylove & Mary Ann Coffman, spin., were married, per license —

Marriages. 226

Whitesides & Rand

Apr. 29th. 1778, Edward Whitesides & Esther Rand, spinster, were married, per license —

Lawyer & Kirk.

Apr. 29th. 1778, Thomas Lawyer & Martha Kirk, spinster — were married, per license —

Nisbett, & Scott.

Apr. 30th. 1778, William Nisbett & Jane Scott, spinster, were married, per license —

Adler & Rodgamon.

May 3rd. 1778, Stolberg Adler & Ann Rodgamon, spinster, were married, per lic. by the Rev. F. Moreau. —

Walker & Byers.

May 12th. 1778, Joel Walker & Elizabeth Byers, widow, were married, per license —

Rout & Parker,

May 14th. 1778, George Rout & Ann Parker, widow, were married, per license —

Russel & Mason.

June 1st. 1778, Andrew Russel & Mary Mason, widow, were married, per lic. by the Rev. C. F. Moreau —

Gilmore, & Hartman.

May 28th. 1778, John Gilmore & Elizabeth Hartman, were married, per lic. by Rev. Alexander Garden —

Lessesne, & Frederick.

July 2nd. 1778, John Lessesne & Mary Frederick, were married, per lic. by Rev. F. Moreau—

Fordham & Sharp.	July 9th. 1778, Richard Fordham & Mary Sharp, widow, were married, per license —
Sullivan & Shackleford.	July 9th. 1778, Philip Sullivan & Susanna Shackleford, spins., were married, per license —
Johnson & Pitt.	July 9th. 1778, George Johnson & Rowdy Pitt, widow, were married, per license —
Deevees & Forgey.	July 14th. 1778, William Deevees & Frances Forgey, spinster, were married, per license —
Cattell & Webb.	July 22nd. 1778, Benjamin Cattell & Rose Webb, were married, per license —

Smith & Crips.	Aug. 8th. 1778, Nicholas Smith & Mary Abel Allen Crips, widow, were married, per license —
Glaze & Nevin.	Aug. 23rd. 1778, William Glaze & Ann Nevin, widow, were married, per license —
Mondey & Duncan.	Sept. 13th. 1778, William Mondey & Eleanor Duncan, widow, were married, per license —
O'Reilly & McMillor.	Sept. 19th. 1778, John O'Reilly & Elizabeth McMillor, spinster, were married, per license —
Gabeau & Henley.	Sept. 23rd. 1778, Anthony Gabeau & Elizabeth Henley, spinster, were married, per license —
Rhodes & Pittman.	Sept. 24th. 1778, Joseph Rhodes & Sarah Pittman, spinster, were married, per license —
Ladson & Smith.	Oct. 1st. 1778, James Ladson & Judith Smith, spinster, were married, per license —

Gadsden & Fenwicke.	Oct. 16th. 1778, Thomas Gadsden & Martha Fenwicke, spin., were married, per license —
Jacob & Younker.	Oct. 20th. 1778, Frederick Jacob & Mary Younker, spinster, were married, per license —
Stocks & Young.	Nov. 10th. 1778, John Stocks & Margaret Young, spinster, were married, per license —
Grenier & Younker.	Nov. 24th. 1778, Peter Francis Grenier & Margaret Younker, spin., were married, per lic. by the Rev. Jno. Lewis.
Herman & Gutstrings.	Dec. 12th. 1778, Michael Herman & Barbary Gutstrings, widow. were married, per license —
Muncrief & Young.	Dec. 17th. 1778, Richard Muncrief & Elizabeth Young, spin., were married, per license —

More, & Sweeny.	Dec. 24th. Stephen More & Mary Sweeny, were married —
Trusler & Anderson.	Dec. 31st. 1778, William Trusler & Jane Anderson, were married, per license —
Ashton & Preston.	Jan. 7th. 1779, John Ashton & Catharine Preston, were married, per lic. by the Rev. C. F. Moreau —
Tobin & Merchant.	Feb. 3rd. 1779, Michael Tobin & Mary Merchant, widow. were married, per license —
Vickers & Rion.	Feb. 9th. 1779, James Vickers & Hannah Rion, widow, were married, per license —
Toomy & Simmons.	Feb. 18th. 1779, Michael Toomy & Mary Ann Simmons, widow, were married, per banns.

Jones & Goodson,	Feb. 20th. 1779, Edward Jones & Margaret Goodson, spin., were married, per license —
Bellinger & Evans.	Feb. 21st. 1779, John Bellinger & Rebecca Evans, were married, per license —
Ellis & Mills.	Feb. 24th. 1779, Henry Ellis & Sarah Mills, widow, were married, per license —
Cole & Turner.	Feb. 26th. 1779, Joseph Cole & Rebecca Turner, spinster, were married, per License —
Patton & Tom.	Mar. 8th. 1779, Andrew Patton & Katharine Tom, spinster, were married, per License —
Hughes & Bothwell.	Mar. 28th. 1779, Henry Hughes & Susannah Bothwell, widow, were married, per license —
Martin & Scott.	Apr. 1st. 1779, Laughlin Martin & Margaret Scott, widow, were married, per license —
Lemon & Watts.	Apr. 3rd. 1779, George Lemon & Esther Watts, were married, per license —

Taffe & Bury.	Apr. 5th. 1779, Aaron Taffe & Margaret Bury, spinster, were married, per license —
Harvey & Delany.	Apr. 8th. 1779, Andrew Harvey & Sarah Delany, widow, were married, per license —
Quelch & Fyfe.	Apr. 22nd. 1779, Andrew Quelch & Sarah Fyfe, widow, were married, per license —
Boone & Boid.	Apr. 22nd. 1779, Capers Boone & Mary Boid, spinster, were married, per license —

Bourke & Miller.	May 24th. 1779, Alexander Bourke & Jane Miller, were married, by the Rev. John Lewis.
Antony & Cook	June 19th. 1779, Abraham Antony & Margaret Cook, were married, by the Rev. John Lewis —
Friend & Muckenfuss.	June 29th. 1779; George Friend & Catharine Muckenfuss, widow, were married, by the Rev. John Lewis —
Mills & Williams.	July 4th. 1779, John Mills & Elizabeth Williams, were married, by the Rev. John Lewis —
Berwick & Johnson.	July 20th. 1779, John Berwick & Sarah Johnson, widow, were married, per license —
DuBarthas & LeBoulinger.	July 20th. 1779, William DuBarthas & Mary Jane LeBoulinger, were married —
Pinckney & Motte.	July 22nd. 1779, Thomas Pinckney & Elizabeth Motte, spinster, were married —[1]
Roland & Benet.	July 23rd. 1779, Malachi Roland & Martha Benet, widow, were married —
Harth & Holson.	Aug. 1st. 1779, John Harth — Elizabeth Holson, widow, were married —
McCarty & Budge.	Aug. 9th. 1779. Thomas McCarty & Jane Budge, were married —

Marriages. 230

Rolins & Green	Aug. 17th. 1779, Thomas Rolins & Ann Green, were married —

[1]He was a son of Charles Pinckney, sometime chief-justice of the province, by his second wife, Elizabeth ("Eliza:") Lucas, and was born October 23, 1750. (See *Life of Gen. Thomas Pinckney*, by C. C. Pinckney; *The South Carolina Historical and Genealogical Magazine*, II, 148-151.)

Petrie & Peronneau.	Aug. 22nd. 1779, Edmund Petrie & Ann Peronneau, spinster, were married —
Bull & Reid.	Aug. 26th. 1779, William Bull[1] & Elizabeth Reid, spinster, were married —
Sutter & Tippin,	Sept. 11th. 1779, John Sutter & Susannah Tippin, spinster, were married —
Akon & Cameron.	Sept. 19th. 1779, Thomas Akon & Mary Cameron, widow, were married —
Sulivan & Sprowl.	Sept. 21st. 1779, Cornelius Sulivan & Abigail Sprowl, were married —
Farr & Smith.	Sept. 24th. 1779, Nathaniel Farr & Elizabeth Smith, widow, were married —
Stafford & Oliver,	Oct. 4th. 1779, Elijah Stafford & Elizabeth Oliver, were married —
Moultrie & Lynch.	Oct. 10th. 1779, William Moultrie[2] & Hannah Lynch, widow, were married —
Mitcham & Herrington.	Oct. 14th. 1779, Colin Mitcham & Dorcas Herrington, were married —

[1]This was a son of Stephen Bull, of Newberry (plantation), by his second wife, Judith Mayrant, and a half-brother of Gen. Stephen Bull, of Sheldon. He inherited Ashley Hall, St. Andrew's Parish, from his uncle, Lieutenant-Governor William Bull (1710-1791), and resided there until his death in 1805. (See *The South Carolina Historical and Genealogical Magazine*, I, 82.)

[2]This was Gen. Moultrie's second marriage, his first having been with Elizabeth Damaris de St. Julien, December 10, 1749. This second marriage was to the widow of Thomas Lynch, late delegate to the Continental Congress and father of Thomas Lynch, Jr., signer of the Declaration of Independence. She was a daughter of Jacob Motte, for many years Public Treasurer of the province, and sister of Col. Isaac Motte and Major Charles Motte, of the South Carolina Line, Continental Establishment. (See *The South Carolina Historical and Genealogical Magazine*, V. 257.)

Hancock & Elsinore. — Oct. 14th. 1779, Robert Hancock & Elizabeth Elsinore, widow, were married —

Smith & Clarke — Nov. 1st. 1779, William Smith & Elizabeth Clarke, were married —

Sharp & Baldwin. — Nov. 2nd. 1779, Joseph Sharp & Jane Baldwin, widow, were married —

Bury & Roberts. — Nov. 4th. 1779, John Bury & Susannah Roberts, were married —

Izard, & Fenwick — Nov. 7th. 1779, Walter Izard & Mary Fenwick, spinster, were married —

Keith & Bullin — Dec. 2nd. 1779, Alexander Keith & Susanna Bullin, spinster, were married —

Fraser & Corker. — Dec. 13th. 1779, William Fraser & Eleanor Corker, widow, were married —

Marlow & Green — Dec. 16th. 1779, John Marlow & Mary Green, spinster, were married —

Wifer & Davie. — Dec. 18th. 1779, Henry Wifer & Mary Magdalen Davie, widow, were married —

Bolton & Lynch. — Dec. 29th. 1779, William Bolton & Mary Lynch, were married.

Harris & Carpenter. — Dec. 30th. 1779, Thomas Harris & Martha Carpenter, were married —

Stedman & McLean. — Dec. 30th. 1779 James Stedman & Sarah McLean, were married —

Moore & Drew.	Jan. 19th. 1780 Robert Moore & Elizabeth Drew. widow, were married —
Elliott & Prioleau.	Jan. 27th. 1780, Thomas Elliott & Elizabeth Prioleau, spinster, were married — £200 —
Cobia & Rumph.	Feb. 8th. 1780, Nicholas Cobia & Ann Rumph, spinster, were Married — £260 —
Crawford & James	Feb. 22nd. 1780, Bellamy Crawford & Susannah James, were married, by the Rev. J. Lewis — £260 —

Marriages 233[1]

N. B. The records of the parish from February 6th. 1780 to 1787 have not been found up to this date, August 20th. 1889., Reference will be made to them if they shall be found.[2]

Godfrey and Donnom, (spinster)	January 14th. 1787 Thomas Godfrey and Sarah Donnom were married per Lic. by the Revd. Thomas Frost.
Todd and Ball	Jany 16 1787 John Todd, widower, and Agnes Ball, spinster, were married, per Lic.
Lindsay and Pendervais (widow)	Jany 27. 1787 Barnard Lindsay and Mary Pendervais were married
Todd and Bell	Jany 30. 1787 James Todd and Anna Bell, Spinster, were married per Lic. by the Rev'd Thomas Frost.
Walker and Baris (or Bans)	February 25 1787 William Walker and Susannah Baris or Bans were married.

---

[1]Page 232 is blank.

[2]This note was inserted above the records.

Axon and You	March 1. 1787 Samuel Jacob Axon, M. D. of St. Paul's parish, and Eliza You, Charleston, Spinster, were married per Lic. by the Rev'd Thomas Frost.
Gordon and Reilly	March 14. 1787 John Gordon and Elizabeth Reilly, widower, were married per Lic.

Marriages.

Marriages Continued 234

Hunt and Nott.	January 31. 1787 Thomas Hunt and Hannah Nott were married per Lic.
Woodberry and Scott	April 5. 1787 John Woodberry and Ann Scott, widow, were married per Lic.
Vandle and Oliphant	April 12 1787 James Vandle and Elizabeth Oliphant, widow, were married, per Lic.
Richards and Ralph	April 29. 1787 William Richards and Mary Ralph, spinster, were married per Lic.
Thompson and Frear	May. 3 1787 John Thompson and Rebecca Frear, spinster, were married per Lic.
Harleston and Moultrie	May 31. 1787 Edward Harleston and Anna Bella Moultrie by the Rev'd Thomas Frost.
Browne and Forster	June 17. 1787 Daniel Browne and Margaret Forster, widow, were married per Lic.
Lang and Crawford	June 21. 1787 William Lang and Susannah Crawford, widow, were married per Lic.

Marriages.

Marriages Continued 235

McGuire and McThie	July 5th. 1787 John McGuire of Ashepoo, and Mary McThie of the same place were married per Lic.

Wyatt and Lebby.	July 12. 1787. Richard Wyatt and Elizabeth Lebby Spinster, were married per Lic.
Morris and Gadsden.	July 26th. 1787 Thomas Morris and Mary Gadsden spinster, were married per Lic.
Quinby and Binnie	August 19th. 1787 Joseph Quinby and Rebecca Hannah Binnie, widow, were married per Lic.
Miller and Trenholm.	October 2. 1787 James Miller and Mary Trenholm were married per License by the Rev'd Thomas Frost.
Wilson and Drayton.	October 10th. 1787 Daniel Wilson and Mary Drayton, Spinster, were married per License.
Revd. Thos. Frost and Downes	November 15th. 1787 The Rev. Thomas Frost[1] and Elizabeth Downes, Spinster, were married per License.
Thomas and Burrington	December 11. 1787 Edward Thomas and Elizabeth Burrington, Spinster, were married per License.

Marriages.

Marriages continued 236

Love and LLoyd.	December 20. 1787, John Love and Elizabeth LLoyd, Spinster, were married per Lic.
Loveday and Butler.	January 6. 1788 John Loveday and Sarah Butler, widow, were married per Lic.
Carr and Yeadon.	January 10. 1788, James Carr and Mary Yeadon were married per Lic.
Coward and Hayes.	January 24. 1788 Jeremiah Coward and Elizabeth Hayes were married per Lic.

[1]He was born in the County of Norfolk, England, in 1759; came to Charleston in 1786 and was elected Assistant Rector of St. Philip's, and rector upon the death of Bishop Smith in 1801; died July 18, 1804. (See Dalcho's *Protestant Episcopal Church in South Carolina.*)

Baas and Smith.	January 26. 1788, John Baas and Frances Rosalie Smith, widow, were married per Lic.
Thorne and Stocks	February 16. 1788, John Gardener Thorne and Sarah Stocks, were married per License by the Rev'd Thomas Frost.
Medforth and Boast	February 20. 1788 George Medforth and Sarah Boast, widow, were married per License by the Rev'd Thomas Frost.
Heyward and Manigault	February 27. 1788, Nathaniel Heyward[1] and Henrietta Manigault, spinster, were married per License.
Donovan and Cobia	March 6. 1788 Isaac Donovan and Mary Cobia, Spinster, were married per License.

Marriages.

Marriages continued 237

Bacot and Dessaussure	March 6. 1788 Thomas Wright Bacot[2] and Jane Dessaussure, spinster were ma ried per License.
Eayres and Ripley.	March 12. 1788 William Eayres, and Rebecca Ripley, spinster, were married per License.
Bell and O'Quin.	March 17. 1788 Elijah Bell and Elizabeth O'Quin, Spinster, were married per License.
Kelsey and Murrah.	March 25. 1788 William Kelsey and Eleanor Murrah, spinster, were married per License by the Revd. Thomas Frost.
Rout and Houston.	March 27. 1788, George Rout and Catharine Houston, Spinster, were married per Lic.

[1]He was a son of Col. Daniel Heyward and a half-brother of Thomas Heyward, Jr., a signer of the Declaration of Independence. He was an extensive planter and the largest slave holder in the state. See his portrait in *Charles Fraser*, by Alice R. and D. E. Huger Smith.

[2]He was appointed postmaster of Charleston by President Washington, in 1794, and served continuously as such until his death in 1834; succeeded by Alfred Huger.

Vale and Alexander.	John David Vale and Elizabeth Alexander, spinster, were married per Lic.
Meeks and Fittermus.	March. 31. 1788 Joseph Meeks and Mary Fittermus, were married per License, by the Rev'd Thomas Frost.
Cook and Forbes.	April 10. 1788 Thomas Cook and Hannah Forbes, widow, were married per License.
Pinckney and Laurens.	April 27. 1788 Charles Pinckney and Mary Eleanor Laurens, spinster, were married per Lic.
Mowbray and Darby	April 8. 1788 William Mowbray and Martha Darby, widow, were married per Lic. by the Rev'd Thomas Frost.

Marriages.

Marriages continued 238

Higgins and Lockens.	April 30. 1788 Seth Higgins and Isabella Lockens, spinster, were married per Lic. by the Rev'd Thomas Frost.
Harris and Donner.	May 29. 1788 John Harris and Margaret Donner, widow, were married, per Lic.
McComb Junr. and Stoll	June 10. 1788 James McComb Junr. and Mary Stoll, spinster, were married per Lic.
Sutcliffe and Gowdy.	June 12. 1788 John Sutcliffe and Elizabeth Gowdy, spinster, were married per Lic.
Glaspell and O'Hearne	June 16. 1788 Neal Glaspell and Elizabeth O'Hearne, spinster, were married per Lic.
Russell and Hopton	June 19. 1788 Nathaniel Russell[1] and Sarah Hopton, spinster, were married per Lic.

[1]He came to Charleston from Bristol, R. I., and had in Charleston a long and successful business career. He built the house on Meeting Street next south of the Scotch Presbyterian Churcn. The wrought-iron balcony thereof bears his initials—N. R.

Scott and Cattell.	July 3. 1788 David Scott and Sarah Cattell, spinster, were married per Lic.
Rayner and Slowman	July 18. 1788 David Rayner and Mary Slowman, spinster, were married per Lic.
Braly and Bramston.	July 20. 1788 Thomas Braly and Mary Bramston, widow, were married per Lic.
Parker and Rombert.	August 14. 1788 Joseph Parker and Florida Rombert spinster, were married per Lic.

Marriages

Marriages continued 239

Paggett and Folker.	August 21. 1788 Thomas Paggett and Peggy Folker, spinster, were married per License.
Whilden and Robinson	August 24. 1788 Joseph Whilden and Charlotte Robinson, Spinster, were married per Lic.
Mayer and Theus	August 27. 1788 John George Mayer and Charlotte Theus, Spinster, were married per Lic.
Oats and Middleton	September 8. 1788, Charles Oats and Mary Middleton, Spinster, were married by the Rev'd Thomas Frost.
Rutledge and Huger.	October 4. 1788 Hugh Rutledge[1] and Mary Huger were married per Lic.
Moles and Caveneau.	November 2. 1788 James Moles and Elizabeth Caveneau, spinster, were married per Lic.
Horry and Burnett.	November 5. 1788 Jonah Horry and Sarah Burnett, spinster, were married per License.
Lloyd and Trusler.	January 1. 1789 John Lloyd and Mary Trusler, spinster, were married per Lic. by the Rev'd. Thomas Frost.

[1]A brother of Governors John and Edward Rutledge and himself sometime Judge of the Admiralty of the state and one of the chancellors of the Court of Chancery. This was his third marriage.

Simons and Simons	January 6. 1789 Maurice Simons and Elizabeth Simons, Spinster, were married per Lic. by the Rev'd Thomas Frost.
Course and Prince.	January 14. 1789 Isaac Course and Ann Prince, spinster, were married per License.

Marriages

Marriages continued 240

Zahler and Cobia	January 15. 1789 Jacob Zahler and Ann Cobia, spinster, were married by License.
Dawson and Huger	February 10. 1789 John Dawson Junr. and Mary Huger, Spinster, were married per License.
Gillon and Purcell	Alexander Gillon[1] and Ann Purcell, Spinster were married per Lic.
Gregory and Hopton	February 23. 1789 James Gregory and Mary Christina Hopton, Spinster, were married per Lic. by the Rev'd Thomas Frost.
McQueen and Crawley	March 18. 1789 Robert McQueen and Eleanor Crawley, were married per License, by the Rev'd Thomas Frost.
Von Peterson and Brown	March 22. 1789 Lewis Von Peterson and Mary Anne Brown, were married per Lic. by the Rev'd Thomas Frost.
Cruger and Kirk	April 4. 1789 Charles Frederick Cruger and Martha Kirk, were married per Lic. by the Revd Thomas Frost.
Garrett and Davis	April 26. 1789 Richard Garrett and Mary Davis, widow, were married per Lic. by the Rev'd Thomas Frost.

[1]He was born in Rotterdam, August 13, 1741, and came to South Carolina in 1765. This was his second marriage. He died October 6, 1794, at his plantation, Gillon's Retreat, in Orangeburgh District, where he is buried. (See *The South Carolina Historical and Genealogical Magazine,* IX, 189-219; X, 92-115.

Oliver and McKay	May 2. 1789 James Brush Oliver and Sarah McKay, were married per Lic. by the Rev'd Thomas Frost.
Cumming and McCormick. (spinster)	June 24. 1789 Alexander Cumming and Lucy McCormick were married per Lic.

Marriages.

Chisolm and Maxwell.	July 6. 1789 Alexander Robert Chisolm and Sarah Glaze Maxwell were married per Lic. by the Rev'd William Smith. (on July 6. 1789)
Hanly and Duggan.	August 2. 1789 John Hanly and Margaret Duggan, widow, were married per Lic. by the Rev'd Thomas Frost.
Swindershore and Bowler	August 6. 1789 Andrew Swindershore and Sarah Bowler, widow, were married per Lic. by the Rev'd Thomas Frost.
Prince and Dearle	August 9. 1789 Charles Prince and Sarah Dearle were married per License by the Rev'd Thomas Frost.
Barnett and Smith	August 20. 1789 William Barnett and Catharine Smith were married per Lic. by the Rev'd William Smith.
McAlister and Keith.	August 23. 1789 John McAlister and Ann Keith were married per Lic. by the Rev'd Thomas Frost.
Bowen and Robinson	September 2. 1789 John Bowen and Mary Robinson were married per Lic. by the Rev'd William Smith.
Ditcham and McPherson	September 7. 1789 George Ditcham and Ann McPherson were married per Lic. by the Rev'd Thomas Frost.
Dobbins and Pots.	John Dobbins and Ann Pots were married per License, by the Rev'd Thomas Frost.
Monk and Weston	September 13. 1789. James Monk and Margaret Elizabeth Weston were married per Lic. by the Rev'd Thomas Frost.

Marriages continued 242

Butterton and Tousiger	November 3. 1789 Joseph Butterton and Elizabeth Margaret Tousiger were married per Lic. by the Rev'd Thomas Frost.
Neufville and Simons	December 1. 1789 William Neufville and Ann Simons, widow, were married per Lic. by the Rev'd Thomas Frost.
Nicolls and Yarnold.	December 2. 1789. Thomas Nicolls and Sarah Yarnold were married per Lic. by the Rev'd Thomas Frost.
Harleston and Pinckney.	December 9th. 1789. William Harleston and Elizabeth Pinckney were married per Lic. by the Rev'd Thomas Frost.
Jones and Farquhar.	January 28. 1790. Alexander Jones and Mary Farquhar, spinster, were married per Lic. by the Rev'd Thomas Frost.
Granville and Forbes.	March 14. 1790 James Granville and Elizabeth Forbes, spinster, were married per Lic.
Hort and Simons	March 23. 1790. William Hort and Catharine Simons, spinster, were married per Lic.
Quin and Fitzgerald.	April 5. 1790. James Quin and Mary Fitzgerald, were married
Frogatt and Wood.	April 11. 1790. Addin Frogatt and Ann Wood Spinster, were married per Lic.
Findley and Jerry.	May 22. 1790. Henry Findley and Martha Jerry, spinster, were married per Lic.
Harrison and Gladdin.	June 17. 1790. Isaac Harrison and Hannah Gladdin, widow, were married per Lic. by the Rev'd William Smith.

Marriages.

Marriages Continued 243

Forest and Clancy.	June 26. 1790. Michael Forest and Joanna Clancy widow, were married per Lic.

Mayers and Jonson. — August 15. 1790. Thomas Mayers and Elizabeth Jonson, spinster, were married per Lic. by the Rev'd Thomas Frost.

Bessileu and Young — August 19. 1790. Lewis Bessileu and Elizabeth Young, Spinster, were married per Lic. by the Rev'd Thomas Frost.

Snyder and Harvey. — October 2. 1790. Paul Snyder and Ann Harvey, Spinster, were married per Lic.

Gadelius and Banister. — October 4. 1790. Sven Gadelius and Abbey Everott Banister, Spinster, were married per Lic.

Moultrie and Moultrie — October 4. 1790. James Moultrie and Catharine Moultrie, Spinster, were married per Lic.

Gibbes and Ball — October 20. 1790. Benjamin Gibbes and Elizabeth Ball, Spinster, were married per Lic. by the Rev'd Thomas Frost.

Morris and Singletary. — October 28. 1790. George Morris and Martha Singletary, spinster, were married by Lic.

Quinby and Darby. — January 13. 1791. Henry Quinby and Mary Darby, Spinster, were married per Lic. by the Rev'd Thomas Frost.

Allston and Motte. — February 24. 1791. William Allston and Mary Motte, Spinster, were married per Lic.

DeBow and Darby. — March 10. 1791, John DeBow and Ann Darby, Spinster, were married per Lic.

Calwel and Rivers. — March 11. 1791. Henry Calwel Senr. and Sarah Rivers Spinster, were married per Lic. by the Rev'd Thomas Frost.

Marriages.

Rust and Honour. — March 27. 1791. Thomas Rust and Susannah Honour were married per Lic. by the Rev'd Thomas Frost.

Lees and Granttin.	April 14. 1791. Robert Lees and Kitty Ecklin Granttin, Spinster, were married per Lic.
Sims and Duncan.	April 18. 1791. Patrick Sims and Catharine Duncan were married per Lic. by the Rev'd. Thomas Frost.
Thackam and Gready	May 1. 1791. Thomas Thackam and Judith Gready, widow, were married per Lic. by the Rev'd Thomas Frost.
Ham and Ralph.	June 1791. Thomas Ham and Margaret Addison Ralph, Spinster, were married per Lic. by the Rev'd Thomas Frost.
Neilson and Barthe	July 10. 1791 Francis Neilson and Elizabeth Barthe, widow, were married per Lic. by the Rev'd Thomas Frost.
Welsh and Cotton	July 15. 1791. John Lewis Welsh and Maria Cotton, widow, were married per Lic. by the Rev'd Thomas Frost.
Grainger and Eckall.	August 20. 1791 James Grainger and Eleanor Ekall, were married per Lic.
Gibbes and Dunbar.	August 30. 1791 Henry Gibbes and Mary Dunbar, widow, were married per Lic. by the Rev'd Thomas Frost.
Hales and Johnson.	September 6. 1791. Daniel Hales and Sarah Johnson, Spinster, were married per Lic. by the Rev'd Thomas Frost.
Smith and Clifford.	September 15. 1791 John Press Smith and Elizabeth Clifford, widow, were married per lic.

Marriages

Marriages continued 245

Rivers and Pitt.	October 5. 1791. James Rivers and Frances Pitt, widow, were married per Lic. by the Rev'd Thomas Frost.
Murphy and Starnes	October 7. 1791 Roger Murphy and Minta Starnes, widow, were married per Lic. by the Rev'd Thomas Frost.

Parker and Drayton.	October 25. 1791. Thomas Parker[1] and Mary Drayton, Spinster, were married per Lic.
Duval and Addison	November 3. 1791. John Duval and Martha Addison, Spinster, were married per Lic.
Garden and Lesesne	November 3. 1791. Alexander Garden and Sarah Lesesne, Spinster, were married per Lic.
Johnson and Webb	November 9. 1791. William Johnson and Mary Webb, Spinster, were married per Lic.
Steel and Chovin.	November 17. 1791. Peter Steel and Sarah Chovin, widow, were married per Lic.
McCarthy and Collins.	November 24. 1791. Garman McCarthy and Jane Collins, widow, were married per Lic.
Gaillard And Lord.	November 24. 1791. John Gaillard and Harriott Lord, Spinster, were married per Lic. by the Rev'd Thomas Frost.
Rutledge and Smith.	December 26. 1791 John Rutledge Junr. and Sarah Motte Smith, were married per Lic. by the Rev'd Thomas Frost.

Marriages.

Marriages continued. 246

Pepoon and Nott.	January 5. 1792 Benjamin Pepoon and Lucy Nott, were married per Lic.
Graeser and Clements	January 7. 1792. Conrad Jacob Graeser and Ann Maria Clements, Spinster, were married per Lic.

[1]He was a son of John and Mary (Daniell) Parker, and was born November 8, 1760. He was appointed U. S. District Attorney, by President Washington, in 1792, and served as such for twenty-eight years. He died August 25, 1820. His wife was a daughter of William Henry Drayton, a leader of the Revolution.

Meeks and McNabb	January 20. 1792. Joseph Meeks and Jane McNabb, Spinster, were married per Lic. by the Rev'd Thomas Frost.
Jackson and Minott	January 21. 1792. John Jackson and Martha Crofts Minott, Spinster, were married per Lic. by the Rev'd Thomas Frost.
Fairchild and Noble	Morris Fairchild and Kate Noble were married per Lic. by the Rev'd Thomas Frost.
Collins and Taylor	Manasseh Collins and Ann Taylor, widow, were married per Lic. by the Rev'd Thomas Frost.
Kershaw and Breton.	March 24. 1792 Charles Kershaw and Mary Eyre Breton, were married per Lic.
Pagett and Gibson	April 5. 1792. Thomas Pagett and Eliza Gibson, Spinster, were married per Lic.
Alexander and White	April 10. 1792, David Alexander and Mary White, spinster, were married per Lic.
Morris and Murphy.	April 17. 1792. James Morris and Martha Murphy were married per Lic. by the Rev'd Thomas Frost.
Heriot and Thomas.	Mar. 21. 1792. William Heriot and Mary Thomas Spinster, were married per Lic.

Marriages.

Laurens and Rutledge	May 26. 1792. Henry Laurens Junr. and Eliza Rutledge, spinster, were married per Lic.
Wish and Singletary.	June. 14. 1792. John Wish and Catharine Singletary, Spinster, were married per Lic.
Speisseger Jr. and Ladson.	July 8. 1792. John Speisseger Junr and Sarah Phoebe Ladson, Spinster, were married per Lic.
Williams and Lemming	July 12. 1792. Charles Williams and Rachel Lemming were married per Lic.

Bradford and Woodruffe	July 12. 1792. Charles Bradford and Mary Woodruffe were married per Lic. by the Rev'd Thomas Frost.
Singletary and Pedrio	August 2. 1792. James Singletary and Lydia Ann Pedrio, spinster were married per Lic. by the Rev'd Thomas Frost.
Purcell and Bonsall.	September 20. 1792. Joseph Purcell and Ann Bonsall, widow, were married per Lic.
Toole and Jones.	September 25. 1792. John Toole and Susannah Jones, spinster, were married per Lic. by the Rev'd Thomas Gates.
Dashiell and Howeth.	September 30. 1792. Charles Dashiell and Esther Howeth were married.
Porcher and Mazyck.	October 25. 1792. Thomas Porcher and Charlotte Mazyck, Spinster, were married per Lic.

Marriages.

Marriages continued. 248

Kirkedge and Eveleigh	October 28. 1792 Edward Kirkedge and Mary Eveleigh, widow, were married per Lic.
Gaillard and Doughty.	November 1. 1792 Theodore Gaillard Junr. and Martha Doughty, Spinster, were married per Lic. by the Rev'd Thomas Frost.
Pinckney and Shubrick	November 8. 1792. Roger Pinckney and Susannah Shubrick, Spinster, were married per Lic.
Gates and Postell.	November 1792. The Rev'd Thomas Gates and Elizabeth Postell, were married per Lic.
Pritchard and Hamilton	November 1792. William Pritchard and Elizabeth Hamilton, Spinster, were married per Lic. by the Rev'd Thomas Frost.
Calhoun and Cattell.	November 21. 1792. William Calhoun and Lydia Cattell, Spinster, were married per Lic.

Gaillaird and Loyd.	November 22. 1792. John Gaillaird and Mary Loyd[1] Spinster, were married per Lic.
O'Kane and Seagrove	December 4. 1792. Henry O'Kane and Margaret Seagrove, widow, were married per Lic.
Brown and Eyre.	December 25. 1792. Squire Brown and Maria Eyre were married per Lic. by the Rev'd Thomas Frost.
Winn and Gissendanner.	December 26. 1792. Thomas Winn and Mary Ann Gissendanner, were married per Lic. by the Rev'd Thomas Frost.

Marriages.

Marriages continued. 249

Slatter and Mordah.	December 27. 1792. John Slatter and Frances Mordah, Spinster, were married, per Lic.
Prince and Morgan.	December 21. 1792. Clement Prince and Mary Morgan were married per Lic. by the Rev'd Thomas Frost.

McKee and Rivers.	January 1. 1793. John McKee and Harriott Rivers were married per Lic. by the Rev'd Thomas Frost.
Flagg and McCleish	January 3. 1793. Samuel Hawk Flagg and Elizabeth McCleish were married per Lic. by the Rev'd Thomas Frost.
Anderson and June.	January 10. 1793. John Anderson and Rebecca June, widow, were married per Lic.
Grainger and Eyre.	January 13. 1793. James Grainger and Ann Eyre were married per Lic.

[1]Lord. John Gaillard was subsequently United States Senator from December 6, 1804, to his death, February 26, 1826—21 years, 2 months and 20 days. Only one South Carolina senator has served longer—B. R. Tillman, 23 years, 4 months.

Hunter and Wiatt	January 26. 1793 Thomas Hunter and Mary Lingard Wiatt, Spinster, were married per Lic.
Snelling and Phipps.	February 19. 1793. John Snelling and Elizabeth Fitzgerald Phipps, were married per Lic. by the Rev'd Thomas Frost.
Mason and Timothy	March 24. 1793 William Mason and Sarah Timothy, Spinster, were married per Lic.
Schepelere and Clement.	April 18. 1793. George Schepelere and Sarah Clarke Clement, spinster, were married per Lic.

Marriages.

Weyman and Turpin	May 6. 1793. Edward Weyman and Catharine Turpin, Spinster, were married per Lic.
Hill and Finlayson	May 19 1793. Charles Hill and Charlotte Finlayson, Spinster were married, per Lic.
Spurr and Crawford	May 30. 1793. Benjamin Spurr and Sarah Crawford, Spinster, were married per Lic.
Greenland and Hamilton.	June 2. 1793. Walter Mondet Greenland and Ann David Hamilton, Spinster, were married per Lic.
Hunter and Kennedy.	June 27. 1793 William Hunter and Mary Kennedy, Spinster, were married per Lic.
Peck and Pierson.	July 3. 1793. Daniel Peck and Mary Pierson, widow, were married per Lic.
McDougall and Morgan.	July 14. 1793. Duncan McDougall and Mary Morgan, Spinster, were married per Lic.
Quinby and Buluck	July 20. 1793 Henry Quinby and Elizabeth Buluck, Spinster, were married per Lic.
Story and Pierfore	August 28. 1793. Abril R. Story and Mary Pierfore, widow, were married per Lic.

Simons and Wilson.	September 29. 1793. Keating Simons and Eleanor Wilson, widow, were married per Lic.

Marriages.

Marriages continued. 251

Beckman and Lee.	October 11. 1793. Samuel Beckman and Ann Lee, Spinster, were married per Lic.
Pressman and Cattell	November 4. 1793. William Pressman and Ann Ferguson Cattell, spinster, were married per Lic.
Gourdin and Doughty.	November 7. 1793 Samuel Gourdin and Mary Doughty, Spinster, were married per Lic.
Roberts and Johnson.	November 9. 1793. John Roberts and Ann Johnson were married per Lic.
Dwight and Moore.	November 20. 1793. Samuel Dwight and Elizabeth Moore were married per Lic.
Tucker and Buchanan.	November 28. 1793 Daniel Tucker and Mary Elizabeth Buchanan, were married per Lic.
Perry and Drayton.	December 10. 1793. Edward Perry Junr. and Ann Drayton, Spinster, were married per Lic.
Vicyra and Florentine	December 22. 1793. Joseph Vicyra and Ann Florentine, widow, were married per Lic.

Cutler and Hyrne	January 9. 1794. Benjamin Clarke Cutler and Sarah Hyrne, widow, were married per Lic. by the Rev'd Thomas Frost.
Neyle and Villepontoux.	January 11. 1794. William Neyle and Hariett Villepontoux, spinster, were married per Lic. by the Rev'd Thomas Frost.

Marriages.

Marriages continued. 252

Rutledge and Harleston	January 14. 1794. Edward Rutledge and Jane Smith Harleston, were married per Lic.

Ummensetter and Snider, February 1. 1794. Gabriel Ummensetter and Jane Snider, widow, were married per Lic. by the Rev'd Thomas Frost.

Burrows and Torey February 2. 1794 Frederick Burrows and Mary Torey, widow, were married per Lic. by the Rev'd Thomas Frost.

Smith and Rambert February 4. 1794. Henry Smith and Mary Rambert, spinster, were married per Lic.

Marshall and Chanler. February 19. 1794. Thomas Marshall and Mary Susanna Chanler, Spinster, were married per Lic. by the Rev'd Thomas Frost.

Whitaker and Sinkeler February 26. 1794 Samuel Whitaker and Hannah Sinkeler, widow, were married per Lic. by the Rev'd Thomas Frost.

Purcell and Blake. March 1. 1794 Henry Purcell and Sarah Blake, Spinster, were married per Lic.

Harleston and Quash March 13. 1794. William Harleston and Sarah Quash, Spinster, were married per Lic. by the Rev'd Thomas Frost.

Greene and Flagg July 25. 1794. Ray Greene and Mary Magdeline Flagg, Spinster, were married per Lic.

Young and Haig April 4. 1794 Thomas Young and Eliza Maria Haig, Spinster, were married per Lic. by the Rev'd Thomas Frost.

Marriages.

Kay and Moore June 10. 1794. Joseph Kay and Jane Moore, widow, were married per Lic. by the Rev'd Thomas Frost.

Havey and Henry. June 13. 1794. Dennis Havey and Mary Henry, widow, were married per Lic. by the Rev'd Thomas Frost.

Jarmin and Wilkinson. August 7. 1794, John Jarman and Jane Wilkinson, widow, were married per Lic. by the Rev'd Thomas Frost.

Bunness and Jaudon	September 9. 1794. James Bunness and Sarah Jaudon, Spinster, were married per Lic. by the Rev'd Thomas Frost.
Bruce and Smith.	October 2. 1794, Daniel Bruce and Susanna Smith, Spinster, were married per Lic.
Smith and Camrow.	October 2. 1794, John Smith and Elizabeth Camrow, Spinster, Were married per Lic.
Bryant and Thornton	October 8. 1794, John Bryant and Jane Thornton, Spinster, were married per License by the Rev'd Thomas Frost.
Brindlay and Pope.	October 21. 1794, John George Brindlay and Sarah Pope, widow, were married by License.
Drayton and Tidyman.	November 6. 1794. John Drayton[1] and Hester Rose Tidyman, spinster, were married per Lic.
Grierson and Wasson.	November 8. 1794, James Grierson and Elizabeth Wasson, spinster, were married per Lic.

Marriages

Marriages continued. 254

DeHon and Rice	November 9. 1794, Peter DeHon and Grace Rice, widow, were married per Lic. by the Rev'd Thomas Frost.
Chichester and Powell.	November 11. 1794, John Chichester and Mary Beatrix Powell, spinster, were married per Lic.
Todenhaver and Canton	December 4. 1794. Lewis Todenhaver and Christiana Canton, widow, were married per Lic. by the Rev'd Thomas Frost.
Self and Lefoy.	December 6. 1794, Samuel Coffin Self and Mary Lefoy, widow were married per Lic. by the Rev'd Thomas Frost.

[1]He was a son of William Henry Drayton whose *Memoirs of the Revolution* he edited. He was born at Drayton Hall plantation, June 22, 1766, and died November 22, 1822; was Lieutenant Governor, 1798-1800, Governor, 1800-1802, 1808-1810; U. S. District Judge, 1812-1822.

Clarkson and Harris,	December 30. 1794, William Clarkson and Elizabeth Anderson Harris, spinster, were married per Lic. by the Rev'd Thomas Frost.

Brown and Floyd.	January 13. 1795. Ross Brown and Elizabeth Floyd, widow, were married by the Rev'd Thomas Frost.
Courty and McKenzie.	February 6. 1795. Jacques Courty and Mary McKenzie, spinster, were married per Lic. by the Rev'd Thomas Frost.
Terence and Yeulin.	February 14. 1795. Robert Terence and Sarah Yeulin, spinster, were married per Lic. by the Rev'd Thomas Frost.
Bowls and Drayton.	March 10. 1795, Tobias Bowls and Susannah Drayton, spinster, were married per Lic.
Gill and Pearce.	March 11. 1795, John Gill and Rebecca Pearce, widow, were married per Lic.

Marriages.

Marriages continued. 255

Kirkland and Guerard.	March 12. 1795. Joseph Kirkland and Maryanne Guerard, widow, were married per Lic.
Corbett and Harleston.	May 21. 1795. Thomas Corbett and Elizabeth Harleston, spinster, were married Per Lic.
White and Walter.	May 21. 1795. Christopher Gadsden White and Martha Walter, spinster, were married per Lic.
Harvey and Greenland	May 21. 1795. Samuel Harvey and Ann Greenland, widow, were married per Lic. by the Rev'd Thomas Frost.
Rhodes and Grant	May 26. 1795. Thomas Rhodes and Sarah Grant, widow, were married per Lic. by the Rev'd Thomas Frost.
Izard and Middleton	June 1. 1795 Henry Izard and Emma Philadelphia Middleton, spinster were married per Lic. by the Rev'd Thomas Frost.

Rhodes and Wright	July 10. 1795. Thomas Rhodes and Mary Wright Spinster, were married per Lic. by the Rev. Thomas Frost.
Browne and Cole.	July 12. 1795. William Browne and Margaret Cole, spinster, were married per Lic. by the Rev'd Thomas Frost.
Reynolds and Myers.	July 14. 1795. James Reynolds and Elizabeth Myers, Spinster, were married per Lic. by the Rev'd Thomas Frost.
George and Hamilton.	September 17. 1795, James George and Elizabeth Hamilton, widow, were married per Lic. by the Rev'd Thomas Frost.

Marriages.

Marriages continued. 256

Frink and Kirk	September 20. 1795. Thomas Frink and Rebecca Eliza Kirk, spinster were married per Lic. by the Rev'd Thomas Frost.
Derby and Trimble	September 27. 1795, John Derby and Arabella Trimble, spinster, were married per Lic. by the Rev'd Thomas Frost.
Greene and Hansor.	December 24. 1795. Russell Greene and Ann Hansor, widow, were married per Lic. by the Rev'd Thomas Frost.
Ditmore and Holmes	December 24. 1795. Henry Ditmore and Abigail Holmes, spinster, were married per Lic. by the Rev'd Thomas Frost.
Gissendanner and Bessileau.	December 31. 1795. John Gissendanner and Susannah Bessileau, spinster, were married per Lic. by the Rev'd Thomas Frost.
Bell and Lenneau.	December 31. 1795 David Bell and Sarah Lenneau, Spinster, were married per Lic. by the Rev'd Thomas Frost.
Giles and Cameron	December 31. 1795, Robert Giles and Matilda Cameron, widow, were married per Lic. by the Rev'd Thomas Frost.
Ehrick and Wightman.	January 6. 1796. John Mathias Ehrick and Peggy Africana Wightman, spinster, were married per Lic. by the Rev'd Thomas Frost.

Newton and Morton

February 8. 1796. William Newton and Mary Morton, widow, were married per Lic.

Darrell and White.

February 16 1796 Edward Darrell and Sarah White, Spinster, were married per Lic.

Marriages.

Walter and Whilder

February 21. 1796. Bayfield Walter and Charlotte Whilder, widow, were married per Lic. by the Rev'd Thomas Frost.

Smith and Downes

March 1. 1796, Roger Moore Smith and Ann Downes, Spinster, were married per Lic.

Garden and Cochran,

March 9. 1796 Alexander Garden and Harriett Hockley Cochran, Spinster, were married per Lic.

Irving and Corbett

April 19. 1796. Jacob Emelius Irving and Hannah Margaret Corbett, spinster, were married per Lic.

Fall and Welsh.

April 20. 1796. John Fall and Margaret Welsh, spinster, were married per Lic.

Glenn and Bocquet

April 21. 1796. John Glenn and Mary Bocquet, spinster, were married.

Greenwood and Lord.

April 28. 1796. William Greenwood and Ann Lord, widow, were married per Lic.

Barns and Gowens.

May 1. 1796. Henry Barns and Massy Gowens, a black woman, were married.

Nowell and Chalmers.

May 2. 1796. Edward Broun Nowell and Margaret Chalmers, spinster, were married per Lic.

Webb and Pinckney.

September 15. 1796 Benjamin Webb and Rebecca Pinckney, Spinster, were married per Lic.

Marriages.

Marriages continued. 258

Roux and Buckle.	September 15. 1796 Lewis Roux and Ann Buckle, widow, were married per Lic.
Simons and Lowndes	November 15 1796, Francis Simons and Ruth Lowndes, Spinster, were married per Lic.
White and Purcell.	November 15. 1796. John White and Jane Pogson Purcell, spinster, were married per Lic.
Edwards and Wakefield	December 8. 1796 Edward Edwards and Mary Wakefield, Spinster, were married per Lic.

Hickey and Lestargette.	February 25. 1797. James Hickey and Charlotte Lestargette, spinster, were married per Lic.
Cordes and Jamieson	May 3. 1797 Thomas Cordes Junr. and Rebecca Jamieson, spinster, were married per Lic.
Murray and Frigay.	July 20. 1797 Daniel Murray and Elizabeth Frigay, spinster, were married per Lic.
Darby and Evans	August 17. 1797 William Darby and Margaret Evans, spinster, were married per Lic.
Rutledge and Cosslet.	September 12. 1797 William Rutledge and Ann Cosslet, Spinster, were married.
Rutledge and Horry	October 11. 1797, Frederick Rutledge and Harriott Pinckney Horry, spinster, were married per Lic.

Marriages.

Marriages continued. 259

Pinckney and Middleton	October 19. 1797 Thomas Pinckney and Frances Middleton, widow, were married per Lic.
Bull and St. John	November 2. 1797. John Bull and Elizabeth St. John, spinster, were married per Lic.

Nowell and Lord.	November 28. 1797. John Nowell and Mary Lord, spinster, were married per Lic.
Johnston and Pinckney.	December 5. 1797, William Johnston and Anna Maria Pinckney, spinster, were married per Lic.
Read and Young.	December 7. 1797. James Bond Read and Louisa Young, spinster, were married.
Kershaw and Ramage.	December 24. 1797 Charles Kershaw and Frances Ramage, spinster, were married.
Lowndes and I'on.	March 8. 1798, Thomas Lowndes and Sarah Bond I'on, spinster, were married per Lic.
Shepheard and Perry	April 10. 1798. Thomas Radcliffe Shepheard and Sophia Frances Perry, spinster, were married per Lic.
Logan and Webb.	April 26. 1798. William Logan Junr. and Mary Doughty Webb, spinster, were married per Lic.
McCay and Bacot.	May 9. 1798. Joseph Ringland McCay and Frances Bacot were married

Marriages.

Marriages continued. 260

Noble and Markley.	September 2. 1798 Ezekiel Noble and Mary Markley, spinster, were married per Lic.
Deas and Izard	November 2. 1798. William Allen Deas and Ann Izard, were married per Lic.
Lord and Lord.	December 27. 1798. Richard Lord and Maria Lord, Spinster, were married per Lic.

Helldrup and Larry	April 6. 1799. Thomas Goseelin Helldrup and Susannah Eliza Larry, Spinster, were married per Lic.

Matthews and Rutledge.	May 5. 1799. John Matthews[1] and Sarah Rutledge, spinster, were married.
Macracken and McGee	July 28. 1799 Arthur Macracken and Ann McGee, widow, were married.
Bynum and Miller.	August 13. 1799 Turner Bynum and Eliza Miller, spinster, were married per Lic.
Miles and Rose.	November 3. 1799 William Miles and Mary Ann Blake Rose, Spinster, were married per lic.
Roulain and Givingston	November 7. 1799. Robert Roulain and Hannah Givingston, spinster, were married per Lic.
Bonnetheau and Petsh,	November 26. 1799, Gabriel Manigault Bonnetheau and Anna Maria Petsh, spinster, were married per Lic.

Marriages.

Marriages Continued. 261

Ball and Gough	February 20 1800. Archibald Scott Ball and Mary Gough, Spinster, were married per Lic.
Serisier and Smith	October 24 1800 Louis Arvengas Serisier and Sarah Smith, widow, were married by the Rev'd R. Smith.
Jackson and Chalbo	November 11 1800 Josiah Jackson and Maryan Chalbo, Spinster, were married.
Wilson and Latham	November 20 1800 Robert Wilson and Charity Latham Spinster, were married per Lic.
Aspray and Nelson	December 9 1800 John Faledo Aspray and Jane Nelson, widow. were married.
Ravenel and Mazyck	December 11 1800 Stephen Ravenel and Catharine Mazyck, spinster, were married per Lic.

[1]Mathews was the way he spelled his name. His father and the other members of the family, which was a prominent one, spelled the name Mathewes. See "Gibbes Family of South Carolina", in *The South Carolina Historical and Genealogical Magazine*, XII, 83; *The House of Plant*. He was governor of South Carolina, 1782-1783.

Simons and Harris	December 30 1800 James Simons and Sarah Tucker Harris, spinster, were married per Lic.
Wragg and I'on	February 19 1801 Samuel Wragg and Mary Ashby I'on, spinster, were married per Lic.
Smylie and Bruce	October 8 1801 Andrew Smylie and Susanna Bruce, widow, were married per Licence.

Marriages.

Marriages 262

Boaund and Gibson	April 27. 1796 Samuel Boaund, of Charleston, Factor, and Mary Gibson, of the same place, spinster, were married.
Veronee and Byrd.	May 20 " William Veronee, of Charleston, Gentleman, and Elizabeth Byrd, of the same place, spinster, were married per Lic.
Beard and Higgins	July 17 " Robert Beard, of Charleston, Tin plate worker, and Elizabeth Higgins, of the same place, widow, were married per Lic.
Smith and McCredy	Sept. 29. " William Smith, of Charleston, Merchant, and Catharine McCredy, of the same place, were married by Lic.
Jones and Jamieson.	Decr. 28. " Edward Jones, of Charleston, phsician, and Ann Janieson, of the same place, spinster, were married.
Henry and Flemming.	Jany 5. 1797. Alexander Henry, of Charleston, Merchant, and Elizabeth Flemming, of the same place, spinster, were married.
Manson and Milligan	" 28. " George Manson, of Charleston, ship Carpenter, and Sarah Milligan, widow, were married per Lic.
McCready, and Johnson	March 2. " John McCready, of Charleston, Attorney at Law, and Jane Johnson, of the same place, spinster, were married.

Pritchard and Geyer	" 12. " Paul Pritchard, of Charleston, Ship-wright, and Mary Geyer, of the same place, spinster, were married per Lic.
Greer and Farquhar.	" 17. " James Carey Greer, of Charleston, Merchant, and Margaret Manson Farquhar, spinster, were married per Lic.

Marriages.

Frazer and Eairr,	April 6 1797. John Milligan Frazer, of Charleston, House carpenter and Rebecca Eairr, of the same place, widow, were married per Lic.
Roberts and Philips.	" 17. " William John Roberts, Mariner, and Sarah Philips, widow, were married.
Meylly and Black.	" 20. " John Meylly, of Charleston, Constable, and Ann Black, of the same place, widow, were married.
Gillibeau and More	" 22. " James Gillibeau, of Charleston, Taylor, and Elizabeth More, of the same place, spinster, were married.
Wish and Johnston	" 24. " William Wish, of Charleston, Merchant, and Anna Johnston, of the same place, Spinster, were married per Lic.
Sitton and Davis.	" 26 " Philip Sitton, of Charleston, Mariner, and Elizabeth Davis, of the same place, spinster, were married per Lic.
Nichols and Rivell	May 27. " George Nichols, of Charleston, Grocer, and Margaret Rivell, of the same place, spinster, were married per Lic.
Corker and Glew.	" 31. " Thomas Corker, of Charleston, ship wright, and Elizabeth Glew, of the same place, spinster, were married per Lic.

Heyward and Villepontoux	June 1. " William Heyward, of Prince Winyaw parish, plantation,[1] and Charlotte Manby Villepontoux, of Charleston, spinster, were married per Lic.
Sparks and Kimmelgo	August 23. " Thomas Sparks, of Charleston, Harness Maker, and Rachel Kimmelgo, of the same place, widow, were married per Lic.

Marriages.

Baudrop and Benson.	October 1. 1797 Joseph Baudrop, of Charleston, Gentleman, and Matilda Benson, of the same place, spinster, were married.
Hickbo and McCleith	" 13. " Isaac Barre Hickbo, of Charleston, Mariner, and Catharine McClieth, of the same place, Spinster, were married per Lic.
Bonneau and Legare	December 7 " Francis Bonneau, of Charleston, House Carpenter and Eleanor Sarah Legare, of the same place, widow, were married per Lic.
Griffith and Wyatt,	" 10. " Thomas Jones Griffith, of Charleston, Gentleman, and Elizabeth Brewer Wyatt, of the same place, spinster, were married per Lic.
Stoll and Douglas,	" 30. " Justinus Stoll, of Charleston, Brick-layer, and Elizabeth Douglas, Spinster, were married per Lic.
Bougler and Soverince	January 4. 1798 John Edward Boulger, of Charleston, Gentleman, and Ann Elizabeth Soverince, of Christ Church, spinster, were married by Lic.
Footman and Turpin	" 10. " John Waggaman Footman, of Charleston, Gentleman, and Mary Turpin, of the Same place, spinster, were married by Lic.

[1]An evident attempt to write "of Prince William's Parish, planter."

Yates and Hall — February 5. " William Yates, of Charleston, Innkeeper, and Ann Hall, of the same place, Spinster, were married by Lic.

Wyatt and Wood — " . 6. " Lemuel Wyatt, of Charleston, Baker, and Elizabeth Wood, of the same place, widow, were married by Lic.

McGrath and Kennedy. — " 8 " James McGrath, of Charleston, Mariner, and Jane Kennedy, of the same place, widow, were married by Lic.

Marriages.

Bee and Ward — March 16. 1798 Peter Smith Bee of Charleston, Gentleman, and Frances Ward, of the same place, spinster, were married per Lic.

Logan and Creighton — " 22. " George Logan, of Charleston, Carpenter, and Lydia Creighton, of the same place, spinster, were married by Lic.

Doane and Finlayson. — " 28. " Joseph Doane, of Charleston, Mariner, and Mary Finlayson, of the same place, spinster, were married by Lic.

Mongin and Rivers — April 15. " Daniel William Mongin of St. Luke's Parish, Planter, and Shepaliah Rivers, of Charleston, Spinster, were married by Lic.

Taylor And Grissel — May 15. " Capt. Alexander Taylor, of Charleston, Mariner, and Sarah Grissel, of the same place. widow, were married by Lic.

Culliatt and Treaggy — " 17. " James Culliatt, of Charleston, Coachmaker, and Jane Treaggy, of the same place, spinster, were married by Lic.

Holmes and Simons. — June 6 " Jack Holmes, of Charleston, Gentleman, and Mary Esther Simons, of the. same place, Spinster, were married by Lic.

Galloway and Gleeason — " 27. " Alfred Galloway, of Charleston, Pilot, and Elizabeth Gleason, of same place, widow, were married by Lic.

Sunborn and Thomas. October 9 ” Ebenezer Sunborn, of Charleston, mariner, and Ann Thomas, of the same place, widow, were married by Lic.

Mathews And Wells November. 17. ” Edmund Mathews, of Edisto, Clergyman, and Miss Mary Winborn Wells, of Charleston, spinster, were married.

Halliday and Halliday December 12. 1798 Hugh Halliday, of Charleston, Grocer, and Eleanor Halliday of the same place, widow, were married by Lic.

Beale and Bagnall ” 29 ” Joseph Beale, of Charleston, Merchant, and Mary Bagnell, of the same place, widow, were married by Lic.

Waterry, and Lequet. February 3. 1799. Francis Waterry, Lieut. of the British Navy, and Caroline Lequet, of Charleston, spinster, were married by Lic.

Burk and Salter ” 12. ” Capt. Walter Burk, of Philadelphia, Mariner, and Elizabeth Salter, of Charleston, spinster, were married by Lic.

Racine and Harris. ” 22. ” Thomas Racine, of Charleston, storekeeper, and Mary Harris, of the same place, spinster, were married by Lic.

Spedle and Askew. May 7. ” John George Spedle, of Charleston, House carpenter, and Caroline Ann Askew, of the same place, Spinster, were married by Lic.

Richey and Birkett ” ” ” Louisa Birkett, of Doopland County, East river, North Carolina, and John Richey, of Charleston, Artillerist, were married.

Cordier, and Stonestreet. ” 18 ” Peter Cordier, of Charleston, Merchant, and Julia Felicity Stonestreet, of the same place, Spinster, were married by Lic.

Smith and Ladson, " 22. " John Rutledge Smith, of Charleston, Gentleman, and Susanna Elizabeth Ladson, of the same place. Spinster, were married.

Gruber, and Finley. June 23. " Samuel Gruber, of Charleston, House Carpenter, and Elizabeth Finley, of the Same place, Spinster, were married by Lic.

Marriages.

Dolliver and Hazard. July 14. 1799. Capt. Henry Dolliver, of Charleston, Mariner, and Margaret Hazard, of the same place, widow, were married by Lic.

Taylor and Hamilton, " 25. " Capt. Joseph Taylor, of Charleston, Mariner, and Serezel Agnes Hamilton, of the same place, Spinster, were married by Lic.

Haslett and Wilson, August 2. " John Haslett, of Charleston, Painter, and Mary Wilson, of the same place, spinster, were married by Lic.

Handy, and Gilchrist " 6 " Thomas Handy, of Charleston, Rigger, and Dorothy Gilchrist, of the same place. widow, were married.

Smith and Norris, September 2 " John Smith, of Charleston, upholster, and Elizabeth Norris, of the same place, widow, were married by Lic.

Mitchell and How " " " James Mitchell, of Charleston, Gentleman, and Ann How, of the same place, spinster, were married.

Reid and Brindley October 11. " John Reid, of Charleston, Tin plate worker, and Mary Brindley, of the same place, widow, were married by Lic.

Rutledge and Middleton. " 15 " Major Henry M. Rutledge of Charleston, and Septima Santa[1] Middleton, were married by Lic.

[1]Sexta was the name.

Butler and Tash — " 26 " Joseph Butler, of Charleston, Mariner, and Maria Tash, of the same place, spinster, were married by Lic.

Davis and Oswald — " 31 " Capt. Harman Davis, of Charleston, and Mrs. Dorothy Oswald, of the same place, widow, were married by Lic.

Maul and Bessilew. — November 2 1799. David Maul, of Charleston, and Mary Bessilew of the same place, spinster, were married by Lic.

Gibbes and Smith — " 28 " Robert Reeves Gibbes, of Charleston, planter, and Anne Smith, of the same place, spinster, were married by Lic.

Stewart and Wish — December 22 " John Stewart, of Charleston, Vendue Master, and Elizabeth Wish, of the same place, spinster, were married by Lic.

Browne and Chitty — " 24 " Charles Fowler Browne, of Charleston, Bricklayer, and Sarah Chitty, of the same place, spinster, were married by Lic.

Vesey, and Morris. — " " " Charles Morgan Vesey, of Charleston, Gentleman, and Mary Morris, of the same place, spinster, were married by Lic.

Blake and Middleton — February 1 1800 Daniel Blake Esq, of Charleston, Gentleman, and Anna Louisa Middleton, of the same place, spinster, were married.

Sharp and Doré — March 3 " John Sharp, of Charleston, Clock-maker, and Elizabeth Doré of the same place, spinster, were married by Lic.

Gaillard and Doughty. — " 6 " Bartholomew Gaillard Esq. Merchant, to Miss Rebecca C. Doughty, Spinster, were married.

Rutledge and Smith	" 25 " Charles Rutledge, M. D., of Charleston, and Caroline Smith, of the same place, Spinster, were married.
Burrows and Harvey.	April 24 " George William Burrows, of Charleston, Mariner, and Sarah Harvey, of the same place, widow, were married.

Marriages.

Holmes and Gray.	May 22 1800 Andrew Holmes, of Charleston, Gentleman, and Margaret Gray, of the same place, Spinster, were married by Lic.
Torrey and Prince	" 30 " Capt. William Torrey, of Charleston, and Ann Prince of the same place, Spinster, were married by Lic.
Purdy and Besselleu	June 5 " Joseph Purdy, of Charleston, Mariner, and Johanna Bessilleau, of the same place, Spinster, were married by Lic.
Jenkins and Austin	" 21 " Elias Jenkins, of Charleston, Brick-layer, to Mrs. Elizabeth Austin, of the same place, widow, were married.
Jackson and Jurdon.	July 19 " William Jackson, Soldier, and Margaret Jurdon, widow, were married.
Parker and Milligan.	" 20 " Isaac Parker, House Carpenter, and Mary Milligan, of the same place, Spinster, were married.
Darrell and McDougal.	August 9 " Capt. Nicholas Darrell and Mrs. Mary McDougal, both of Charleston, were married.
Bessilleu and Williams	September 11 Mark Anthony Bessilleu, of Charleston, Mariner, and Maria Williams, of the same place, Spinster, were married by Lic.
Woodrupp and McCall	October 1 1800 John Woodrupp, of Charleston, Merchant, and Ann McCall, of the same place, Spinster, were married.

Derby and Sinclair.	" 23 " Robert Derby, of Charleston, Taylor, and Rebecca Sinclair, of the same place, Spinster were married by Lic

Rodman and Scott	October 24 1800 Thomas Rodman, of Charleston, Mariner, and Mary Scott, of the same place, widow, were married. by Lic.
Hutson and Miller	November 8 " William Hutson, of Charleston, Millwright, and Mary Ann Miller, of the same place, Spinster, were married.
Ford and Prioleau	" 20 " Timothy Ford, of Charleston, Attorney, and Mary Magdalene Prioleau, of the same place, Spinster, were married.
Clark and Simonson.	" 27 " James Clark, of Charleston, Mariner, and Mary Simonson, of the same place, Widow, were married by Lic.
Clark and	December 18 " Mathew Clark, of St. Paul's Parish, planter, and Mary of the same place, Spinster, were married.
Johnson and Clement	" " " David Johnson, of Charleston, Gentleman, and Eleanor Clement, of the same place, Spinster, were married by Lic.
Chandler and McCord	" 20 " Dr. Isaac Chandler, of Charleston, Physician, and Catharine McCord, of the same place, widow, were married.
Patterson and Halliday	January 1 1801 Capt David Patterson and Ann Halliday, of the same place, Spinster, were married.
Gregorie and Ladson.	February 3 " James Gregorie, Merchant in Charleston, to Miss Ann Ladson, of the same place, Spinster, were married.
Johnson and Will	" " James Johnson, of London, Mariner, and Elizabeth Will, of Charleston, Widow, were married by Lic.

Greet and Allen	April 12 1801 James Greet, of Charleston, Mariner, and Jane Allen, of the same place, Spinster, were married.
Oswald and Oliphant	" 18 " David Oswald, of Charleston, Taylor, and Elizabeth Oliphant, of the same place, Spinster, were married by Lic.
Church and McDonald	June 28 " Slocum Church, of Charleston, Carpenter, and Mary McDonald, of the same place, Spinster, were married by Lic.
Butcher and Gabriel	uly 4 " Abraham Butcher, of Charleston, Mariner, and Mary Gabriel, of the same place, widow, were married by Lic.
Quin and Reed	September 27 " James Quin, of Charleston, painter, and Ann Reed, of the same place, widow, were married by Lic.
Aiken and Wyatt	November 11 " William Aiken, of Charleston. Merchant, and Henrietta Wyatt, of the same place, Spinster, were married.
Richards and Singleton.	December 6 " Samuel Richards, of Charleston, Broker. and Mary Singleton, of the same place, Spinster, were married by Lic.
Trapier and Shubrick	January 7 1802 Paul Trapier Esq. of Georgetown, to Miss Sarah Shubrick, of Charleston, were married.
Huger and Pinckney	" 14 " Capt Francis Huger,[1] of Waccamaw, to Miss Harriott Lucas Pinckney, Santee were married.
Bowhay and Jarman.	" 19 " Joseph Procter Bowhay, of Charleston, Butcher, and Charlotte Jarman, of the same place, Spinster were married by Lic.

Marriages

[1]Francis Kinloch Huger, son of Major Benjamin and Mary (Kinloch) Huger. He was born in 1773 and died February 14, 1855. Noted for an attempt to rescue Lafayette from the Austrian fortress of Olmutz.

Browne and Boucheneau	January 30 1802 Mr. George William Browne, Rope Maker, and Mary Ann Boucheneau, of the same place, Spinster, were married.
Smith and Reynolds	February 19 1802 John Smith, of Charleston, Upholster, and Elizabeth Reynolds, of the same place, Widow, were married.
Howard and Grathan	" 25 " Richard Francis Howard, of Charleston, Cooper, and Eliza Grathan, of the same place, Spinster, were married.
Woolcock and Taylor	March 2 " William Woolcock, of Charleston, House Carpenter, and Ann Taylor, of the same place, widow, were married.
Parmele and Snyder.	April 6 " John Parmele, of Charleston, Shipwright, and Ann Snyder, of the same place, widow, were married by Lic.
Laight and Huger	" 22 " Edward William Laight Esq. of New York, and Ann Elliott Huger, of Charleston, Spinster, were married.
Cowan and Basilleau	May 25 " John Cowan, of Charleston, Rigger, and Maria Basilleau of the same place, widow, were married by Lic.
Bradley and Harvey	June 14 " Charles Bradley, of Charleston, printer, and Elizabeth Harvey, of the same place, Spinster, were married by Lic.
Hall and Howard	July 20 " Thomas Hall, of Charleston, Bricklayer, and Sarah Howard, of the same place, Spinster, were married.
Theving and Wolf	" 25 " Edward Theving, of Charleston, House Carpenter, and Margaret Wolf, of the same place, widow, were married.

Marriages.

Ackis and Hogarth.	August 19 1802 John Ackis, of Charleston, Shoemaker. and Charlotte Hogarth, of the same place, Spinster, were married.

Henniguin and Olman.	September 9 " John Baptiste Henniguin, of Charleston, Confectioner, and Mary Josepha Olman, of the Same place, widow, were married.
Lowndes and Pinckney.	" 10 " William Lowndes Esq.[1] of Charleston, Gentleman, to Miss Elizabeth Pinckney, of the Same place, Spinster, were married.
Ricard and Capdeville	October 3 " Francis Ricard, of Charleston, Merchant, to Mrs. Mary Capdeville, of the same place, widow, were married.
Baker and Kennedy	" 14 " John Jonathan Baker, of Charleston, plaisterer, and Susanna Kennedy, of the same place, widow, were married.
Poincignon and Conlon.	" 16 " Peter Anthony Poincignon, tin plate worker, and Jeane Conlon, of the same place, widow, were married.
Gabbeux and Smith	December 23 " James Gabbeux, of Charleston, and Doratha Smith, of the same place, Spinster, were married.
Dawson and Prioleau	" 29 " William Dawson, M. D., and Miss Caroline Prioleau, were married.

Burials. 280[2]

1753	th.	
November	19	Was buried James Nisbett Child.
	23	Was buried Cockram Parish
	25	Was buried Renney Soldier.
	27	Was buried Uyl
Decemr	4	Was buried Charles Pinckney, Child
	7	Was buried Mrs. Cray.
	8	Was buried John Royer
	22	Was buried Daniel Logan
	24	Was buried Charles Marino
	25	Was buried William Coomer

[1]Son of Rawlins Lowndes by his third wife. (See *Life* of by Mrs. Harriott Horry Ravenel.)

[2]Pages 274-279 are blank.

	28	Was buried Samuel Smith
1754	29	Was buried Jane Carne Child
January	2	Was buried Elizabeth McDowel
	4	Was buried Samuel Evans, Soldier.
	9	Was buried Mrs. Dixon Parish
	11	Was buried David Guerard
	12	Was buried George Salter
	16	Was buried Mrs. Ruck
	18	Was buried Mary Rose
	21	Was buried a Sailor
	25	Was buried Martha Price
	28	Was buried Thomas Dunn Parish
	30	Was buried Elizabeth Sarrazin
February	1	Was buried Mrs. Neufville
	3	Was buried William Bissett
	6	Was buried Peter Reaston
	8	Was buried Mary Bissett
	12	Was buried Capt. Thos. Riggs
	13	Was buried Henry Sarrazin Child
	20	Was buried Francis Brown
	22	Was buried Mary Ragnous
	25	Was buried John Watson
March	4	Was buried Joseph Anon Parish
	5	Was buried Elizabeth Quincy
	5	Was buried Vaughan Child
	13	Was buried Mrs. Bond

1754		
March	16	Was buried Mary Cooper Child
	25	Was buried Thomas Poole
	26	Was buried Mary Dowling Parish
	28	Was buried William Wedlock do.
	29	Was buried Peter David
		Was buried Mrs. Clarke
	30	Was buried Yarnold Child
April	5	Was buried Rolens James Sailer
	12	Was buried Eunice Clark Child
		Was buried Mrs. Poyas
	25	Was buried John Badger Parish
May	20	Was buried Mary Brown do.
	29	Was buried James McMurdon Sailer
	30	Was buried Patrick Reid. Mrcht.
June	4	Was buried Elizabeth Rodgers.
	8	Was buried William Air.
	9	Was buried Mary Bush Parish.

	16	Was buried John Lightfoot
	29	Was buried Joseph Lea Parish
July	2	Was buried Joseph Crofts, butcher.
	4	Was buried William Gordon.
	7	Was buried Virtue Baker, widow.
	9	Was buried James McLeod Sailer
	10	Was buried John McGlester Parish
		Was buried George Ewin Soldr. Child.
	12	Was buried John Campbell Parish
		Was buried Mrs. Barnes,
	13	Was buried Ann D'harriette
		Was buried John Cray Child
	19	was buried James Doughty Child
August	1	Was buried Crokatt Child
		Was buried Elizabeth Boyd Child
	3	Was buried Sarah Andrews,
	14	Was buried Mary Butler Parish
	16	Was buried Elizabeth Marley
	30	Was buried Peter Larey

Burials. 282

1754		
September	1st.	Was Buried Mary Fergus
	10	Was Buried Thomas Bright
		Was Buried Thomas Themis Psh.
		Was Buried Jane Gadsden child
	13	Was Buried Robert Christie
		Was Buried William Chorus Sailer
	20	Was Buried John Ball child
	23	Was Buried Long Child
	25	Was Buried Ann Izard widow.
		Was Buried John Elbeck
	30	Was Buried Elizabeth Mason
		Was Buried John Moultrie Child
October	3	Was Buried Richard Roberson Sailer
	9	Was Buried Thomas Drummond Child
	13	Was Buried Clemmons do.
		Was Buried Mrs. Page.
	15	Was Buried John Drayton Child
	16	Was Buried Shekell do.
	19	Was Buried Abraham Shaw
	20	Was Buried Marianne Godin
	22	Was Buried John Ewin
	24	Was Buried Richard Timberly, painter
	26	Was Buried Susanna Hume Child
	27	Was Buried Daniel Brunett Child

		Was Buried Fleming Child
	28	Was Buried Samuel Kynaston, Mrcht.
November	1st.	Was Buried Capt. Lawrence Wheeler, **Masr. of** the Snow Neptune
	8	Was Buried Collin McCollough Sailer
	12	Was Buried Mrs. Hext.
	18	Was Buried John Montjoy Sailer
	27	Was Buried Peter Oliver, Butcher
December	3	Was Buried David Hext.
	9	Was Buried Benjamin Race, Taylor
	18	Was Buried Mary Pitts Psh.
	22	Was Buried Morris Psh.
	25	Was Buried Psh.
	29	Was Buried Abraham Knight, Tallow **Chandler** Psh.
1755	30	Was Buried Mrs. Frazer Psh.
Jany.	1	Was Buried Sarah Lloyd
	2	Was Buried William Pinckney. Child

1755		
January	4	Was buried J. Sturges, Comedian
	5	Was buried Christopher Knowel Psh.
	6	Was buried Moses Tipper Psh.
	8	Was buried William Hamilton Psh.
	11	Was buried Martin Shekell Child
	13	Was buried Edward Swan, Cooper.
	14	Was buried Hester Carrol
	19	Was buried Lee Child
		Was buried Thomas Fairchild Child
		Was buried Abraham Rentfree Psh.
	25	Was buried Mrs. Rice, Solders Widow
	28	Was buried Elizabeth Frowendall Child.
February	14	Was buried William Chicken Child
	17	Was buried William Marrion
	19	Was buried Charles Read Sailer
March	9	Was buried Henry Chapone
	15	Was buried John Goodby
	27	Was buried Elizabeth Richardson
	28	Was buried McCall Child
April	6	Was buried Lupton Child
	9	Was buried Margary Ackles.
	23	Was buried Benjamin Baker Child
May	12	Was buried Roupell Child
	26	Was buried Jane Gadsden
	29	Was buried Jacobina Dellmore Psh.

	30	Was buried Mrs. Fryerson
	31	Was buried Thomas Crokatt
June	6	Was buried Michael Pascoe
		Was buried White Outerbridge
		Was buried William Dennison Parish
	9	Was buried Graham Butler Child
	10	Was buried Hext Roper Child
	12	Was buried John Dixon Psh.
		Was buried Morrison child Psh.
	24	Was buried Elizabeth Wyatt Child
	28	Was buried Mrs. Mason
	29	Was buried Thomas Doughty Victualler
	30	Was buried Morrison Child Psh.
July	1	Was buried Mrs. Bryan
	9	Was buried Webb Child
	11	Was buried Thomas Bonney, Mrcht.

Burials 284

1755		
July	15	Was buried John Garden son of the Revd. Mr. Garden.
	22	Was buried Clarke Child
	23	Was buried Eunice Clarke Child
	28	Was buried Sarah Ward Child
August	19	Was buried Ann Stuart Child
	22	Was buried Mary Dubberly Psh.
	25	Was buried Laurens Child
		Was buried Robert Hancock
Septemr.	2	Was buried Susanna Brewton
	11	Was buried William Randall blacksmith
	13	Was buried Mary Conner, Child
	16	Was buried Bowman Child
	20	Was buried Pritchard Child
	22	Was buried Catherine Lenox
October	8	Was buried Brailsford Child
	13	Was buried William Powel Sailer
	23	Was buried Edward Smith
	24	Was buried Poyas Child
	25	Was buried Margaret Mahlony Psh.
	26	Was buried James Donnett Psh.
		Was buried Psh.
	28	Was buried Mary Burrows Child
	31	Was buried John Bradley, Hatter,
November	3	Was buried Susanna Powers
	9	Was buried Charles Fox Sailer
	12	Was buried Sarah Serug, child

	14	Was buried Miller child
	17	Was buried a Dutch Doctor Psh.
	20	Was buried Andrew Rutledge Esqr. Attorney at Law.
	21	Was buried James Williams Sailer
	23	Was buried Sarah Neville Psh.
	26	Was buried Ann Hilliard
	28	Was buried Alexander Wood
Decemr	6	Was buried Rodgers Child
	8	Was buried a man from the Workhouse
	10	Was buried Thomas Easton, Gunner
	16	Was buried James Doughty Child
	17	Was buried Skirving Child.
	18	Was buried a man from the Workhouse
	20	Was buried Richardson
	24	Was buried Robert Dunbar
	25	Was buried Thomas Cart, Taylor.

1756		
January	2	Was buried Mayrant Child
	6	Was buried Joseph Samms
	9	Was buried Mary Stongen
		Was buried Irving Child
	21	Was buried Frances Child
February	2	Was buried John Older Sailer
	3	Was buried Fitzgerald Sailer
	6	Was buried Hinds Child
	16	Was buried Moultrie Child
		Was buried Mrs. Morgan
	18	Was buried Benjamin D'harriette Mercht.
	20	Was buried Mrs. Champlet Psh.
	22	Was buried Mrs. Gegee Psh.
	28	Was buried Colin Sharpe, shoemaker
	29	Was buried Plant
March	2	Was buried William Doble
	5	Was buried Dorothy Wire, the famous Curtezan
	6	Was buried Jno. Plant Child
	15	Was buried Lingard do.
		Was buried Foskey do.
	18	Was buried Francis do.
	22	Was buried Mrs. Rieley
	29	Was buried Ben Harvey
		Was buried Wm. Shepherd
April	1	Was buried Mary Beckett
	2	Was buried Mrs. Denison

281

	5	Was buried Marshall Child
	9	Was buried a Child on ye Parish
	12	Was buried Mrs. Creighton Sol. wife
		Was buried a Sailers wife
	14	Was buried Mrs. Shekell
	18	Was buried Cannon Child
	30	Was buried Priscilla Joyner Child
May	7	Was buried O'Connor do. Parish
	8	Was buried Dennison do
	9	Was buried Smith do
	13	Was buried John Edwards Psh.

Burials 286

1756		
May	24	Was buried James Withers
June	4	Was buried Mrs. Miles
		Was buried Baker Ch.d
	8	Was buried Benj. Dixon Psh.
	9	Was buried Dart Ch.d
	15	Was buried Ann Hamilton Psh.
		Was buried Thomas Crosthwaite
	16	Was buried Richard Powers
	18	Was buried John Brown Psh.
	21	Was buried John Gunter
		Was buried Mrs. Hatcher Psh.
	23	Was buried Lewis Timothy Ch.d
	25	Was buried Margaret Leigh Ch.d
July	3	Was buried Rose do
	7	Was buried Busby do.
	13	Was buried Pritchard do.
	16	Was buried Laurens do.
	18	Was buried Joshua Hattrick
	25	Was buried John Lockyearn
		Was buried John Philips
	27	Was buried Batsman
	28	Was buried John Simpson
		Was buried Alexr. Brown
		Was buried Mary Yerworth
Augt.	4th.	Was buried Williams Child
	12	Was buried William Harris
	13	Was buried Hope
	15	Was buried Sarah Denison Ch.d
	19	Was buried Bullea Psh.
	22	Was buried Burrows Ch.d
	24	Was buried Marshal do.
	28	Was buried John Glouster

Sept.	4	Was buried Kitty Cranmor Child
	6	Was buried Jordan Roche
		Was buried Hart Child
	12	Was buried Gordon do
	22	Was buried John Sheed do.
		Was buried Royal
		Was buried Honeyhorn

Burials 287

1756		
Sept.	29	Was Buried The Rev'd Mr. Alexr Garden late Rector of this Parish[1]
Octr.	3	Was Buried Rose Ch.d
	6	Was Buried Wilson Psh.
	11	Was Buried Christopher Freyer
	13	Was Buried Pinckney Child
	18	Was Buried Chd. on ye Psh.
	20	Was Buried Farrindon Lurcock
		Was Buried Henry HardCastle a Carver
	24	Was Buried Painter Psh.
	25	Was Buried Berry Psh.
		Was Buried Davidson Psh.
	27	Was Buried Hollyhan Psh.
Novr.	3	Was Buried Grace Stokes.
	15	Was Buried Oliphant Ch.d
	17	Was Buried Nathaniel Tucker
		Was Buried John Harris Psh.
	25	Was Buried Mrs. Bashford
Decr	1	Was Buried William Thompson mr. of the snow Eliza.
	3	Was Buried McEuen Chd.
		Was Buried Mrs. Godfrey
	6	Was Buried Mrs Solloman Parish
	9	Was Buried St. John Chd.
	11	Was Buried Rose do.
	12	Was Buried Robert McDougal
	17	Was Buried Hance Suer
	22	Was Buried John Colcock
		Was Buried Thomas Hall
	26	Was Buried Peter Banbury,
	28	Was Buried Ann Robeson.

[1]Bishop of London's Commissary for North and South Carolina and the Bahama Islands. There is a tombstone to him in St. Philip's churchyard. (See Dalcho's *Protestant Episcopal Church in South Carolina.*)

		Was Buried James Creighton ....
1757	31	Was Buried Meller St. John ....
Jany.	1	Was Buried Charles Stuart ....
	9	Was Buried Mrs. Smith ....
	14	Was Buried Hart ....
		Was Buried Mitchel Robarts ....
	15	Was Buried James Miles ....
	19	Was Buried Mrs. Deas ....
	20	Was Buried Robert Henderson ....

Burials 288

1757			
January	22	Was buried George Lea.	
	23	Was buried James Burt.	
		Was buried James Elsinore.	
	30	Was buried John Orman	Psh.
	31	Was buried Elizabeth Lea	
		Was buried a Sailer	
Feby.	5th.	Was buried Edmund Cain	
	11	Was buried Mrs. Motte	
	27	Was buried Mrs. Easton	
March	9	Was buried a Sailer	
	10	Was buried Middleton	Chd.
	16	Was buried a Sailer	
	20	Was buried Thomas Price	
	28	Was buried a Sailer	
April	2d.	Was buried John Fryer	
	4	Was buried Elizabeth Timothy[1]	
	5	Was buried John Tucker.	
	9	Was buried William Burch	
	21	Was buried Henry Smith	
		Was buried a Soldier.	
		Was buried Thomas Miller	Psh.
	28	Was buried a Daughter of Thomas Tucker	
May	5	Was buried Pollard	Psh.
	12	Was buried Carr	Psh.
	26	Was buried John Bounetheau	
	27	Was buried Mrs. Lee.	
	28	Was buried Mrs. Meredith	
	29	Was buried Susanna Beazeley	

[1]She was the widow of Lewis Timothy, sometime proprietor of *The South-Carolina Gazette.* (See "A Century of the Courier", by A. S. Salley, Jr., Centennial Edition of *The News and Courier*, April 20, 1904.)

June	3	Was buried Jos. Lassey Psh.
		Was buried Mrs. Sharpe Psh.
	17	Was buried Elizabeth Smith
	23	Was buried John Daniels
	24	Was buried a Person on the Psh.
	28	Was buried Peter Ripault Psh.
		Was buried Thompson
	30	Was buried Mrs. Rhoda
July	3	Was buried Trezvant Chd.
		Was buried Sarah North. Psh.
	4	Was buried Peter Deboin
		Was buried James Barry
		Was buried Samued Woodside
	17	Was buried Mr. Hart
	18	Was buried Mrs. Holmes. Psh.
	30	Was buried Cranmer Chd.
Augst.	2d.	Was buried Barbary Honskitly Psh.

1757		
Augst.	3d.	Was buried a Soldier
	7	Was buried Edward Spikeman Psh.
	8	Was buried Evance Chd.
	15	Was buried Peter Leigh Chd.
		Was buried Ann Airs Chd.
		Was buried Mrs. Douxsaint
	18	Was buried John Ryder Psh.
	23	Was buried Rodger Chd.
	25	Was buried Gabriel Guignard
		Was buried John Ragnois
	27	Was buried a Soldier
		Was buried King Chd.
		Was buried Ryboult Psh.
	29	Was buried a Soldier
Sept.	1	Was buried Hume Chd.
	4	Was buried Peter Poinsett
	5	Was buried Raber Psh.
	9	Was buried Perdriau Chd.
		Was buried Alexander Ffraser Chd.
		Was buried Two Soldiers
	12	Was buried Phebe Jones Psh.
	15	Was buried a Soldier
	16	Was buried a Soldier
	18	Was buried a Soldier
		Was buried Lingerd Chd.
	19	Was buried a Soldier

	20	Was buried Jos. Alsey Psh.
		Was buried Ann Grant Psh.
		Was buried a Soldier
	21	Was buried John Scott.
	23	Was buried four Soldiers
		Was buried Bozzard Psh.
	24	Was buried a Soldier
		Was buried Cooper a Chd.
	25	Was buried a Soldier
	26	Was buried three Soldiers
		Was buried Mrs. Bryan
	27	Was buried a Soldier
	28	Was buried three Soldiers
		Was buried Esaie Brunett
	30	Was buried three Soldiers
		Was buried Collis Chd.
Octr	3d.	Was buried two Soldiers
		Was buried Francis Corterman Psh.

Burials 290

1757		
October	5	Was buried John Grant Psh.
		Was buried Conrad Long Psh.
	6	Was buried two Soldiers.
	7	Was buried a Soldier
	10	Was buried two Soldiers and a wife
	11	Was buried a Soldier
	12	Was buried a Soldier
	13	Was buried a Soldiers Wife
	14	Was buried two Soldiers
	15	Was buried a Soldier
		Was buried John Romain Psh.
	16	Was buried a Soldiers Child.
		Was buried John Flemming
		Was buried William Irish
		Was buried Barsheba Tattle
	17	Was buried a Soldier and Sailer
	18	Was buried two Soldiers
	19	Was buried three Soldiers
		Was buried Ann Raber Psh.
	20	Was buried two Sailers
	24	Was buried A Soldiers Wife
		Was buried Thomas Chd
	27	Was buried Cranmer Chd
		Was buried Timothy Chd

Novr.	2d	Was buried a Soldier
	3	Was buried Elizabeth Hailey Psh
	4	Was buried Elizabeth Gibbons Psh
	5	Was buried a Soldier
	7	Was buried a Soldier
	9	Was buried a Soldier
		Was buried Philip Welch Psh
	13	Was buried a Soldier
		Was buried a Sailer
	14	Was buried Rice Price
		Was buried Dart Chd
	15	Was buried Hammet Chd
		Was buried a Soldier
	16	Was buried Samuel Bowman Esqr Justice ' Peace
	17	Was buried four Soldiers
	22	Was buried Barbary Pinckley Psh.
	24	Was buried Richard Mason
		Was buried John Rigland
		Was buried Two Soldiers
	25	Was buried Bryan Chd
	28	Was buried a Sailor two Soldiers & one of their Wifes.

1757		
Novr.	29th	Was buried 2 Soldiers
	30	Was buried Ann Creighton Chd
Decr.	1st.	Was buried a Soldier
	2d	Was buried Moore Chd
	3	Was buried a Soldier
	5	Was buried Isaac Abraham
	7	Was buried a Soldier
	9	Was buried Mrs. Moultrie Junr.
		Was buried Catherine Spencer
	11	Was buried two Soldiers
		Was buried Mrs. Singleton
		Was buried Conrad Raber Psh
	13	Was buried Daniel Hill Psh
	15	Was buried a Soldier
		Was buried Mrs. Smith Psh
	18	Was buried Margaret Pharo Psh
	20	Was buried a Soldier
	22	Was buried a Soldiers Chd
		Was buried two Soldiers
		Was buried Cannon's Chd.
	24	Was buried a Soldier

	26	Was buried Mrs. Neyle
1758		Was buried a Sailer
Jany	1st.	Was buried William Dalton Indian Trader
		Was buried a Sailer
	4	Was buried Mrs. Metheringham.
		Was buried Walter Patterson
	5	Was buried Fenwick Chd.
	6	Was buried a Soldier
	10	Was buried Francis Spencer
	11	Was buried Frances Carragin Psh
	12	Was buried A Man from Prison
		Was buried a Soldier
	15	Was buried a Sailer
	17	Was buried Francis Dandridge
	22	Was buried a Sailer
	24	Was buried Banbury Chd
	25	Was buried Nellson
	30	Was buried Sarah Burrows
Feby	1st.	Was buried Davis Chd
	2	Was buried Richd. Dun Lawrence
		Was buried a Soldier
	9	Was buried Two Soldiers

Burials 292

1758		
Feby.	10	Was buried a Soldier
	11	Was buried Two Soldiers
	16	Was buried Angel Harding Alias Snow
	19	Was buried Two Soldiers
	19	Was buried Robert Colles
	22	Was buried John Moore
	24	Was buried Mrs. Allen
	28	Was buried Mrs. Bennett
March	1st.	Was buried a Sailer
	3	Was buried a Sailer
		Was buried Two Soldiers
	6	Was buried Two Soldiers
	8	Was buried a Soldier
	9	Was buried John Ward
	10	Was buried Arenout Schermehorne
	26	Was buried a Sailer
		Was buried a Soldier
	30	Was buried Richard Wainwright
April	2	Was buried William Farley Psh
	3	Was buried Peter Oliver
	4	Was buried a Soldier

	10	Was buried William Godard	
		Was buried three Soldiers	
	12	Was buried Margaret Boone	
		Was buried Elizabeth Poole	
	13	Was buried Margaret Hughes	
		Was buried a Soldier	
		Was buried Margaret Reid	
	14	Was buried Sarah Trezvant	
		Was buried John Phillips	Psh
	15	Was buried William Edwards	
		Was buried Andrew McDowdle	Psh
	16	Was buried Cavenos Chd	
	17	Was buried Rachel Fryer	
		Was buried David Snelling	Psh
	18	Was buried James Kean	
		Was buried a Chd	Psh
		Was buried a Soldier	
	20	Was buried John McKinzie	
		Was buried a Soldier	
	22	Was buried Dominic Rock	Psh
	26	Was buried Catherine Schurlock	
	28	Was buried a Soldier	
	29	Was buried James Beard	
May	5	Was buried Elizabeth Smith	Psh
	6	Was buried Moore a Chd	

1758

May	8	Was buried a Soldier	
	12	Was buried Elizabeth James	Psh
	17	Was buried a Sailer	
	20	Was buried a Sailer	
	25	Was buried William Gold	
	29	Was buried a Sailer	
		Was buried William Looke	
June	2	Was buried Chalmers a Chd	
	6	Was buried Barnaby Ripault	
	10	Was buried Mrs. Handlin	
	13	Was buried Easter Rager	Psh
		Was buried John Thomas Chd	
	24	Was buried a Sailer	
	26	Was buried Peter Calveti	
July	1	Was buried Marrineau a Chd	
	2	Was buried William Shrubsole	
		Was buried a Soldier	
	3	Was buried Patrick Boyland	

	4	Was buried Mary Linthwaite a Child
		Was buried a Chd Psh
	6	Was buried two Sailers
	13	Was buried a Sailer
		Was buried Charles Pinckney a Chd
		Was buried William Oven Psh
	14	Was buried a Chd Psh
		Was buried William Buchanan.
		Was buried William Jones
		Was buried Mrs. Camble, Dancing Mistress
	17	Was buried Bowman a Chd
	22	Was buried William Wyatt a Chd
	23	Was buried Wainwright a Chd
		Was buried a Chd Psh
		Was buried Nicholas Psh
	24	Was buried a Soldier
	26	Was buried a Sailer
August	1	Was buried Henry Laurens a Chd
	2	Was buried Elfe a Chd
	4	Was buried two Soldiers
	10	Was buried Capt Hail's Chd
		Was buried Capt Whitburn

1758		
August	16	Was buried William King
		Was buried a Sailer
	21	Was buried a Soldier
		Was buried Buticar a Chd
		Was buried a Soldier
		Was buried the Revd. Mr. Clarke's Child
	29	Was buried Mrs. Partridge
	30	Was buried Mrs. Brown
		Was buried Mrs. Palmer Psh
	31	Was buried William Jones Psh
Sept	4	Was buried a Soldier
		Was buried Elizabeth Jourdin Psh
	20	Was buried a Soldier
		Was buried Free Jane's Chd
	21	Was buried Pattons Chd
		Was buried Doctr. David Caw
	22	Was buried Henry Fendles Chd
	25	Was buried a Soldier
		Was buried John Mills Psh
	27	Was buried a Soldier
October	1	Was buried David Johnson Psh

	5	Was buried Joseph Dextor
	7	Was buried a Sailer
	12	Was buried a Soldier
	13	Was buried Mrs. Carne
		Was buried a Sailer
		Was buried A Soldier
	21	Was buried Mrs. Tuffts
		Was buried a Soldier
	22	Was buried Mrs. Clifford
	24	Was buried a Sailer
	29	Was buried Mrs. Mitchell
	30	Was buried Abraham Peragar Psh
	31	Was buried a Soldier
		Was buried Underwood a Chd
November	3	Was buried Valicut Mannis Psh
		Was buried a Sailer
	5	Was buried John Lloyd Commander of Johnstons Fort
		Was buried a Soldier
	15	Was buried a Soldier
	20	Was buried Augustin Cox
	27	Was buried a Sailer
		Was buried a Soldier
		Was buried John Crokett
December	1st.	Was buried a Sailer

1758		
December	11	Was buried a Sailer
		Was buried Barnard McQuire Psh
		Was buried Joseph Prince
	16	Was buried a Sailer
		Was buried Richard Easton Psh
		Was buried a Soldier
	22	Was buried George Anderson Psh
1759	27	Was buried a Sailer
Jany	1	Was buried a Sailer
	4	Was buried a Soldier
	7	Was buried William Jenkins Psh
	14	Was buried Richard Walters Psh
	15	Was buried Mrs. Hargrove Psh
	16	Was buried Mrs. Remington Junr.
	19	Was buried a Sailer
		Was buried a Soldier
	27	Was buried James Scott
		Was buried Sarah Summers

Feby	4	Was buried a Soldier
	8	Was buried a Soldier
	11	Was buried a Woman on the Psh
	14	Was buried Ambrous Gibbons Psh
		Was buried Austin Robert Lockton
		Was buried a Soldier
	24	Was buried a Soldier
	26	Was buried a Soldier
		Was buried Michael Barns Psh
		Was buried a Sailer
		Was buried a Soldier
March	2	Was buried a Sailer
	11	Was buried a Soldier
		Was buried Leopold Nealy
	13	Was buried a Soldier
		Was buried a Soldier
	16	Was buried a Soldier
	22	Was buried Mrs. Brailsford
	27	Was buried John Scott Gun Smith
		Was buried John Sheriff Psh
	28	Was buried John Whitlock
April	4	Was buried John Pope
	8	Was buried a Sailer
	12	Was buried Abraham Bartout

Burials 296

1759

April	16th.	Was buried Walters Child
	17th.	Was Buried Benja Philips Wife
	19th.	Was Buried Mrs. Deveaux
May	7th.	Was Buried Stephen Hartley
	25th.	Was Buried Henry Laurens' Child
	31th.	Was Buried Thomas Tucker's Child
	do.	Was Buried Samuel Thomas' Child
	do.	Was Buried Francis Bremer's Child
June	3d.	Was Buried ditto's Child
	do.	Was Buried Charles Dewer's Child
	6th.	Was Buried Christopher Roger's Child
	22d.	Was Buried John Poinsett's Child (Sarah)
	do.	Was Buried Thomas Rose's Child
	26th.	Was Buried Peter Leigh Esqr's Child
July	1st.	Was Buried Jonathan Sarrazin's Child
	8th.	Was Buried Walkers Child
	12th.	Was Buried Hopkins' Child
	17th.	Was Buried Elizabeth Bullard
	27th.	Was Buried Dupnee's Child

	31st.	Was Buried Thomas Hall
August	8th.	Was Buried Robert Hardey's Child
	9th.	Was Buried Isaac Holmes
	15th.	Was Buried Miss Fairchild
	20th.	Was Buried John Wilson
	21st.	Was Buried Robert Brewton[1]
	22nd.	Was Buried Peter Leigh Esqr. Chief Justice.[2]
	27th.	Was Buried John Logan's Child
	do.	Was Buried Frederick Holsendorff's Child
	do.	Was Buried John Evans
Septemr.	3d.	Was Buried a Sailor

E. Poinsett (Registr.)

1759		
Septemr	4th.	Was Buried a Sailor
	6th.	Was Buried Mrs. Stronick
	15th.	Was Buried Thomas Fox
Octr.	13th.	Was Buried Guiniyard
	28th.	Was Buried Jacop Motte Junr. Child
	do.	Was Buried Stephen Hartleys Widow.
Novr.	4th.	Was Buried Mrs. Carden
	do	Was Buried Joseph Keally
	do	Was Buried John Mayrants Child
	13th.	Was Buried Mrs. Tamplet
	20th.	Was Buried Mary Parris
decemr.	4th.	Was Buried John Neufville's Child
	10th.	Was Buried Mrs. Gibbs
	20th.	Was Buried William Patridge's Child
	25th.	Was Buried Henry Fendle's Child
1760		
Jany	6th.	Was Buried William Logan's Child
	8th.	Was Buried Mr. Hill's Child
Feby.	7th.	Was Buried James Nichols
	14th.	Was Buried Thomas Linning's Child
	do.	Was Buried William Lawrence's Child
	17th.	Was Buried William Blackridge's Child
	do.	Was Buried Doctr. Ecpard
	21st.	Was Buried Elizabeth Smith
	do	Was Buried William Middleton
	22nd.	Was Buried Widow Pickering's Child

[1]See *The South Carolina Historical and Genealogical Magazine,* Vol. II, 130-142.)

[2]Appointed February 6, 1753.

23d. Was Buried Mallery Brandford ....
27th. Was Buried Mrs. Brandford ....
28th. Was Buried Daniel Cannon's Child ....
29th. Was Buried Robert Williams Junr Child ....

E. Poinsett (Regstr.)

Burials 298

1760

March 1st. Was Buried Benjamin Smith's Wife ....
2d. Was Buried Mr. Hill's Child ....
do. Was Buried Abraham Remington's Child ....
3d. Was Buried John Remington Junr. Child ....
do. Was Buried Isaac Mazyck's Child ....
Do. Was Buried Benja. Smith's Child ....
do. Was Buried John Moultrie Junr. Child ....
4th. Was Buried James Laurence's Wife ....
do. Was Buried James Williams ....
5th. Was Buried Mrs Burnett's Child ....
do. Was Buried Lawrence Sanders ....
do. Was Buried Benjamin Gardens Wife ....
do. Was Buried Jacob Varné ....
6th. Was Buried Samuel Perkins' Child ....
do. Was Buried Mrs. Blake ....
do. Was Buried Benjamin Mazyck's Child ....
7th. Was Buried Sarah Ward ....
do. Was Buried Richard Weaver ....
do. Was Buried William Richards ....
do. Was Buried Joseph Maxcey's Child ....
8th. Was Buried Mrs. Burnett ....
do Was Buried Miss Deamond ....
9th. Was Buried John Nelmes ....
do. Was Buried Mrs. Wilson's Child ....
do. Was Buried Peter Shaw ....
do. Was Buried James Rodger's Child ....
10th. Was Buried Susanna Rose ....
do. Was Buried Widow Benoist ....
do Was Buried Mr. Bakers' Child ....
11th. Was Buried Thomas Evance's Child ....
do. Was Buried Henry St. Martin's Son ....

E. Poinsett (Register)

Burials 299

1760

March 12th. Was Buried William Moultries Child ....
do. Was Buried Benjamin Yarnolds Child ....

	do.	Was Buried Stephen Smiths Child
	do.	Was Buried Laughlin Shaw's Child
	13th.	Was Buried John Perdriau's Child
	do.	Was Buried Doctr. Lionel Chalmers' Child
	do.	Was Buried John Poinsett's daughter Mary
	14th.	Was Buried John Guerard's Child
	do.	Was Buried Mrs. Stevenson
	do.	Was Buried Mary Goff
	15th.	Was Buried Doctr. David Oliphant's Child
	do.	Was Buried Henry Cornish
	17th.	Was Buried Thomas Radcliff's Child
	18th.	Was Buried John Remington's Child
	19th.	Was Buried Egerton Leigh's Child
	do.	Was Buried Jarvis Williams
	20th.	Was Buried Capt. McGillevray's Child
	21st.	Was Buried Ralph Atmore's Child
	do.	Was Buried Charles Dewer's Child
	22d.	Was Buried Mrs. Pritchard's Child
	24th.	Was Buried Francis Bremar's Child
	do.	Was Buried Mrs. Wyatt
	do.	Was Buried Laughlin Shaw's Child
	do.	Was Buried George Roupell's Child
	do.	Was Buried Mr. Hart's Apprentice
	do.	Was Buried Mrs. Golding
	do.	Was Buried Mrs. Lewis
	25th.	Was Buried Jacob Motte Senr. Child
	do.	Was Buried David Jones
	26th.	Was Buried Richard Berrisford's Child

E. Poinsett (Registr.)

Burials 300

1760		
March	26th.	Was Buried Mary Bowers
	do.	Was Buried Darby Pendergrass' Child
	do.	Was Buried Mrs. Gowdey
	do	Was Buried Michael Jeanes
	do.	Was Buried Archibald Thompson
	do.	Was Buried William Carpenter's Child
	27th.	Was Buried Elizabeth Spencer
	do.	Was Buried Mrs. Atmore
	28th.	Was Buried Mrs. Deamond
	do.	Was Buried William Squires
	do.	Was Buried Christopher Easton
	do.	Was Buried William Lawrence's Child
	29th.	Was Buried James Britton
	30th.	Was Buried Daniel Doyley's Child

do. Was Buried a Sailor ....
do. Was Buried John Stevenson's Child ....
31st. Was Buried Mrs. McKelvey's Child ....
do. Was Buried Ann Buckmaster ....
do. Was Buried Mr. Colliss ....
April 1st. Was Buried William Nelmes ....
2d. Was Buried Miles Teddar ....
do. Was Buried John Nodding's Child ....
do. Was Buried William Edden ....
3d. Was Buried Widow Smith ....
do. Was Buried John Calvert's Child ....
do. Was Buried Mrs. Wortzer ....
4th. Was Buried Mrs. Hardey ....
6th. Was Buried John Bates ....
7th. Was Buried Mr. Gowdey's Child ....

E. Poinsett (Registr.)

Burials 301

1760
April 9th. Was Buried Capt. Nicholson ....
do. Was Buried Henry Fendle's Child ....
do. Was Buried Benjamin Hawes' Child ....
10th. Was Buried Richard Berrisford's Child ....
do. Was Buried James Laurens' Child ....
13th. Was Buried Elizabeth Fox ....
do. Was Buried Robert Hardey's Child ....
15th. Was Buried Mrs. Merineau's Child ....
do. Was Buried John D'Harriette's Child ....
do. Was Buried Widow Jones ....
17th. Was Buried John Snelling's Child ....
20th. Was Buried Thomas Raven's Child ....
21st. Was Buried Robert Hardey's Apprentice ....
do. Was Buried John Cart's Child ....
22nd. Was Buried William Wyatt ....
do. Was Buried Widow Hutchens ....
23rd. Was Buried Abigail Benoist ....
do. Was Buried James Sharp's Child ....
24th. Was Buried Theodore Trezvant's Child ....
May 1st. Was Buried Mrs. Johnston's Child ....
7th. Was Buried John Ward (Taylor's) Wife ....
13th. Was Buried John Barker's Child ....
do. Was Buried Mrs. Outerbriges Child ....
do. Was Buried Mr. Ball's Child ....
June 4th. Was Buried Mr. Rawlins' Child ....
do. Was Buried Mr. Ball's Child ....
do. Was Buried Mrs. Legare ....

	10th.	Was Buried Mrs. Crow
	21st.	Was Buried Thomas Smith's Child
July	19th.	Was Buried John Waitus

E. Poinsett. (Registr.)

Burials 302

1760		
July	30th.	Was Buried Mrs. Hindes
	31st.	Was Buried a Sailor
August	8th.	Was Buried Mrs. Handlin
	16th.	Was Buried a Sailor
	20th.	Was Buried Royce
Septemr	12th.	Was Buried Mr. Wright's Child
	13th.	Was Buried Mr. Howarth's Child
	do.	Was Buried Mrs. McQueen's Child
	16th.	Was Buried John Caveneau
	17th.	Was Buried Gibbon Wright
	18th.	Was Buried Mrs. Prioleau's Child
October	6th.	Was Buried a man
	7th.	Was Buried Mrs. Bolton
	do.	Was Buried Mr. Brailsford's Child
	13th.	Was Buried Thomas McLeoad
	22d.	Was Buried William Jordan
	do.	Was Buried Vincent Rape
	25th.	Was Buried Morton Brailsford
	29th.	Was Buried Mrs Carroll
Novemr.	3d.	Was Buried Sarah Hughes
	21st.	Was Buried Walter Webb
decemr.	5th.	Was Buried Mrs. Chalmbers
	do.	Was Buried A Sailor
	15th.	Was Buried Mrs. Hazlewood
	24th.	Was Buried Mrs. McLoughlin
1761		
Jany.	2d.	Was Buried Mrs. Wilson's Child
	11th.	Was Buried A Sailor
	19th.	Was Buried A Sailor
	23d.	Was Buried Two Sailors

E. Poinsett (Regstr.)

Burials 303

1761		
Jany.	29th.	Was Buried A Sailor
Feby.	4th.	Was Buried Moreau Sarazin
	6th.	Was Buried Richard Elrington

	16th.	Was Buried Henry Joynes ....
	20th.	Was Buried Mr. Elliott ....
	30th.	Was Buried Mrs. Lovell ....
Mar.	5th.	Was Buried Mrs. Lockton ....
	16th.	Was Buried Mrs. Bates ....
	19th.	Was Buried Mrs. Honnour ....
	21st.	Was Buried Mrs. Savage ....
	....	Was Buried John Hunt the 20th. Novr. 1759 ....
	26th.	Was Buried Mary Boyd ....
	27th.	Was Buried—A Man (say two men) One a Soldier the Other on the Parish ....
	29th.	Was Buried—A Boy Soldier. ....
	30th.	Was Buried—A Boy Soldier ....
	31st.	Was Buried A Girl ditto ....
	do.	Was Buried John Bassnett ....
April	3d.	Was Buried A Woman on the Parish ....
	6th.	Was Buried Eliz. Boodington On Ditto ....
	7th.	Was Buried Joseph Merideth ....
	14th.	Was Buried A Man Sailor ....
	do.	Was Buried A Man & A Boy, On the Parish ....
	27th.	Was Buried Mr. Rose's Child ....
	28th.	Was Buried Margaret Finlay's Child ....
May	2d.	Was Buried Jane Connoway a Soldiers Child ....
	6th.	Was Buried A Soldier ....
	do.	Was Buried A Soldier's Child ....
	8th.	Was Buried William Wilson ....
	9th.	Was Buried Archibald Berwick ....

E. Poinsett (Regstr.)

Burials 304

1761		
May	17th.	Was Buried A Soldiers Child ....
	20th.	Was Buried A Boy on the Parish ....
	22d.	Was Buried Martha Dawson's Child ....
	do.	Was Buried A Child on the Parish ....
	23d.	Was Buried A Woman On ditto ....
	26th.	Was Buried A Child on ditto ....
	29th.	Was Buried A Parish——Child ....
	30th.	Was Buried Henry Gray's Child ....
June	8th.	Was Buried John Patience ....
	16th.	Was Buried Robert Bunning ....
	22d.	Was Buried John Harper ....
July	2d.	Was Buried Ann Hall on the Parish ....
	do.	Was Buried Mrs. Wilson On ditto ....
	do.	Was Buried John Laird ....
	24th.	Was Buried A Child On the Parish ....

	do.	Was Buried Mr. Outerbridges Child
	do.	Was Buried A Man on the Parish
	25th.	Was Buried A Woman On ditto
	26th.	Was Buried A Man on ditto
	31st.	Was Buried A Child on ditto
August	1st.	Was Buried A Woman on ditto
	6th.	Was Buried Mr. Finch
	do.	Was Buried A Man on the Parish
	do.	Was Buried Jarvis William's Child
	10th.	Was Buried Mrs. Colcock
	11th.	Was Buried A Soldier
	12th.	Was Buried John James
	13th.	Was Buried A Man On the Parish

E. Poinsett (Registr.)

Burials 305

1761		
August	14th.	Was Buried A Woman On the Parish
	15th.	Was Buried A Child On ditto
	17th.	Was Buried A Child On ditto
	19th.	Was Buried A Child On ditto
	20th.	Was Buried Two Children On ditto
	21st.	Was Buried William Poole
	do.	Was Buried Jordan Roche
	do.	Was Buried A Woman On the Parish
	do.	Was Buried Mrs. Morrison's Child
	26th.	Was Buried A Child On the Parish
	27th.	Was Buried A Woman On ditto
	do.	Was Buried Mr. Smith a Soldier
	28th.	Was Buried A Soldier
	30th.	Was Buried Mrs. Caveneau On the Parish
	do.	Was Buried Mrs. Jeanes
	31st.	Was Buried A Woman On the Parish
	do.	Was Buried William Johnston
Sept.	1st.	Was Buried Mr. Greenland
	do.	Was Buried A Man from Prison
	do.	Was Buried A Man On the Parish
	6th.	Was Buried Robertson Day
	7th.	Was Buried Mrs. Kirk & Mrs. Pusley on the Parish.
	do.	Was Buried Henry Burnett
	8th.	Was Buried A Woman & A Man On the Parish
	9th.	Was Buried A Woman On ditto
	do.	Was Buried Mrs. Massey
	10th.	Was Buried A Man On the Parish
	do.	Was Buried A Sailor

	13th.	Was Buried Mr. Kielley's Apprentice
	do.	Was Buried James Hill

E. Poinsett (Regstr.)

Burials 306

1761		
Septemr.	14th.	Was Buried A Sailor
	do.	Was Buried Mrs. Reiley
	15th.	Was Buried Mr. Flurrys Child
	do.	Was Buried A Man On the Parish
	do.	Was Buried John Becketts Child
	19th.	Was Buried William Burley
	do.	Was Buried A Boy of Pendergrasses
	22d.	Was Buried A Soldier
	24th.	Was Buried James Gage
	do.	Was Buried Capt. Darvil
	27th.	Was Buried Joseph Maxseys Child
	do.	Was Buried A Sailor
	do.	Was Buried A Soldier
	29th.	Was Buried A Child of Ann Jane On the Parish
	do.	Was Buried A Soldier
	30th.	Was Buried A Soldier
Octr.	1st.	Was Buried A Soldier
	3d.	Was Buried A Soldier
	do.	Was Buried Doctr Bayley
	do.	Was Buried Martha Weaver
	4th	Was Buried Two Men On the Parish
	6th.	Was Buried Reuben Cunningham
	do.	Was Buried A Child On the Parish
	7th.	Was Buried Edward Newman
	11th.	Was Buried Abraham Remingtons Child
	13th.	Was Buried A Soldier
	14th.	Was Buried A Soldier
	17th.	Was Buried Richard Miles, & A Child On the Parish
	do.	Was Buried Mary Smith

E. Poinsett (Regstr.)

Burials 307

1761		
Octr.	17th.	Was Buried Nathaniel Hockley
	18th.	Was Buried Simon Murphy
	24th.	Was Buried A Man On the Parish
	do.	Was Buried Mary Roberts
	do.	Was Buried William Page a Soldier

	27th.	Was Buried Thomas Bennett
Novr.	1st.	Was Buried John Colston
	do.	Was Buried John Fraser
	5th.	Was Buried A Child On the Parish
	do.	Was Buried A Soldier
	do.	Was Buried Thomas Fogg A Soldier
	6th.	Was Buried A Boy On the Parish
	do.	Was Buried Andrew Tate
	7th.	Was Buried Mrs. Allen
	8th.	Was Buried Two Soldiers
	9th.	Was Buried Mrs. Banbury
	13th.	Was Buried A Soldier
	14th.	Was Buried Patrick Laird
	18th.	Was Buried Benjamin Garden's Wife
	do.	Was Buried Miss Butler
	21st.	Was Buried A Soldier
	23d.	Was Buried Two Children On the Parish
	26th.	Was Buried John Jones A Soldier
	28th.	Was Buried A Soldier
	29th.	Was Buried Mary Brewton
decemr	2d.	Was Buried A Woman & A Child On the Parish
	4th.	Was Buried Mary Hill
	do.	Was Buried James Nicholson
	7th.	Was Buried A Woman On the Parish
	8th.	Was Buried A Man On ditto
	do.	Was Buried Mrs. Shubrick

E. Poinsett (Registr.

Burials 308

1761		
decemr	7th.	Was Buried John Grant
	9th.	Was Buried A Soldier
	11th.	Was Buried John McGriger
	12th.	Was Buried Mrs. Rogers
	do.	Was Buried A Soldier
	do.	Was Buried Mr. Greenland
	do.	Was Buried Robert Hardey
	14th.	Was Buried A Soldier
	15th.	Was Buried A Soldier
	do.	Was Buried A Soldier Boy
	18th.	Was Buried Nathaniel Broughton
	do.	Was Buried Sarah Williams
	20th.	Was Buried A Woman On the Parish
	do.	Was Buried A Soldier
	24th.	Was Buried Samuel Carne's Child
	25th.	Was Buried Mrs. Rose

301

	27th.	Was Buried A Woman On the Parish
	28th.	Was Buried Edward Randell, A Soldier
1762		
Jany	3d.	Was Buried A Woman On the Parish
	do.	Was Buried William Wyatt
	9th.	Was Buried A Soldier
	11th.	Was Buried William Raiford
	do.	Was Buried Thomas Shubrick's Child
	14th.	Was Buried A Sailor
	15th.	Was Buried John Gordon (Vintner)
	18th.	Was Buried Mr. Spinks On the Parish
	do.	Was Buried Capt. James Rodgers
Feby.	12th.	Was Buried Sarah Rookes On the Parish
	17th.	Was Buried John Hail
	24th.	Was Buried Mrs. Scott

E. Poinsett (Registr.)

Burials 309

1762		
Feby.	26th.	Was Buried Joseph Loocock
Mar.	1st.	Was Buried A Sailor
	do.	Was Buried A Man from Prison
	11th.	Was Buried Mrs. Oakley On the Parish
	14th.	Was Buried Mrs. Dudley
	19th.	Was Buried Charles Stevenson
	20th.	Was Buried Mrs. Mills
	do.	Was Buried James Chalmers
April	12th.	Was Buried John Cammer
May	8th.	Was Buried Mrs. Cart.
	9th.	Was Buried A Man & A Woman On the Parish
	17th.	Was Buried Mrs. Place
	18th.	Was Buried James Edes
	25th.	Was Buried Mrs. Holson
	do.	Was Buried Samuel Hopkin's Child
June	4th.	Was Buried Mrs. Gibbs
	8th.	Was Buried John Fripp
	14th.	Was Buried Samuel Wallace
	do.	Was Buried John Dawson's Child
	17th.	Was Buried Joseph Nicholson's ditto
	21st.	Was Buried Andrew Wills
	30th.	Was Buried Mrs. Nelmes' Son
July	5th.	Was Buried Andrew Sillivant
	do.	Was Buried Samuel Hodsons, Son
	do.	Was Buried Charlotte Sarazin
	do.	Was Buried Miss Lucia Boone's daughter
	8th.	Was Buried Ann Croft

	11th.	Was Buried Charles Shinners Child
	do.	Was Buried Miss Isabella Chalmers Child
	do.	Was Buried Benjamin Bakers Child

E. Poinsett (Registr.)

1762		
Augst.	10th.	Was Buried Benjamin Harvey
	16th.	Was Buried Richard Park Stobo's Child
	do.	Was Buried James Rodger's Child
	22d.	Was Buried Thomas White
	24th.	Was Buried John Blackney
	do.	Was Buried John McQueen's Son
	do.	Was Buried Agnes Dawson
	30th.	Was Buried A Child
Septr	3rd.	Was Buried Elizabeth Harrison
	do	Was Buried A Child
	13th.	Was Buried James Keally
	20th.	Was Buried A Man
	24th.	Was Buried Sarah Ramsey
	28th.	Was Buried James Richards' Child
Octobr.	3d.	Was Buried Darby Pendergrass' Child
	6th.	Was Buried Benjamin Allen's Son
	14th.	Was Buried Bastian Eugo
	15th.	Was Buried Mrs. Flemming' Son
	21st.	Was Buried Capt. Benson
	22d.	Was Buried Ann French
	28th.	Was Buried James Davies
Novr.	12th.	Was Buried John McQueen
	19th.	Was Buried A Child
	do.	Was Buried William Monroe
decemr.	12th.	Was Buried James Warren
	13th.	Was Buried A Man
	18th.	Was Buried A Woman & A Child
	21st.	Was Buried A Man
	24th.	Was Buried Elizabeth Hawkins
	do.	Was Buried Mrs. Johnson
	do.	Was Buried Thomas Rodey
1763		
Jany.	17th.	Was Buried William Scott

E. Poinsett (Regstr)

1763

Jany.	27th.	Was Buried Sarah Belshaw On the Parish
	28th.	Was Buried Margaret Cocklin
	30th.	Was Buried Charles Smith On The Parish
	do.	Was Buried Robert Luckus
Feby.	4th.	Was Buried Alexander Young
	11th.	Was Buried Hannah Gordon On the Parish
	do.	Was Buried Daniel Cannon's Son
	do.	Was Buried Thomas Linthwaite
	16th.	Was Buried Lachlan Blackneys Wife
	26th.	Was Buried John Jones
	29th.	Was Buried John Burrows' Wife
	do.	Was Buried William Stone On the Parish
Mar.	3d.	Was Buried A Child On the Parish
	9th.	Was Buried Ellis On ditto
	12th.	Was Buried Daniel Grant
	14th.	Was Buried Capt. Burton
	16th.	Was Buried Robert Hill On the Parish
	19th.	Was Buried Mr. Cannons Apprentice
	do.	Was Buried Doctr. Heweth
	20th.	Was Buried John Sturgeon On the Parish
	26th.	Was Buried John Delack On ditto
	do.	Was Buried Stephen Smith's Child
	28th.	Was Buried Hugh Anderson
	31st.	Was Buried Nancy Smith On the Parish
	do.	Was Buried Benjamin Backhouse's Child
April	14th.	Was Buried Andrew Hickley
	do.	Was Buried Elizabeth Hockwell's Child
	do.	Was Buried Henry West
	19th.	Was Buried Mrs. Railey
	21st.	Was Buried John Wood
	do.	Was Buried Mr. Burges daughter

E. Poinsett (Registr.

1763

April	22nd.	Was Buried Mrs. Walkers Child
	do.	Was Buried Samuel Liddle
	do.	Was Buried Jarvis Williams Child
	28th.	Was Buried Mrs Brown Child
May	4th.	Was Buried David Green A Soldier
	do.	Was Buried A Soldiers Child
	11th.	Was Buried Simeon Feild
	do.	Was Buried Benjamin Godfrey's Child

	19th.	Was Buried Alexander Stewart, Justice of the Peace
	28th.	Was Buried A Man On the Parish
	do.	Was Buried James Tonge's Wife
June	2d.	Was Buried John Russell
	3d.	Was Buried John Shaw's Child
	5th.	Was Buried Robert Fairweather
	9th.	Was Buried Margaret Russell On the Parish
	19th.	Was Buried A Man On the Parish
	24th.	Was Buried Elizabeth Woolford
	do.	Was Buried Richard Holland
	do.	Was Buried Daniel Easton
	30th.	Was Buried Mrs. Corbett
July	2d.	Was Buried A Man On the Parish
	3d.	Was Buried Mary Uskwood On ditto
	8th.	Was Buried Mary Welch On ditto
	do.	Was Buried George Sheeds Child
	15th.	Was Buried Henry Loockus On the Parish
	29th.	Was Buried Eleanor French's Child
Aug.	3d.	Was Buried James Glover
	4th.	Was Buried Thomas Batty
	5th.	Was Buried A Man On the Parish
	12th.	Was Buried Mr. Moss On ditto
	do.	Was Buried Nicholas Farrit On ditto

E. Poinsett (Registr.)

1763		
Septemr.	3d.	Was Buried James Owen & Leonard Cample
	do.	Was Buried Mr. Robertson's Child
	7th.	Was Buried John Springer
	9th.	Was Buried Anthony Sahlers Child
	do.	Was Buried Stephen Carmon
	do.	Was Buried Mary Jones
	do.	Was Buried Elizabeth Knowles
	do.	Was Buried Margaret King
	15th.	Was Buried Thomas Linning
	17th.	Was Buried Thomas Evance's Child
	do.	Was Buried William Coats Child
	22d.	Was Buried John Thompson
	24th.	Was Buried A Man On the Parish
	do.	Was Buried Patrick Bryan On ditto
	do.	Was Buried Mrs. Guthrie
	do.	Was Buried Mr. Gadsdens Child
Octor.	5th.	Was Buried Mrs. Creightons Child
	6th.	Was Buried Samuel Robins On the Parish

do. Was Buried James Richards Child
8th. Was Buried Jacob Viart
11th. Was Buried Robert Bolton
do. Was Buried Samuel Conyers
12th. Was Buried Mr. Martin
15th. Was Buried Capt. Butler
17th. Was Buried Elizabeth Kings Child
18th. Was Buried John Greenwood
19th. Was Buried Edward Fenwicke's Child
do. Was Buried John Huffs Child
do. Was Buried Thomas Tucker's Child
25th. Was Buried Rachael Fairchild
do. Was Buried Darby Pendergrass' Child
do. Was Buried Mary Hannah & Daniel Sillivan On the Parish
28th. Was Buried Doctr. August Jehné

E. Poinsett (Registr.)

Burials 314

1763
Octor.
28th. Was Buried Mrs. Linthwaites Child
do. Was Buried William Watson
31st. Was Buried A Man On the Parish
Novr. 5th. Was Buried Henry Hext
do. Was Buried Henry Crouch Senr.
12th. Was Buried Henry Lybert
14th. Was Buried Francis Fisher
16th. Was Buried John Irvin
22d. Was Buried Thomas Bolton
30th. Was Buried John Hewes Child
do. Was Buried Henry Hollwell
decemr. 4th. Was Buried Sarah Martin On the Parish
5th. Was Buried A Man On ditto
8th. Was Buried Alexander Garden Revd's Wife
14th. Was Buried Hannah Obryan & Barnd. Drougpt. On the Parish
1764
Jany 4th. Was Buried John James
do. Was Buried Lydia Clerk
6th. Was Buried Joseph Powells Child
do. Was Buried Mrs. Kirkwood
10th. Was Buried Mrs. Griffith
13th. Was Buried Thomas Sibson
16th. Was Buried Joanna Davies & A Man On the Parish
do. Was Buried James Jarvis On the Parish
19th. Was Buried Thomas Fletcher

	21st.	Was Buried John McCoy ....
	22d.	Was Buried Benjamin Simmons Junr's Wife ....
	....	
1763		
August	5th.	Was Buried William Jones ....
Octr.	15th.	Was Buried Samuel Brailsford's Child ....
1764		
January	21st.	Was Buried A Man of Capt. Love ....
	26th.	Was Buried Mrs. Burk ....
February	4th.	Was Buried Thomas Lambe ....
	6th.	Was Buried Jeremiah VanRansselear ....

E. Poinsett (Regstr.)

1764		
February	15th.	Was Buried Capt. Parker ....
	19th.	Was Buried George Walker ....
	25th.	Was Buried Ann Air ....
March	7th.	Was Buried George Lewis ....
	do.	Was Buried A Man from Mrs. Nelme's ....
	11th.	Was Buried Mrs. Lance ....
	14th.	Was Buried Thomas Raven ....
April	2d.	Was Buried James Stewart ....
	do.	Was Buried Samuel Perkins ....
	20th.	Was Buried A Man from Mr. Cantle's ....
	do.	Was Buried Arnold Harvey ....
	do.	Was Buried Henry Laurens' Child ....
	27th.	Was Buried Mrs. Coulliette ....
May	11th.	Was Buried Mrs. Gordon ....
	12th.	Was Buried Thomas Coulliette ....
	15th.	Was Buried Margaret Furgus ....
	do.	Was Buried Mr. Leques Child ....
	do.	Was Buried Francis Grenick ....
	do.	Was Buried John Guerard ....
	do.	Was Buried Edward Handbury ....
	21st.	Was Buried Charles Dawson's Child ....
	23d.	Was Buried Mrs. Scott ....
	27th.	Was Buried William Draytons Child ....
June	1st.	Was Buried William Beles Child ....
	2d.	Was Buried John Burk ....
	3d.	Was Buried John Hume's Son ....
	4th.	Was Buried Thomas Bell ....
	do.	Was Buried John Lee ....
	do.	Was Buried Charles Pinckneys Child ....
	8th.	Was Buried Henry Lyberts Child ....
	12th.	Was Buried Thomas Nightingle's do. ....

	do.	Was Buried James Phillips ....
	23d.	Was Buried Mrs. Linning ....

E. Poinsett (Registr.)

Burials 316

1764		
June	23d.	Was Buried John Martins Child ....
	28th.	Was Buried William Forbes ....
July	3d.	Was Buried Thomas Lloyd' Child ....
	do.	Was Buried George Logans do. ....
	9th.	Was Buried Thomas Harberson ....
	10th.	Was Buried Elsinore' Child ....
	12th.	Was Buried Thomas Osburn ....
	16th.	Was Buried John Torrans' Child ....
	19th.	Was Buried Charles Crouch's do. ....
	28th.	Was Buried Francis Nicholson's do. ....
	do.	Was Buried John Baileys do. ....
	do.	Was Buried Mrs. Hatfield ....
Aug.	6th.	Was Buried Mr. Lambert' Child ....
	14th.	Was Buried Mrs. Calvert ....
	do.	Was Buried Doctr. Chalmondely Dering's Child ....
1764		
Jany	26th.	Was Buried John McNeyle (on the Parish) ....
	do.	Was Buried Mrs. Burk do. .... } These are already registered
Feby.	4th.	Was Buried Sarah Smith .... }
	do.	Was Buried Thomas Lambe .... }
	25th.	Was Buried Ann Bowles ....
Mar.	14th.	Was Buried Daniel McDaniel, (Parish) ....
April	23d.	Was Buried Mrs. Gibbs do. ....
	do.	Was Buried Michael Legaree do. ....
June	22d.	Was Buried Miss Benfield ....
	23d.	Was Buried Langridge ....
Augst.	14th.	Was Buried Susanna Whims (Parish) ....
Septemr.	1st.	Was Buried John Norman do. ....
	5th.	Was Buried Joseph Green do. ....
	do.	Was Buried John Wisher ....

E. Poinsett (Registr.)

Burials 317

1764		
Ball		On the 12th. September 1764 Was Buried Mrs. Ball
— — — —	do.	Was Buried Benjamin Yarnolds Child ....
Septr.	13th.	Was Buried Mrs. Cunningham (Parish) ....
	16th.	Was Buried James Marshall ....
	19th.	Was Buried Daniel Horry's Child ....

	do.	Was Buried Samuel Hopkins Child
	25th.	Was Buried Tunis Tebout's Child
	28th.	Was Buried Margaret Hickey (Parish)
Octr.	2d.	Was Buried Alexander Broughton[1]
	do.	Was Buried John Hatfield's Child
	7th.	Was Buried Abraham Andersons
	do.	Was Buried Robert Walker
	9th.	Was Buried John Conner (Parish)
	11th.	Was Buried Benjamin Smiths Child
	14th.	Was Buried A Man On the Parish
	do.	Was Buried John Oxendines Child
	do.	Was Buried William Coats Child
	24th.	Was Buried A Man On the Parish
	26th.	Was Buried a man on Do.
	do.	Was Buried Samuel Thomas' Child
Novr.	5th.	Was Buried Mrs. Washing
	10th.	Was Buried Mrs. Walker
	11th.	Was Buried a man on the Parish
1764		
Mar	7th.	Was Buried John Bullman
Septr.	25th.	Was Buried Ward (Hatters Child)
Novr.	4th.	Was Buried Sarah Bullock — —
1764		
Octor.	16th.	Was Buried Frederick Grenswicke
Novr.	19th.	Was Buried Philip Lake (Parish)

Burials 318

1764		
Novemr.	20th.	Was Buried Elizabeth Reason
	28th.	Was Buried John Lamb (Parish)
	30th.	Was Buried John Stevenson (do.)
	do.	Was Buried Francis Bowles (Sailor)
Decemr.	2d.	Was Buried John Conner
	8th.	Was Buried Mrs. Wood
	16th.	Was Buried Rebecca Retattle
1765	24th.	Was Buried Mary Peeke
Jany	9th.	Was Buried Mrs. Roulain
	10th.	Was Buried Martha Young
	do.	Was Buried Edward Richardson
	do.	Was Buried Robert Surly
	16th.	Was Buried Mrs. Atkinson
	25th.	Was Buried Mrs. Smith

[1]Of Kibblesworth (plantation), son of Capt. Nathaniel Broughton, of Mulberry, and grandson of Lieutenant Governor Thomas Broughton, of Mulberry.

26th. Was Buried Guerard Kean
31st. Was Buried Tayler (Parish)
Feby. 4th. Was Buried Silvey Dore
7th. Was Buried Robert Minors
17th. Was Buried Saml. Pickerings daughter
25th. Was Buried Mrs. Trezvant.
26th. Was Buried Joseph Ball Senr's son
do. Was Buried Robert Williams Junr's daughter
29th. Was Buried Samuel Porter
March 5th. Was Buried Mrs. Day
8th. Was Buried Frances Constable & Sarah Chardwell (Parish
13th. Was Buried Joseph Austin
do. Was Buried William Ellis
14th. Was Buried Francis Gillmore's Child
17th. Was Buried John McPhearson

1765
April 7th. Was Buried Mark Anthony Besseleu
do. 3d. Was Buried Mrs. Brady (Parish)
1765
Mar. 31st. Was Buried Mrs. Nightingale
April 15th. Was Buried William Stinson (of Ireland)
22d. Was Buried John son of Learon Foster
27th. Was Buried Joseph Willcocks
28th. Was Buried James Lewis
May 1st. Was Buried John West (Parish)
3d. Was Buried Joseph Smith
April 1st. Was Buried Abraham Remington's son
May 6th. Was Buried Esther Martin (Parish)
7th. Was Buried Joseph, son of Joseph Powell
10th. Was Buried Peter Manigault's Child
12th. Was Buried Sarah of George Day
do. Was Buried Esther Ray (Parish)
14th. Was Buried Thomas Hams daughter
19th. Was Buried William Testard's Son
do. Was Buried John Oxendines son
27th. Was Buried Frances Grunswicke.
June 2d. Was Buried Esther Simmons
do. Was Buried Mr. Nicholsons daughter
10th. Was Buried George Austins Widow
15th. Was Buried Jarvis Williams Child
do. Was Buried Thomas Derbus (Parish)
do. Was Buried John Moultrie Junr' Child

	do.	Was Buried Richard D'harriette' daughter
	do.	Was Buried Jonathan Sarrazins daughter
	16th.	Was Buried Joseph Varree's Child
	do.	Was Buried Elizabeth Plunkett

Burials 320

1765		
June	16th.	Was Buried Todhunter (of York shire)
July	3d.	Was Buried Michael Bryan (Parish)
	19th.	Was Buried Isaac Motte's Child
	20th.	Was Buried John Ward (hatters) Child
	do.	Was Buried Edward Cruse (Parish)
July	1st.	Was Buried John Ward (hatters) Wife
	do.	Was Buried William Testards Wife
	10th.	Was Buried James Geter
	16th.	Was Buried William Willson (Parish)
	19th.	Was Buried William Rawlins (do.)
	do.	Was Buried Eliz Woolford's Child
	do.	Was Buried John of John Harrison
	7th.	Was Buried William Summerfield
	do.	Was Buried Sarah, the wife of John Poinsett
	20th.	Was Buried Richard of Richard Joice
	24th.	Was Buried Jonathan Sarrazins Wife
	30th.	Was Buried Mr. Freeman (of Ireland)
	do.	Was Buried William Hawkes
	31st.	Was Buried John O'kay
Augst.	10th.	Was Buried Elizabeth, the Wife of Lionel Chalmers
	12th.	Was Buried Thomas Newgent (Parish)
	15th.	Was Buried Singen Smiley
	do.	Was Buried Thomas of John Hughs
	do.	Was Buried Walter Wingate (of England)
	19th.	Was Buried Cooper (Parish)
	do.	Was Buried Jarvis Williams Wife
	25th.	Was Buried Thomas Johnston
	do.	Was Buried Eliz. Mary of Arthur Neyle
	30th.	Was Buried Henry Gregorious (Parish)

E. Poinsett (Regstr.)

Burials 321

1765		
Septr.	2d.	Was Buried John Hilton
	9th.	Was Buried Charles Dawson' Child
	10th.	Was Buried John Thompson (Ship Carpenter)
	do.	Was Buried Mary Morrison
	17th.	Was Buried James Gillman

	do.	Was Buried James Simpson (Shoemakers) Child
	do.	Was Buried Joseph of Samuel & Ann Thomas
	30th.	Was Buried Mary Giles
Octor.	2d.	Was Buried John Harcutt
	3d.	Was Buried Jemima of Jemima Adams (Parish)
	7th.	Was Buried Richard Jones (of New London)
	do.	Was Buried Judith of Daniel Horry
	do.	Was Buried Susanna of Mrs Clarke
	11th.	Was Buried Charles of Jonathan Sarrazin
	13th.	Was Buried Mary of Charles Wilman
	14th.	Was Buried Ann of John & Mary Bowen
	do.	Was Buried Mary Williams (Parish)
	17th.	Was Buried Jemima Adams (Parish)
	22d.	Was Buried Elizabeth Clements
	do.	Was Buried John Shuttleworth (of Lankershire)
	do.	Was Buried George Whiten (of Liverpoole)
	do.	Was Buried Charles Reileys Child
	do.	Was Buried James Hunters Child
	27th.	Was Buried William Ellis (of London)
	29th.	Was Buried James Willis
Novr.	2d.	Was Buried Stephen Tough (Parish)
	5th.	Was Buried John Taylor (do.)
	7th.	Was Buried Anson of Elizabeth Lebbay
	do.	Was Buried Gasper Streach (of Holland)

E. Poinsett (registr.)

Burials 322

1765		
Novemr.	9th.	Was Buried Robert Mowles (of Dover)
	10th.	Was Buried John French (of Ireland)
	15th.	Was Buried Isabella wife of Thomas Mills
	16th.	Was Buried George Lee (Parish)
	17th.	Was Buried Magdilene Prioleau Senr.
	18th.	Was Buried John Burger (of Scottland)
	do.	Was Buried Jane Mathias.
	do.	Was Buried Margaret Moore
	19th.	Was Buried Robert Mills (of London)
	25th.	Was Buried Margaret Doyley
	28th.	Was Buried Ann wife of Abraham Remington
Decemr.	2d.	Was Buried James, of Dan'l. Lessesne (of St. Thomas Parish)
	do.	Was Buried McKeman
	30th.	Was Buried Mrs. Bampfield (Widow)
	7th.	Was Buried Sarah Freeman (Parish)
	do.	Was Buried Elizabeth of John & Elizabeth Logan
	13th.	Was Buried Sarah Edes

	17th.	Was Buried Thompson (Parish)
	28th.	Was Buried Robert Williams, Child
1766	do.	Was Buried Joshua Wards Child
Jany.	3d.	Was Buried John Witchouse (Parish)
	4th.	Was Buried John Mackenzie, Capt.
	6th.	Was Buried James Stewart (Parish)
	12th.	Was Buried Lidia Hankinson
	do.	Was Buried Frances, wife of Charles Shinner Esqr.
	14th.	Was Buried Dunken Kirkland
	16th.	Was Buried Wm. Johnston of Geo Milligan
	20th.	Was Buried Mary, of Ben & Catherine Backhouse

E. Poinsett. (Registr.)

1766		
Jany	20th.	Was Buried Patrick Jourdan (of Ireland)
	do.	Was Buried James Sullivan (of do.)
	31st.	Was Buried Thomas, of Edward & Rebecca Weyman
Omitted		
1764		
Sept.	5th.	Was Buried John Clintons wife
	do.	Was Buried John Wilsher
1766		
Feby.	3d.	Was Buried Hugh of William Storland
	5th.	Was Buried James Gillman (Parish)
	13th.	Was Buried William Henderson (Do.)
	14th.	Was Buried William Hart
	16th.	Was Buried William Hamilton (of Ireland)
Mar.	7th.	Was Buried Richard Burnes (of Yorkshire)
	21st.	Was Buried John Bishop (of Liverpoole)
	do.	Was Buried John Campbell (Parish)
	do.	Was Buried Thomas Mills (of Scottland
	do.	Was Buried William Varner (of Falmouth) (Parish)
	25th.	Was Buried Peter Brass
	do.	Was Buried Elizabeth Balding
	do.	Was Buried Charles Grissam (Parish)
	30th.	Was Buried George Eden (of England)
April	13th.	Was Buried William Jackson (of Jamaica)
	do.	Was Buried Joseph Smith
	13th.	Was Buried Rachel Lawrence
	do.	Was Buried Alexander Fife
May	28th.	Was Buried Joseph Scott
	do.	Was Buried Edward Pierce

June	2d.	Was Buried Richard Spell
	do.	Was Buried John Champney's Son
	do.	Was Buried William McDonalds Son
	19th.	Was Buried John Shaw
	do.	Was Buried James Campbell (Parish)

E. Poinsett (Registr.)

Burials 324

1766		
June	24th.	Was Buried Son of Egerton & Leigh
July	2d.	Was Buried Eleanor Kelly (Parish)
	14th.	Was Buried Elizabeth Banbury
	15th.	Was Buried James Bishop
	16th.	Was Buried Robert Boyd
	28th.	Was Buried Ephraim Rice
	do.	Was Buried Joseph Parker
Augst.	4th.	Was Buried William Ogle (of Bristoll)
	5th.	Was Buried John Bartlett
	7th.	Was Buried Jane Perry
	do.	Was Buried Andrew Allen (of Ireland)
	do.	Was Buried Peter Norton (Parish)
	12th.	Was Buried Sarah Kendle (do.)
	13th.	Was Buried Nicholas Flood
	14th.	Was Buried Robert Price Godfrey
	do.	Was Buried Lewis, son of Peter & Timothy
	15th.	Was Buried Mary Thomas (Parish)
	17th.	Was Buried Eleanor Gillmore's Child
	18th.	Was Buried Mary Foster.
	do.	Was Buried William McDonard (of Ireland)
	do.	Was Buried Christopher, son of Christopher & Gadsden
	19th.	Was Buried son of Charles & Dewer
	25th.	Was Buried Alexander Hurbert (of London)
	26th.	Was Buried Peter, son of Peter & — Manigault
	27th.	Was Buried Samuel, son of Samuel & Pickering
	28th.	Was Buried Mary Massey of Mrs. McLean
	31st.	........Ditto........a Woman on the Parish ....
Septr.	3d.	........Ditto........Thomas Lloyd ....
	do.	........Ditto William (a Child of John Cole on the Parish

E. Poinsett (Registr.— —

1766		
Septemr.	5th.	Was Buried Daughter of Mary Hughes, on the Parish
	14th.	Ditto James Powers (on the Parish)
	do.	Ditto James Green Ditto
	do.	Ditto John Denton
	15th.	Ditto Mary a child of Learon Foster
	24th.	Ditto John Hopkins (of Ireland)
	29	Ditto Thomas Stokes
	do.	Ditto Thomas McCreth (of London)
	31st.	Ditto Richard Tuckerman
Octor.	1st.	Ditto John Macklish
	do.	Ditto John Shaw
	5th.	Ditto Daughter of Thomas Atkins ——Parish.
	do.	Ditto James Stevens — —
	do.	Ditto John Brown —
	6th.	Ditto Corley Adam, of Charles Mitchell, Parish,
	do.	Ditto Mary White — —
	do.	Ditto Elizabeth, Child of Philemon Waters —
	8th.	Ditto John of Thomas Bennett — —
	do.	Ditto James of Francis Longwood
	12th.	Ditto John Morrisson
	14th.	Ditto James Greeme (Parish)
	do.	Ditto Hector Berrenger[1] DeBeaufain
	17th.	Ditto William White (Parish)
	do.	Ditto Cornelius Donovan (Ditto)
	18th.	Ditto Nathaniel Nicholl's (Ditto)
	do.	Ditto William Bissett (Ditto —
	20th.	Ditto Henry Smith (of Scotland)
	21st.	Ditto of Charles Shinner,
	22d.	Ditto Richard Elliott (Parish)
	23d.	Ditto John Lancefield (Ditto)

E. Poinsett. (Registr. —

[1]Berenger is the correct spelling. DeBeaufain was born at Orange, France, and came to South Carolina in 1733. He was appointed Collector of His Majesty's Customs at Charles Town in 1743, and to His Majesty's Council for South Carolina in 1747. He died October 13, 1766. He was "allied by blood to the family of our late gracious Queen Caroline". In 1786, by Act of the General Assembly, John Rutledge was authorized to sell his lands for the benefit of his nephew, the Baron de Berenger de Beaufain. A street in Charleston bears his name. See *The Dwelling Houses of Charleston* (Smiths).

1766		
Octor.	24th.	Was Buried Robert Hume — — —
	28th.	Ditto . . Catherine of James Mathews
	29th.	Ditto Caleb Hutson (Parish)
	30th.	Ditto John Burrows
Novr.	3d.	Ditto Catherine of John Mitchell (Parish)
	do.	Ditto Stephen Streeter (Parish)
	8th.	Ditto John Eurin (Ditto)
	10th.	Ditto Joseph Atkinson
	do.	Ditto Doctr. Johnson
	12th.	Ditto Adam Howell (Parish)
	13th.	Ditto William of John & Abigail Watson (of London)
	do.	Ditto Richard Johnson
	14th.	Ditto Martin Solloman (Parish)
	22d.	Ditto Hannah of John & Mary Ward (Hatter)
	28th.	Ditto John Vine (Parish)
	29th.	Ditto James Rippen Ervin (Parish)
	do.	Ditto William Greeme (of Ireland)
	do.	Ditto Mary Hughes (Parish)
Decemr.	2d.	Ditto Thomas Sinnote (Ditto)
	3d.	Ditto James Rowling.
	8th.	Ditto Rebecca of Anthony Gillmore
	9th.	Ditto George Edwards
	12th.	Ditto of John Logan —
	14th.	Ditto James Mathews of Ireland —
	15th.	Ditto Jane a Child of Thos. Norwood (Parish)
	do.	Ditto David Williams —
	16th.	Ditto Elizabeth Payne
	18th.	Ditto Elizabeth of John Jones.

E. Poinsett. (Register)

1766		
Decemr.	18th.	Was Buried Jane Monroe —
	do.	Ditto Margaret Fraser —
	30th.	Ditto John Field —
1767		
Jany.	1st.	Ditto Thomas Waldren —
	10th.	Ditto John Stewart Parish
	14th.	Ditto Ruth Hartman
	do.	Ditto James Walder —
	do.	Ditto Duncan Shaw. Parish —
	16th.	Ditto George Carpenter

	18th.	Ditto	Rachael Waldren —
	19th.	Ditto	Edward Bullard
	do.	Ditto	Gasper McGregor —
	22d.	Ditto	William McGau —
	do.	Ditto	Mary Watson, wife of Archibald Watson
	23d.	Ditto	William Trewin
	24th.	Ditto	Patrick Carrill —
	26th.	Ditto	Thomas of Thos. Lemarr
	28th.	Ditto	Ann Thomas (wife of Samuel Thomas —
	do.	Ditto	Barbara Burkett Parish
	do.	Ditto	William Porter Parish
Feby.	8th.	Ditto	John Cromedy —
	10th.	Ditto	Sarah Williams (wife of John Williams
	11th.	Ditto	Martin Rivers—Parish
	12th.	Ditto	Caleb Lloyd — —
	13th.	Ditto	Thomas Beckett, Parish
	16th.	Ditto	John, son of Mathew Collins, Parish —
	20th.	Ditto	Joseph Runner, Parish,
	21st.	Ditto	Mary Runner, Parish —
	26th.	Ditto	Henry Erven, Parish —
Mar.	1st.	Ditto	Mary, Daughter of Robert Reid, Parish

E. Poinsett. Registr. —

Burials 328

1767			
Mar.	2d.	Was Buried	Thomas of William & Agnus Sloan, Parish
	3d.	Ditto	John Gruber, Parish
	do.	Ditto	Agnus Sloan, Wife of William Sloan —Parish
	do.	Ditto	Susanna, Daughter of Daniel Burgett
	8th.	Ditto	Sarah Fisher
	11th.	Ditto	Andrew Johnston
	do.	Ditto	Daniel Long
	do.	Ditto	of & Robertson (Chairmaker)
	do.	Ditto	James Wiker, Parish)
	15th.	Ditto	Michael Shirer, Parish
	30th.	Ditto	Elizabeth Marshall
	do.	Ditto	Thomas Sheppard
	do.	Ditto,	Thomas, son of the Widow Adams, Parish
April	5th.	Ditto	Collins (a Woman) Parish
	do.	Ditto	John St. John, Parish
	do.	Ditto	William Dormand, Parish,
	do.	Ditto	Elizabeth White, Daughter of Mrs. Hakett
	do.	Ditto	Francis Magau (of France,
	do.	Ditto	William Lackey —

	do.	Ditto Moses Dixcey
	19th.	Ditto Jane (of Edward & Mary Cryer
	do.	Ditto Anna Maria, of Charles Shinner
	26th.	Ditto Thomas Brickles (of Sarah Meeke
	30th.	Ditto Mrs. Barrow, Parish
May	8th.	Ditto William Greeme
	13th.	Ditto John Dunkin, of New England
	do.	Ditto John Johnson
	15th.	Ditto William of Moses & Sarah Mitchell

E. Poinsett. (Registr—

Burials 329

1767

May	15th.	Was Buried William, of Capt. Dawson
	26th.	Ditto John Connoway P.
	do.	Ditto William Hawkens
	27th.	Ditto Warwell P.
	29th.	Ditto Grace of James & Margaret Moffet of Ireland P.
	do.	Ditto Jane Gillin a Child of Do. P.
	do.	Ditto Mary Connoway P.
June	4th.	Ditto Richard Burn (of Barbades
	do.	Ditto Elizabeth of Charles & Martha Dawson
	7th.	Ditto Sarah of James & Barbara Simpson
	do.	Ditto Jacob of Isaac & Ann Motte
	9th.	Ditto Mary of Thomas & Elizabeth Campbell P.
	12th.	Ditto Thomas Morris (Ship Master)
	do.	Ditto Martha (wife of Peter Boquet Junr.
	do.	Ditto Samuel Kerby P.
	do.	Ditto of John & Champneys
	13th.	Ditto Edward Harley (of New Castle in England. P.
	14th.	Ditto Robert of Robert & Agnus Hanneu P.
	do.	Ditto William of John & Christian Almond P
	15th.	Ditto John Hockstal P.
	do.	Ditto Isabella of Henry & Mary Lybert —
	20th.	Ditto Damond, of London —
	21st.	Ditto Hugh Fee (of Ireland
	do.	Ditto John of John & Christian Almond P.
	23d.	Ditto Thomas Crotty P.
	do.	Ditto Susanna of William & Elizabeth Hay, of Ireland P.
	24th.	Ditto Robert of Ditto P.
	do.	Ditto Rebecca of William & Mary Bonner (of Ireland P.

	do.	Ditto Elizabeth, wife of Hugh Morrison of Ireland P.

E. Poinsett, (Registr. ———

1767		
June	25th.	Was Buried, William Kelly of Ireland
	26th.	Ditto, Luke Blakey of Ireland P.
	do.	Ditto, Mary, Wife of James Laufin of Ireland P.
	do.	Ditto, John of James & Grizel Robertson of Ireland P.
	do.	Ditto, Lydia wife of Robert Rawlins
	27th	Ditto, Philip Dougherty,
	do.	Ditto, William of James Laufin of Ireland P.
	do.	Ditto, A Child of Eleanor Burts of Do. P.
	do.	Ditto, Jacob Watts P.
	28th.	Ditto, David of Richard & Elizabeth Scott of Ireland P.
	29th.	Ditto, Francis of Francis & Nicholson
	do.	Ditto, George Spender (of London
	do.	Ditto, William Channon P.
	30th.	Ditto, Martin Fomatu P.
	do.	Ditto, William of William & Mary Seal (of Ireland p.
	do.	Ditto, George of James & Grizel Robertson of Ireland P.
	do.	Ditto, Mary wife of John Cox of Ireland P.
July	1st.	Ditto, Sarah of Hugh Morrison of Ireland P.
	do.	Ditto, Margaret of Hugh Morrison of Do. P.
	do.	Ditto, Robert of William & Mary Downes of Ireland P.
	do.	Ditto, Elizabeth Rodgers of Ireland P.
	2d.	Ditto, Margaret wife of John Maitland of Ireland P.
	3d.	Ditto, John Oliver, of England
	4th.	Ditto, Jane of John and Elizabeth Martin of England P.
	do.	Ditto, Margaret of Richard & Elizabeth Scott, of Ireland P.
	5th.	Ditto, Catherine of John & Jane Rodgers of Do. P.
	do.	Ditto, Abraham of the Widow Trumble of Do. P.
	6th.	Ditto, Rachael of Hugh Morrison
	do.	Ditto, Amarinthia Wife of Benjamin Elliott
	8th.	Ditto, James of Robert & Mary Montgomery

	8th.	Ditto, John of Robert & Margaret Young of Ireland P.
	do.	Ditto, Agnus of John & Jane Turk of Do. P.
	9th.	Ditto, Mary Wife of Mathew Reid of Do. P.
	do.	Ditto, John of James & Grizelle Robinson of Do. P.

E. Poinsett. (Registr. —

Burials 331

1767		
July	10th.	Was Buried, William Webster of England —
	do.	Ditto, Elizabeth of John & Jane Rogers of Ireland P.
	do.	Ditto, George of John & Elizabeth Hollis of Do. P.
	12th.	Ditto, Sarah a Child of Mathew Reid of Do. P.
	do.	Ditto, Esther, wife of Philip Brackinridge of Do. P.
	do.	Ditto, John of the Widow Trumble of Do. P.
	do.	Ditto, Margaret, of David & Elizabeth Cannady P.
	do.	Ditto, Benjamin of John & Sophia Packrow
	13th.	Ditto Elizabeth of Nathl. White of Ireland P.
	do.	Ditto, John Owens of Ireland P.
	14th.	Ditto, Ann Owens of Do. P.
	do.	Ditto, Robert of John & Mary Varnon of Ireland P.
	do.	Ditto, William of John & Isabella Martin of Ireland P.
	15th.	Ditto, James Elsinor
	do.	Ditto, Elizabeth Andrews of Ireland P.
	16th.	Ditto, Mary Smith (Carolina Born Aged 74 years
	17th.	Ditto, Jane of John & Mary Vernon, of Ireland P.
	do.	Ditto, John of John & Jane Ordd of Do. P.
	do.	Ditto, Mary of John & Elizabeth Rogers of Do. P.
	do.	Ditto, Jane of William & Mary Seal of Do. P.
	18th.	Ditto, David of Elizabeth Sloan of Do. P.
	do.	Ditto, William Thompson (of England
	20th.	Ditto, Sarah Black, of Ireland P.
	do.	Ditto, Mary Mongomery, of Do. P.
	do.	Ditto, Ann Anson P.
	21st.	Ditto, Jane of James & Jane Johnson of Ireland P.

	22d.	Ditto, Mary of & Gordon of Do. P.
	23d.	Ditto, Sarah of Philip Brackinridge of Do. P.
	do.	Ditto, Robert Rodgers of Do. P.
	24th.	Ditto, Walter Stewart of Do. P.
	25th.	Ditto, William Andrews of Do. P.
	26th.	Ditto, Mary of John & Jane Ordd of Ireland P.
	do.	Ditto, Susanna of Robert Peacock of Do. P.
	do.	Ditto, John Rogers, of Ireland, Father Mother, Brothers, & Sisters all dead.

E. Poinsett, (Registr. —

Burials 332

1767		
July	27th.	Was Buried, Mary of William & Mary Seal of Ireland P.
	28th.	Ditto, of & Hutchens
	29th.	Ditto Richard of Philip Brackinridge of Ireland P.
	do.	Ditto James Sullavan of Do.
	30th.	Ditto, Elizabeth of Hugh & Elizabeth Morrison of Ireland P
	31st.	Ditto James Carr, of Ireland P.
Aug.	1st.	Ditto, a Child of Judith Protertent
	3d.	Ditto, William White P.
	4th.	Ditto, Sarah Meek & Deborah Trail
	do.	Ditto, Sheeling a Soldier —
	do.	Ditto, Frances Burley P.
	5th.	Ditto, Elizabeth Crawford of Ireland P.
	8th.	Ditto, Benjamin Backhouse,
	12th.	Ditto, James Wright, P.
	13th.	Ditto, Peter Kelley from Santee
	16th.	Ditto, Elizabeth Carline, P.
	17th.	Ditto, John Harris, P.
	do.	Ditto, Montgomery Fee, of Ireland
	27th.	Ditto, Ann Mathews.
	do.	Ditto, Arnold Witherholt, Soldier,
	do.	Ditto, a Child of William Gibbs
	25th.	Ditto, John Dimes, P—
	27th.	Ditto, Elizabeth McClanachan
	30th.	Ditto, A child of Benjamin Webb,
	31st.	Ditto, Samuel Walker,
Septemr.	1st.	Ditto, Richard Barnsby Skett,
	4th.	Ditto, A Child of William Gibbes,
	do.	Ditto, George Row,
	do.	Ditto, Rebecca Johnson,
	11th.	Ditto. Soldiers Wife

do.	Ditto,	Rhett of Thomas & Smith
13th.	Ditto,	Eleanor, of Catherine Backhouse
do.	Ditto,	Balguy Littlewood,

E. Poinsett, Registr. —

1767			
Septemr.	14th.	Was Buried,	William Grant
	17th.	Ditto,	Patrick MacDowell of Ireland,
	23d.	Ditto,	Joseph of Benjamin & Yarnald
	do.	Ditto,	Rhoda Dean
	do.	Ditto,	James Doucherty, of Ireland
	24th.	Ditto,	David, of David Wise.
	do.	Ditto,	Stephen Chipchase,
	do.	Ditto,	of Henry & Laurens
	26th.	Ditto,	John Neyle
	27th.	Ditto,	Martha Blott
	29th.	Ditto,	William, of Samuel & Jane Groves
Octor.	1st.	Ditto,	Peter Butler,
	2d.	Ditto,	Martha Staten
	do.	Ditto,	Samuel Witton, P.
	do.	Ditto,	Edward Cole, P.
	6.	Ditto,	Thomas Farrell, P.
	do.	Ditto,	The Revd. Mr. Joseph Dacre Wilton,[1]
	7th.	Ditto,	John Lynah, of Ireland,
	10th.	Ditto,	Jacob Smith, P.
	do.	Ditto,	Thomas Sanders P.
	15th.	Ditto,	Alexander Strattenberry, P.
	19th.	Ditto,	Thomas, of Michael & Catherine Spaldron, Soldiers Child
	do.	Ditto,	James Fling.
	22d.	Ditto,	Catherine Backhouse
	do.	Ditto,	Hannah, Hurst —
	do.	Ditto,	Mongin of Robert & Elizabeth Harvey,
	27th.	Ditto,	Hugh MacFarling, of Ireland
	29th.	Ditto,	William Smith P.
Novr.	3d.	Ditto,	Edward Greeme, of England
	do.	Ditto,	Nathaniel Dean.
	do.	Ditto,	John Levingston
	do.	Ditto,	Lucia Grissam P.

[1]He arrived in Charles Town in 1761 and was made Assistant Rector of St. Philip's in January, 1762. He died October 6, 1767. (See Dalcho's *Protestant Episcopal Church in South Carolina*, 189-198.)

	13th.	Ditto,	Samuel of Abraham & Jane Jones P.
	do.	Ditto,	William Niell P.
	16th.	Ditto,	Jane, Wife of Abraham Jones
	do.	Ditto,	Sarah Lacey of Ireland.
	18th.	Ditto,	George Boon, of Ireland.
	do.	Ditto,	Sarah, Wife of Monro

E. Poinsett, (Registr.

Burials 334

1767			
Novemr.	22d.	Was Buried,	Ann Clements, Wife of White Outerbridge.
	do.	Ditto,	John Balligo P.
	24th.	Ditto,	Mary Legg,
	do.	Ditto,	Mrs. Turner P.
	27th.	Ditto,	Thomas Giventon, of London
	28th.	Ditto,	James Clark, of New England,
	29th.	Ditto,	James Chain P.
	30th.	Ditto,	Francis Lee, son of Thomas Lee,
Decemr.	2d.	Ditto,	Daniel Burget Junr.
	3d.	Ditto,	Thomas Burton
	do.	Ditto,	Elias Todut P.
	6th.	Ditto,	Obedience Sullivan P.
	8th.	Ditto,	James Johnson P.
	10th.	Ditto,	Wife of Andrew Lord
	11th.	Ditto,	George Falckner, of England
	12th.	Ditto,	Mary, wife of Jacob Ham,
	14th.	Ditto,	Elizabeth, Daughter of Peter Boquet Senr.
	17th.	Ditto,	Mary of Jacob & Rebecca Motte.
	18th.	Ditto,	Mary Bailly P.
	24th.	Ditto,	Mary, Wife of William Wragg
	29th.	Ditto,	Thomas of James & Jane Grey P.
1768			
Janry.	1st.	Ditto,	Zacharia of Thomas & Catherine Lamar
	do.	Ditto,	Mary of James & Mary MacDowell P.
	9th.	Ditto,	Elizabeth of Adam & Mary Harbinson P.
	14th.	Ditto,	John of James & Sarah Wiley P.
	15th.	Ditto,	A Child of Peter & Ann Manigault
	20th.	Ditto,	Mark of Paty & Elizabeth Holmes,
	23d.	Ditto,	Henry St. Martin
	25th.	Ditto,	George Chapple P.
	30th.	Ditto,	Wife of Oliver Cromwell
	27th.	Ditto,	Jesty Daughter of James & Mary Shackels P.
	29th.	Ditto,	Christiana, of Abraham Jones P.

Febry.	4th.	Ditto, Margaret Lavender,
	12th.	Ditto, John Crosbey, of Yorkshire, in England, Sailer
	14th.	Ditto, Samuel Faris of Philadelphia
	18th.	Ditto, Wife of John Bennett.

E. Poinsett (Registr. —

1768		
Febry.	18th.	Was Buried, William of Thomas & Margaret Connelly
Febry.	21st.	Ditto, Richard Booker Colthuard
	do.	Ditto, George Moon
	26th	Ditto, Mary Ross, P.
	do.	Ditto, Wife of James Ried
	do.	Ditto, Lucia Child of Mrs. Clark
	27th.	Ditto, Ogil Smith, P.
	28th.	Ditto, Charles Shinner Esqr. Chief Justice[1]
	do.	Ditto, Joseph Mitchell P.
	do.	Ditto, Mary White,
Mar.	5th.	Ditto, James Cook
	do.	Ditto, John Ellis —
	do.	Ditto, Lucia Kent —
	6th.	Ditto, Grace Connelly —
	do.	Ditto, William Widows
	do.	Ditto, Jonathan Brazell, of London
	12th.	Ditto, John Fowler,
	14th.	Ditto, George Coleman P.
	18th.	Ditto, Louisa Wife of James Richards
	22d.	Ditto, A child of Robert Howard
	25th.	Ditto, Isabella Orr,
	26th.	Ditto, John Davis,
	Do.	Ditto, Mary of Richard & Catherine Clark,
	27th.	Ditto, Mark Welsh
April	1st.	Ditto, George Barcolt P.
	8th.	Ditto, Allcie Coker P.
	do.	Ditto, William Middleton
	9th.	Ditto, Richard Grandle
	11th.	Ditto, Mary Taylor P.
	do.	Ditto, William Hall (Carpenter)
	13th.	Ditto, John Boone of Catherine Holmes
	do.	Ditto, Sarah Stoughtenbourgh,

[1]He had been appointed in 1762. (See McCrady's *South Carolina under Royal Government.*)

May	1st.	Ditto,	Jeremiah of Joseph & Martha Roper,
	2d.	Ditto,	Richard Towell .... P.
	15th.	Ditto,	Alexander Blank .... P.
	19th.	Ditto,	Robert Franshaw .... P.
	do.	Ditto,	Ann Breedlove ....

E. Poinsett, (Registr — — —

Burials — — 336

1768			
May	22d.	Was Buried Owen Duckett	P.
	31st.	Ditto,	Willm. Richd. Forde of Pon Pon
	do.	Ditto,	Lewis of James Richards — —
June	3d.	Ditto,	Margaret Hughs — —
	do.	Ditto,	Isaac Lloyd, of Rebecca Widow of Thomas
	6th.	Ditto,	Mary of Mary Veritett —
	do.	Ditto,	James Sinclair P —
	11th.	Ditto,	William Newman —
	12th.	Ditto,	John of & Elizabeth Lynch —
	do.	Ditto,	Ann Martha of John & Mary Beale
	15th.	Ditto,	Stephen of Edward & Rebecca Shrewsberry — —
	22d.	Ditto,	Mongo of Elizabeth Butler Widow of Peter
	23d.	Ditto,	John of William & Elizabeth Clark —
	25th.	Ditto,	Sarah, wife of James Skirving Senr. —
	do.	Ditto,	Martha of William & Martha Edwards —
	do.	Ditto,	Ann of David & Margaret Swanson —
	28th.	Ditto,	William of John & Logan —
July	4th.	Ditto.	Sarah Evans P —
	9th.	Ditto,	of Oliver Cromwell — —
	11th.	Ditto,	Francis Thody (of New York —
	18th.	Ditto,	Mary May P —
	21st.	Ditto,	Samuel Merideth — —
	22d.	Ditto,	John Evans P —
	24th.	Ditto,	John Ackions P —
	do.	Ditto,	Isabella of the Widow Campble —
	26th.	Ditto,	Rencha (say Amarinthia, of John & Waring
	do.	Ditto,	Lucretia of Lucretia Connely P —

Burials 337

1768			
Augst.	1st.	Was Buried	Wife of John Williams Ship Carpenter

	2d.	Ditto,	John Cantle —
	3d.	Ditto,	Lambert Lance —
	4th.	Ditto,	Henry of Theodore Trezvant —
	do.	Ditto,	Leonard Bodell —
	9th.	Ditto,	Robert Mills —
	10th.	Ditto,	Henry Glass —
	11th.	Ditto,	Susanna of William Lake
	13th.	Ditto,	Samuel Fitzherburt —
	15th	Ditto,	Susanna Wife of Roger Pinckney —
	28th.	Ditto,	John of Lowry & Hannah Prince
	31st.	Ditto,	John Price — P.
Septemr.	2d.	Ditto,	John Denniston P —
	do.	Ditto,	Martha of Joseph & Martha Roper —
	do.	Ditto,	Daniel of Daniel Roberts, P.
	5th.	Ditto,	Mathew Cross —
	do.	Ditto,	Ann, Wife of Mathew Dunlap P.
	8th	Ditto,	Edward Picking —
	do.	Ditto,	Mary Mitchell (Free Negroe)
	do.	Ditto,	Patrick Griffin P.
	do.	Ditto,	Sarah of & Mary Campbell — —
	12th.	Ditto,	Mary Obrian —
	16th.	Ditto,	Sarah of William & Ann Phillips — —
	19th.	Ditto,	Robert Spence P.
	20th.	Ditto,	John Welch — — —
	22d.	Ditto,	Robert Holson — —
	25th.	Ditto,	William Punting P. —
	do.	Ditto,	Henry Richardson — —
	26th.	Ditto,	Mary, Wife of Probart Howarth — — —.

E. Poinsett Registr.

Burials 338

1768			
Septemr.	26th.	Was Buried	Christian, Wife of William McCullor
	28th.	Ditto,	Hannah of Elizabeth Cooper P.
	do.	Ditto,	Lining — —
	30th.	Ditto,	Abigail, Wife of Lawrence
October	4th.	Ditto,	John Shenton P.
	8th.	Ditto,	Samuel Kingwood P.
	do.	Ditto,	Lydia McCarthy — —
	10th.	Ditto,	James Galloway P.
	13th.	Ditto,	John Walter P.
	do.	Ditto,	Rachael Daughter of James & Gordon (Carpenter)
	do.	Ditto,	Hugh Dalley (of London)
	14th.	Ditto,	Samuel of Thomas & Elizabeth Tomlinson — —

	18th.	Ditto,	Hugh Ballentine — —	
	19th.	Ditto,	of Samuel & Hopkins —	
	25th.	Ditto,	Mary Edgill — — —	
	31st.	Ditto,	of Mrs. Oldridge	P.
Novemr.	1st.	Ditto,	Mary Bolter	P.
	do.	Ditto,	Margaret Stephens (daughter in Law to Jac. Faris)	
	2d.	Ditto,	Andrew Birk (Child)	P.
	do.	Ditto,	James Peto (Child	P.
	6th.	Ditto,	Daniel Hindes	P.
	do.	Ditto,	John Farrer (of England)	
	do.	Ditto,	William Kenny (Captain)	
	7th.	Ditto,	Precilla Burrows	P.
	9th.	Ditto,	Catherine Moffett (Ireland)	
	11th.	Ditto,	Jane Young (of Ireland)	P.
	12th.	Ditto,	Samuel Henry (of Ireland)	P.
	do.	Ditto,	John of John & Harisson (Captain)	
	do.	Ditto,	Thomas Gunter — — —	
	do.	Ditto,	of William & Kelsey	
	20th.	Ditto,	Ann Mitchell	P.
	21st.	Ditto,	Thos. Howell — — —	

E. Poinsett (Registr. —

Burials — — 339

1768				
Novempr.	22d.	Was Buried	Mary Newman	P.
	do.	Ditto,	John Golding	P.
	23d.	Ditto,	James Russ	P.
	28th.	Ditto,	Archibald McCoy	
	29th.	Ditto,	William Thornton	
Decemr.	1st.	Ditto,	Eliz. of Anthony & Pheeba Duesto	P.
	do.	Ditto,	Joseph of Jno. Fraser	
	do.	Ditto,	Mary Robins	P.
	14th.	Ditto,	George Beard —	
	15th.	Ditto,	of John & Isabella Nevine —	
	23d.	Ditto,	Agness Walter	P.
	25th.	Ditto,	Catherine Croft	
	26th.	Ditto,	A Man at Jno. Bureys	P.
	do.	Ditto,	A Child of George Shipping —	
	27th.	Ditto,	Archibald Wilson — —	
	28th.	Ditto,	Daniel Tresvant —	
	do.	Ditto,	Wife of Saml. Hopkins	
	do.	Ditto,	George Gordon — —	
1769				
Janry	4th.	Ditto,	James Dove — —	
	do.	Ditto,	Robert Davis — —	

	5th.	Ditto,	Mary Sterling	P.
	do.	Ditto,	Martha of Charles & Dawson	
	do.	Ditto,	James Tebout	P.
	8th.	Ditto,	Ruben Pring — —	
	14th	Ditto,	John Wells	
	do.	Ditto,	Edward Beale — —	
	do.	Ditto,	Elizabeth Woolford — —	
	22d.	Ditto,	Hammilton Cummings of Jane Martin	
	27th.	Ditto,	Mary Gadsden — — —	
	do.	Ditto,	Wife of Thos. Williams	
	30th.	Ditto,	Christian Applesack — —	
Febry.	2d.	Ditto,	George Seaman	
	do.	Ditto,	John Buttery — — —	
	7th.	Ditto,	Eleanor Rynd	
	11th.	Ditto,	Frances Prue — — —	

E. Poinsett (Registr. —

Burials 340

1769				
February	23d.	Was Buried	of John Brown.	P.
	do.	Ditto . .	of James Fitts	P.
	25th.	Ditto, .	Catherine Cotteral	P.
	do.	Ditto . .	Ephraim Brown	P.
Mar.	3d.	Ditto.	A Man Drowned at Roper's Wharf	P.
	4th.	Ditto.	Edward of Edward & Ann Thomas	
	do.	Ditto,	Edward Newbald	P.
	7th.	Ditto.	Mary MacDonald	P.
	do.	Ditto.	Richard Elliott	P.
	9th.	Ditto	Mary Castolo	P —
	12th.	Ditto,	Frances Gutting	P —
	do.	Ditto.	William Bolton	P —
	do.	Ditto,	Margaret MacDugal	P —
	do.	Ditto,	Thomas Colman	
	do.	Ditto.	James Rogers	
	do.	Ditto.	John Hill	
	23d.	Ditto,	Mary Harleston	
	do.	Ditto,	Elizabeth Bartley	P —
	25th.	Ditto.	George Higgins	
	29th.	Ditto,	of Joseph Maxsey	
April		Ditto.	Stephen Smith	
		Ditto.	Sarah Rose	
	8th.	Ditto.	John Murray	P —
	12th.	Ditto.	Arthur of John Watts	P —
	13th.	Ditto.	Sarah Dixon	P —
	do.	Ditto.	John Ferritt	P —
	21st.	Ditto.	Thomas Clifford	

	26th.	Ditto. Christian Handle	P —
	do.	Ditto. William Davis	
	27th.	Ditto. of John & Harrison	Doctr.
May	3d.	Ditto. Jacob Motte of John & Dart	— —
	5th.	Ditto, Mrs. Massey	P.
	7th.	Ditto. Mary Smith	P —
	do.	Ditto. of Catherine Martin	P.
	10th.	Ditto. Martha Bremar	
	11th.	Ditto. Moses Audibert	
	20th.	Ditto. Jane Douxsaint	
	do.	Ditto. Harriett Eliz. of Lord Charles Graville Montagu[1]— & Lady —	
	25th.	Ditto. John of John & Sarah Holford	
	do.	Ditto. Mary Wife of Samuel Pickering	

E. Poinsett (Registr. —

Burials 341

1769			
May	25th.	Was Buried Catherine Wilson	P.
	do.	Ditto. David of David & Mary Huston	P.
	30th.	Ditto, Edward Bowen, of Wales —	
	do.	Ditto. of Egerton & Martha Liegh —	
	do.	Ditto, Peter Cusack	P.
June	3d.	Ditto, John Bond	
	5th.	Ditto, William Harrisson	
	do.	Ditto, Thomas Fowler	
	14th.	Ditto, Susanna, Wife of John Donalson —	
	17th.	Ditto, Thomas, Son of John & Neufville	
	23d.	Ditto, John Piggott —	
	25th.	Ditto, Christopher Simpson —	
	do.	Ditto, John, son of James Moultrie Junr	
	do.	Ditto, John St. Leger —	
	do.	Ditto, Richd. Barton —	
	29th.	Ditto, Mary of Benjamin & Mary Guerard	
	do.	Ditto, of Daniel Price —	
July	7th.	Ditto, James Stuart (of Scotland)	
	12th.	Ditto, Thomas of John Oxendine Parish	
	17th.	Ditto, Mary Lewis —	
	do.	Ditto, Elizabeth Hackett —	
	22d.	Ditto, James Devall —	

[1]Harriet Elizabeth, daughter of Lord Charles Greville Montagu. The latter was the second son of the Duke of Manchester and was governor of South Carolina, 1766-1773. He returned to England in 1773.

	23d.	Ditto,	Jane Harriss —	
	do.	Ditto	Wife of John Waring —	
	28th.	Ditto	William Miller	P. —
	30th.	Ditto,	Robt Mills	P. —
Augst.	1st.	Ditto,	Sarah Pett —	
	do.	Ditto,	Ann Allen	P. —
	4th.	Ditto,	Mary Hodge	P. —
	9th.	Ditto,	Isaac Leger — —	
	do.	Ditto,	James Laden —	
	do.	Ditto,	Robert Duncan —	
	8th.	Ditto,	Thomas Lee — —	
	do.	Ditto,	John Baker —	
	do.	Ditto,	Martha of Wm. & Martha Edwards	
	10th.	Ditto,	Mary Tousegers — —	
	16th.	Ditto,	James Tonge	P.

E. Poinsett. (Registr. —

Burials 342

1769				
August	17th.	Was Buried.	William Alexander	Parish.
	do.	Ditto,	Frederick Wingate	P—
	26th.	Ditto.	John son of Pott & Eliza. Shaw — —	
	27th.	Ditto,	Mary Wife of John White — —	
	do.	Ditto.	John Cargill — —	
	do.	Ditto.	Thomas of Miss Ives —	
	do.	Ditto.	Charles of John Oxendine. — P —	
	do.	Ditto.	Thomas Peek (of Boston P —	
Septemr.	1st.	Ditto.	William Rhen	P —
	9th.	Ditto.	Catherine Christie	P —
	do.	Ditto.	Thomas Smith (on the Bay) — —	
	11th.	Ditto	John Bradberry	P —
	do.	Ditto.	Ann Clinock — —	
	14th.	Ditto.	John Henry Jackson — —	
	do.	Ditto.	Ann, Wife of John Ward (Taylor) — —	
	do.	Ditto.	Catherine McLoughling.	P. —
	18th.	Ditto.	Martha Clase — —	
	21st.	Ditto.	Alexander Hext — — —	
	do.	Ditto.	Thomas of Thos. & Eliz. You — —	
	24th.	Ditto.	Joseph Ball Senr. — — —	
	25th.	Ditto.	John Merritt — —	P —
	27th.	Ditto.	Drayton Hermond Wood, Hurst — — —	
Octor.	1st.	Ditto.	Dinnis Shaw (of Ireland)	
	2d.	Ditto.	Isabella, Wife of John Wish — —	
	do.	Ditto.	John Davereau	P —
	5th.	Ditto.	Catherine Karr —	P —

	do.	Ditto. David of David & Hannah Wise — —	
	7th.	Ditto. John Pointer	P —
	do.	Ditto. Thomas Foiles	P —
	do.	Ditto. Daniel of Charles & Mary Galahan — —	
	14th.	Ditto. Edward Lightwood Senr. — — —	

E. Poinsett. (Registr. —

1769			
Octobr.	15th.	Was Buried. Catherine, of Thomas & Mary Smith (Founder.)	
	20th.	Ditto. Charlotte Mariane Porcher — —	
	do.	Ditto. Isaac Jerman Parish —	
	22d.	Ditto. Catherine Emery —	
	25th.	Ditto. John Greenwood — — —	
	27th.	Ditto. Samuel Weldon —	P. —
Novr.	3d.	Ditto. Ezra Waite — — —	
	4th.	Ditto. Thomas Nightingale — — —	
	8th.	Ditto. John Snelling — —	
	do.	Ditto, Elizabeth, Wife of William Creighton —	
	9th.	Ditto. David Mitchell.	P —
	do.	Ditto. William Regate.	P. —
	10th.	Ditto. Elizabeth, Wife of Robert Williams Junr.	
	12th.	Ditto. Henry Lloyd (from Prison)	
	13th.	Ditto. William Flemming	P —
	18th.	Ditto. George Legg —	P —
	21st.	Ditto. Mary Emery (of Goose Creek)	
	28th.	Ditto. Mary Doyle —	P —
Decemr.	1st.	Ditto. William Allen	P —
	2d.	Ditto. Edward Henley —	P —
	8th.	Ditto. Elijah Prioleau — — —	
	12th.	Ditto. Dougard Stewart —	P —
	14th.	Ditto. John Chapman — —	
	19th.	Ditto. Francis Gale, Phillips — —	
	20th.	Ditto. Judith Wragg Senr —	
	24th.	Ditto. Joseph Cart — —	
	25th.	Ditto. Alexander Brodie (of Scotland)	
	27th.	Ditto. Mary Burrows.	P —
	29th.	Ditto. Ann Rothmahler — —	
	do.	Ditto. Alexander of William & Catherine Tweed — —	
1770			
Janry.	5th.	Ditto. Thomas Sneed's Wife Elizabeth — —	
	6th.	Ditto. Mary Austin — —	

E. Poinsett. (Registr. —

1770		
Janry.	9th.	Was Buried. Daniel Mackensey P —
	10th.	Ditto. Hannah Eva.
	14th.	Ditto. Richard Seaton P —
	16th.	Ditto. Thomas Welsh P —
	17th.	Ditto. Peter Burt — —
	18th.	Ditto. Andrew, son of Andrew & Eliz. Ried — —
	20th.	Ditto. William Baker — — —
	do.	Ditto. Samuel Mills — —
	22d.	Ditto. Mary, Wife of John Bishop — —
	do.	Ditto. Daniel Bourgett — — —
	24th.	Ditto. Peter Orrat — P — —
	do.	Ditto. Ann West (a Child) P — —
February	1st.	Ditto. Elizabeth Yaw. P — —
	4th.	Ditto. Edward Franklin P — —
	10th.	Ditto. Thomas Courtain (Ship Master) —
	13th.	Ditto. John Dearing — — —
	do.	Ditto. John (Son of Doctr. John Farer)
	do.	Ditto James (Son of Richard & Ann Nicholls)
	15th.	Ditto. Elizabeth (Daughter of William Creighton)
	17th.	Ditto. Paty Holmes — — —
	do.	Ditto. John Oldfather P.
	19th.	Ditto. John Minott — — —
	21st.	Ditto. John Evans, the Revd. — — — —
Mar.	5th.	Ditto. Arminal (Wife of John Billings — —
	do.	Ditto. John Johnson P —
	7th.	Ditto. Thomas Gadsden — — — —
	16th.	Ditto. A Man Drowned at Mazycks Rope Walk P — —
	do.	Ditto. George Greenwood — — —
	18th.	Ditto. A Man Drowned at Burns Wharf
April	8th.	Ditto. George (Son of Mary Hartley P — —
	11th.	Ditto. Mary (Daughter of John Bishop)
	do.	Ditto. Thomas Mills P. ——
	20th.	Ditto. Jeremiah Burrows — — — — — —
	do.	Ditto. Mary Griffith. P — —
	do.	Ditto. Sarah Mitchell P — —
	do.	Ditto. Mary (Daughter of Abraham Jones — —

E. Poinsett. (Registr. — —

1770		
April	22d.	Was Buried. Edward (Son of Thos. & Mary Butler) P —
	26th.	Ditto. Margaret Sloan P —
	27th.	Ditto. Mary, of John & Ann Hume (of Georgia)
	do.	Ditto. Sarah Clark (A Child) P —
May	3d.	Ditto. John Burtee P —
	11th.	Ditto. Mahetable, Daughter of Benj. & Mahetable Brackett — —
	do.	Ditto. Elizabeth Cummins P —
	13th.	Ditto. William Henry (Son of William Henry & Dorathy Drayton — —
	do.	Ditto. Enoch Answorth — — — —
	23d.	Ditto. Elizabeth (Daughter of Stephen & Elizabeth Prosser — —
	do.	Ditto. Boston Shinner P —
	do.	Ditto. Eleanor Laurens (Wife of Henry Laurens — — —[1]
	27th.	Ditto. John Weston — — — —
	30th.	Ditto. Joseph Brown (of Bristol) — — —
June	1st.	Ditto. John King P —
	5th.	Ditto. John Lynch P —
	do.	Ditto. Jacob Wiitzer
	7th.	Ditto. Peter, Son of Peter & Ann Timothy —
	8th.	Ditto. William of William & Catherine Fair
	do.	Ditto. Catherine, of Peter & Catherine Horlbeck — — —
	do.	Ditto. Joseph Docharty P —
	do.	Ditto. Christian Myre P —
	9th.	Ditto. Ann Hume — — —
	14th.	Ditto. Thomas Cluling P —
	18th.	Ditto. John, son of Paty & Jane Elizabeth Holmes — — — —
	do.	Ditto. Sabina Charlotte, Daughter of Benj. & Smith — — — —
	19th.	Ditto. Jacob Motte (Public Treasurer) — — —[2]
	20th.	Ditto. Catherine, Daughter of Christianna Almond P — —

[1]See *Life of Henry Laurens*, by D. D. Wallace.

[2]He was born in 1701 and came with his father (John Abraham Motte) to South Carolina from Antigua in 1704; was appointed Public Treasurer in 1743.

	21st.	Ditto. Mary Daughter of Ditto P — —
	do.	Ditto. Edward Miles (of Bristol)
	27th.	Ditto. Daughter of Mongo Finlingson — — —
	28th.	Ditto. John Mackenzie P—
	30th.	Ditto. John Nox (of Scotland) — —
July	1st.	Ditto. Mary, Daughter of of Oldridge P —
	do.	Ditto. James, son of Alexander & Wright — — —
	3d.	Ditto. William, son of Collins P — —
	do.	Ditto. William, son of Brown P — —
	do.	Ditto. son of Jonathan Cooper — — — —
	4th.	Ditto. John Martin P — —

E. Poinsett. (Registr. — —

Burials 346

1770		
July	5th.	Was Buried. Peter, son of Peter & Williamson — —
	8th.	Ditto. Rachel Goven — — —
	do.	Ditto. Sarah Woodsides (late Williams)
	9th.	Ditto. Catherine, Daughter of William & Susanna Moore — — —
	do.	Ditto. Lucresia, Daughter of Collins — — —
	do.	Ditto. Edward Davis — P — —
	11th.	Ditto. Nathaniel Kent — P — —
	12th.	Ditto. Whinny Daughter of James & Frances Carter — — —
	13th.	Ditto. John Mongomery P — —
	14th.	Ditto. Mary Gordon — P — —
	15th.	Ditto. William, Son of William & Margaret Gowdey — — —
	do.	Ditto. John Stewart P — —
	21st.	Ditto. John, Son of Jeremiah & Hester Sharp —
	22d.	Ditto. Anthony Fox — P— —
	do.	Ditto. Daughter of William & Susanna Moore — — —
	27th.	Ditto. Thomas White, Son of Doctr. Hackett —
	do.	Ditto. Sarah, Daughter of Mrs. Mills — — P —
	do.	Ditto. Catherine Martin — P — —
	do.	Ditto. William Moses — P — —
	28th.	Ditto. Mary McHugh — P — —
	do.	Ditto. James Crowley — P — —

	29th.	Ditto.	George, Son of George Robinson — — —
	31st.	Ditto.	James Telfair (of Edinburgh) — —
	do.	Ditto.	William Amory — — —
	do.	Ditto.	James Agnew (of Ireland)
Augst.	1st.	Ditto.	Thomas Docharty — P — —
	7th.	Ditto.	Hannah, Wife of Thomas Newby — — —

Burials 349[1]

1772

April 1st. Was Buried Samuel Trouncer

Burials 370[2]

1779

		Was Buried	
Octobr.	29	Daugr. of George Spencer	
	"	Evey Digo	Soldier
	"	William Cassaday	Soldier
	"	John Robertson	prisoner of War
Novr.	3	Empry Wheeler	Soldier
	4	George Pratt	
	6	Dumpry Oldfield	Soldier
	8	John Gordon a Sailor	
	9	Son of Lebs. Whitney	
	11	John Chappel	
	"	William Manners	Soldier
	12	William Conway	Soldier
	14	Adam Creighton	Soldier
	15	Erneast Stear	Soldier
	"	Maria Bennet	
	"	Child of Farro	
	16	Philip Shulzer	Parish
	21	William Wilkinson & Jno. Hutson soldiers	
	"	Mary Ann Dugay Pereneau	
	"	Capt. Dean	
	"	William Woodhouse	
	22	Wife of Robt. Jones	
	"	Margt. Warden	
	"	John Williams	Parish
	23	Margaret Robertson	Parish
	25	Katherine Smith	Parish
	"	Henry Bulleaux soldier	

[1]Pages 247 and 248 are blank. There are no entries between August 7, 1770, and April 1, 1772.

[2]Pages 350-369 are blank.

27 John Atkins Miller Parish

30 Dury Sims prisoner of War

N. B.* As it is of little or no consequence to Register Soldiers or Sailors' funerals & would fill up the Register too soon shall from this date leave them out & those registered shall be Inhabitants old or new, Parish poor, officers of the Army & Navy, Capts. Masters & Mates of vessells & passangers—refering the names of the first mentioned to my daily entry Book.

Decr. 1 William Jones Parish

" Thos. Snellings

8 Child of Wm. Phillips)

" Bedaulx a Lt. Col.[1]

16 Fanny Ailey . . . . . . Parish

20 a portuguise man ——— Parish

22 DeTroy a Lieut.[2]

24 Mrs. Troutte

Geo. Denholm (Registr.

Burials 371

1779[3]

Was Buried

Decemr. 25 son of John Sarrazin

William Wilson Mercht.

brought from the Country & burried 22d. Curt.)

29 Child of Eltred Lawrence

John Wipple 26th. Parish

29 James Mitchell Parish

1780

Janry 4 Rebecca, daughter of Alexr. Alexander

" Elizabeth Woodhouse

6 James Smith (Carpenter)

" a Sailor Parish

" a Woman Parish

7 Lovely (Mr.) Parish

8 Child of Saml. Legare

9 Peter Chozin Parish

10 Philip Coram

---

[1]Charles Frederick de Bedaulx, Lieutenant-Colonel of Pulaski's Legion.

[2]Francis de Troy, a lieutenant in Pulaski's Legion.

[3]The date 1782 in the register has been stricken out and 1779 written over it in pencil.

	"	Ann daughter of Alexr. Alexander
	11	Child of Major Pierce Butler
	12	Benjamin Darling
	21	Peggy Sept. 21st. Parish
	17	a Woman Octbr. 17th Parish
	18	Peter Quinn Octbr. 18th. Parish
	25	James Anderson
	"	Chappel wife of John Chappel
	30	Bershebah Tattle
Febry.	13	Ann Waller
	19	Child of Mrs. Wilkins
	20	Peter son of Peter Bacot
	24	Calvert wife of John Calvert
March	5	Child of Ruger
	8	Child of Fair
	31	Bowman a Capt.[1]
April	7	Marrow (Mr.)
	"	Ferguson (Mrs.)
	14	daughter of Benja. Rivers
	18	Neil a Major[2]
	24	Thos. Moultrie a Capt.[3]
	25	Parker a Col.[4]
	27	John Shingleton a Col.

Geo. Denholm (Registr.

Burials 372

1780		
April	28	Was Burried
		Emanuel Gonzaliz
	"	Jonathan Paterson
May	1	Andrew Lord
	4	Samuel Philips a Lieut.[5]

Since the Capitulation

	13	Henry Latham
	"	Archibald Risk

[1]Capt. Joseph Bowman, 1st Regiment, North Carolina Line, Continental Establishment.

[2]Philip Neyle, aide to Gen. Moultrie.

[3]He was a captain in the 2nd Regiment, South Carolina Line, Continental Establishment, a younger brother of Gen. Moultrie. He was killed in action.

[4]Col. Richard Parker, 1st Regiment, Virginia Line, Continental Establishment.

[5]Of the 7th Regiment, Virginia Line, Continental Establishment.

	14	Templeton a Capt.[1]
	15	David Boulliat son of Mrs. Harvey
	"	Wife of Daniel Jenkins
	17	William Mitchell a Capt.
	18	Neufville Doctor[2] (in the french C. yard)
	20	John Fell
	"	John Howe
	"	Thomas Page
	25	Samuel Wainwright
	"	William, son of William Weston
	27	William Hinckley
	30	Sarah Robertson
	"	Monck wife of Monck
	"	Mary Collins
	31	Samuel McKinley a Lieut.
	"	Noy Wolly Hutchins
		Child of Henry Hainsdorff
June	6	a female Child of Spencer
	"	a female Child of Stewart
	7	a female Child of Willm. Dewees
	9	a female Child of Lauchlan McNeil
	"	Parham a Lieut.
	13	a female Child of Eltred Lawrence
	"	Judith Wragg
	"	Edward son of Edward McCready

Geo. Denholm (Registr.

Burials 373

Was Burried

1780		
June	15	Jonathan Giles
	"	a Child of William Glaize
	17	a female Child of John Calvert
	18	a female Child of Chapman
	21	John son of David Mitchell
	23	Hinson Port
	"	a female Child of Willm Jennings
	24	Latham a Serjt. of Artillery
	26	Thomas son of Baldwin
	"	Margery Hogg
	27	John Minton

[1]Capt. Andrew Templeton, Georgia Line, Continental Establishment.

[2]Zachariah Neufville.

	"	a female Child of Doctr. Logan
	28	Polly Austin Daugr. in Law to Jas. Arnold
	"	Bryan (Mrs.)
	29	a female Child of Darby
	"	a female Child of Thos Higgans
	30	Son of Middleton
July	1	John Weir of Artillery
	"	a male Child of Robert Weyman
	2	a female Child of Edwd. McCready
	"	Child of Joseph Dill
	4	a female Child of George Vane
	"	Garrick (Mrs.) of Artilly.
	7	a male Child of James Bentham
	"	a female Child of Isaac Lesesne
	8	Sarah Jennings
	"	James Craig
	9	Nancy MacBride
	"	Child of Cornels. Sulivan
	"	Sarah Thomson
	10	a male Child of Peter Bounetheau
	"	son of Peter Prow
	"	Allen McCaskell
	11	William Seltridge

Geo. Denholm (Registr —

Burials 374

Was Burried

1780		
July	11	a female Child of John Coils
	12	James Carry
	"	William Evans son of the Widdw. Evans
	"	Robert Curley
	13	Catharine McDonald
	"	a female Child of Ann Govan
	14	a female Child of Mrs. Knight
	15	a Male Child of Charles Harris
	"	a female Child of Thos. Holmes
	17	a female Child of John Roilly
	"	Gilbert Hare
	"	William Roberts
	"	male Child of Chas. Burnham
	18	male Child of Robt. Balcanqual of Artilly.
	19	wife of H. McKellan of Artilly.
	"	wife of George Virgent
	"	male Child of John Bennet
	20	a female Child of Thos. Tims.

339

	21	Katharine Braithwaite
	"	Samuel son of Middleton
	"	male Child of John Thomson
	"	male Child of James Leeson
	22	Child of Abm. Shecut
	"	Wife of Serjeant
	"	male Grand Child of Christr. Gadsden
	23	Wife of Willm. Wyatt
	"	Elizabeth Johnston
	"	male Child of Thos. Hall
	"	male Child of Willm. Prowas
	24	Charles Hay a Serjeant of 17 Reg.
	"	William Easton's Child

Geo. Denholm (Registr.

Burials 375

		Was Burried
1780		
July	25	William Osbourn
	"	male Child of Garrick of Artilly.
	26	James Brown
	"	Susannah Goddat
	"	male Child of Philips
	27	Melican Rowland
	29	male Child of Latham of Artilly
	"	Child of Goddat
	"	Sarah Simpson
	"	Wife of Snead
	30	male Child of Crawford
	31	male Child of Darby Pendergrass
	"	Edward Price
	"	Richard Price
	"	male Child of John Muncrieff
Augst.	1	male Child of Joseph Tipplin
	"	Joseph Fisher Capt. of the Brigg Peters
	"	Coats Serjeant of 7th. Reg.
	"	Wife of Thos. Tims.
	2	George Lee
	"	Child of Moncks.
	3	a female Child of Mrs. Dew
	"	Child of John Carston
	4	a female Child of Warnock,
	6	Low (Mrs.)
	7	a female Child of Thos Ellfe
	8	Polly Hammet

	"	male Child of James Arnold
	"	Isabella Jefferett
	9	Michael Bowell

Geo. Denholm (Registr —

Burials 376

1780		
		Was Buried
Augst.	9	Mrs. a poor Woman
	"	wife of Carston
	10	William Lake Wheeler of Artilly.
	"	male Child of Willm. Such
	"	male Child of Lauchlan McNeil
	"	a female Child of Harleston
	11	a female Child of Alexr. Cuthill of Artilly
	"	a female Child of Belisle a mulattoe
	13	George Goslin Mercht.
	"	Star Capt. of the Schooner East Florida
	"	a female Child of James Bentham
	"	male Child of Robert Muncreef
	16	a female Child of James Potts
	17	Mary Henderson
	19	a Grand Child of Doctor Wm. Keith Senr.
	"	George Thomson of Artilly
	21	John Francis
	"	Catharine McLeod
	22	John Henderson
	"	male Child of Dr. Baker
	24	Sarah Mòre
	26	male Child of James Potts
	28	William Glaize
	"	Ailey (Mrs.) of Artilly.
	29	female Child of Dr. Wilson
	"	James Magahan
	"	Robert Burd's female Child
	31	Thomas Holmes
	"	Neddy Henderson
Sept.	1	Darby Pendergrass

Geo: Denholm (Register —

Burials 377

1780		
		Was Burried
Sept.	1	Beck a Capt.

	9	Andrew Wilson of Artilly
	11	Macky (Mrs.)
	12	Elizabeth Furneau
	13	Jonathan Olds
	"	John Bennet
	17	Child of Robt. Conoway
	18	Beccy Weyman
	20	Wife of Willm. Donaldson from New York
	"	Robert Jones
		Jenkins (Mrs.) Octbr. 20 Parish
	21	a poor refugee Boy from Jas. Simpson Esqr's
	24	Woodhouse a Capt.
	27	a female Child of Richd Wayne
	28	a male Child of Richd. Wainwright
	"	a Child of Willm. Glaize Octbr. 28th. Parish
	30	a female Child of Willm. Weston
Octbr.	1	Mary Ann Walker of Artilly.
	"	James McClanaghan
	6	Child of Lieut. Charleston of Artilly.
	8	male Child of Capt. Riddle
	"	Mathias Ross a Lieut. of the P. W. A.[1] Regt.
	"	Cousins a Capt. of a vessell
	9	Wife of Willm. Cotes
	"	Wife of Willm. Trussler
	"	James Chillman of Artilly.
	"	Willm. Lamson Doctor of the P. W. A.[1] Regt.
	"	Moses Mitchell
	10	Lewis (Mrs.)
	11	Benjamin Baker
	13	McKnight (Mrs.)

Geo. Denholm (Registr.

Burials 378

Was Burried

1780		
October	15	William Marquois a Lieut of Artilly
	16	John Spreggs
	"	Andrew Miller
	20	Julian daughter of Isaac Lesesne
	"	Henry Loan
	"	wife of Foran Master Armourer
	"	Peter Christian
	21	Charles son of William Goudey

[1]Prince of Wales's American Regiment.

	"	male Child of Ralph Izard
	"	William Hopkins
	"	Child of Robt. Conoway
	22	wife of Creighton
	"	Clouddsdale (Mrs.)
	"	Stephen Duvall
	23	Child of Bottiton
	"	Child of Geo. Brewton
	26	Wife of John Egan
	"	male Child of Willm Cameron
	26	George son of Isaac Lesesne
	"	Francis Nicholson
	29	Hugh Irvine
	30	Larry (Mr.) Parish
	"	Child of Kanes adjutt.
Novr.	1	Constable a Capt.
	3	Reikie a Capt. of a vessell
	"	a female Child of Dr. Steel
	"	John Anderson a sailor Parish
	4	a female Child of Sisk
	"	sister of Isaac More
	6	Ann Wood
	7	Hannah Wainwright Parish
	8	male Child of Roger Smith

Geo. Denholm (Registr.

Burials 379

1780

		Was Burried
Novr.	8	Haukes (Mrs.)
	11	Smith (Mrs.) Parish
	12	Child of Isaac Dutilly
	15	John Clark (Stranger)
	16	James Pritchard
	18	
	23	Daughter of McKennery
	"	John Remington
	26	Peter Parish
	"	Joseph son of Patk. Hinds
Decemr.	5	Dutilly (Mrs.)
	"	Wife of Willm. Cameron
	6	Daniel McMullin
	7	Child of Geo. Harriot (of Georgetown)
	11	Child of Willm. Long
	12	a female Child of Lewis Joner

	13	Wilkins (Mrs.)
	"	Henry Carry
	14	Joseph Farley (of Georgia)
	15	John Poaug
	16	John Frew
	"	male Child of Lundgon
	19	James Rowlain
	20	a female Child of Thos. Higgans
	22	Susannah Johnston
	24	wife of Eden
	29	William Thomson of Artilly.
	"	wife of Coppithorn
	"	John Fee Parish
	30	wife of Noddings
1781		
Jany.	3	wife of Robert Pilmore a Capt. of a Vessell
	"	Isaac Packeton
	"	Dawson a Capt. of a Vessell

Geo. Denholm (Registr.

Burials 380

1781		
		Was Burried
Jany	6	Robert Wilkinson (servant to Majr. Berry)
	7	Atkinson (Mr.) a Stranger)
	"	male Child of Doctor Harris
	"	male Child of David Taylor
	9	male Child of Willm. Roper
	10	Robert Stringer
	11	Neil McKeller Parish
	"	a son of Moses Vinters
	18	Charles Elliott (burried at Stonno)
	21	male child of Dr. Wilson
	23	Wife of a Soldier Parish
	27	Wife of Dewees
	28	male Child of John Bennet
Feby.	1	Mcdonach (Mrs.) of Engineer Depart.)
	2	female Child of John Singleton
	"	Peggy McDougall Parish
	10	McGraw (Mr.)
	14	Andrew Harvey (Carpenter)
	18	Child of Belly. Crawford
	19	John Tipplin
	21	Child of Turbott
	23	wife of James Keith

	24	female Child of Jameson
	"	Alexander Poaug
	27	wife of Robt. Wm. Powell
		James Meads Parish
March	2	daughter of Hencock (Mrs.)
	"	James Repult
	3	male Child of McMahon (Mrs.)
	4	Allen Cameron a Capt.
	9	Annus Duffey
	11	female Child of Jas. Guy
	12	Mary Jones Stevenson

Geo. Denholm) Registr.

Burials 381

1781		
		Was Burried
March	13	female Child of Francs. Bonneau
	17	Daniel Rowlain
	23	David Richardson
	24	George Adamson
	25	wife of John Heningburgh of the Artilly.
	"	James Welsh
	26	Anthony Cartman
	28	wife of Willm. Harvey
	29	male Child of John Harrison (Conductr. of artilly.)
	30	male Child of Capt. Alexr. McLean
	"	male Child of Philip Thorn
April	1	wife of Jesse Dean
	"	John Lion (barber)
	"	Peggy Barn a mulattoe Child
	6	John Lodge Parish
	"	Peter Touchecar
	7	Betty Pitts. Parish
	9	David Wolfe
	10	Lewis Imer
	"	female Child of Jas. Strickland
	"	female Child of Roderick McKennon a Lieut.
	11	Joseph Loyd
	14	John Keating
	15	William Sharp
	16	Elizabeth Clifford
	18	Ann Walker
	19	Catharine Berwick
	21	Thomas Shutter

	25	female Child of Pott Shaw
	28	wife of Willm. Sharp
	"	a Sailor Parish
	29	male Child of Alexr. Davidson
May	1	female Child of Dr. Kendrick
	2	Jeremiah Wane

Geo. Denholm (Registr.

Burials 382

1781		
		Was Burried
May	5	John Nixon (armourer)
	7	John Callaghan
	8	Benjamin Haas
	9	male Child of Lieut. Oneil
	10	Abigail Godfrey
	11	female Child of Joseph Yates
	"	OEneas McLeod Ensign of the 71st. Regt.
	"	son of Dr. Thos. Honnor
	12	male Child of E. Hannahan
	"	a Man Parish
		Thomas Mellichamp (22d. April)
	13	Andrew Lord
	"	Nancy Shepherd
	"	a Sailor Parish
	16	William Cotes
		female Child of Nicholas Smith
	17	Hariotte Somervaille (daughter of a Clergyman in Dublin)
	19	Thomas Atkin
	20	John son of John Rose
	"	Thomas Evans (Qr. master Genls. department)
	23	male Child of Dr. Harris
	28	Peggy Veal
June	3	male Child of John Gabriel
	"	female Child of Willm. Goudey
	4	female Child of Henry Hughes
	"	Hannah Robinson
	6	Gabriel Manigault
	8	wife of Thomas Scottowe
	9	female Child of John Hughes
	10	male Child of Joseph Bee
	11	male Child of Robt. Wm. Powell
	12	wife of John Howe (deceas'd)
	"	female Child of Mrs. P. Tidyman

Geo. Denholm (Registr.

1781		
		Was Burried
June	12	Richard Dicky
	13	William McDuff
	15	William Kennedy
	19	Charity Russell (Mrs.)
	"	female Child of David Taylor
	"	child of Wilkins
		Dr. Thomas Honnor 18th. Curt.
	20	Stephen Rogers
	"	Bowers Capt. of a vessell
	21	John Dalley
	"	male Child of Moses Barnes a refugee
	22	Peggy McCormick Parish
	24	James Bennet
	"	wife of Walter Izard
	25	Elizabeth Stevenson
	"	William Hales
	"	Walter Hodge
	"	Theodore Gaillard Senr.
	26	Wilkins (Mrs.) a refugee
	27	John Collston a refugee
July	2	female Child of John Cunningham a refugee
	"	wife of Dr. Thos. Honnor deceas'd
	10	James Campbell
	"	Sarah Sanders
	11	George Forbes
	16	William Trussler
	"	female Child of James Wisdom
	19	Donald McLeod a Lieut.
	20	William Rudhall
	"	James Kirkwood
	25	George Clayton a refugee
	27	female Child of James Love

Geo. Denholm (Registr.

1781		Was Burried
July	26	Samuel Hopkins
	27	John Potts
	"	William Green a Lieut. of the 30th. Regt.
	30	Bellinger (Mrs.) Parish

Augst. 2 William Giles
" female Child of St. John
" Patrick Rush
5 Dr. William Loocock
" a Sailor Parish
7 wife of Fredk. Glazier
9 Ebenezer Bagnell
20 female Child of William Mills a refugee
23 James Bryan Capt. of a small vessell
25 John Lanneau
26 male Child of Franc's. Mainard
28 John Barton Parish
Septr. 1 Robert Paris a Capt of the So. Carolina Loyalists
3 male Child of John Harrison
" Andrew Galley a Capt. of a vessell
6 male Child of Thomas Ellfe
7 Ann Goodale
" Thomas Hodd
11 wife of John Wilson Mercht.
12 James Roach Parish
13 William Cunningham a refugee's son
14 Ensign Ruxton of 30th. Regt.
16 John Johnson
17 Sir Egerton Leigh Bart.
" male Child of Thos Neilson
19 James Schaw a Capt. in the provincial light Infantry
" wife of James Hepburn Atty. at Law
20 Betsey Cionn
23 William Cunningham a refugee

Geo. Denholm (Registr.

Burials 385

Was Burried

1781
Septr. 23d female Child of Capt. Arnold of the Nancy
" Judith Swinton
25 male Child of John Hughes
" female Child of John Oats
27 Judith, wife of Major Carden of the P. W. A. Regt.
29 Elizabeth Elmes
30 Child of Henry Mascall
Octbr. 1 Peter Thomson
" wife of Major Peter Traile of the Artilly.

3 wife of Joseph Jones
4 David Henderson mate of the schooner Sally
" James Martin a refugee
6 William Long
7 Thomas Wilkie a Lieut of the 30th. Regt.
8 male Child of Willm. Hanscomb
9 male Child of Lieut. Serjeant
" male Child of Robt Fanting a refugee
10 female Child of William Morgan
11 a poor Woman Parish
" Peter Smith Tavern keeper Union Street
12 Dennis Holland
" wife of Mr. McConnell a refugee
" Robert Cunningham a refugee
13 Elizabeth Cole a free-mulattoe
15 Robert Howard a Cadet in the Volunteers of Irland[1]
" George Kerr
16 Connic a Capt. of a vessell
17 Garginie Augustus, female Child of McCartan Campbell
" John Rick
21 Catharine daughter of Benjn. Eddy
23 female Child of Thos. Hopper
24 Hugh Campbell a refugee
" male Child of Archd. Murray a Refugee

Geo. Denholm (Registr.

Burials 386

1781

Was Burried

Octbr. 27 John More (Engineer Depart.)
" wife of James Butler
30 male Child of Dr. Destalleur of the Artilly.
" male Child of Capt. Bingham of Lord Roden's Core
31 Andrew Rutlidge (dancing Master)
Novr. 1 George Morris' male Child
4 John Frederick Dubbert a refugee Clergyman
" male Child of Ishom Williams a refugee
" Elizabeth Lamb
5 Alexander Lynch (Butcher)
6 female Child of Maurice Simmons

[1]Lord Rawdon's regiment.

7 Elizabeth Hutchings Parish
" female Child of John Harrison
8 Samuel Bours (Comy. Genls. department)
10 Geo. McCoull (Quarter mr. Genls depart.)
12 female Child of Cotton a refugee
13 female Child of Barnard McGuires
18 Child of Henry Gower
20 Alexander Rantowle
21 Daniel Jacqueri Parish
22 George Thompson (Master of a vessell) Parish
25 male Child of John Evans (Drayman)
" male Child of Michael Nugent
26 James Butler Parish
" female Child of Dr. Destalleur of the Artilly.
22 Glazier (Mrs.)
24 wife of Woodward Engineer depart.
27 John Pattison
29 John Pitcher (Serjt. of the Guard)
" William Dickson of the Ship Polly
30 Mrs. Francs. Williams
Decemr. 1 Keating a refugee's daughter
" male Child of Lieut. McKinnon

Geo. Denholm (Registr.

Burials 387

1781

Was Burried
Decemr. 2 male Child of Martin a refugee Capt.
" Gregory
4 Hugh Jones Serjt. of the 1st. Regt. Guards
" Joseph Smith Serjt. of the Cold Stream Guards
" male Child of Thos. Scott a refugee
5 male Child of Henry Hammond
" John Oneil
" female Child of Thos Radcliffe Junr.
6 female Child of Richard Martin
9 Black a Lieut. of the Volunteers of Irland
10 Elizabeth Knox
" George Bakers Gibbes
11 Mary Mouat
" William Stent a refugee
14 John McCoy
16 Mrs, Adam
" Esther Schaw
" Hopkin Prise

	17	George Vane
	18	Mrs. Thompson
	"	Margaret Sawyer
	19	female Child of Henry Hammond
	21	Robert Muncrief
	"	Child of Mrs. Andw. Lord
	22	male Child of Evans
	23	wife of Samuel Rivers
	25	Ann Manley
	26	Ann Thomas
	28	David Dick
	30	wife of Vanashendeleft Mr.
	31	female Child of Richd. Martin
1782		
Janry.	2	Peter Sinkler[1]

Geo. Denholm (Registr.

Burials 388

1782		Was Burried
Janry	3	Alexander McLeod Capt. of the North Carolina Highlanders
	"	William male Child of Robt. Morton Serjt. 7th. Regt.
	4	Ann Clarke child of Robt. Napier's Wife's first Husband
	"	Child of John Schaw
	5	Alexander Murray
	7	John Davis
	10	male Child of Arthur Benning
	13	male Child of Thos Ackron
	14	James Baillie a refugee
	16	female Child of Robt. Morton Serjt. 7th Regt.
	18	Joseph Younghusband Capt. of a vessell
	20	Ann Britt
	"	female Child of James Carmichael
	21	William Pall
	22	Male Child of Robert Williams
	23	Benjamin Dart
	"	Henry McGriggor

[1]A prominent patriot of the Revolution. He had been arrested at Lifeland, his plantation in St. Stephen's Parish, and taken to Charles Town and imprisoned in the Exchange (the postoffice of later years) which was used as a provost prison. There he died of typhus fever. (See Samuel DuBose's *Reminiscences of St. Stephen's Parish.*)

	24	Magnus Murchison a Lieut of the 71st. Regt.[1]
	25	Williams a refugee Capt.
	30	Dawson Capt. of a vessell
	"	Wife of John Hanisay (a drayman)
		male Child of Mrs. Mills. Parish
	31	wife of George Rout
	"	Margaret wife of Gilbert
	"	male Child of John Simpson
Febry.	1	Elizabeth Sanders
	4	William Lawrence of the Artilly.
	10	Rachel Neilson
	13	male Child of John Phillips
	14	male Child of Willm. Ellfe
	19	Donald Campbell Capt of the 74th. Regt.[1]
	20	John Steel an orphan Child
	21	Walter Lorve of the Artilly.

Geo. Denholm. Registr.

Burials 389

1782		Was Burried
Febry	22	wife of William Roach
	23d	Farrell Parish
	24	Edward Dean
	25	female Child of Willm. Ellfe
	27	Josiah Bonneau
March	2	Charles Mynaird a refugee
	9	female Child of Donald McKenzie
	11	Thomas Torrop an orphan Child Parish
	12	male Child of Daniel Sinclair a refugee
	18	Col. Lechmere[2]
	19	Daniel Boyne
	23	David McKenzie (Master of a small Craft vessell)
	25	female Child of John Axom
	27	male Child of Willm. Ranken a refugee
	"	Isabella Child of Alexander Inglis
	29	Sarah Ellis
April	1	Hannah Smith
	8	Elizabeth wife of Hendry Bookless
	10	Abigail daugr. of Etsell Lawrence (a child)
	14	Nathan Legare

---

[1]British.

[2]Col. Nicholas Lechmere, formerly Collector of Customs at Beaufort, then a colonel (principally on paper) of Loyal militia.

	"	Andrew son of Roger Smith Esqr. (a Child)
	21	Sally daugr. of Andw. Cunningham (Refugee (a Child)
	"	Mary daugr. of George Eden Refugee (a Child)
	25	Ann wife of the deceast. Gabriel Manigault Esqr.
	28	son of John Banks refugee (a Child)
May	3	James Smith a pilot
	4	Ensign John Mcdonald
	5	Samuel, son of Samuel Rivers (a Child)
	6	William son of John Watson (Gardner)
	8	Mary Elizabeth, daugr. of Rhd. Kaylor
	9	John Newton Hartley
	12	Andrew Reid

Geo. Denholm (Registr.

Burials 390

		Was Burried
1782		
May	13	Elizabeth wife of John Gilmore Tavern keeper
	16	Catharine widow of Franc's Johnston a mariner
	20	William Smith (a mate of a vessell)
	21	Thomas Harding 2nd. Lieut. of a vessell[1]
	26	Elizabeth wife of William Scott, buried at James Island
	28	Ann wife of John Williams a refugee
	29	Thomas son of John Coram (a Child)
June	5	Elizabeth wife of William Conroy Lieut. of the P. W. A. Regt.
	8	Catharine wife of John Watson (Gardner)
	11	Ann wife of James Smyth
	16	William Wilkins (sail maker)
	24	Bethea Daughter of Fredk. Stage (Baker) a Child
	26	Elizabeth Daugr. of Anthy. Gabbeau (a child)
	29	James son of James Steadman (a Child)
	30	George Boles
July	2d.	Hester wife of James Jaudon
	3	James Farrell
	4	Margaret Daugr. of Willm. McKennon (a Child)
	5	Michael Keating (Shoe maker)
	6	James son of James Wisdom (a Child)
	8	Roger Galey Capt. of a vessell
	"	Thomas Grissom
	9	Sally Middleton (a Child)

[1]An officer of the British Navy.

10 Thomas Dutchfield
12 John son of John Thompson
15 Ann Gray daugr. in Law of Willm. Hanscomb
16 Betsey Daugr. of John McKenzie (a Child
19 Samuel son of John Gaillard (a Child)
21 Thomas Hutchinson
25 Sarah Paris
27 Alexr. McMartin

Geo. Denholm (Registr.

Burials 391

1782

Was Burried
July 29 Sarah wife of John Quinley Junr.
" John son of the deceast John Matthews
30 Sarah wife of John Evans
31 Allice wife of John Maromet
" Arthur Fitzharris
John Keating burried 14th. April—81 Parish
18 male Child of Do. burried this day Parish
Augst. 2d. female Child of William Prowes
3 Dougal Campbell
4 an orphan refugee Child Parish
5 John McCulloch
6 Doctor Luke D'Evelin[1] of the P. W. A. Regt.
9 Hugh McCartney
" Joseph Wright a Coll. of the Refugees
10 John Christie
12 Elsie daugr. of Charles Miller (a Child)
17 Robert Bryson
18 Alexander Dunbar
20 Margaret Woods
24 William Walby
25 Rhoda Badger
" John Richards
26 Charles Darrell son of Benjn. (a Child)
27 Margaret Daugr. of Rodk. McKennon
28 Martha wife of James Miller a refugee Capt.
29 John Williams a refugee
31 Hugh son of John McCall (Taylor) a Child
Septr. 2 Philip son of Philip Thorn (a Child)
" Frances daugr. of Col. Saml. Campbell (a Child)
4 Nancy Stocks (a Child)
" Child of John McCall (Taylor)

Geo. Denholm (Regr.

---

[1] D'Elevin.

1782

		Was Burried
Sept.	5	Seymore Hood (sail Maker)
	7	Mary (relict of Artemus) Elliott
	"	Harriette Cannon (daugr. of John) Webb (a Child)
	10	John Beale (a Carpenter)
	11	Sarah Daugr. of Henry McKiven (a Child)
	14	Hugh McMurchy
	15	Charles Roilley
	16	Keith Williamson
	19	James (son of John, Murphy (a Carpenter) a child
	25	James Riddle
	27	Sarah (wife of Jacob). Miley
	29	Benjamin Godfrey
October	2	Dorothy (daugr. of John) Hugill (a Child)
	3	Thomas (son of Thomas) Simpson (a refugee's Child
	4	Nelly (wife of John) Helbert
	"	Alice Wilson
	"	Hector McNeil (a refugee Capt.)
	5	Joel (son of Joel) Poinsett (a child)
	"	William Hipple
	7	daugr. of Thomas Holmes (a child)
	11	Nicholas Boden
	12	Christian (daugr. of Col. Saml. Campbell (a refugee's Child)
	13	George Wilkins of the Royal Artilly.
	18	Elizabeth Carne
	19	John (son of John) Muncrief (a Child)
	"	Samuel Goldsthwait
	"	Benjamin Blackham (a bombadn. of the Royal Artilly.)
	"	George (son of Wm.) Roach

1782		Was Burried
October	24	Mary (Wife of John) Webb
	25	Nathaniel (son of Nathaniel) Jones (a refugee's child)
	26	Edward Fairchild (a Serjt. in the P. W. A. Regt.)
	27	George Powell
	31	Robert Graham of the Royal Artilly.

November	1	Major Carden[1] of the P. W. A. Regt.
	4	James (son of Patrick) Cunningham
	5	Margaret (wife of William) Glen (burr'd at Scotch meet'g yard)
	9	John Botsford (a Serjt. of the P. W. A. Regt.
	"	John Gaborial
	12	William Morgan

Burials 411[2]

1796, Aug.	24	Was Buried		Ann Wrighter
	"	"	"	Doctor Lynah's child
	25	"	"	Andrew Williamson
	30	"	"	Mary Glen
Sept.	1	"	"	Joseph Lloyd's child
	3	"	"	Mr. Foster's child
	5	"	"	Elizabeth Cowell
	6	"	"	Capt. Mayberry's child
	8	"	"	Ann Crafts (child)
	12	"	"	Mr. Clarkson's child
	13	"	"	James Wyatt
	"	"	"	James Milligan
	16	"	"	Mr. Wilson Glover's child
	"	"	"	Frances Davis
	20	"	"	Henry Hainsdorff
Oct.	6	"	"	Mrs. Davis' child
	18	"	"	Mrs. Holder's child
Nov.	16	"	"	Catherine Holmes
	21	"	"	Samuel Legare
	"	"	"	Robert Beard
	30	"	"	Ann Pickering
Dec	10	"	"	Joseph Oldman
	30	"	"	Samuel Bonsall
Jany	10	"	"	Walker Hall
	17	"	"	John Major
	25	"	"	Ann Mason
Febry	7	"	"	Alexander Moorehead
	21	"	"	Henry Halleday
	28	"	"	Mary Simmons
March	24	"	"	James Hayes
April	23	"	"	George Gresle

[1]Major John Carden. (See *Marriage Notices in The South-Carolina and American General Gazette from May* 30, 1766, *to February* 28, 1781 *and in its successor The Royal Gazette* (1781-1782), 35, 36.

[2]Pages 394-410 are blank. No burial records are entered between November 12, 1782, and August 24, 1796.

May	13	"	"	Elizabeth Harrisson Bay
	"	"	"	Eliza Shubrick

Burials

Burials 412

1796 June	7	Was	Buried	Blake Leay White
	25	"	"	John Wragg
July	1	"	"	Elizabeth McCredie
	7	"	"	Mary Boddy
	18	"	"	Revd. Peter Daniel Bourdillon
	24	"	"	Elizabeth Bowler — child
	25	"	"	Benedict Bergman
	27	"	"	Pier Bouchet
	28	"	"	John Roberts
Aug.	1	"	"	John Poague
	2	"	"	Capt. John Holland
	4	"	"	Richard Sutton
	"	"	"	George Bamfield
	10	"	"	Felix Pownall
	12	"	"	Mary Ann Pownall (formally Mrs. Wrighten)
	13	"	"	Mr. Love's Child
	"	"	"	Mrs. Bonneau
	15	"	"	Mr. Armstrong's Child
	16	"	"	Mr. Richard Wrainch's child
	17	"	"	Mary Jones
	18	"	"	James Earle (portrait painter)[1]
	21	"	"	William Flood Hampton (child)
	22	"	"	Sara Eastmede
	"	"	"	Joseph Stewart
	23	"	"	Robert Blakely
	"	"	"	George Houston
	24	"	"	Rebecca Collis
	"	"	"	Elisha Egleston
	"	"	"	Benjamin Corbett
1797 Jany.	10	Was	Buried	Barnard Richardson
	12	"	"	Susanna Bee

[1]One of the gazettes published in Charleston at the time states (August 20) that he was a native of Paxton, Massachusetts; that he had lived nearly two years in Charleston; that he had resided in London ten years and was a "Royal Academician". He left a wife and children in London. His will is recorded in Charleston. Among the portraits painted by him were those of Edward Rutledge and Bishop Robert Smith.

	"	"	"	Capt. Daniel Anthony
Feby.	3	"	"	William Newcome

Burials 413

1797		Was Buried
Febry.	4	John Timms
	10	Major Thomas Watkins
	16	Mr. Clarkson's child
March	16	Mary King
April	2	Mr. Frazier's child
	12	George Gardiner
May	5	John Wagner
	9	Mr. Buchanan, child
	11	Martha Custer
	19	Emanuel Pencile
	20	Dr. Moultrie's child
	28	John Magnan
	29	Elizabeth Thomas
June	14	James Patterson
	22	Child (Priscilla Thompson)
	23	Elizabeth Long
	28	Matthew Arnold
	30	Robert Fielding
July	2	Col. Barnard Bee Donan
	3	Child, Louisa Delia Pownall
	7	Letitia Pearse
	8	Child, Samuel Smith
	"	Do. Roger Moor Smith's
	20	Do., Mr. Cleapor's
	"	Do., Mr. Purses
	26	Henry Dale
	30	Miss Harleston
Aug.	1	Child, Mr. Carts
	3	Mrs. Mary Bullock
	8	Ann Lee
	10	Mrs. Richman
	11	John Leindhall

Burials

Burials 414

		Was Buried
1797. Aug.	11	Child, Daniel Kelly
	12	Richard Hall
	19	Aaron Pond
	21	Sarah Hadley

	23	John Lawrence
	26	Lewis Rogers
	27	Mr. T. Middleton
	28	Mr. Paul Hadley
	29	Mr. T. O Elliott
		Dr. Deveaux's child
Sept.	1	Peleg P. Hall
	7	Mary Anderson (child)
	12	Thomas Williamson
	13	Ann Wall
	14	James Poyas
	16	John Gowndry
	22	Jethro Todd
	24	Rebecca Motte Pinckney
(omitted)	18	Charles Beekman
Oct.	1	William Pritchard's child
	7	John Weaver
	8	Joseph Wenalquest
	23	Peter Smith Junior
	24	Thomas Coo
	25	Matthew Sims
	29	Mrs. Hazel
	30	William Tresler
Nov.	1	John Wyatt
	9	Mr. Greaker's child
	22	Mr. Tool's child
Dec.	8	John Bithup
	11	John Y. Mayer

Burials

		Was Buried
1797. Dec.	1[illegible]	Margaret Woodward
	30	Joseph White
1798. Jany.	4	Ann Foster
	19	James Gibbs
	21	Sarah Lessesne
	"	Isaac C. Harleston
Febry	5	Mr. Shippin
March	14	Peter Saul Ryan
	15	Child, Mary Hennesee
April	24	Lightfoot Harrison
May	2	Peter Marshall Neufville
	5	William Darby
	22	Joseph Rumney
	"	Frederick Grunzweig

June	1	James Steadman
	2	Child, Catherine Eliza Hussy
	5	George Browne
	8	Mary McDowall
	10	Child, John Clement Schepler
July	7	Thomas Pearce
	8	Child, Matilda Teasdale
	17	Mary Keith
	18	Thomas Brodie
	20	Child
Aug.	2	Mrs. Sarah Moore
	"	Richard East
	3	Maria G. Turnbull
	14	Thomas Collis
	19	John Langstaff
	20	John Lewis Gervais
	22	Child, William Mason
	25	Thomas Dawson

Burials

Burials 416

		Was Buried
1798, Aug.	29	A Man
	30	Elizabeth Cripps
Sept	12	Teressa Harrigare (child)
	"	Christopher Hart
	17	James Stapples
	23	Anna Maria Lord
	"	Child, John Phipps
	26	Daniel Dueston
	27	Joseph Kay
Oct.	4	William Gowdy
	11	William S. Roe
	12	Samuel Bryan
	23	Child, Rebecca Pinckney
	"	William Barnfield
	27	William Halliday
Nov.	6	Elizabeth Timms
	7	A man from Mrs. Lingard
	8	Benjamin Castell
	17	Mrs. Mary Matthews
	"	William Neufville
	20	Major Peter Bonnetheau
1799 March		
	12	Thomas Tate
	"	Robert Howard

	"	Mrs. Mary Wall
	15	Mrs. Anna Ross
	17	Mr. Thomas Akeen
	21	Mrs. Margaret Weaver
	27	Mr. Jesse Daniel
April	2	Mr. Squire Brown
	6	Mrs. Mary McHugo
	17	Mr. Peter Thompson
		Mrs. Sarah Keating
	24	Mrs. Mary Cameron

Burials 417

1799		Was Buried
April	24	Mrs. Mary Martin
	26	Mr. John McLean
	28	Majr. John Hamilton
	29	Mr. Henry Ditmor
	30	Mrs. Mary Quyn
	"	Mr. James Granville
May		Wm. Alexander (son) of Wm. and Sibble Davidson
	5	Mary daughter of and Kemp
	12	William son of John and Harriot Leescombe
	"	John Samuel son of John and Elizabeth Smith
	16	Wm. Henry son of Richard and Eliza Smith
	17	Mr. Samuel Johnson
	30	Catherine daughter of William and Mary Halliday
June	2	Mr. James Cross
	4	Mr. John Connoly
	8	Mr. John Gissendanner, but buried in the French Church yard
	10	Sarah Phebe Field daughter of John Cato Field
	"	Mrs. Haig
	12	Ewing son of James and Mary Miller
	25	Mrs. Susanna Toale
	26	Mr. Mungo Finlayson
July	1	son of Joseph and Nevell
	"	Mrs. Elizabeth Touseger
	7	Mr. Daniel Huger
	9	Miss Ann daughter of and Miller
	14	Mr. Francis F. Taylor
	15	Eliza daughter of John and Elizabeth Tarver
	18	George Sheed Esq.
	19	Stephen Roberts
Aug	7	John Booth
	"	John Whittick
	8	Margaret Crafts

Burials 418

		Was Buried
1799 Aug.	9	Maryann daughter of Charles and Mary O'hara
	11	Maryann daughter of Jeremiah and Madelen Josephs
	12	Wm. Moore James
	13	of Wm. Lee
	14	Rufus Williams
	"	Mr. Parish
	15	Elizabeth daughter of James and Mary Miller
	16	John Burrage
	"	James Crawford
	18	William King
	"	Elizabeth daughter of Davis
	19	Samuel Jerman
	"	Francis son of Smith
	20	Robert Dowthwaite
	"	James King
	"	Stevens
	"	William Johnson
	21	Harriet Hales
	22	Lucretia Munro
	"	Joseph Jones
	24	Richard Young
	"	J. B. Rickets
	25	Elizabeth daughter of Miles
	"	John son of John Debow
	26	Samuel Mishow
	27	Samuel Dyre
	29	Miss Palmer
	30	Henry C. Manley
Sept.	1	Bailey
	"	Mary daughter of Joseph and Elizabeth Turner
	2	Miss Susannah Ryan
	"	Jane Camp

Burials 419

1799		Was Buried
Sept.	2	Elizabeth Turner
	3	Mary A. daughter of Smerdon
	4	Martha daughter of James & Ann Berisley Kennedy
	"	Archable Ball son of John and Agnes Todd
	6	Harriet daughter of William and Harriet Lee
	"	Mrs. Harriet Luscomb

	7	John son of John & Rebecca Fields
	"	Mr. Severs' child
	8	M. German
	9	Dr. Stephen Dickson
	"	Dr. Daniel Tucker
	12	Robert Norris
	13	Rachell daughter of Flagg
	14	Catherine Hughes
	15	A Child
	"	Stephen son of Dr. Stephen Dickson
	16	Catherine Elizabeth daughter of Job St. Julian and Obadiah Marian
	17	William Miles
	19	Mary Stephens daughter of William and Eliza Marlen
	"	Eliza Bacot[1]
	"	Eliza Marlir
	20	Thomas Gordon son of Joseph and Jane Dill
	21	Mary Gibbes
	24	Nancy Murray
	"	Cynthia West
	23	Ann Smith
	26	Carolina M. daughter of William Clarkson
		Mrs. Dickson
		Mrs. Catherine Maverick
	8	Benjamin Hossfield
	"	Benjamin Channer
	12	Capt. West's child

Burials 420

1799 Sept		Was Buried
	12	Mr. John S. Cripps' child
	15	Ann daughter of William and Sarah Moore
	16	Harict Pierce
	18	Thomas King
	22	Henry son of William and Maryan Gappin
	23	Mrs. Henrietta Gabriel
	"	John Mortimer Williams
	24	Joseph son of Jonathan Lucas
	26	Mrs. Ann Williams
	27	Thomas Broom
	"	John Moss
Nov.	1	Mrs. Louisa Williamson

[1]In pencil has been added; "beth (neé Harramond) widow of Peter Bacot who predeceased her on the 7th. Sept. 1787."

	5	Ann daughter of Samuel Pease
	"	Mrs. Ann Ball
	8	Mrs. Sarah Simons (service at the house and interred in the Country)
	10	Martha Mathews
	11	John Frew
	13	Thomas Bennet son of William and Sarah Johnson
	15	Harriet Day
	17	Mrs. Elizabeth Thompson
Dec	13	Mrs. Ann O'Neal
	15	John Michael Servers
	17	Drury Clark
	20	John son of George and Jane Lamb
	29	Capt Alexander McDowell
	"	Elijah Clark
1800 Jan	12	was Buried Richard Roberson.
	18	William Calvert
	25	His Excellency Edward Rutledge, Governor of South Carolina.[1]
	26	Harriett Moore.
	27	Polly Jackson Warsor.

Burials

Was Buried Burials 421

1800 Jan	28	Edward Hare.
Feby	2	Alexander Alexander Esq.
	4	Mary Jones
	5	Harriott Jones
	7	Henry Kershaw.
	14	Mary Ponteaux.
	15	Clement Richard,
	20	Nevell.
	22	Seth S. Chambers.
	23	Mrs. Elizabeth Radcliffe.

[1]He was born November 23, 1749; entered as a student in the Middle Temple, London, January 12, 1767, and was called to the English bar, July 3, 1772, and to the bar of South Carolina in January, 1773; was a delegate to the Continental Congress, 1774, 1775, 1776, 1777, and was one of the four signers for South Carolina of the Declaration of Independence; was sometime captain in the Charles Town Battalion of Artillery and while so acting participated in the Battle of Port Royal Island, February 4, 1779; was taken prisoner at the fall of Charles Town, May 12, 1780, and later sent a prisoner to St. Augustine; was elected governor in December, 1798.

	26	Lucy T. Niroth.
March	8	Rebecca Martin
	9	Smerdon.
	13	Elizabeth Hart.
	17	James Wilkinson.
	21	Ann Lemarque.
	24	Margaret Gillespie.
	"	William Lockey
	25	Joseph Knox
	"	Thomas Oswald.
April	3	Mary Champneys.
	5	Elanor Tool.
	13	Frances Bass.
	15	Revd John Callaghan.
	"	Capt. William Main.
	26	James B. Reynolds.
May	4	Charles Hill.
	8	Hort.
	26	Mrs. Elizabeth Joell
	30	Elizabeth Evengton.
June	7	Robt Norman.
	14	Christopher Cart.

Burials.

Was Buried 422

1800		
June	14	Benjamin Wish.
	21	Catherine Abercromby.
	27	Samuel Burrows.
	29	John Robertson.
July	9	Mariannie Van Assendelf.
	11	John Todd.
	12	Samuel Weld.
	17	Joshua Crofts Lockwood.
	19	Bridget Moles.
	22	John Doar.
	23	Francis Augustine Bacot.
	"	Micah Johnston.
	27	Peter Lane.
	29	Elizabeth Lockwood.
August	1	Louisa Dalton.
	2	James Richards.
	10	James Warden.
	14	Berry Flagg.
	15	Elizabeth Smith, deposited in Logan's Vault. The Ceremonies performed at Cain Hoy.

" John Payne Sargeant.
16 Elizabeth Kelly.
19 Capt. John W. Purcell.
" Elizabeth Jeannerett.
22 James Bailey.
24 Mary Death.
25 The Hon. Rawlins Lowndes Esq.[1]
29 Daniel White.
" Joseph Watson.
31 Mr. Henry Izard's child.
Sept 1 Mary Independentia Logan.
2 Stephen Bull.

Burials

Was Buried 423

1800
Sept 3 Henry DeBerrae.
" Juliana Moser.
4 Elizabeth P. Channer.
5 John Dinsdale.
6 Johannah R. Groves.
" George Sugden.
10 Mary Everingham.
12 George Clark.
" Emilia Esmuard.
13 Mrs. Hort.
16 George Bague.
17 Sidney Walker.
18 Mary Ann Whitney.
23 Ann Brown
" The Revd Robert Woodbridge.
29 Mary Williams.
Oct 2 William Thorny.
4 John J. Remsen.
28 Coecelia daughter of Edward and Annabella Harleston.

---

[1]He was born in 1721. A few years later his father, Charles Lowndes, came to South Carolina from the island of St. Christopher's (St. Kitt's). Rawlins was Provost Marshal of South Carolina for many years; was speaker of the Commons House of Assembly; a member of the Provincial Congresses; a member of the Council of Safety, and president of South Carolina, 1778-1779. He was three times married. First to Amarinthia Elliott, who died January 1, 1750; second to Mary Cartwright, and, after her death, to Sarah Jones. See *Lowndes of South Carolina* (Chase).

	"	Rawlins, son of Thomas and Sarah Lowndes.
	29	William Heyward, son of James and Margaret Green
	"	Irving Norrell.
	30	Margaret daughter of James and Eleanor Peebles.
	31	William Hicks.
Nov.	1	William Pritchard, son of Samuel and Ann Harvey.
	2	Elanor Davis.
	4	Margaret Ann Hrabowski.
	6	Emma daughter of William and Crafts.
	14	Benjamin Gabriel.
	15	Margaret daughter of Philip and Catharine Gadsden.
	22	Ellenor daughter of Joseph F. and Henrietta C. Barker
	24	John Mason.

Burials.

Was buried 424

1800 Nov	26	Mrs. Wyatt
Dec	11	William Long
	14	James Davidson.
	17	Sarah Williams.
	20	John Sutton.
	22	Beekman, son of Thomas and Elizabeth Joell.
	25	Rawlins Lowndes Jun.
	26	Mrs. Miller.
	29	Henry, son of Thomas W and Bacot.
1801 Jan	12	John Clark.
	29	Mary Quin.
	30	Robert Shedden.
Feb	9	Washington Collins.
	16	William Prosser.
	18	John Kennedy.
	22	Clifford, son of Joseph and Sarah Lewis.
	24	Robert, son of Robert and Hannah Roulain.
	26	Thomas Heyward son of Ebenezer and Caroline Thayer.
March	9	Susannah Clay.
	10	Beranger Francois de Courtin.
	"	Matilda daughter of John and Harriot Miot.
	14	William Haley.
	"	Hamilton son of Benjamin and Margaret Seabrook.
	19	Alexander Ross.
	20	Miles Dodson.
	24	John Wish.

25 John Williams.
30 Jeremiah John son of William and Margaret Lovely
April 6 Jane Stevenson.
May 5 John Fletcher.
15 Theodore Trezevant.
19 John Lahiffe.

Burials.

Was Buried. 425

1801 May 19 Merreot (stranger)
19 Mrs. Mary Pritchard.
20 J. L. Hussy, a child. (stranger)
23 Thomas Drayton. "
27 Thomas, child of Edward & Elizabeth Woodrouffe (stranger)
28 Mrs. Elizabeth Verree. "
June 2 Stephen, child of James and Ales Oliver.
2 Sack Holmes (stranger)
5 Jane, child of Joseph & Frances Mackey.
7 Mrs. Sarah Lowndes.
9 Susanna, child of Peter & Susanna Fisher (stranger)
18 Miss , child of William & Chambers. (stranger)
25 Daniel Gibbs (stranger)
27 Elizabeth Lebby.
28 Dr. Thomas Marshall, M. D. (stranger)
28 Ann Eliza, child of Saml & Selina Houston "ditto
28 Martha Richards.
30 Ameliam Ann Pringle.
July 11 Sebastienne Pebarte (stranger)
12 Deelia Leewis. "
13 Daniel Bell, child of John & Elizabeth Tarver (stranger)
14 Margaret Lane (stranger)
17 Thomas Williams, child of Thomas & Rebecca Allen. (stranger)
17 Joseph Butterton. (stranger)
17 Mrs. Mary Cape. "
18 Edward Gardner "
20 Cornelia E. Richardson "
22 Lambert G. Lance.
26 Child of Thomas & Cave.
27 David Gaillard. (stranger)
30 John, child of John & Mary Bourgneuf. (stranger)

Burials

Burials.

Was buried			426
1801 July	31	Margaret Dolliver. (French Church)	
Aug.	4	Silas Norris	(stranger)
	6	Daniel Sinclaire	"
	7	George, child of John and Eliza Geyer (stranger)	
	11	Mrs. Charlotte Izard.	
	11	and Delia Lewis	(stranger)
	14	Thomas M. Waring.	"
	17	Sarah Lightbourne.	"
	17	Edward G. F. Green	"
	20	Joseph Dill	"
	22	Charles Maylie	"
	22	Mrs. Margaret Buckle.	
	23	Susan. child of John Cart.	
	24	Charles Wheeler.	(stranger)
	24	Alexander Shivas	"
	25	William Charles child of William & Tunno (stranger)	
	26	Benjamin, child of William Hasell & Eliza Gibbs.	
	28	Phinehas Parmele.	(stranger)
	28	Capt Ames	"
	28	Miss Mary Cape	"
	29	John Randoll, child of Theodore & Cornelia Gaillard (stranger)	
	29	Nucellimus Ambrosy	(stranger)
	31	Joseph Torree	"
	31	Peter Hill.	"
Sept	1	John Travers.	"
	2	Amelia Niroth, a child.	"
	4	B. DuPont. (French Churchyard,)	
	5	John, child of Thomas & Sarah Nichols. (stranger)	
	5	Christopher, child of Christopher & Catherine FitzSimons (carried to the Country)	
	5	Charles child of Thomas & Sophia Sheppard.	
	6	Child of & Ball	(stranger)[1]

Burials.

Was buried			427
1801 Sept	10	Henry Allen.	(stranger)
	10	William Dennison.	"

[1]Those marked "stranger" had died of yellow fever, then commonly called "stranger's fever".

	12	John Stollard	”
	13	William Smith.	”
	14	Joseph Gutterie.	”
	14	Tucker Harris, child of James & Sarah Tucker Simons.	
	15	Cornelia Van Rhyn	(stranger)
	15	Andrew Jurgen.	”
	18	Catherine M. child of Jacob & Catherine Stoll. (stranger)	
	18	Charles Thomas, child of Charles & Mary Cleapor.	
	20	Edward Broun Nowell,	(stranger)
	20	Henry Caldwell.	”
	21	William, child of John & Rebecca Gell. (stranger)	
	22	Frances Maria, child of Francis & Ann Motte.	
	23	Henry M. Snipes. (carried to the country)	
	23	Folkert Hoes.	(stranger)
	23	Mrs. Honoria Mills, spouse of the Rev. Mr. Mills.	
	24	William Ham.	(stranger)
	25	Jennet, child of William & Louisa Marshall. (stranger)	
	28	Jesse Jones.	(stranger) (entombed)
	29	John Clement.	
	30	John Press Smith, M. D.	
	30	John Ralph.	(stranger)
	30	Jane Hamilton,	”
Oct	2	Eliza, child of Kennedy & Ann McKenzie. (stranger)	
	4	Mrs. Sarah Hopton.	
	5	Antoine Elie.	(stranger)
	6	Ina Castinel	”
	6	Amon. Johnson	”
	7	John, child of Isaac & Statira Weatherby. (stranger)	
	7	Theodore Latapie.	”

Burials.

Burials.

Was Buried. 428

1801 Oct.	8	John Bolton Rook.	(stranger)
	11	Anthony Carriere.	”
	12	Alcey Jones	”
	12	Sarah Guy.	”
	12	Thomas Peech.	”
	12	Thomas, child of Edward & Catherine Weyman.	
	12	Samuel Allen.	(stranger)
	17	John Paul Boutenor De Risveau.	”

		Robert James Turnbull	”
	26	Mary Ann Thompson.	”
	26	Peter Cap de Ville.	”
	28	Robert Alleanan.	”
	29	Right Rev. Robert Smith, Bishop of S. C. & Rector St. Philips Church.	
Nov.	1	Benjamin McKenzie.	(stranger)
	2	Thomas Cope.	”
	10	Capt. Luke Snain.	”
	13	Mrs. Mary Ann Finlayson.	
	21	Elizabeth Millne.	(stranger)
	23	Capt. Thomas Curlin.	”
	30	Thomas Hall.	
Dec	4	Dr. Daniel Weatherby.	(stranger)
	6	Andrew, child of James & Eleanor Gale Reid. (stranger)	
	18	Sanford William, child of J. S. & Henrietta Catherine Barker. (stranger)	
	19	James Andrews.	(stranger)
	22	James Horne	”
	25	Joseph, child of & Elizabeth Moles. (stranger)	
	26	John Grant.	(stranger)
	27	Mrs. Elizabeth Elliott.	
	27	Nicholas Silberg.	(stranger).

Burials.

Burials.

Was Buried. 429

1802 Jan.	3	John Phipps.	
	6	Elizabeth Moles.	(stranger)
	8	Elizabeth Wallace.	”
	9	Mary Wall.	”
	10	Statira Weatherby	”
	12	Richard Augustus, child of William & Margaret Lobeey. (stranger)	
	12	Magdalane Ruth, child of William & Magdalane Brown.	
	13	Victor, child of Joseph & Ladervize (stranger)	
	27	Maria, child of John & Esther Barron.	”
	27	Joseph Horlock.	(stranger)
	28	Miss Mary, daughter of John Hume Esq. (Only service in St. Philips)	
	30	William Theodore, child of Bartholomew & Rebecca C. Gaillard.	
Feby.	5	Mary Ivrin.	(stranger)

	12	Ann Scott, child of Archibald & Mary Ball, (stranger)
	14	Ann McConnoly. (stranger)
	17	William Kelsey, Senior.
	22	Judith Wrainch.
	22	Charlotte, child of Daniel & Sarah McGivrin. (stranger)
	24	John Mills (stranger)
	24	James Killin. (stranger)
	24	Robert S. Timothy "
	28	Louisa Frederica, child of William & Louisa Frederica Marshall (stranger)
March	1	Francis Bonneau Esq.
	2	Mary, child of John & Mary Wilkinson. (stranger)
	21	Mary, child of Mary & Adam Rebb. "
	22	Lawrence Tragay. "
	25	Nathaniel Lebby.
	27	Sophia Edin. (stranger)
	29	John B. Williamson. "
	31	Crofton Shepheard. "
April	2	Edward Powell "
	3	Emilie, child of Peter & Louisa Blomberg. (stranger)

Burials.

Burials.

Was Buried. 430

1802 April	13	Dr. Isaac Chanler.
	7	Morris Clayton (stranger)
	10	Mrs. Olevy Garnet "
	10	Alexander Pringle.
	11	Ann, child of William & Ann Hall
	13	Elizabeth, child of James & Ann Grainger. (stranger)
	17	Thomas, child of Joseph & Sarah Lewis. (stranger)
	17	Joseph, child of Joseph & Carew "
	19	Frances Amelia, child of Thomas & Amelia Baker (stranger)
	19	Eliza, child of Thomas & Mary Shubrick.
	27	John, child of John & Jane Phipps.
	28	Joseph Haylegar. (Stranger)
	29	Andrew Weaver. "
May	1	Casper Antichon. "
	2	George Verree "
	5	Benjamin Simons. "
	6	Mary, child of John & Jane Phipps.
	6	John, child of John & Judith Wrainch. (stranger)

	7	Caroline, child of Joseph & Esther Lloyd ”
	9	Capt. John Robert Foster.
	10	Elizabeth, child of & Timothy. ”
	15	Sarah Elisa, child of William and Anna Maria Johnson.
	19	William Doughty, child of Samuel & Mary Gourdin (stranger)
	21	Mrs. Davis (stranger)
	26	William, child of William & Judith Calvert.
	29	Mrs. Elise Fitzgerald. (stranger)
June	1	Henry William, child of Charles & Mary Cleapor.
	6	William, child of William & Ann Wish.
	6	William Logan Senior, Esq.
	7	Thomas, child of Capt William & Ann Hall.
	9	Mrs. Amelia Munro. (stranger)

Burials.

Burials.

Was Buried. 431

1802 June	10	Ann Maria, child of Elias & Elizabeth Jenkins. (stranger)
	12	John, child of John & Mary Hunter.
	14	Thomas Jefferson, child of John & Frances Palmer.
	14	Louis Mozet. (stranger)
	17	Sarah Ethridge. ”
	18	Horatio, child of Andrew Brown. ”
	26	Mrs. Susanna Cross. ”
	30	Henry Tool. ”
July	7	Thomas, child of Capt. Thomas Simons.
	8	Felix, child of John B. & Elizabeth Williamson (stranger)
	8	Etienne Bellemeau De Lavincendiere. (stranger)
	9	Frances, child of Alexander & Frances Gray.
	16	John, child of Richard Claybrook.
	24	Rev Peter H. Parker, Asst of St. Philips Church.[1]
	29	William, child of David & Eleanor Johnson.
	30	Thomas, child of Thomas & Corbett.
	30	Jeremiah Clark (stranger)
	16	Miss Mary Newman. ”
	23	Ann, child of William P. & Ann Chambers (stranger)
	30	Frances Pinckney, child of William & Mary Alston.

[1]Rev. Peter Manigault Parker. See page 220 of Dalcho and note page 88.

Aug	14	Mary Eliza Shaw.	(stranger)
	14	Dennis Hagarty	"
	25	John Bull Esq.	"
	23	Daniel McGivrin.	"
	27	Isaac Auld, a child.	"
	27	Elizabeth McNeill	"
	28	Richard Wainwright.	"
Sept.	3	John Martin Lenion.	"
	5	Daniel, child of John Tarver.	"
	6	James Wilkerson.	"
	8	Preservad Saunders.	"

Burials.

Burials.

Was Buried. 432

1802 Sept	11	Simon Ferry.	(stranger)
	13	John Jones.	"
	13	Robert Maxwell Dabney.	"
	14	Robert Willson.	"
	17	Son of Spratt Cripps Esq.	
	18	John Wallis	(stranger)
	19	Charles Shilberk.	"
	20	James Swain	"
	21	Miss M. C. Ashby.	"
	21	John D. Porter.	"
	23	Robert Lamont.	"
	25	Robert Taylor.	"
	26	Sarah Wilkinson.	
	29	Elizabeth Axon.	
	30	Peter Swain.	(stranger)
Oct.	1	Mrs. Sarah Pritchard.	
	2	Mrs. Mary Frierson.	(stranger)
	2	Miss Dorothea Broadhurst.	"
	2	Federick Karnes.	"
	4	William Weaver	"
	5	Daniel Cannon Esq. (late vestryman of St. Philips.)	
	6	Mozia Kezic.	(stranger)
	7	Maria S. child of Hon. Judge Bay.	
	7	Capt. David Quiggin	(stranger)
	7	Jacob Stoll	"
	9	Susan Thompson	"
	10	Susanna Mason.	
	11	Rebecca Gell.	(stranger)
	11	Amos Ellmore.	"
	12	Mary Stevens.	"

	13	Elizabeth Weatherston.	"
	18	Isaac Parker.	

Burials.

Burials.

Was Buried. 433

1802 Oct	22	Mary Thompson.	(stranger)
	26	Capt Shuball Haws, aged 32 years.	(stranger)
	27	Nathaniel Hathaway, aged 27 "	"
	29	Anthony Icle " 55 "	"
Nov.	3	James Russell.	"
	5	Thomas Tappier,	"
	5	Richard Burford Halsell aged 6 days.	"
	8	Robert Limehouse " 18 months	"
	11	William Jones " 40 Years	"
	12	Anna Lane " 20 months	"
	13	John Stewart, " 24 years.	"
	14	John Barron " 28 years	"
	17	Joseph, child of Joseph & Mary Ann Doane Aged 14 days.	"
	21	George Rout Esq. Aged 49 years.	
	26	Elizabeth Nevill, aged 26 years	
	29	Thomas Fowler, aged 24 years.	
Dec	1	Jane A., child of Richard & Ann Cheevers, aged 18 months.	
	5	Mrs. Rebecca Bampfield, aged 70 years.	
	6	Oliver Stevens, a child, aged 5 years—stranger.	
	8	Mary Adams, a child aged 2 years	"
	14	Catherine McLeod, aged 30 years	"
	22	Thomas Jefferson, child of William & Jane McBlair, stranger, aged 2 yrs.	
	24	Mary Butcher, aged 9 weeks.	stranger.
	28	Richard Holmes Chevers, aged 27 years	"
1803 Jan	1	Edward Rogers, aged 46 years, stranger.	
	3	Miss Susannah Poinsett, aged 59 years.	
	10	Edward Thomas Butt, aged 3 months.	
	16	Richard Preston, aged 33 years.	
	19	Ann, child of John & Frances Palmer, aged 16 days, stranger.	
	23	Jane Boiles, aged 40 years, stranger,	

Burials.

Burials.

Was buried.			434
1803 Feby.	2	George Buckle, aged 50 years,	stranger.
	7	Mary Roberts, aged 66 years.	"
	7	Susannah Jourdin, aged 66 years	"
	8	Mrs. Ann Motte, aged 73 years.	
	10	John, child of Rev. Thomas Frost.	
	10	Mrs. Lee, stranger.	
	11	Elizabeth, child of Roger & Elizabeth Pinckney, aged 4 years.	
	12	Mrs. Amelia Dart, aged 70 years.	
	18	Alexander Tweed, aged 69 years.	stranger.
	19	Mathew Fowler.	"
	23	Robert Koan, aged 2 years	"
	23	John Logan Esq. aged 37 years.	"
	28	Joshua Hargreeves, aged 43 years,	Stranger.
March	1	Christian Grovenstone, aged 29 years	"
	9	John Wolf, aged 16 years	"
	15	Robert Smith, aged 17 years	"
	17	Louis Graeser, aged 30 years	"
	21	James, child of James & Elisa McIllhenny, aged 2 months.	
	23	Mary, child of John & Mary Kenny, aged 4 months, (stranger)	
	24	William Gray aged 31 years	Stranger.
	26	Hannah Roulain, aged 29 years	"
	29	Francis, child of Francis & Mary Kearne aged 14 months.	"
April	7	Richard Claybrook aged 33 years	"
	7	Theodal Frederick Tavel, aged 5 days	"
	12	Jane E., child of Benjamin & Harriet Leefe aged 18 months.	"
	22	Thomas, child of William & Jane Dewees, aged 17 years.	
	28	Mrs. Ellas Campbell, aged 47 years	Stranger.
		Frantz Jacob Foltz, stranger.	
May	7	Ella Crask, aged 18 years "	
	13	Angale Santi, aged 40 years "	
	13	Jonathan Cape, aged 23 years "	

Burials.

Burials.

Was Buried.			435.
1803 May	14	Jan. B. Landre, aged 45 years stranger.	
	18	A child of Mrs. Elisha Jenkins, aged 1 day.	

18 Benjamin Snipes, aged 31 years, stranger.
21 James C Green aged 31 years, "
22 Mary Russell, aged 2 years.

For originial see long book
(Burials Indexed
To and including May 22, 1803)

Thomas Cole doth make oath and say that on the fifteenth day of Febru'y 1763 William Raper in the Prescence of the said deponent and Mrs. Wilton Nesbit and the widow of the late Rev. Mr. Joseph Dacre Wilton deceased at the house of the said Mr. Wilton deceased was married to Elizabeth Raper wife of the said William Raper then Elizabeth Marchand, according to the Rites and Ceremonies of the Church of England.
Sworn this 11 of Sept.
1769 before me.

John Troup J. P.

(Registered Folio 193)

INDEX

[1]This was evidently the pronunciation of the name of the then Chief Justice of South Carolina. Many writers persist in making the name Skinner, his autograph to the contrary notwithstanding.